# A Delicate Experiment

The Harvard Business School 1908-1945

Jeffrey L. Cruikshank

# A Delicate Experiment

The Harvard Business School
1908-1945

Foreword by
Dean John H. McArthur

HBS
PRESS

Harvard Business School Press
Boston, Massachusetts

The paper used in this publication meets the requirements
of the American National Standard for Permanence of Paper for
Printed Library Materials Z39.48-1984.

Harvard Business School Press, Boston 02163

91  90  89  88  87     5  4  3  2  1

Library of Congress Cataloging-in-Publication Data

Cruikshank, Jeffrey L.
   A delicate experiment.

   Bibliography: p. 287
   Includes index.
   1. Harvard University. Graduate School of Business
Administration—History.   I. Title.   II. Title: Harvard
business school, 1908-1945.
HF1134.H4C78     1987     650'.07'1174444     86-20953
ISBN 0-87584-135-X

*To Ann, Benjamin, and Meredith:*
*all truth-tellers*

# Contents

# Foreword

This history of the Harvard Business School concludes with the introduction of a revised MBA curriculum at the end of the Second World War. My own relationship with the School began over a decade later, and many of the people introduced in this volume had already left the School when my classmates and I entered the MBA program in 1957. Dean Donald K. David, for example, had retired two years earlier. Melvin T. Copeland, the last active member of the School's original faculty, had become an emeritus professor in 1953.

For those of my generation and younger, therefore, the material in the following pages predates personal experience and memory. I think it is important to bring some elements of the School's story up to date. I would also like to recount the origins of this book, and to identify some of the lessons it contains which may be useful to us today.

One such lesson, it seems to me, is that ideology and strategy are inextricably linked. Dean Stanley F. Teele, who succeeded Don David, grappled with that fact toward the end of his deanship. "Planning for Change," a 1961 faculty committee report which advocated a number of changes in the MBA program, caused a local uproar. It seemed to many on the faculty that our most basic ideological tenets were under attack. As an aside, for example, the report suggested that the name of the School be changed. But symbols embody ideology, and we ignore them at our peril.

It fell to Stan Teele's successor, George P. Baker, to deal with the turmoil resulting from "Planning for Change." As Dean, George's first priority was to rebuild a cohesive faculty at Soldiers Field. He did so with great skill, in part by ensuring that all faculty members had ample opportunity to express their particular concerns about the report. During his tenure, furthermore, the faculty appointments process was decentralized, and significant responsibility for appointments was delegated to the newly created "areas."

The decentralization process was substantially modified by Lawrence E. Fouraker, who succeeded Dean Baker in 1970. Larry envisioned and implemented a sophisticated matrix organization for the School. This structure not only made our increasingly complex affairs manageable, but also served to involve a new generation of faculty in the administration of the School. But changing circumstances outside Soldiers Field, including two sharp economic recessions in the early 1970s, necessitated retrenchments on other fronts. Appropriately, Larry effected economies in the School's operations, and recaptured some measure of control over both our rate of growth and the quality of our faculty appointments. Simultaneously, our executive education activities were brought into sharper focus, and again, effective quality controls and standards were put in place.

I suggest that this brief summary of relatively recent developments illustrates several of the themes which recur time and again in this volume. First, strategies are derived from the power of ideas. Ideas, in turn, are empowered by historical circumstance, and can't be considered apart from their context. Finally, many of the apparent discontinuities in this School's history are in fact not radical departures at all. Our tactics may change, but our strategy has been remarkably enduring.

When I began my term as Dean, I saw the need to reinforce a wavering consensus regarding our goals, activities, and purpose. It seemed then that many people who were involved with the School were uncertain about some of the most fundamental characteristics that have made this institution so special. As a member of Larry Fouraker's administration, I had seen first-hand how the 1970s—a period characterized first by social unrest, and later by a widespread cynicism toward institutions—had affected our School. Those external pressures had led us to extensive internal questioning. What were we about? What was our most appropriate mission as a School? How should we organize ourselves to accomplish that mission, once defined? Whom should we hire and promote?

Insofar as such questioning leads to hypotheses and fruitful experimentation, I think that we at Soldiers Field have always supported the process. In fact, this volume supplies ample evidence of that trait. But when dialogue and self-criticism verge on self-absorption, we are less patient. I think that is appropriate. By 1980, I personally felt that we were spending far too much time worrying about our "identity." As Dean, I was determined to initiate a number of activities to clarify that identity, to build consensus, and to allow us to move on to more pressing issues.

Toward these ends, I was determined to encourage a concentrated research and development effort. In addition to clarifying our joint purpose, I felt, such an effort would help meet the rapidly changing knowledge-based needs of the School and its constituencies, and further the professional development of individual faculty members and staff. I also hoped that the products of such an effort might serve as a useful antidote to the irrelevance of much contemporary business research. In connection with that effort, I asked Jeffrey L. Cruikshank—then editor of the Harvard Business School *Bulletin*—to prepare an illustrated summary of the School's research activities, past and present.

The resulting publication, issued in the spring of 1982, was a clear success. It made a number of us at the School more aware of our longstanding research traditions. Unexpectedly, it also evoked once again the abiding loyalty and affection with which many of our alumni regard this institution. Both at Soldiers Field and elsewhere, friends of the School found it helpful to have laid out before them the institution's intellectual history and traditions. I was therefore encouraged to begin an additional experiment in consensus-building. I asked Jeff Cruikshank to write a new history of the Harvard Business School.

I had no clear idea about what form such a history might take, or when it might become available. It seemed obvious, though, that it should be both festive and instructive. The reader with an affection for the School should learn more about the roots of this institution, and should find that learning process rich, challenging, and unpredictable. That is, after all, how many of us have experienced the School personally.

The first fruits of that experiment follow. Those of us who had worked with Jeff in the past were not surprised when he redefined and expanded upon his assignment. I, for one, am persuaded that the story deserves a full telling. This volume covers the School's history from its formative years to the end of World War II. The most striking thing that emerges from the text is the creativity and responsiveness of the institution it describes. "The School to succeed must be in close touch with the business world," wrote Harvard's Professor (and later President) A. Lawrence Lowell in 1907. His prescription has proved a good one. Most of the subsequent initiatives of the School's faculty, whether successful or unsuccessful, have had it at their heart.

This volume tells only half a story. The reader will be struck by the distance traveled by the School in its first four decades; my personal conviction is that it has traveled greater distances since. Since the Second World War, the range and significance of our activities have increased exponentially. Even in 1945, the School was relatively simple, graspable, parochial, and precarious; today we are immensely more complex, elusive, catholic, and established.

But our predecessors took giant steps. Before we can understand the present or the recent past, we have to understand the challenges and the legacy of those earlier days. It was indeed, as Lowell, phrased it, "a delicate experiment." I invite you to read, to enjoy, and to learn from the following pages. We at the School would welcome your comments upon them.

JOHN H. MCARTHUR,
*Dean*

*Harvard Business School*
*Soldiers Field, Boston, Massachusetts*
*November, 1986*

# Acknowledgments

In many ways, this book grows out of an unusual conception. To the degree that it is successful, it is so because many people have lent their time and talents to that conception. I would like to thank those people here.

Discussions about a new school history began in 1982. Dean John McArthur helped define the content of the book as both an intellectual history of the School and a study in institution building. Along with Professor Thomas McCraw, Dean McArthur envisioned a book which would use both words and pictures to tell a relatively complicated story. Through the book's many transformations, those original ideas and devices have survived intact. This is in part due to the efforts of Senior Associate Dean Hugo Uyterhoeven and Associate Deans Timothy Armour and Charles Sethness, who lent the project their support at every juncture.

Two researchers helped immeasurably. Questions concerning the University and Boston's Brahmins were answered by Helen Kessler, who in many cases was able to call upon her own accumulated store of Harvard lore for answers; in other cases, she scoured the Harvard and Business School archives for needed information. Photographs and other visual materials were entirely the responsibility of Robin Ray. Her success in finding, obtaining permission to use, and simply keeping track of hundreds of images lends beauty and authority to this volume. Working with Robin, photographers Tom Wedell and Ken Raynor gave our jumble of objects and images a coherent visual treatment; they also climbed to dizzying heights for a dust-jacket image.

Special thanks are due to those in the Business School and University archives. Florence Lathrop, assisted by Gregory Pano and Mark Mastromarino, made Baker Library's extensive records and photographic collection accessible to us. At the Harvard archives, curator Harley Holden allowed us to consult the papers of various Harvard professors and presidents, and steered us toward other helpful material. Robin Carlaw, Tom Sexton, and Barbara Meloni unearthed the documents we needed, while Robin McElheny met our many requests for pictures.

Words and pictures were elegantly integrated by the firm of Logowitz + Moore. Nancy Allen, and later Judy Kohn, designed the book's five chapters into statements that were both clear and subtle. Steve Logowitz conceived a design that imparts information on many levels; he also provided continuity, good humor, and a steadying hand.

Tom McCraw and John March had the unenviable task of responding to the rough drafts of each chapter. They were demanding editors, and I have learned a lot from them. On the administrative side, Bob Burakoff was equally demanding. Anne O'Connell and Joan O'Connor deciphered dozens of tapes with patience and discretion. As a result of their collective efforts, the book is much the better.

I would especially like to thank three gentlemen, all retired Business School faculty members, for their extraordinary efforts on behalf of this history. Up to the time of his death, the late Malcolm P. McNair was listening and responding to each chapter as it became available. George E. Bates similarly spent many hours with the text, correcting misperceptions and tempering unwitting exaggerations. And last, Edmund P. Learned —known to his many friends as a man of strong opinions—provided a remarkably fair and balanced commentary on my version of forty years at the Harvard Business School. Professors McNair, Bates, and Learned helped define the character of the institution; it is fortunate and appropriate that they have also helped shape this book.

JEFFREY L. CRUIKSHANK

*Boston, Massachusetts*
*November, 1986*

# A Delicate Experiment

The Harvard Business School 1908-1945

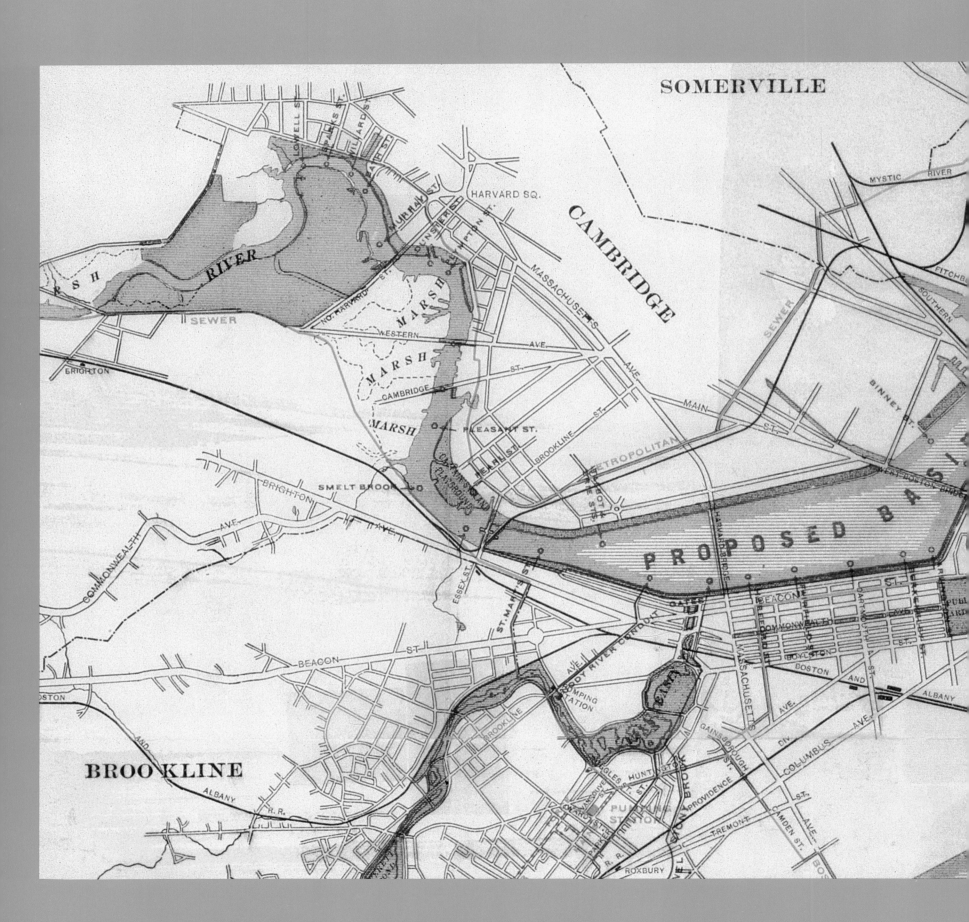

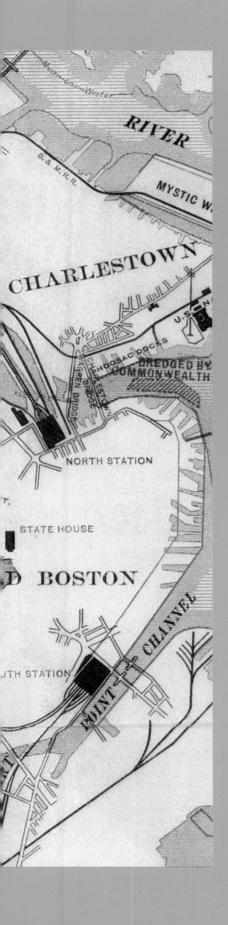

IN THE SUMMER OF 1895, Harvard University President Charles W. Eliot found himself reviewing the lengthy paragraphs of a short magazine article. The article — in the June issue of the *Harvard Graduates' Magazine* — had an unusual premise: that railroad management should be acknowledged as a science. The author of the article, George Bridge Leighton, was a member of the Harvard College class of 1888.

"Let us see," wrote Leighton, "what a responsible official in a railway ought to know, whatever may be his special department. He should know that those who own the property expect and believe that, if properly managed, their investment can derive the usual rate of profit. The railway must have an economic reason for its existence, and be operated to secure economic success. He must understand the relation of the railway to the owners, to the public, and to the state. Again, he must understand the importance of managing men, the results of experience in the organization of departments, and selection of proper and efficient subordinates. The railway official must be broadly versed in the principles of the railway from a

George Bridge Leighton,
Harvard senior. From his
1888 Class Book.
In addition to his educa-
tional and business interests,
George B. Leighton was also
a part-time politician: he
turned down the 1905 New
Hampshire Democratic
gubernatorial nomination,
and ran unsuccessfully
the following year (as a
Republican) for one of
New Hampshire's U.S.
Senate seats.

Overleaf:
A 1902 Metropolitan
District Commission map of
the proposed Charles River
Basin submitted to Henry
L. Higginson, James J.
Storrow, and others.

mechanical and engineering viewpoint. When called upon to examine a new line, he must be able to pass upon its merits intelligently. He must satisfy himself whether it will be better to build a new line at all; whether it will be better to build a cheap line, but one more expensive to operate, or an expensive one, yet one cheaper to operate. He must know the theories of rates and traffic, must pass intelligently upon such questions as whether a certain traffic is worth doing or not, the true theory of competition, and the limit of competitive business. He will have to know what to leave to subordinates and how to direct them. These are but a few of the qualifications necessary for an efficient manager. His profession is one of the most versatile of all professions. In a broad way, he must be not only a man of affairs, but lawyer, engineer, financier, economist, accountant."

The *Graduates' Magazine* was not a forum that would ordinarily engage the attention of the University's president. Operated by and for alumni, the publication featured short articles by Harvard graduates, and devoted many pages to various class activities. The University — and certainly its president — had no direct involvement in it.

Eliot, furthermore, was a prominent national figure: then in his twenty-sixth year as Harvard's president, he was renowned for his relentless campaigns to reform education, and particularly the education offered at Harvard. Two decades earlier, he had revived the University's moribund elective system. Over storms of faculty protest, he had rebuilt Harvard's law and medical schools. He had commenced a campaign against collegiate football, which he considered brutal and a waste of time. He spoke and wrote precisely, and did not hesitate to voice his opinions. "President Eliot was a kind of perpetual Judgement Day to me," said one long-time Harvard employee. "Something in his look and bearing said plainly, 'I am observing you; you must prove your worth.'"

George Bridge Leighton, however, was undaunted by the president's reputation. In fact, a month after the magazine's publication, he sent a letter to Eliot and

The railroad boom of the
nineteenth century called
into being a new American
profession: management.

recommended that he read the article. In his letter, Leighton explained his motivations for submitting the article and for approaching Eliot. "It is my hope," he wrote, "that Harvard may be in the lead in this as she has so often been, in fitting men to some new and important work in this busy and highly organized life."

Leighton had had some firsthand experience of the work he was describing. A member of a prominent New Hampshire family, he was then halfway through what would prove to be an eleven-year tenure as president of the Los Angeles Terminal Railway, a short line with less than one hundred miles of track. The Terminal Railway's size belied its strategic position, however: three times, battles over the development of Los Angeles' harbor reached the floor of the United States Senate, and each time the Los Angeles Terminal Railway played a prominent role.

**The young President Eliot**

The railroad president, then, began his lobbying of the university president with two strong motivations: a keen sense of the importance of the national railway network in an emerging economic order, and an underlying affection for his alma mater. (That same year, 1895, Leighton founded and was elected president of the Associated Harvard Clubs.) For the next several years, Leighton vigorously pleaded his case, by mail and in person. In October, for example, he learned that Eliot had asked some advisors about the feasibility of "a course of railway instruction" at Harvard — "more properly," chided Leighton in a letter, "a School of Railways." He restated his contention that while building a railroad was a scientific task, *running* a railroad was "almost entirely economic":

"The scientific training is now given at many schools in the country, Harvard, the Tech [MIT], Yale, Cornell, Purdue and others but the economic and financial questions are not there touched upon or if so but lightly and not with the view of making a well rounded course. . . .

**San Pedro Harbor and Terminal Island, Los Angeles, 1906. The terminus of Leighton's railroad is visible at the far left.**

"In the Pennsylvania railroad alone and there in the engineering departments, there are upwards of fifty graduates of Troy. What would be the numbers from a school which not only prepared men for the engineering but the traffic and financial departments?"

It was, as Eliot sensed, an apt argument. Leighton had intuitively grasped what Alfred D. Chandler would document some eighty years later in *The Visible Hand:* that "the operational requirements of the railroads demanded the creation of the first administrative hierarchies in American business." Concerns about safety, and later the need for increased efficiency in the face of heightened competition, had created a demand for a new breed of managers, who were, in Leighton's terms, part lawyer, part engineer, part financier, part economist, and part accountant.

But Eliot was a pragmatic administrator, and he represented an institution mindful of its traditions. "As an institution," business historian N. S. B. Gras would write in 1943, "Harvard is a bit conservative. It rarely does any large institutional pioneering, but when it acts,

it does things differently, sometimes better." Eliot proceeded according to Harvard tradition: he sought counsel from trusted advisors and friends of the University, and estimated what an experiment in railroad education would cost. He sent his tentative conclusions to Leighton in a letter dated March 13, 1896:

"From the estimates which I have been able to procure of the cost of additional instruction which it would be necessary to provide in order to maintain a satisfactory course on railway management, I have come to the conclusion that $4000 a year for five years would enable the Corporation to try an intelligent experiment on the subject. The whole sum would be spent every year for instruction not now provided at the University. . . . It should also be understood that on this basis the instruction would have to be given by teachers not above the grade of assistant professor, — that is, we could not afford to employ professors in the work. The plan would include occasional lectures or short courses of lectures by railway experts.

The telegraph, along with the railroads, created national and international markets of unprecedented scale. The corporations that arose to exploit those markets needed professional managers in ever-increasing numbers.

"Since I saw you at Cambridge, I had the opportunity of talking with two or three railroad men. They see the difficulty of the present situation much more plainly than they see any remedy therefor. You see what you believe to be a remedy."

ELIOT'S REFERENCE to the "difficulty of the present situation" may have had more than one connotation. There was, as Leighton had argued, an unprecedented need for railroad management: some 75,000 miles of track had been laid in America in the 1880s, a record never approached before or since, anywhere in the world. But other facts also illustrated the need for management skills in the railroads: by the mid-1890s, a substantial percentage of American railroad track — some 40,000 miles, representing a capitalization of over $2.5 billion — had been foreclosed upon and sold. The nation's leading investment banking houses, which had secured European capital to help build the roads, were now being asked to refinance them in bankruptcy.

One such firm was Lee, Higginson & Company, based in Boston. Its president and dominant figure was Henry Lee Higginson — known as Major Higginson from the days of his Civil War service — who founded the Boston Symphony Orchestra and was a generous supporter of Harvard throughout his lifetime. His financial acumen was frequently called upon by the University; in addition to his informal advisory role, he served at various times as a Fellow of the Harvard Corporation, as Radcliffe's treasurer, and as one of three members of the University's Finance Committee. In that capacity, he frequently complained to Eliot that his fellow committee members were "timid," and faulted them for their "extreme conservatism" regarding the investments he proposed for the University.

Higginson may have been, of all Boston financiers, most familiar with the state of American railroads. It was therefore natural that President Eliot should consult Major Higginson on the proposed course of instruction in railroading. Higginson's response was characteristically blunt. "I should decidedly object," he wrote to Eliot, "to establishing any such lectureship." Higginson had learned that Leighton proposed to raise funds for the purpose among friends of the University. "This seems to me to be a pity," he continued, "for the object is poor and a dollar spent in this lectureship would be a dollar lost to some other lectureship in all probability."

Henry Lee Higginson — universally referred to as Major Higginson as a result of his Civil War service — dominated Boston's financial circles in the late nineteenth and early twentieth centuries. A benefactor of many causes and individuals, he particularly favored the Boston Symphony Orchestra, which he founded, and Harvard University.

Railroad president Leighton (top) challenged Harvard's President Eliot (above) to teach railroad management in the "broad and proper way."

Higginson's opposition was not immediately fatal. Characteristically, Eliot softened the major's criticisms somewhat, and passed them along to Leighton. Leighton wrote back at once: "The doubts that some people have," he argued, "are to my mind probably just the doubts that were met when the first medical and law schools were established or the doubts that some men have as to the value of colleges at all."

The 1896 McKinley-Bryan presidential campaign —which began with Bryan's "Cross of Gold" acceptance speech at the Democratic convention and ended with McKinley's narrow victory—forced a suspension in Leighton's correspondence with Eliot. By November, though, Leighton was again in communication with Eliot, suggesting that only a man to head up the new school was lacking. "It seems to me," he wrote to Eliot, "that it is really the sole obstacle at present, for I know that much, if not the entire money required is in sight the moment we have selected a person . . . . "

Over the winter of 1896–1897, the railroad president and the university president traded nominations for the proposed position, and each disqualified at least one of the other's candidates. Compensation was a serious obstacle: Harvard could not compete with the railroads' salary scales, and Leighton insisted upon an accomplished railroad manager for the post. (The salary problem was one that Eliot understood from firsthand experience. In 1865 he had declined a post as superintendent of the Merrimac Mills in Lowell, Massachusetts, at a salary of $5000 per year. Three years later, as Harvard's president, he was being paid $3000 per year.) Whether for this reason or another, by the spring of 1897 the correspondence cooled. Leighton pointed out in April that the University of Pennsylvania was inaugurating a new course in railways, and that "the matter has been discussed at Columbia."

Leighton and Eliot corresponded frequently over the next few years, but principally about alumni activities. At the turn of the century the Los Angeles Terminal Railway was absorbed by the Los Angeles and Salt Lake Railroad, and Leighton moved on to St. Louis.

There he assumed the presidency of the Leighton and Howard Steel Company, and helped create the city's network of parks and parkways. The school of railroading remained on his mind, however. In the summer of 1901, Leighton received a letter from a young Japanese student who hoped to come to America for training in railroad management. Leighton, with understandable regret, directed the student to the Massachusetts Institute of Technology.

"I have sent you this letter," he wrote to Eliot, enclosing the Japanese student's inquiry, "showing you that there is a real need for the kind of work, which I hope someday to see instituted in Cambridge in the broad and proper way, that Harvard University and you especially are accustomed to do things."

This note marks the end of Leighton's campaign for a school of railroading. What Leighton did not know, however, was that the definition of the "broad and proper way" to teach management was only just beginning to emerge in discussions at Harvard. When finally realized, it would take a far different form. But George Leighton must have derived some special satisfaction when he was asked, in 1912, to lecture at Harvard, on the subject of "Railway Track and Loading Gauges." The lecture was sponsored not by a School of Railroading, but by an institution then in its fourth year of existence: the fledgling Graduate School of Business Administration.

CAPTAIN JOHN SMITH sailed out of Jamestown, Rhode Island, in 1614 to explore the largely unknown coastline to the north. His report on the Shawmut peninsula— later to become Boston—was succinct: only money, he said, would ever draw people there. Commerce, or the promise of it, was soon in the air along the Massachusetts coast. It was Plymouth Colony, somewhat to the south, which had the distinction of employing the first "commercial teacher" in America. In 1635, the Plymouth colonists dug deep in their pockets to hire one James Morton, who was to teach their children to "read, write, and cast accounts."

**A "chop," or trademark, of a Chinese merchant, from the days of the Boston merchant kings.**

Three years later, Harvard College opened its doors. Although it was for the next six decades the only degree-granting college in the colonies, its existence was at best precarious. Hindered by scant resources and largely ignored by the public, the College graduated only eight students a year, on average, during those early decades.

Throughout the eighteenth century and well into the nineteenth, Harvard's fortunes mirrored Boston's. In 1776, when the British evacuated the city, Boston's population was still under 10,000. But the city flourished in the first half of the nineteenth century. It was during that era that New England's merchant princes made fortunes in the shipping and textile trades, and laid the financial foundations of Boston's First Families. John Murray Forbes may be the outstanding example: at the age of seventeen, he went to China and served as assistant to the Chinese merchant Houqua, then estimated to be worth some $26 million. While helping Houqua with his business correspondence, Forbes also began chartering and loading his own ships, charging ten percent of the profits for his services. He was a millionaire while still in his early twenties.

A new aristocracy had begun to emerge in Boston. An 1846 pamphlet—entitled "Our First Men, A Calendar of Wealth, Fashion and Gentility"—in a sense verified Captain Smith's prediction, and reflected Boston's Puritan tradition: "It is no derogation, then, to the Boston aristocracy that it rests upon money. Money is something substantial. Every body knows that and feels it. Birth is a mere idea which grows every day more and more intangible."

With wealth, however, came responsibilities. One such obligation was ethical conduct in business: for example, most business transactions in Boston were concluded with a handshake. One merchant of the period suggested that mercantile honor could only be compared with a woman's: "delicate and fragile," as he put it, the merchant's honor could not "bear the slightest stain."

**John Murray Forbes made two separate fortunes in his lifetime: first in the China trade, and later in textiles. His son William also contributed to the family fortune by investing in the invention of an obscure young Boston University professor, Alexander Graham Bell.**

Another obligation — and one which may be described as distinctively Brahmin — was service. Harvard historian Samuel Eliot Morison, himself from a distinguished Boston family, described the phenomenon in *One Boy's Boston: 1887–1901*:

"When a family had accumulated a certain fortune, instead of trying to build it up still further, to become a Rockefeller or Carnegie or Huntington and then perhaps discharge its debt to society by some great foundation, it would step out of business or finance and try to accomplish something in literature, education, medical research, the arts, or public service. Generally one or two members of the family continued in business, to look after the family securities and enable the creative brothers or cousins to carry on without the handicap of poverty. Of course there were families like that in other cities, but in Boston there were so many of them as to constitute a recognized way of life."

One of the principal beneficiaries of this tradition was Harvard College, which by the mid-1800s was educating the sons of Boston's successful merchants. In 1859, Abbott Lawrence gave the largest single gift to a college ever recorded, when he donated $50,000 to found the "Lawrence Scientific School" at Harvard. Other institutions were born and benefited as well, including the Perkins Institute for the Blind, the House of Reformation, and many of New England's cultural institutions. Charles Dickens published his *American Notes*, based upon a tour of the United States, in 1843, praising what he considered Boston's relative state of enlightenment: "I sincerely believe that the public institutions and charities of this capital of Massachusetts are as nearly perfect as the most considerate wisdom, benevolence, and humanity can make them. I never in my life was more affected."

Abbott Lawrence began store clerking at the age of 15, and gradually built up the Lowell textile empire. Late in life, he gave two twenty-dollar gold pieces to his grandson Abbott Lawrence Lowell — named Harvard's president in 1909 — who wore them as cuff-buttons until his death.

**The mills of Lawrence and Lowell became the basis of New England's greatest source of wealth, following the decline of the West Indies and China trade.**

Boston had captured the high ground in American life, garnering the title "the Athens of America" in part by defining "culture" as those things that Bostonians did well. The city's trading wealth afforded it the means to attempt the creation of an ideal community; it was this spirit that impressed Dickens. The founders of the Boston Athenaeum, in their statement of purpose, noted that "the class of persons enjoying easy circumstances, and possessing surplus wealth, is comparatively numerous. As we are not called upon for large contributions for national purposes, we shall do well to take advantage of the exemption, by taxing ourselves for those institutions, which will be attended with lasting and extensive benefit, amidst all changes of our public fortunes and political affairs."

But those "changes in fortune" were already underway. New England's second significant wave of industrialization occurred in the fifteen years preceding the Civil War. The city changed: slums began to spring up; smallpox, unknown in Boston since the previous century, returned in 1845. New England's great fortunes grew larger, but by 1855 a third of Boston's residents were Irish immigrants, many of whom were oppressed by poverty and alienated from the city's traditions and institutions.

One such institution was Harvard: in 1870, for example, the College counted seven Catholics among its 563 students. With rare exceptions, few public high schools could send their graduates to Harvard, in part because the College's entrance requirements included a knowledge of Greek. This exclusivity, in turn, was representative of larger problems. In spite of Boston's democratic ideals, the College had earned a reputation as a rich man's college—and, in fact, it had consistently been the most expensive school in the country through the first half of the nineteenth century. By the middle of the century, furthermore, new charges were being leveled at Harvard: in particular, that the institution was teaching little of any practical value. The curriculum was centuries old; learning was by rote; and examinations were largely meaningless, since exams were oral, and the examiners rarely knew anything about the subject at hand.

A Harvard graduating
class of the 1870s. When
Charles Eliot assumed
Harvard's presidency in
1869, Harvard's undergraduate curriculum was mor-
ibund, and its graduate
schools of uncertain quality.

Josiah Quincy, Boston's
second mayor, was elected
president of Harvard in
1829. Quincy, one of the two
Harvard presidents before
Charles Eliot who was
not an ordained minister,
founded both the Divinity
and Law Schools at Harvard.

And broader trends did not seem to favor Harvard. While the College's enrollments climbed in the decades preceding the Civil War, Yale, Princeton, Dartmouth, and Union were all larger institutions. After the Civil War, Harvard's position deteriorated further. Between 1870 and 1880, for example, Princeton's enrollment increased by 60 percent, and Yale's by 37 percent, while Harvard's grew by only 3.7 percent.

While the College still had a core of wealthy and dedicated supporters, even the context within which these benefactors operated was changing irrevocably. Before the Civil War, there were only several dozen millionaires in the country — a large percentage of whom lived in New England — and Abbott Lawrence's 1859 gift to Harvard of $50,000 was considered a princely sum. Between the Civil War and the turn of the century, however, Johns Hopkins received a $3.5 million gift, Stanford a $24 million gift, and Chicago a $34 million gift. American millionaires now numbered in the thousands, and few of the newly wealthy lived in New England.

Harvard College could not be blamed for these external trends. But the institution's internal problems were a different matter: they were in large part the result of short-sighted administration. A succession of conservative presidents had purposefully limited the University's scope. (Harvard had been founded in the seventeenth century to train ministers, and all but two of the University's presidents up to 1869 had themselves been ministers.) This tradition hindered research and course development in practical fields.

At the same time, new standards of scholarship were being established — principally in Europe — and Harvard was failing to keep pace. To compound the error, Harvard's leaders tended to blame this failure on the consumer: as late as the 1860s, for example, Harvard's President Thomas Hill complained that America's talented students seemed unable to attain a truly cultured status "without being transplanted to Europe for a few years."

By the late 1860s, a heated national debate on the subject of education was under way, and Harvard found itself an isolated observer of the discussion. Americans, always inclined toward the practical, had had that impulse greatly reinforced by the industrialization which had begun to transform their country. Educators and laymen alike sought to define a "new education."

**University Hall, Harvard's administration building, circa 1870.**

IT WAS IN THIS CLIMATE that a young MIT chemistry professor, Charles W. Eliot — then 34 years old — published two articles on education, which appeared in the *Atlantic Monthly*. The first article began with a bold question:

"What can I do with my boy? I want to give him a practical education that will prepare him better than I was prepared to follow my business or any other active calling. The classical schools and the colleges do not offer what I want. Where can I put him? Here is a real need and a very serious problem."

The Harvard Corporation — that is, the President and Fellows of Harvard College — agreed, and, on March 9, 1869, Eliot was informed of his pending election by the Corporation as president of Harvard. The University's Board of Overseers — of which Eliot was a member — balked, but the Corporation held firm, and Eliot was installed.

President Eliot first transformed the Medical School's curriculum, and later its campus. Once housed in cramped quarters on Boston's Shattuck Street (facing page, top), by 1906 the School had three new buildings (facing page, bottom). The new campus was underwritten by J.P. Morgan (below, left); John D. Rockefeller (below, right) contributed $1 million to the School's endowment.

The new president defined his first task as the building of a *university* out of the disparate elements of Harvard College and its five graduate schools — of Medicine, Divinity, Law, Engineering, and Dentistry. This would place new demands on the University's administrators, and Eliot soon insisted that his Corporation meet twice a month, instead of once. Then, less than a year into his presidency, he tackled the University's graduate schools.

In 1869, Harvard's Medical School was flourishing: it had, after all, 308 students enrolled, compared with 562 in the College's four classes. An interested observer — such as Eliot — could detect some weaknesses, however. For one thing, there were no entrance examinations; as a result, large numbers of underqualified students were admitted, some of whom could barely read or write. Final examinations were oral, as in the College; at the Medical School, morever, they were only five minutes long, and a student needed to pass exams in only five out of nine subjects to graduate. In short order, Eliot raised the School's standards for admission, instruction, and examination, which gradually elevated it to preeminence in its field. Late in Eliot's tenure, J. P. Morgan, Jr., donated three buildings — completed in 1906 — and John D. Rockefeller contributed a million dollars to its endowment.

**Hastings Hall, at Harvard's Law School, circa 1880.**

The Law School in its turn experienced a similar upheaval. In 1869, half of its students had had no college training; after being enrolled for eighteen months, students were eligible to receive a degree. Again, Eliot pushed for higher standards, and also forced a skeptical faculty to accept the new "case method" of teaching. This experiment became the focus of an international debate; its eventual success brought worldwide acclaim to the Law School. As with the Medical School, enrollments first declined, and then, as standards rose, increased sharply.

Eliot considered his reestablishment of the elective system in the College a key accomplishment of his presidency. Against strong opposition, Eliot gave increasing numbers of undergraduates the opportunity to design their own educations. In these and other policies, the president emphasized the practical and the relevant in education. At a 1905 alumni dinner, he summed up his feelings on the subject:

"We seek at Harvard to put all the various sciences and arts into practice so that public advantage may result. We seek to train doers, achievers — men whose successful personal careers are made subservient to the public good. We are not interested here in producing languid observers of the world, mere spectators in the game of life, or fastidious critics of other men's labors. We want to produce by hundreds and thousands strenuous workers in the world of today — a more interesting world, I venture to say, than has yet offered a field for splendid intellectual and moral achievement . . . .

"The university has a great task on its hands in view of the tremendous advance of the world. That is why we have strengthened every department for immediate effective work in a world that has changed and developed with appalling rapidity."

**Oliver Wendell Holmes, the Medical School's Parkman Professor of Anatomy and Physiology. He noted in December, 1871: "Our new president, Eliot, has turned the whole University over like a flapjack. There never was such a bouleversement as that in our medical faculty."**

*"There is a new president . . ."*

Oliver Wendell Holmes, a prominent member of the Medical School faculty, was surprised to find Harvard's newly installed President Eliot in attendance at the School's faculty meetings. "He presides with an aplomb, a quiet, imperturbable, serious good humor that it is impossible not to admire," he wrote to a friend. Holmes recalled a caustic question posed by a faculty member at one such meeting:

" 'How is it, I should like to ask,' said one of our number the other evening, 'that this faculty has gone on for eighty years, managing its own affairs and doing it well—for the Medical School is the most flourishing department connected with the College—how is it that we have been going on so well in the orderly path for eighty years, and now within *three or four months* it is proposed to change all our mode of carrying on the School—it seems very extraordinary, and I should like to know how it happens.'

" 'I can answer Dr. _____'s question very easily,' said the bland, grave young man' "—as Holmes described Eliot—" 'there is a new president.' "

"**What can I do with my boy?**" Charles Eliot asked rhetorically in the February, 1869, *Atlantic Monthly.* "**I want to give him a prac-tical education that will prepare him better than I was prepared to follow my business or any other active callings.**" Below: Eliot later in life, with his grandson.

BY 1898, PRESIDENT ELIOT was able to enjoy the undis-puted success of his experiments in education. In a quarter of a century, Harvard had moved to center stage in American undergraduate education. Even in gradu-ate education — then dominated by Johns Hopkins — his institution could make claims on excellence. But Eliot remained concerned about the "appalling rapid-ity" of change that he perceived in the world around him. What was Harvard University not doing that it should be doing to prepare itself, and the "doers and achievers" among its students, for the twentieth century?

Discussions with George Bridge Leighton on rail-road education — one tentative answer to this question — were shouldered aside by events in the outside world. Popular sentiment against Spanish rule in Cuba had been growing for several years. War erupted in the spring of 1898, and ended in a stunning American victory within the year. Under the terms of the peace treaty, Spain ceded Puerto Rico, Guam, and the Philip-pines to the United States.

For the first time, America was a colonial power. Annexation became the key campaign issue in 1900: while the Republicans applauded "expansion," the Democrats condemned what they termed "imperial-ism" and "militarism." On January 9, 1900, Indiana's fiery young senator, Albert J. Beveridge, rose on the floor of the Senate to deliver a ringing endorsement of expansion:

"Mr. President," he intoned, "self-government and internal development have been the dominant notes of our first century; administration and the development of other lands will be the dominant notes of our second century. . . . [God] has made us the master organizers of the world to establish system where chaos reigns. . . . He has made us adepts in government that we may administer government among savage and senile peoples."

It was a heady speech, and one which reflected the prevailing mood in America. Unexpectedly, the country had humiliated a proud European power, and had thereby gained a place on the world stage. The Repub-lican victory in 1900 ushered in a sweeping series of international interventions, both large and small. In rapid succession, America set up governmental bodies in the Philippines, Cuba, and Puerto Rico; it brought 1,280 Cuban teachers to Harvard for retraining; it abol-ished polygamy on Guam; it established a territorial government in Hawaii; it negotiated to buy the Dutch West Indies and the Galapagos islands; it participated in the creation of an "Open Door" policy toward China, and subsequently sent 2,400 troops to help crush the Boxer Rebellion; it sent 5,000 tons of corn to relieve famine in India; it sent more exhibits to the 1900 Paris Exposition than any other country (including butter from George B. Leighton's Monadnock Farms, which earned a Silver Medal); and it won 16 of 21 athletic con-tests in the Paris international games. America was flirt-ing with the notion of empire, and it seemed as if the country might indeed be embarking on a campaign to "establish system where chaos reigns."

For forty years, Charles Eliot *was* Harvard, to many. In an undergraduate rowing competition, Eliot and his teammates donned crimson scarfs to distinguish themselves; this was the origin of "Harvard crimson."

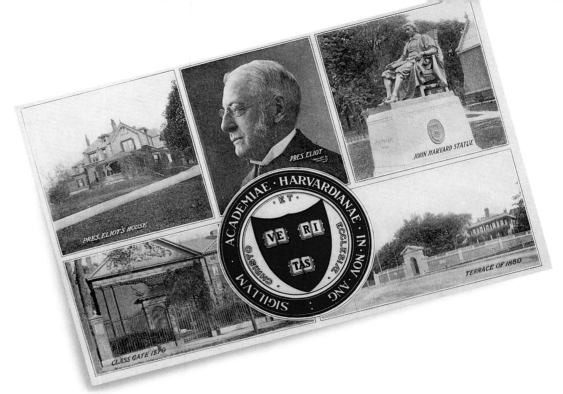

Fourteen years after Eliot's death in 1934, the Post Office included him in its "Famous Americans" series.

American "expansionism" at the turn of the century took many forms. In the summer of 1900, 1,280 Cuban teachers arrived at Harvard for "retraining." President Eliot was called upon to lead a parade celebrating the event.

**Archibald Cary Coolidge was an early advocate of a Harvard school of public administration.**

**A. Lawrence Lowell, who argued strongly against a school of public administration, and strongly in favor of a school of business.**

**F. W. Taussig moderated the debate.**

HARVARD, HOWEVER, WAS NOT CONVINCED. In 1898, President Eliot had broached the idea of a "training school for diplomacy and the government service" to a young professor in the Department of History, Archibald Cary Coolidge. Coolidge had in turn discussed the idea with A. Lawrence Lowell, a prominent Boston lawyer — and grandson of textile king Abbott Lawrence — who since 1897 had been a lecturer in the government department. "I suppose," Coolidge wrote to Eliot on December 2, 1899, "that it would be necessary to create a special department and that department might be made part of the division of history and economics, with some change in title and arrangement."

Several days later, Lowell — who had spent the previous summer in Europe studying the English, French, and Dutch colonial civil services — argued strongly against Coolidge's concept. His letter predated Senator Beveridge's speech by three weeks; his conclusions, like Major Higginson's on railroading education, were blunt:

"When we were talking about the subject last year I had in mind the giving of new courses, which might be valuable in connection with *all* our colonial problems; rather than the systematic training of men for a Colonial Civil Service. In fact it seemed to me that courses such as I had in mind would be quite as valuable for men who were likely to have only commercial relations with the Colonies . . . as for the instruction of aspirants for a Colonial Civil Service.

"[The Coolidge sketch] adds very little to the existing courses, but groups the old ones so as to form systematic departments of study intended solely as a preparation for the public service. On this point I agree with Professor [of Law Henry] Strobel that it would lead to disappointment to give men a training for a special career which might not afterward be open to them."

This argument seems to have carried the day. While there might be some good reason to train young men for *commercial* roles overseas, Harvard apparently would not be called upon to staff the American empire. For the next five years, Eliot floated no more trial balloons about a school for the colonial service.

Instead, in 1900, he picked up another thread in his correspondence. This time, the instigator was Robert G. Valentine, a member of Harvard's Class of 1896, and at that point an instructor of English at MIT. He wrote to Eliot early in 1900 with a proposal for training business leaders. Eliot sent the letter along to Professor F. W. Taussig, a distinguished member of the Department of Economics:

"Will you please let me know," he wrote on March 29, 1900, "what you think of the enclosed letter and of its author? Its view corresponds closely with those of a considerable number of men engaged in corporation business who have told me with a great deal of urgency that the universities were not supplying the great business corporations with well-trained young men who would make responsible managers. These corporate officers have also told me what Mr. Valentine says, that real leaders are as a rule not to be found at present in the graded service of great corporations, the result being that men are put into the highest positions by favoritism pure and simple, sometimes by accident, and sometimes by more or less selection from among the actual managers of similar corporations. Instances of wreck will occur to you at once . . . .

"Alexander Agassiz, of the Calumet and Hecla, John E. Hudson of the Bell Telephone, and almost all the large railroad men I meet complain of the same thing. The difficulty of finding good university presidents is analogous, though not the same. Can Harvard University do anything of a systematic sort to provide from year to year a few young men who can grow into the leaders wanted?"

The "grand old man" of Harvard's economics department, F. W. Taussig: a founder of the Harvard Business School, and advocate of the Socratic method.

## *"I talked too much myself"*

Frank William Taussig was born in St. Louis in 1859, the son of a resourceful Czech immigrant who was, at various points in his life, a wholesale chemist, a physician, a federal tax collector, a banker, and a railroad president.

Young Frank William, however, was drawn to the life of the mind. In his adolescence, he was a voracious reader, and after a year at Washington University, he was able — without having taken the standard entrance examinations — to persuade Harvard College to accept him as a sophomore. He soon distinguished himself as a brilliant undergraduate scholar, taking every available course in economics. He was graduated with the Harvard Class of 1879 — members of which would later contribute, as a group, to Taussig's subscription drive for the Harvard Business School.

After the customary "Grand Tour" of Europe — during which Taussig engaged more in scholarly pursuits than in sightseeing — he returned to Harvard planning to enroll in the Law School. But he decided instead to accept a half-time position as secretary to President Eliot, and to pursue simultaneously a Ph.D. in economics. His studies focused on the historical, legal, and political aspects of economics; he soon developed a preference for the practical solution over the theoretical refinement — a predilection which he would retain throughout his lifetime.

Working with Eliot, Taussig also gained an early exposure to the administrative processes of the University. This served him well when — after earning his doctorate and his postponed law degree — Harvard offered him an instructorship. He declined the post as beneath him, and Harvard was obliged to offer him — in 1886 — an assistant professorship in the economics department. At 27, he was the youngest member of the Harvard faculty. This was, coincidentally, Harvard's two hundred and fiftieth

anniversary. "I seem to have a better chance than any other [faculty] member," Taussig noted in his 1890 class report, "of taking part in the three-hundredth anniversary when that time comes around."

Taussig was promoted to full professor in 1892, and was appointed to the newly established Henry Lee Professorship in 1901. In 1896, he was named editor of the *Quarterly Journal of Economics*, a post which he held until 1936. From this position, and through his published works, he was a dominant figure in economics for over four decades.

But he is best remembered today as a teacher. Three of his distinguished colleagues — J. A. Schumpeter, A. H. Cole, and E. S. Mason — contributed an article to the *Journal* following Taussig's death in 1940. They summarized his approach to teaching as follows:

"He was one of the first to realize that economic theory, like the theoretical part of any other subject, is not a storehouse of recipes or a philosophy, but a tool with which to analyze the economic patterns of real life. Hence the teacher's task consists in imparting a certain way of looking at facts, a habit of mind, an art of formulating the questions which we are to address to the facts. But it is not enough to understand the tool; the student must learn to handle it. Taussig's way of achieving this end was what he himself liked to call the Socratic method. At each meeting of the class, he started discussion on a particular problem which he admirably knew how to make interesting, and allowed his students to fight it out, guiding proceedings with a good-natured firmness that never has had and never will have its like. Returning from a meeting of his course, he once told a friend, 'I am not pleased with my performance today. I talked too much myself.'"

IN A SENSE, of course, business education was as old as business itself. Apprenticeship had been the prevailing means of education in and access to business for centuries, and in some realms of commerce the apprentice system still dominated and served adequately. But early in the nineteenth century, it became clear that the apprentice system was failing on two counts: it was producing inadequate numbers of prospective merchants, and it was failing to accommodate change.

A New York newspaperman, James Gordon Bennett, may have the distinction of having founded formal business education in America. In 1824, with appropriate entrepreneurial fanfare, he announced the founding of his "Permanent Commercial School," which would offer courses in "reading, elocution, penmanship, and arithmetic; algebra, astronomy, history, and geography; moral philosophy, commercial law, and political economy; English grammar and composition; and also, if required, the French and German languages by natives of those countries."

Bennett's school was evidently not permanent—after its founding, it disappears from the record—but it was a model that was soon copied successfully. By the 1830s and 1840s, such commercial schools began to prosper across the eastern and midwestern United States. Peter Duff started his "Duff's Business College" in Pittsburgh in 1839, and his school (still in existence today as Duff's Business Institute) would soon boast many prominent alumni, including catsup king H. J. Heinz. James A. Garfield, later to become President, applauded the efforts of these early schools: "The business colleges which this country originated are a protest against that capital defect in our schools and colleges which consists in their refusal to give a training for business life."

The rapid acceleration of American industrialization, spurred by the railroad and telegraph booms, soon outstripped the capacity of these independent schools. The next stage of development was the "chain school," which offered a standardized curriculum in branches throughout a given geographical region. The first such chain was founded in Cleveland in 1853 by H. D. Stratton and H. B. Bryant, who, by the 1860s, were managing 50 schools. Another, managed by George W. Brown, comprised 30 schools in 22 midwestern towns and cities.

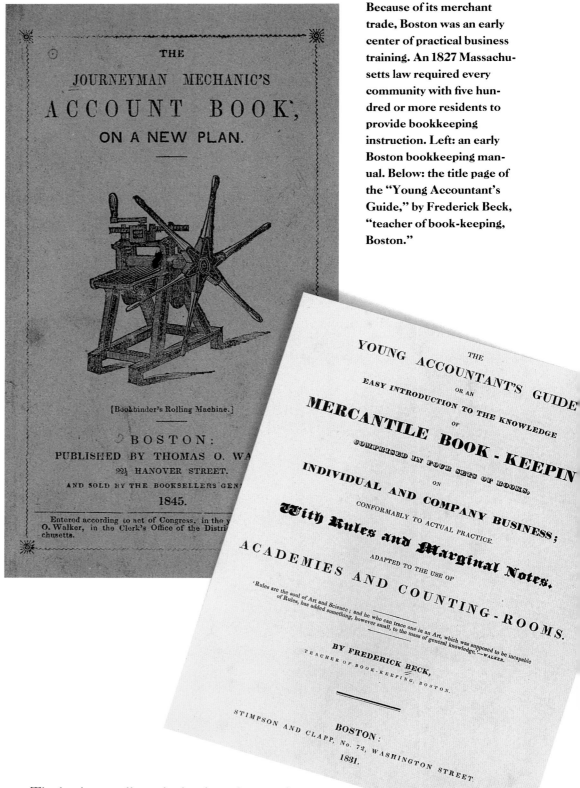

Because of its merchant trade, Boston was an early center of practical business training. An 1827 Massachusetts law required every community with five hundred or more residents to provide bookkeeping instruction. Left: an early Boston bookkeeping manual. Below: the title page of the "Young Accountant's Guide," by Frederick Beck, "teacher of book-keeping, Boston."

The business colleges had serious shortcomings: their standards varied greatly; their curricula were often too parochial, or, in the case of the chain schools, inadequately responsive to local needs. Yet they served a key role, and at least partially educated many of those who would complete the large-scale industrialization of America. When Herbert Hoover enrolled at the new Stanford University, he was already a graduate of the Capital Business College in Salem, Oregon; Thomas D. Watson trained at the Elmira (New York) School of Commerce; Henry Ford attended the Detroit Business University; and John D. Rockefeller and Harvey B. Firestone were fellow alumni of the Dyke College of Cleveland.

Harvard's aloofness notwithstanding, American universities in the nineteenth century were well aware of the popularity—and profitability—of business education. The first course in practical economics was offered in 1849 by the University of Louisiana, later Tulane; the course was described as a combination of "commerce, political economy, and statistics." By 1871, 23 American colleges were offering some form of commercial education.

James Gordon Bennett may have been the first to formalize the idea of business education in America, but Joseph Wharton must be credited with having elevated it. In 1881, Wharton, an imaginative Philadelphia ironmaster, donated $100,000 to the University of Pennsylvania for the creation of the "Wharton School," intended to offer courses of instruction in finance and commerce. The Wharton School began as a three-year curriculum within the university's college of liberal arts, leading to a baccalaureate degree. By 1889, the school's success had led to the creation of a wide-ranging undergraduate curriculum of a full four years.

Other schools followed suit. The University of California and the University of Chicago established business-related curricula in 1898. Business education was, in some ways, an idea whose time had come. But it was also the basis of bitter controversy within the academy, crystallizing as it did two contentious questions at once: what was the role of the university, and what relationship did the professions have to that role? Twenty years later, Thorstein Veblen, in *The Higher Learning in America*, would caustically articulate one point of view:

"The primacy among pragmatic interests has passed from religion to business, and the school of commerce is the exponent of this primacy. It is the perfect flower of the secularization of the universities.

"The professional knowledge and skill of physicians, surgeons, dentists, pharmacists, agriculturalists, engineers of all kinds, perhaps even of journalists, is of some use to the community at large, at the same time that it may be profitable to the bearers of it. . . . But such is not the case with the training designed to give proficiency in business. No gain comes to the community at large from increasing the business proficiency of any number of its young men. There are already much too many of these businessmen, much too astute and proficient in their calling, for the common good. A higher average business efficiency simply raises activity and avidity in business to a higher average pitch and fervour, with very little other material result than a redistribution of ownership; since business is occupied with the competitive acquisition of wealth, not with its production. . . . The work of the College of Commerce, accordingly, is a peculiarly futile line of endeavor for any public institution, in that it serves neither the intellectual advancement nor the material welfare of the community."

COLLEGE PRESIDENTS were also learning, to their dismay, that many businessmen had arrived at the same conclusion as Veblen, although by a very different route. Business practitioners—far from being concerned that such training was too effective—contended instead that higher education was irrelevant to success in business. The nation's colleges, they argued, should stay away from the subject. By the 1890s, Harvard's President Eliot had developed a stock response to such criticisms. A February 12, 1897, letter to a Mr. Oscar Ely, of Holyoke, Massachusetts, is representative:

"I have no adequate statistics," wrote Eliot, "about the success of our graduates in business. From fifteen to twenty percent of every graduating class go into business, including under the term business the service of business corporations; and their success in business is truly remarkable. In my own class, which numbered only 89, fifteen men succeeded eminently in business, being a larger proportion of decided success than my classmates obtained in any other calling. . . . Most of the desirable business corporation appointments in Boston are filled by our graduates. . . . It stands to reason that thorough mental training must give a man an advantage in any business which requires strong mental work."

Four years later, in a letter to R. T. Crane of Chicago, Eliot defined "business" as "banking, transportation, manufacturing, mining, large-scale farming, and engineering in all its branches. These occupations require nowadays in all their higher levels a trained mind, and a good deal of appropriate information. This training and information can only be acquired in colleges and scientific schools. A young man who is going into business had better take an academic course, in my sense of the term, if he has any mind to train. That is an indisputable proposition, and there is no use discussing it."

**Joseph Wharton and the Wharton School: elevating business education on the undergraduate level.**

Harvard University's School of Veterinary Medicine, President Eliot's only unsuccessful experiment in education, had "accommodations for twenty-three horses, a properly fitted room for dogs, and space for a few cows and other animals."

But Eliot's correspondent did not intend to let him have the last word on the subject. Crane, the head of a firm which manufactured pipes, valves, and fittings in twelve branches around the country, included Eliot's response — along with others received from American university presidents — in a small pamphlet produced the following year. Crane called the publication "an investigation" of "the utility of an academic or classical education for young men who have to earn their own living and who expect to pursue a commercial life."

Where Veblen would seek to protect the academy from business, Crane sought to protect would-be entrepreneurs from a fleecing at the hands of the academy. In his pamphlet, he featured Eliot's comments prominently as an example of a "confusion of thought." College authorities, he concluded, "instead of laying the facts before the young men who are preparing to enter college . . . will go right on deceiving as many as they can and taking the money of those to whom they can give nothing in return but useless knowledge. Practically they stand on the same level as the merchant who sells goods which he knows to be shoddy."

R.T. Crane's "investigation," reflecting one businessman's view of business education.

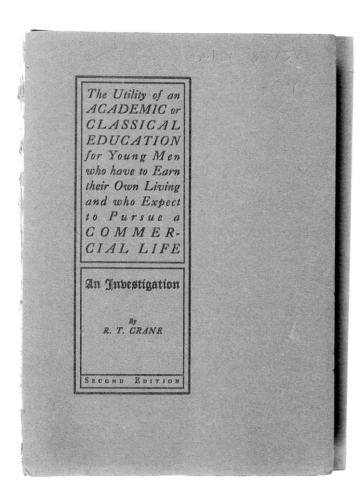

The Utility of an ACADEMIC or CLASSICAL EDUCATION for Young Men who have to Earn their Own Living and who Expect to Pursue a COMMERCIAL LIFE

An Investigation

By R. T. CRANE

SECOND EDITION

Between these two hostile camps, Eliot and his lieutenants took careful steps to begin training students for business careers. The Department of Economics, and particularly Professor Taussig, played an active part in a period of experimentation that began after the turn of the century. In June of 1900, for example, Taussig contacted Higginson, asking for help in securing annual reports from the "great railway corporations":

"You may recall," Taussig wrote, "that we are establishing for next year a course on Principles of Accounting, in which we are making a move toward training designed especially for young fellows who are going into business."

The accounting course was offered in the fall of 1900 by the Department of Economics, and was taught by William Morse Cole. "Everything that I hear about this course is good," Taussig wrote to Eliot in November. "It is taken by considerable numbers, about sixty men. . . . Cole is proceeding now to railway and corporation accounts and auditing. He proposes also to say something about municipal and other public accounts." That spring, Cole made railroads the subject of Economics 5: "I took them from the points of view of the manager and the investor," Cole explained in a letter to Eliot. In the same semester, the Department of Economics also offered "Legal Principles in the Application to Industrial Problems," which Taussig described as "another of those courses designated particularly for students who propose to enter on a business career."

Eliot kept himself well informed of this modest progress, and supported it where he could. But he had at that time a far more pressing concern on his hands: by the year 1900, Harvard's School of Veterinary Medicine had reached a crisis point. Founded with Eliot's blessing in 1882, it had quickly fallen upon hard times. The School's deficit in 1900 was $4,200; to that date, Harvard had paid nearly $40,000 out of its general funds to offset the School's annual deficits. Eliot was faced with a painful and unprecedented task: the termination of a Harvard graduate school, and one which he himself had helped to found.

HARVARD UNIVERSITY.

SCHOOL OF VETERINARY MEDICINE.

A general veterinary establishment for the treatment and care of lame, sick or wounded horses, cattle, sheep, and dogs is maintained in connection with this School.

HOSPITAL.—The hospital is at the corner of Village and Lucas Streets, Boston. It has good accommodations for twenty-three horses, (to which it is proposed to add this season nine more stalls) a properly fitted room for dogs, and space for a few cows and other animals.  The patients will be under the professional charge of Mr. CHARLES P. LYMAN, Fellow of the Royal College of Veterinary Surgeons, London, assisted by ROBERT H. HARRISON, D. V. S.

BUSSEY FARM.—The school also has at its disposal commodious buildings and paddocks at the Bussey Farm, West Roxbury (Forest Hill Station, on the Boston and Providence R. R.), where cattle can be received and cared for, and where horses not required for present use, or suffering from lamenesses or illnesses which require long seasons of rest, can receive all proper care and treatment, together with the benefit grass paddocks in summer and a warm yard in winter.

Any person having sick or lame animals to be cared for ca... benefits of the establishment upon the payment of a fixed... treatment, and medicines.

FREE CLINIC.—On certain days... Hospital on Village St., at wh... charge except the actual cost...

ANNUAL SUBSCRIBERS.—... beginning June 1st and paymen... 70 Water St., Boston), the follow... establishment:—

1.  Each subscriber may have... treatment an unlimited number of... medicines only (not exceeding $1.00... opinion of the surgeons of the school... desire to retain in his own possessio... amining the animal away from the es... amined as to soundness in the course of... surgeons thereon, either verbally or in wri... *patients will not be visited, and ho... away from the establishment.*

The surgeons will visit animals upon th... not under the above arrangement with annua...

For further information address CHARL... Faculty of Veterinary Medicine, 50 Village St...

*May 14th, 1884.*

"I have thus far succeeded in obtaining a reprieve for the School from year to year," Eliot wrote to Dean Charles P. Lyman on October 31, 1900, "but I can do so no longer. . . . I need not say that I deeply regret this ending for the work to which you have devoted yourself for eighteen years." The following month, the Corporation voted to close the hospital in June, 1901, and to take in no new students.

The veterinary school, furthermore, was only the most extreme case among many. In 1903, Eliot was forced to cut the budget of the Department of Government. (This prompted an angry letter from A. Lawrence Lowell, by then a full professor. "When I accepted a professorship four years ago, I was in hopes that we might build up a department of Government worthy of Harvard," he wrote. "At the present moment Government is, I believe, relatively the weakest taught at Harvard.") By 1904, work on Harvard's imposing stadium had stopped, and an athletic committee memo to Eliot said flatly that construction was "not likely to be taken up again until the present debt has been paid off." In December of 1904, Eliot found it necessary to inform ten faculty members that their impending raises would be forthcoming out of a special fund, for one year only, because of the "financial straits" of the Corporation.

IN SHORT, the early years of the twentieth century did not seem to be an auspicious time for new initiatives. But Eliot, then in his third decade as president of Harvard, was as aware as anyone of the cyclical nature of the University's fortunes. The fate of the School of Veterinary Medicine was not repeated: in most cases, once an idea was embraced, Harvard found the resources needed to support it.

Conversely, Harvard was usually able to find an idea to match available resources. This was the happier landscape that Eliot surveyed in 1903, when sewing machine magnate Gordon McKay—himself not a college graduate—left the bulk of his large fortune to Harvard to support education in applied science. The endowment stipulated that the resources "be used to promote applied science [in part] by maintaining professorships, workshops, laboratories, and collections for any or all of those scientific subjects which have or may hereafter have, applications useful to man."

The terms of the endowment left the definition of "useful applied sciences" entirely up to Harvard. Furthermore, the University would have ample time to ponder the question: under the terms of the bequest, a million dollars in interest had to accumulate before Harvard could have access to any of the funds. The most optimistic projections placed that date at least four or five years into the future. What definitions would Harvard arrive at in the meantime?

The 1903 bequest of Gordon McKay inspired President Eliot to define "scientific subjects which have or may hereafter have, applications useful to man." Was business such a science?

Eliot's 1901 letter to manufacturer Crane had suggested that engineering might be considered a sub-specialty of business. This was certainly illustration by exaggeration; Eliot would never have articulated such a point of view to his Harvard peers in the applied sciences. Still, he resisted all efforts to confine the range of fields that McKay's endowment might benefit. When Professor of Mining and Metallurgy H. L. Smyth proposed in late 1905 that Harvard use the McKay funds to establish a school of engineering, Eliot stated categorically that this would not be possible:

"The most striking thing about the McKay bequest is its comprehending every science which can be applied for the benefit of mankind; and the President and Fellows are sure to avail themselves to the utmost of that comprehensiveness. Moreover, the President and Fellows for many years past have refused to create special schools like a school of commerce, a school of mining, a school of finance, a school of journalism, etc. So far as is practicable, they would even like to avoid any deep division between pure science and applied science."

Another factor entered into the process of definition. In 1903, roughly concurrent with the announcement of the McKay bequest, Harvard University and the Massachusetts Institute of Technology were engaged in a third attempt to merge their resources in technical education. (The first such attempt had been made in 1870, and the second in 1897.) This latest version proposed that MIT move from its location on Boston's Boylston Street to a site closer to Harvard, and join Harvard in a cooperative venture in the applied sciences.

The McKay bequest provided additional incentive to both parties in the proposed merger. The planned pooling of resources — although hailed by most observers as selfless and farsighted — was essentially a pragmatic move on the part of both institutions. But ultimately this third merger effort was scuttled on neither practical nor ethical grounds: in October of 1905, the Massachusetts State Supreme Judicial Court ruled that MIT could not legally sell its Boylston Street property, which had been donated to it by the Commonwealth. Without the revenue from that sale, MIT could not move.

"IT PRACTICALLY RESOLVES ITSELF to this: that Professor Gross is the only one who knows you and speaks for you."

President Eliot was brusquely concluding an interview, one day in 1901, with a young job applicant in his office. The scholar he was interrogating was slight in stature, with black hair and brooding dark eyes; the young man's evident nervousness reinforced his fox-like appearance.

"You have two possible sponsors from outside," Eliot continued, "who cannot know your work very intimately, and you have had no previous experience in teaching."

Edwin F. Gay left his first encounter with Harvard's "personal Judgement Day" somewhat shaken. Charles Gross, Harvard's eminent medieval constitutional historian, was waiting in Eliot's outer office to learn how his young protégé had fared. Not well, Gay confessed; the president had seemed more interested in his pedigree than in his academic qualifications. Shortly thereafter, Gay set sail for Europe with little hope of a job at Harvard. He was very surprised to receive, several weeks later, an offer of employment from Eliot.

Eliot's gruffness during their first meeting notwithstanding, the president had been impressed with the young economic historian. But a more pressing argument for retaining Gay was the then dire situation of Harvard's Department of Economics. Recently, one of the department's leading members had died, and two other professors had resigned. Furthermore, Professor Taussig had become seriously ill the preceding year, and had been forced to take a two-year leave of absence. The department was shorthanded, and Gay seemed qualified to fill in. As a result, Eliot offered him a lectureship on the history of economics, beginning in the fall of 1902.

Gay accepted immediately, finished his dissertation, and returned to America in August, 1902. "I shall be happy indeed to be home and to settle down at last," he wrote to his wife. "This Ulysses is tired of wandering." Gay experienced some initial difficulties translating his years of study into lectures for undergraduates, and he soon developed a reputation among Harvard students as a particularly demanding instructor. But

## Swings of the pendulum

President Eliot's notes on his interview with Edwin F. Gay do indeed reflect an interest in his prospective employee's "pedigree," as Gay surmised: "1630 —John Gay," he wrote. "Has some money; has lived on it."

Like Eliot, Edwin F. Gay was the product of a family which had lived in Massachusetts for many generations. But Gay had been born in Detroit and raised in Au Sable, Wisconsin, then a rough and ready sawmill town in which his father had a financial interest. Aaron Gay's financial success had enabled him to send his family to Europe for the children's education. Young Edwin's childhood and early adolescence were characterized by contradictions: he was a Yankee born in Detroit, a relatively wealthy child in a poor town, and then an American boy educated primarily in European schools.

Gay returned to America for high school, where he was most interested in botany; it was not until his junior year at the University of Michigan that he settled upon history as his principal field of interest. This led him to Germany and England, following his graduation in 1890; there he spent nearly thirteen years, filling what he perceived as gaps in his education while also pursuing a doctorate in European economic history.

His various studies gradually transformed his interpretations of economic history. As a college student, Gay had lamented the impact of the Industrial Revolution, and had argued that men should "return to the spirit of such workers as old Nuremberg sent forth, artist workmen with honest pride in their work, whether they tanned hides or carved statues." But eventually he developed a dynamic vision of economic history: it was, he concluded, a record of swings of the pendulum between periods when social controls dominated, and periods dominated by the actions of aggressive individuals. The former periods were static, characterized by security and stability. The latter periods, ushered in by the introduction of new tools, weapons, or other forces, were controlled by the powerful individuals who introduced those forces.

These dynamic periods, Gay now felt, were crucial to economic development. The Industrial Revolution, for all its unwelcome side effects, had made possible new levels of productivity and prosperity. The role of the economic historian, as Gay perceived it, was to study and comprehend these cycles, and to suggest ways of restraining their excesses.

It was this thesis, as well as Gay's knowledge of the medieval economy of England, which earned the attention of Harvard's Charles Gross, and which eventually led to Gay's interview with President Eliot.

his reputation among his colleagues grew. He was promoted to assistant professor in 1903, and to full professor (and acting chairman of the department) in 1906. "Eliot kept promoting Gay so fast," wrote one observer, "that people wondered what was next." Significantly, Gay also overcame some initial skepticism on the part of Professor Taussig, the acknowledged "grand old man" of the department:

"Gay . . . shows a most willing spirit," Taussig wrote to Eliot in September of 1905, "and will undertake anything that seems departmentally advisable. The more I have to do with him, the better I like him and his ways."

LATER THAT MONTH, Taussig received a letter from A. Lawrence Lowell. Both men were influential powers in their respective departments — Taussig in economics, and Lowell in government. They were also social acquaintances, with neighboring summer houses in Cotuit on the south shore of Cape Cod. Lowell's note began with a reference to the train ride to Boston that they occasionally took together:

"I send you this to beguile your way up on the train. An objection to your plan of a course at Harvard to fit for the civil service that appeals to me forcibly is the same one which was raised to a similar plan some years ago, and that is that the course is to fit for a career that does not yet fully exist, and hence may prove a will-o'-the-wisp for a student who follows it.

"The problem in regard to the commercial course," Lowell continued, "is a very different one. The question there, I take it, is whether the course we offer is the best training for general business, or whether a general training in academic studies is better. General business is a pretty vague thing, for which it is probably impossible to give anything like a professional training. When the same question was before the Institute of Technology some years ago (and I happened to be on the committee) I suggested the wisdom of carving out of business some profession, just as the existing professions have been carved out of the general occupations of men. It seemed to me that it might be possible to treat railroads as the subject of a special profession, and train men specially for the work, giving them a

sufficient general knowledge of Engineering and Political Economy, together with a more detailed knowledge of Transportation. The plan found no favor, and very likely did not deserve any."

In part, Lowell was reiterating to Taussig what he had said six years earlier to Eliot: that training for careers in public service was a weak foundation for a school, since such careers might not exist. Once again, as in 1899, Eliot had raised the question of a school of diplomacy to Professors Coolidge and Taussig; once again, Lowell had been consulted informally, and felt compelled to object to the plan that was taking shape. Lowell's own thinking on the subject had clearly evolved, however. In 1899, he had contemplated training in the commercial aspects of the budding American "empire." Now, he supported the "carving out of business of some profession" — perhaps railroading — and the training of men for a career in that new profession.

Lowell's objections to civil service training did not stop developments in that direction, however. On October 24, 1906, at a meeting of Harvard's Division of History and Political Science, Chairman Charles H. Haskins announced the findings of a committee (comprising himself, Edwin Gay, and Archibald Cary Coolidge) appointed to investigate "the feasibility of organizing courses preparatory to the public service." The Division declared itself in sympathy with the committee's favorable report, and appointed a new committee — which would include Professors Taussig, Gay, and Silas McVane — "to consider the possibility of establishing a separate school of public and private business and to report to the division a detailed plan for such a school."

Taussig, with Eliot's blessing, chaired the new committee of three, which went to work on a detailed plan for the new school. They envisioned a school which would draw upon existing or planned courses in the Departments of History, Law, Government, and Economics.

It was also Taussig who showed a new draft of the plan to Lawrence Lowell in December, 1906. Lowell, in spite of his strong and oft-stated objections, was reluctant to criticize the plan:

"In thinking the project over it seems to me that while there are things in it that are well worth trying, there are defects of organization and object likely to endanger seriously its success. But an eleventh hour critic is apt to be nothing but a marplot. To those who have been familiar with a plan through the various stages of its development, and threshed it out, a stranger who comes in newly at the end with suggestions is always more of a nuisance than a help."

But Taussig persisted: he wanted a clearer sense of the "defects of organization and object" that Lowell perceived. The following month, Lowell obliged. "The diplomatic service is not a career," he reiterated in a blunt letter. "The colonial service, also, does not exist, and there is no great reason for supposing that it will.

"In the business side of the plan I take a great deal more interest. Although, as I think I told you, I do not believe much in the value of any special training for general business, I should like very much to see training for particular branches of business which could be

Judge Francis C. Lowell, like his cousin A. Lawrence Lowell, opposed a school of public administration at Harvard. In a January, 1906, *Atlantic Monthly* article, he made public his views on the subject.

## THE
# ATLANTIC MONTHLY

### JANUARY, 1906

## AMERICAN DIPLOMACY

### BY FRANCIS C. LOWELL

At home and abroad there has been much criticism of American diplomatic representatives as compared with those of European countries. It is often said that our men are much inferior to their expert colleagues from Europe, and we are urged to adopt a system like the European, for their careful training and due promotion. That this criticism is valuable cannot be denied. The extreme unfitness of some American envoys has discredited us, but there are advantages in our system, or want of it, which we ought not to overlook. In considering them here, we will pass over the consuls and limit ourselves to the regular diplomatic service.

Let us take a concrete case, and compare the American representatives in London with the English representatives in Washington. Since 1850 we have sent to England Joseph R. Ingersoll, James Buchanan, George M. Dallas, Charles Francis Adams, Reverdy Johnson, J. L. Motley, R. C. Schenck, Edwards Pierrepont, John Welsh, J. R. Lowell, Edward F. Phelps, Robert T. Lincoln, Thomas F. Bayard, John Hay, Joseph H. Choate, and Whitelaw Reid. The English have sent to us Sir Henry Bulwer (Lord Dalling), J. F. T. Crampton, Lord Napier, Lord Lyons, Sir Frederick Bruce, Sir Edward Thornton, L. S. Sackville West, Lord Pauncefote, Sir Michael Herbert, and Sir Mortimer Durand.

Without dwelling on particular names, we see plainly that the Americans have been the more distinguished men. The English representatives have been well educated and trained, and have tried to do their diplomatic duty, with measurable success. No one of them at any time or in any place made considerable mark of any sort upon the history of his country or that of the world. No one held important office outside the diplomatic service. To establish an accurate standard of comparison is impossible. Distinction and importance cannot be weighed. But of the Englishmen we may say that hardly one was of English cabinet rank, that none, say, had the importance which usually belongs in England to a cabinet minister. Among the sixteen Americans there are found one president, one vice-president, and an unsuccessful nominee of his party for the latter office. Five were in our small cabinet: two secretaries, a secretary of war, and two attorneys-general; two others were lawyers at the head of their profession, one was a great man of letters, and one a poet, both of high rank; and one a poet, both of high rank; still we have not classified those who did the greatest service in the list. The difference in the list is great.

It may be answered that we send our best men to England, while, owing to the comparatively low rank of their legation at Washington, England's choice of an English minister is less distinguished than those of our men. Let us make a comparison. The Americans just named are our ambassadors to France, Germany, and England. The most distinguished English diplomatists of the latter have been Cowley, Lyons, Lyttons... Dufferin, Sir Horace Rumbold, Francis Bertie... Dufferin was a...

VOL. 97 – NO. 1

## Getting hold of the marsh

**Major Higginson: "It seems to me an essential part of the plan..."** Eliot did not agree, but others — including Andrew Carnegie and A. Lawrence Lowell — did.

Henry Lee Higginson, one of President Eliot's more pragmatic counselors, followed with special interest Harvard's and MIT's 1904 effort to merge. He was himself a strong advocate of education in the applied sciences, and he had seen two previous efforts at such a merger unravel. In 1903 and 1904, Higginson engaged Eliot in a continuing correspondence on the subject. Higginson had a particular agenda:

"You may be aware that an effort may be made to buy the land opposite to the old boathouse, lying on the Boston bank of the Charles River, for the Institute of Technology," Higginson wrote to Eliot in December of 1903.

"Something was said one day about the usefulness of this land for our purposes. . . . Supposing the Institute does not go there, do you think we should need the land? Do you think it would be of advantage to us to have the land; and if so, would it be worth while for the University to buy it?"

No, said Eliot in a letter the following day: "We ought to look forward to making use of [our] newly acquired ground [along the Charles in Cambridge] before we think of crossing the river to the marsh opposite."

A panoramic view of Cambridge and Boston, looking south and west from a "tall chimney on Boylston Street," Cambridge, on September 18, 1897. The photographs were taken by Harvard senior Edward R. Cogswell, Jr., at the request of the Harvard library.

But Higginson persisted. With Eliot, he recognized the significance of the new dam then being built across the Charles River flats: it would transform the river's tidal basin — then an unsavory stretch of brackish mud flats and marsh — into valuable real estate. The land just downriver from Harvard's new stadium (sited on Soldiers Field, another of Higginson's gifts to the University) would be greatly enhanced. The major tried again in August of 1904: "But I wish to ask you if we had not better consider getting hold of that marsh. Shall we not want it for our purposes if the Technology doesn't want it? . . . .

"It seems to me an essential part of the plan, if the University and Technology are to get together, that the Technology should live on the marsh, for I know of no other place where they can squat; but I remember some of our people saying half a dozen years ago that we needed those marshes for ourselves, if we were to have a great technical school."

Eventually, Higginson and others took matters into their own hands. A subscription drive was organized in 1905, and three interested groups contributed approximately $240,000 to buy the "marsh": friends of Harvard, including Higginson and A. Lawrence Lowell; alumni of MIT, including Charles Stone and Edwin Webster, the founders of the engineering firm of Stone & Webster; and others, like Andrew Carnegie, who supported the concept of the collaboration. This group held title to the property — 1,334,650 square feet of riverfront — as the "Charles River Lands Trust" until 1918.

At that time, the fourth and final effort at a Harvard/MIT merger in the applied sciences was blocked by the courts. When the decision was handed down, A. Lawrence Lowell — then in his ninth year as the president of Harvard — set out to persuade his fellow trustees to donate their shares in the trust to Harvard.

His efforts were successful. Fifteen years after Higginson's first inquiries about the "marsh," the land became available, in Lowell's phrase, for "future inevitable extensions of the University."

The Rogers Building, on the corner of Clarendon and Boylston streets, Boston. This campus was to be sold to enable MIT to move to the marsh adjoining Soldiers Field.

developed into professions. In that direction I should like to see Harvard a pioneer; and by the way, I have very little sympathy with the argument that we hear so often, that we ought to have a school of such and such at Harvard, because someone else has it. On the contrary, I think that we had better do things that nobody else does; but we had better do them under the conditions that will be most likely to ensure success. Now, a school for any branch of business is likely to be a pretty large one if successful. Therefore, if it is worthwhile to try the experiment at all, it is worthwhile to try it under the best conditions for permanent success; and the more I think of it, the more I am convinced that to do that we must have, not a department of the Graduate School [of Arts and Sciences] or the College, but a separate professional school, with a separate faculty, whose object would be purely to train men for their career, as the Law and Medical Schools do. I think we could learn a great deal from the most successful of our professional schools; that is, the Law School. Its success is, I think, due very largely to the fact that it takes men without any previous requirements, save a liberal education in any field, and then teaches them law, not jurisprudence; and it has been coming across my mind that if we are to have a successful school of business we must do the same thing. We must take men without regard to what they have studied in college, and we must teach them business, not political economy."

The Law School, continued Lowell, had "jealously kept itself free from contact with academic students and professors. Could we create a school which could teach certain branches of business, — let us say railroading and banking, — on such a basis? If we could, I think we might make a great success, and mark an era for education in business. But I feel very doubtful whether any such idea would commend itself to the economists any more than a law school of our type would ever commend itself to professors of jurisprudence."

For the moment, Lowell's cogent argument did commend itself to economist Taussig, however. Within a few weeks, Taussig and Eliot decided to drop the public service side of the proposal for the time being. Harvard's president summarized the debate, and his own conclusions, in a February, 1907, letter to the University of Illinois' President Edmund J. James:

"The present movement to improve the training we have been giving for business started, not from me, but from two or three of our professors who were particularly interested in training for the diplomatic and consular service. I think the movement is likely to take the direction of a general training for business pursuits without any special regard to government service. The general business training with a training in modern languages is the best preparation for the consular service which ought to be in the main a business service."

WHAT TAUSSIG AND LOWELL may not have realized, early in 1907, was that their successful lobbying for a school of business would make them, in Eliot's eyes, the plan's logical sponsors. This role brought with it at least one unwelcome new task: fundraising. As Eliot and his fellow members of the Corporation saw it, the proposed school should be given a five-year trial run, funded by contributions to a subscription drive. At the end of that period, the school would presumably have proven its worth to the business community, and have become self-sustaining.

Taussig shouldered most of the burden. "I have considered again the financial aspects of it," he wrote to Eliot on March 9, 1907, "and am still of the opinion that an additional income of $15,000 would justify us in going ahead. I am so hopeful as to the attraction of additional students that I should be disposed to go ahead with an endowment of $250,000 and an additional income guaranteed for five years of $5000 annually. Very possibly, in view of recent financial experiences, the Corporation would wish to proceed more conservatively."

In 1906, a group of Harvard faculty members with administrative duties organized the "Tuesday Evening Club," which met once a month at the Union Club in Boston. There were two qualifications for membership: "personal congeniality," and representation of a particular faculty. Most members of the club received their faculty appointments during the presidency of Charles Eliot — who joined the club upon his retirement in 1909 — but President Lowell continued Eliot's tradition of appointing Tuesday Evening Club members to significant administrative posts at Harvard.

In all, six of the fourteen club members pictured above became Harvard deans: Gay (Business), Sabine (Applied Science), Christian (Medical), Haskins (Graduate School), Moore (Arts and Sciences), and Ropes (University Extension).

## Spreading the word: a "highly intellectual calling"

In February, 1908, Harvard's President Eliot set off on an extended national tour, intending to speak at Harvard alumni association gatherings across the country. His first stop, on February 21, was in New Haven, Connecticut.

The Harvard Club of Connecticut had been organized only two months before, and this was its first meeting. A third of its 143 members convened in the New Haven House — "just across the street from Yale University," as the *Harvard Alumni Bulletin* pointedly noted — to hear speeches by Eliot, by Connecticut's lieutenant governor Everett J. Lake, and by Anson Phelps Stokes, Jr., the secretary of Yale University.

In his keynote address, Eliot pointed out the growing national, and even international, service of America's great universities. He suggested that these institutions all wanted "to serve in a high degree all the learned and scientific professions."

Why? "The future in our country is for those professions, gentlemen. They are to be the leaders of the people, the controllers of our industries, the directors of our finances and our commerce, the managers of the great public services. The professional men are to have a great future in our country. So all the American universities that look forward desire to serve all the professions, divinity, law and medicine, but also the new ones: engineering in its various specialties, architecture, landscape architecture, forestry, and business administration."

Eliot then marked the New Haven club's first meeting with the first public announcement of the Harvard Business School on record:

"Our newest effort in Cambridge is to establish a graduate school of business administration, a graduate school requiring for admission a preliminary degree, — that is, open only to persons that hold the A.B. or the S.B. What leads us to that new undertaking? In the first place, the prodigious development of many corporate businesses in our country; in the next place, the fact that more than half the recent graduates of Harvard College have gone immediately into business. Last June, for example, more than half the graduates of the year went directly into business. The explanation of that new phenomenon is that business in its upper walks has become a highly intellectual calling, requiring knowledge of languages, economics, industrial organization, and commercial law, and wide reading concerning the resources and habits of the different nations. In all these directions we propose to give professional graduate instruction."

Eliot went on to discuss the importance of continuing education for adults, among other subjects. But being "just across the street from Yale University," Harvard's president couldn't resist offering Yale a concluding suggestion:

"As I have already said, what we want to do next at Harvard is to have a graduate school, with a course of two years, on business administration. There lies a great field for the American universities yet to cover. I hope Mr. Stokes will see in the next forty years this field covered by Yale University, and broadened, and cultivated highly. And I hope the same thing will take place at Harvard, and at every other American university."

**The New Haven House.**

In fact, the Corporation was then engaged in reducing the number of teachers employed and courses offered by Harvard College. Eliot had recently terminated three full professorships and one assistant professorship—economies which he loathed, describing them as "mutilations." The Corporation, which had been running at a deficit for several years, had in the previous year experienced the worst deficit in its history. Much of the deficit—some $60,000—had been incurred in the departments under the Faculty of Arts and Sciences, the proposed administrative "home" of the new school of business.

Nevertheless, the Corporation approved Taussig's financial outline in March, 1907. "You may consider yourself and your supporters," wrote Eliot, "as free to undertake to raise this money." What followed for Taussig was more than fourteen months of sustained fundraising, with intermittent assistance from Lowell. During that first summer, the subscription effort went slowly; following the October panic on Wall Street, it proved even more difficult. Indeed, if the Panic of 1907 had come in May instead of October, the Corporation might well have turned the plan down.

Other difficult questions had to be solved during this same period. "I have been thinking over the Business School matter," Taussig wrote to Eliot on July 18, "and have talked it over further with Lawrence Lowell. I believe it is time that we were thinking carefully about the personnel of the instructing staff, and especially about the head. . . . We ought to make a selection for the Head of the School very early in the autumn, so as to have plenty of time to get together the rest of the staff and launch the project before the public as early as possible in the winter."

**Edward King, president of Bankers Trust in New York, made the first donation to the Harvard Business School, to pay for printing and other administrative expenses.**

For the purchase of books on foreign missions, from
Mrs. J. Scott Boyd, Jr. . . . . . . . . . . . . . . . . . . . . . . $15
Mrs. David R. Craig . . . . . . . . . . . . . . . . . . . . . . . . 5
Gates D. Fahnestock . . . . . . . . . . . . . . . . . . . . . . . . 5
Mrs. Francis C. Lowell . . . . . . . . . . . . . . . . . . . . . . 10
Mrs. S. V. R. Thayer . . . . . . . . . . . . . . . . . . . . . . . 10
Herbert A. Wilder . . . . . . . . . . . . . . . . . . . . . . . . . 10
                                                                   $55

From an anonymous giver, $50, for the purchase of books for the Psychological Laboratory.

From members of the Division of Philosophy, $110, for the purchase of books for the Library of Philosophy in Emerson Hall.

From Archibald Cary Coolidge, $1,300, for the payment of a salary in the College Library for 1907–08.

From Howard P. Arnold, $110 additional, towards special equipment for the College Library.

From the Rose Bindery, $100, for lectures on book-binding given by Mr. Cobden-Sanderson.

From Edward King, $1,000, towards the expense of organizing the Graduate School of Business Administration.

Towards the current expenses of the Graduate School of Business Administration, from
Arthur T. Lyman . . . . . . . . . . . . . . . . . . . . . . . . . $500
Members of the Class of 1879

From the Society
$1,510.71

Right: the Bird mills.

Below: F. W. Bird, founder
of the Bird mills and grandfather of an original subscriber to the Harvard
Business School.

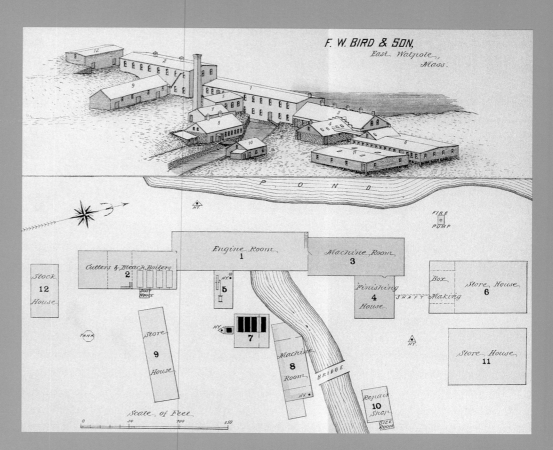

## To the cabin windows— ethically

In June, 1907, Lawrence Lowell wrote to his friend and classmate Charles Sumner Bird, a Massachusetts paper manufacturer. Lowell was seeking financial support for the proposed school of business.

"Dear Charlie," wrote Lowell, "I do not know whether you feel any interest in the enclosed [prospectus] or not, but I write to you on the chance. Professor Taussig and I are trying to get up this school, the idea being that while it is absurd to try to teach those things in business which make the chief difference between the successful and unsuccessful man . . . nevertheless, we believe that it is possible to teach in a comparatively short space of time a great deal that a young man going into business must take much longer to learn by the present system. I mean such matters as accounting in a large sense; that is, not book-keeping, but how to tell from accounts just what the cost of

any branch of the business is, and just what the cost depends on. Such things, also as the methods of organization, which after all depend upon certain general principles that are more or less applicable to all large concerns. We can also teach the method of using official and company reports, accounts, etc. so as to find how business is going. In short, we feel that although we could not give your son, for example, any special knowledge of manufacturing paper, we could give him a great deal that would make him more immediately useful to you in the office. Every professional school is really a ladder or short cut to the cabin windows; and now that everyone begins business or a profession so late in life, it is almost necessary to shorten the time before one becomes valuable.

"We are trying to raise enough money to run the school for five years, believing that at the end of that time, if

successful, we shall be able to raise the money needed for any buildings, while the tuition fees ought to pay current expenses. We are trying to get $25,000 for five years, and I have agreed to give $1,000 a year for five years.

"If you are not interested, or do not feel that you can help, I know you will say so frankly, and feel no offence at my asking you."

And, in a handwritten post-script, Lowell added a final thought: "The school to succeed must be in close touch with the business world, and have among its instructors men from active life."

While Charles Sumner Bird did not subscribe to the new school, his son, F. W., did. "Something should be done to teach a higher code of business

morals," he wrote to Lowell, promising $500 in support of the experiment. "Running through the scheme that idea [of ethics] should be kept alive."

Lowell agreed, with a proviso: "I feel that the way to inculcate good morals is not so much formal preaching as letting them appear an integral part of the principles that are explained or demonstrated."

173

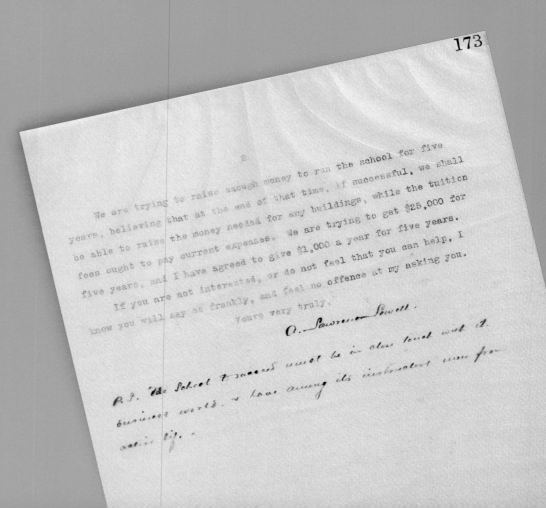

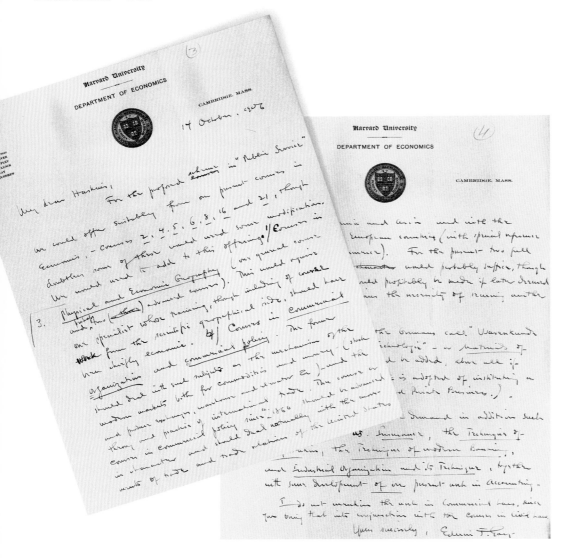

Joseph F. Johnson, Taussig's first choice as business school dean, headed New York University's School of Commerce, Accounts, and Finance, which sponsored a very successful part-time program in business education.

On the same day, Taussig solicited Henry Lee Higginson's suggestions for a head of the school. To that point, Higginson had not been involved in the business school discussions. (He had specifically been spared a fundraising solicitation: "You have been so constantly and lavishly generous," Taussig had written to him earlier in the year, "that we did not propose to ask you even for a nominal contribution.") But now Taussig wanted advice from a representative of the business community, and again Higginson was the obvious candidate:

"I take it you know about the project for a School of Business Administration, which has reached the stage where it seems probable that we shall establish something of the kind. A very important problem in connection with this scheme, perhaps the most important of all, is to find a suitable man to be the Head of it. That Head will have to organize the details of instruction, and will have most to do in securing the other members of the teaching staff. I have myself a possible person in mind, whom I have mentioned to President Eliot; a man of academic associations, but experienced in just this sort of thing. A suggestion, however, has been made, and particularly dwelt upon by my colleague, Lawrence Lowell, that we get hold of a non-academic person. Can there be found a business man, who has shown capacity in the actual work of the world, who has intellectual interests and a love of the University, preferably a graduate of our own, who would be capable of taking hold of this object? Does any man of this sort occur to you?"

To Taussig's dismay, this question would not be settled until the following spring — a scant seven months before the new school was scheduled to open. Taussig's candidate for the post was Joseph F. Johnson, then dean of New York University's School of Commerce, Accounts, and Finance. Lawrence Lowell favored Boston banker and philanthropist John Moors, who had recently distinguished himself during relief efforts in San Francisco following the 1906 earthquake. Eliot's first choice was apparently Taussig himself; when Taussig declined, Eliot offered the post to William Lyon Mackenzie King, a Canadian, then the deputy minister of labor in Ottawa.

The private proof was circulated among influential friends of Harvard in December, 1906 for their endorsement — or criticisms. Both President Roosevelt and Senator Lodge lent their names in support of the proposal; however, internal resistance to the public service aspect stalled the plan at Harvard.

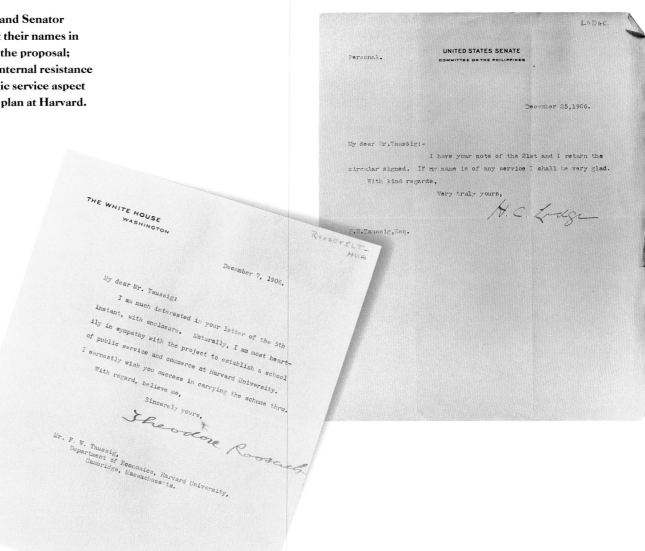

Taussig opposed the choice. Why, he asked Eliot, appoint a Canadian with no business experience to head an American business school? King, in any case, declined the deanship.

On February 19, 1908, Eliot asked Edwin Gay to take the position. "I asked time to consider my decision," Gay wrote in his diary. "The president was good enough to speak highly of my administrative ability when I urged my lack of experience for this task." (According to some accounts, Eliot countered this objection by saying, "I know all that, but I've noticed you have an inventive mind.") Gay was concerned about further postponements of his long-delayed opus on economic history; Eliot replied that the job would take no longer than two years.

Five days later, Gay accepted Eliot's offer, with some reservations. "I told him that his offer seemed to open to me an opportunity for service which perhaps I ought to accept, and I would take it on the chance that this might be the best service that I could do in the next four years." To a friend, H. M. Bates, Gay admitted that he wanted to see if he had "the guts to do it."

"Your vocabulary," replied Bates, "is already beginning to sound like a businessman's."

Taussig and Lowell worked together to influence one additional decision: the degree of autonomy to be enjoyed by the proposed business school. On the one hand, the new school's near-total lack of resources, intellectual and financial, suggested that it should be tied closely to an existing department or faculty. The two professors, though — and particularly Lowell — feared the impact of an overly "academic" faculty.

Eliot apparently had no such misgivings. And, in a letter to Taussig dated August 9, 1907, he suggested an argument for a lesser degree of autonomy:

"The most difficult question is that of an entirely separate organization. My mind is open on that question. It is not clear to me that business administration, including public service, is as distinct from arts and sciences as law or medicine or divinity or engineering is. Business administration seems to me to cover a great variety of studies of industries and of public interests. Its possible range is so great that it may need close connections with almost any subject in the group called arts and sciences."

**William Lyon Mackenzie King studied economics under Taussig, and earned a Harvard doctorate in 1904. He turned down the deanship of Harvard's proposed business school, preferring to remain in the Canadian government. He later became head of the Liberal Party and prime minister of Canada.**

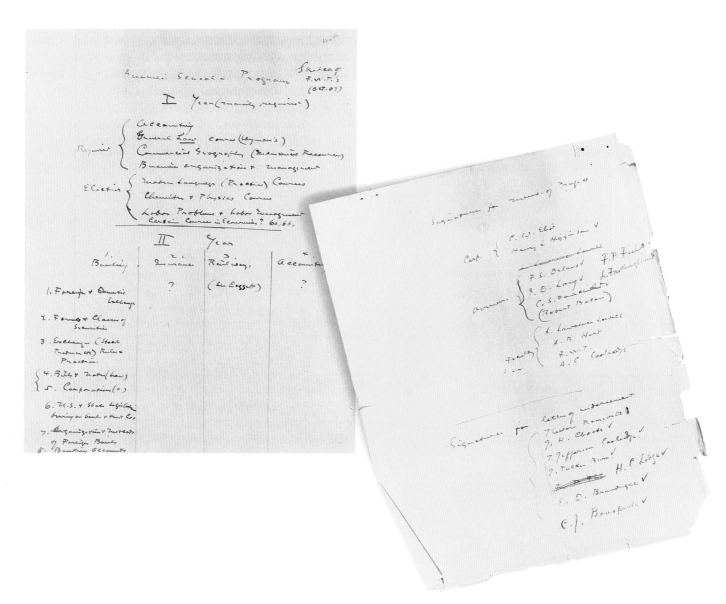

**By October, 1907, Taussig was outlining a fairly specific curriculum for a "Business School," even sketching out a second-year program of electives. He suggested that the faculty of the proposed school might include A. Lawrence Lowell, A. C. Coolidge, A. B. Hart, and himself—a guess which proved incorrect. Coolidge, for one, declared himself uninterested in a school that did not include the public service component.**

Taussig responded two days later, arguing for a "completely separate organization" not subservient to any existing Harvard faculty. He also outlined his vision of the proposed school's curriculum: "The instruction ought to be as professional as possible. The first-year's work ought to be in good part required, — principles of accounting, law for business men, industrial organization and commercial geography. Our courses in economics ought not to appear on the list of the Business School's courses, except so far as transferred thither once for all (e.g. the accounting course). Most of our existing courses, such as those on money and banking, railways, labor questions, consider the *public* aspects of these subjects, and should continue to do so. The practical and managing aspects of them can and should be treated separately."

With Taussig's encouragement, Lowell added his perspective, writing Eliot: "Professor Taussig showed me your letter in regard to the School of Business Administration; and I want to say that I dread very much the effect of a committee of the faculty. It is not easy to make a success of the thing by making it an academic instead of a professional school, as has been

the case, I believe, in other institutions, where something of a lower grade but perhaps easier of accomplishment has been attempted. We are trying a great, but, I think, delicate experiment; and I feel that it would be wise to leave the framing of the plan in the hands of those who originated it and see clearly what they want. After a good deal of consideration, Taussig and I are thoroughly agreed upon the details of the project, and one thing that seems to us vital is that the new school shall be under a separate professional faculty; and, in fact, my support of the scheme from the first has been made conditional upon that."

It was an argument that Taussig and Lowell would lose, at least in the short run, despite their strong feelings. The Corporation was reluctant to launch an entirely independent entity under the prevailing economic conditions. Eliot, for his part, must have had in mind the fate of the School of Veterinary Medicine. But the voice which swayed the decision belonged to the proposed school's designated dean:

"While it is in the experimental stage of development," Gay wrote to Eliot in the spring of 1908, supporting a tie with the Faculty of Arts and Sciences,

Even as late as 1908, "public service" was finding its way into organizational memos regarding the Business School. However, public service careers began to be

subsumed under the larger "business" umbrella — in keeping with President Eliot's sense that the consular service, for example, "ought to be in the main a business service."

The Corporation vote to establish a "Graduate School of Business Administration," April 8, 1908.

"I can perceive no tangible disadvantage, but only advantage, in giving it the shelter and support of this connection . . . .

"It may be a little presumptuous for the School to make a great flourish as a separate department when its foundation is laid on such a modest scale and its actual obligations to the Faculty of Arts and Sciences are so great."

EDWIN GAY HAD SET TO WORK immediately, even before the official Corporation vote, on March 30, "to establish a Graduate School of Business Administration, the ordinary requirement for admission to which shall be possession of a bachelor's degree, and for graduation a course of study covering two years." (Gay's appointment as dean was confirmed at the same meeting.) After all, aside from Taussig's preliminary outlines, no planning had been done on behalf of the School, which was still scheduled to open in October. As of April, the School had no curriculum, no faculty (other than its dean) and no assigned quarters.

This last need was addressed first, through a process that one participant described as "burrowing." Extra space was loaned by other departments; several neglected rooms were rehabilitated and pressed into service. Most important, three small rooms in University Hall, then Harvard's central administration building, were set aside for the Dean of the Business School. Located one floor below the president's office, this suite of offices would for the next two decades give the struggling school a great advantage: access to Harvard's president.

In the spring and summer of 1908, Gay addressed the School's curriculum and faculty needs simultaneously. Concentrating exclusively on the first-year curriculum, and drawing to a large extent on Taussig's scheme, he decided that three courses would, indeed, be required. The first was Principles of Accounting, still taught by William Morse Cole, and since 1905 a full-credit course in the Department of Economics. (Cole accordingly moved to the Business School faculty, from which he retired in 1933.)

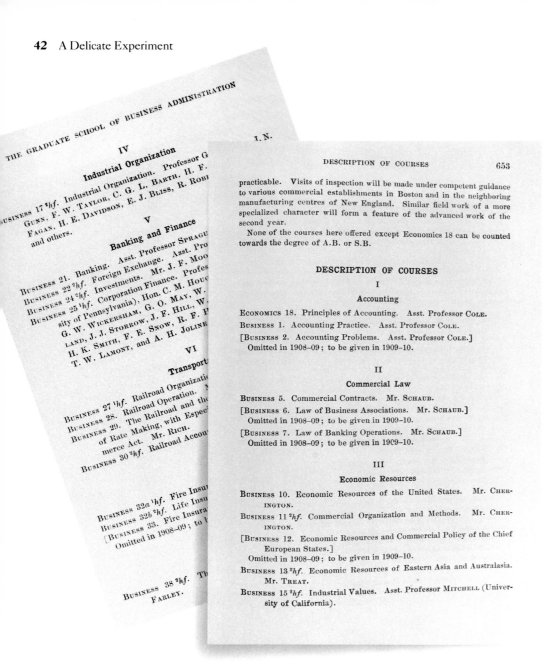

THE GRADUATE SCHOOL OF BUSINESS ADMINISTRATION

IV
Industrial Organization

BUSINESS 17 ²hf. Industrial Organization. Professor G
GUNN, F. W. TAYLOR, C. G. L. BARTH, H. F.
FAGAN, H. E. DAVIDSON, E. J. BLISS, R. ROB
and others.

V
Banking and Finance

BUSINESS 21. Banking. Asst. Professor SPRAGU
BUSINESS 22 ²hf. Foreign Exchange. Asst. Pro
BUSINESS 24 ²hf. Investments. Mr. J. F. MOO
BUSINESS 25 ¹hf. Corporation Finance. Profes
sity of Pennsylvania), Hon. C. M. HOUG
G. W. WICKERSHAM, G. O. MAY, W.
LAND, J. J. STORROW, J. F. HILL, W.
H. K. SMITH, F. E. SNOW, R. F. H
T. W. LAMONT, and A. H. JOLINE

VI
Transport

BUSINESS 27 ¹hf. Railroad Organizatio
BUSINESS 28. Railroad Operation.
BUSINESS 29. The Railroad and the
of Rate Making, with Especi
merce Act. Mr. RICH.
BUSINESS 30 ²hf. Railroad Accou

BUSINESS 32a ¹hf. Fire Insur
BUSINESS 32b ²hf. Life Insu
BUSINESS 33. Fire Insura
[BUSINESS 33. Fire Insura
Omitted in 1908–09; to

BUSINESS 38 ²hf. Th
FARLEY.

---

I. N.

DESCRIPTION OF COURSES                653

practicable. Visits of inspection will be made under competent guidance to various commercial establishments in Boston and in the neighboring manufacturing centres of New England. Similar field work of a more specialized character will form a feature of the advanced work of the second year.

None of the courses here offered except Economics 18 can be counted towards the degree of A.B. or S.B.

### DESCRIPTION OF COURSES

#### I
#### Accounting

ECONOMICS 18. Principles of Accounting. Asst. Professor COLE.

BUSINESS 1. Accounting Practice. Asst. Professor COLE.

[BUSINESS 2. Accounting Problems. Asst. Professor COLE.]
Omitted in 1908–09; to be given in 1909–10.

#### II
#### Commercial Law

BUSINESS 5. Commercial Contracts. Mr. SCHAUB.

[BUSINESS 6. Law of Business Associations. Mr. SCHAUB.]
Omitted in 1908–09; to be given in 1909–10.

[BUSINESS 7. Law of Banking Operations. Mr. SCHAUB.]
Omitted in 1908–09; to be given in 1909–10.

#### III
#### Economic Resources

BUSINESS 10. Economic Resources of the United States. Mr. CHER-
INGTON.

BUSINESS 11 ²hf. Commercial Organization and Methods. Mr. CHER-
INGTON.

[BUSINESS 12. Economic Resources and Commercial Policy of the Chief
European States.]
Omitted in 1908–09; to be given in 1909–10.

BUSINESS 13 ²hf. Economic Resources of Eastern Asia and Australasia.
Mr. TREAT.

BUSINESS 15 ²hf. Industrial Values. Asst. Professor MITCHELL (University of California).

---

The Harvard Business School's course descriptions in the University's 1908–1909 catalogue reflect two influences: an evolution of the concept of the School, up to its founding, and an opportunistic use of available resources.

The Accounting courses, for example, were an outgrowth of the economics department's efforts in the field of practical training. Commercial Law took advantage of existing Law School cases. Economic Resources and Industrial Organization brought aspects of classical economic theory (as well as Scientific Management) to the school.

Banking, Transportation, and Insurance were the fields first proposed for "carving out" of the general business arena to be upgraded into professions. Railroading — George Leighton's special cause — dominated the Transportation curriculum.

Finally, the "public administration" theme, out of which the Business School originally grew, manifested itself in one course on Public Business.

---

The second, Commercial Contracts, was to draw upon existing Law School cases to acquaint business students with legal issues. It would be taught by Law School graduate Lincoln F. Schaub. (Schaub, who served as secretary of the new school, remained on the Business School faculty until 1921.)

The third required course was entitled Economic Resources of the United States. This course — which evolved into Marketing — would be offered by Paul T. Cherington, a graduate of the University of Pennsylvania and then an officer of the Philadelphia Commercial Museum. (Cherington remained on the Business School faculty for more than a decade.)

A group of elective courses was also planned. Oliver W. M. Sprague, a graduate of Harvard's Department of Economics then teaching in Japan, would offer a full-year course in banking and finance. (Sprague — whom Eliot was reluctant to bring back to Harvard because of Sprague's extreme nearsightedness — later filled the School's first endowed professorship, and remained on the faculty until his retirement in 1941.)

Two other half-courses in the banking field — which both Eliot and Lowell thought might be "carved out" as a profession — were also offered: one by Boston banker (and one-time candidate for the Business School deanship) John F. Moors, and the other by a series of sixteen businessmen. These sixteen included two men important in the next phases of the School's development: Thomas W. Lamont, then with Bankers Trust; and Wallace B. Donham, an officer of Boston's Old Colony Trust.

Gay's appointments to the faculty were eclectic, and often adventurous. This was partly a result of the School's circumstances: as Eliot had anticipated, established academics were reluctant to sign on with a school which might well expire after five years. But the new dean also enjoyed the bold stroke. To teach Railroad Accounting — also a potential "profession" within business, according to Lowell — Gay hired William J. Cunningham, then working in the Boston and Albany Railroad's statistical department. Cunningham (who remained on the faculty until 1946) did not hesitate to point out that he had "no academic antecedents whatever"; upon joining the Business School faculty, he became the only Harvard University professor without a bachelor's degree.

## The model at McGill

A letter from Corporation Secretary, Jerome D. Greene, written to Henry Lee Higginson barely a month after Gay's confirmation in the deanship, gives a sense both of Gay's methods and the infant school's goals. The subject, once again, was railroading:

"Professor Edwin F. Gay, who is taking up energetically his new work as Dean of the Graduate School of Business Administration, is looking about for good teachers. I have advised him to inquire into the qualifications of Clarence Morgan, AB Harvard 1894, who was connected with the New York Central Railroad for several years after his graduation . . . .

"Four years ago he was appointed a Professor at McGill University, Montreal, and given the job of organizing a Railroad Department on a three-year contract. This he accomplished with such success that the Canadian Pacific and Grand Trunk railroads are paying $14,000 a year toward the support of the new Department, and have made definite arrangements for providing opportunities for practical work on their lines, as well as taking the graduates of the Railroad Department into their employ. In other words, it is just the sort of relation which our new Business School wishes to establish with the business world generally, and a promising demonstration of the confidence of practical business men in the usefulness of university instruction."

**An illustration for a lecture at McGill's Department of Railroading.**

Oliver M. W. Sprague taught the Business School's first courses in banking, and remained on the faculty for more than three decades.

William Morse Cole, Harvard's resident expert in accounting, left the economics faculty for the Business School faculty.

There were numerous dead ends and setbacks. Mackenzie King—having previously declined the deanship—now declined a faculty position offered by Gay. Judge Gary, president of U.S. Steel, said he was too busy to lecture at Harvard's new school. One temporary disappointment was Frederick Winslow Taylor—promulgator of the theory of "scientific management"—who had been trying for over a year to capture President Eliot's attention. ("If you can spare me some of your valuable time," he wrote to Eliot in April of 1907, "it would give me great pleasure to come to Cambridge and talk on the subject with you.") But when Gay sought to hire one of Taylor's assistants to lecture on a part-time basis, Taylor turned him down flat. "Taylor does not think my chances of being useful in your University are comparable with my present usefulness in the industrial world," wrote Carl G. Barth, the assistant and proposed lecturer. "Nor does he believe I would be happy working under the kind of administration Harvard University shares with similar institutions."

According to his biographer, Gay developed two basic ideas which governed his design of the School. First, he defined "business" as the activity of making things to sell at a profit—decently. The modifier suggested a number of qualities which the businessman should possess, including courage, good judgment, and a "sympathetic tact, a certain kindness of spirit which unites the other two elements, which purifies courage by removing its grosser belligerency and tempers judgement by the understanding heart." The cultivation of these qualities, Gay concluded, was a central purpose of the School.

Second, the "great opportunity" of an institution such as Harvard's new business school was to experiment with ways of training students for the tasks of manufacturing and selling. Through such experimentation, the School would develop a rational approach to business, "a habit of intellectual respect for business as a profession, with the social implications and heightened sense of responsibility which goes with that."

The new School's faculty numbered fifteen, and was augmented by numerous lecturers from the business community. This latter group included such diverse speakers as Frederick W. Taylor, founder of scientific management, and J. O. Fagan, signalman on the Boston and Maine Railroad.

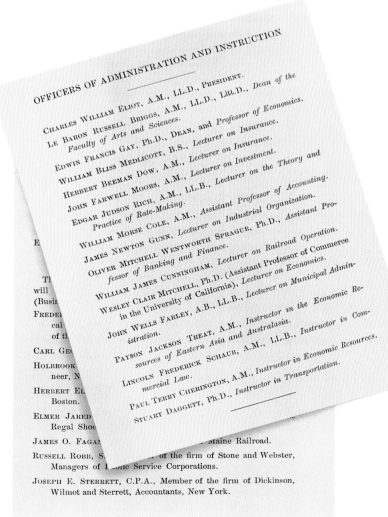

Thomas W. Lamont agreed to lecture in February, 1909, at the fledgling Harvard Business School. He was, at the time, one of four vice presidents working at the First National Bank of New York. His employer was George F. Baker—the "Sphinx of Wall Street"—and one of his fellow vice presidents was Baker's son, George F. Baker, Jr.

CORPORATION FINANCE
("Business 25")

LECTURE XXXII---REORGANIZATION OF CORPORATIONS.

February 5, 1909.

By T. W. Lamont,
(Vice-President of the First National Bank, New York.)

DEFINITIONS AND OBJECTS OF REORGANIZATION
and
PRELIMINARIES TO REORGANIZATION.

The Reorganization of a corporation is, as the word implies, doing over again the work of organization. All of you gentlemen here have followed the lectures upon the organization of a corporation, and are familiar with just what that means. But probably the term Reorganization conveys to your mind something not the case at all, and we shall if complex. Now, this entirely different, something subtle and make a great advance in our definition of Reorganization if, first of all, we get in mind that it is simply doing over again, with certain definite aims to accomplish, what we did in organization.

Coincident with its reorganization there is frequently a radical change in all the business affairs of the corporation---in its management, its system, its methods; and in the eyes of the public the word "Reorganization" generally implies these business changes.

But the legal evidences of Reorganization usually are the readjustment of the corporation's debt or of its capitalization, or of both its debt and capitalization. So that, when Reorganization has been accomplished, we frequently find that the corporate structure presents a radically different appearance. The funded debt has very likely been increased or diminished in amount and the form of it changed; while the capital---that is to say,

Copyright, 1908, by
President and Fellows of Harvard College,
Boston.

---

Wallace B. Donham, a lawyer employed by Boston's Old Colony Trust, accepted Dean Gay's invitation to lecture on banking practices.

CORPORATION FINANCE
("Business 25")

LECTURE XII---UNDERWRITING SYNDICATES AND THE PURCHASE AND SALE OF SECURITIES THROUGH BANKING HOUSES.

November 13, 1908.

By Wallace B. Donham, Esq.,
(Vice-President of the Old Colony Trust Company, Boston, Mass.)

I am going to begin today with a little about the internal relations of syndicates, that is, management, etc. Naturally after the initial purchase or the negotiations for the initial purchase by the banking house which is responsible for the syndicate, that is, which initiates the syndicate, are well along, the first step is for that banking house to choose its associates.

Internal relations of syndicates. Ordinarily the banking house which initiates the negotiations, or some of its individual members, become the syndicate manager or managers, and they choose their associates, either individuals or corporations, or both, according to the nature of the particular problem and what they feel they need to accomplish with reference to that problem. A small matter, that is, an undertaking not involving a very large amount, would very likely be offered by a banking house to some of its individual clients. That has a double effect. If it is a successful syndicate, it has the effect of strengthening the hold of that banking house on those clients. Individuals appreciate an opportunity to get in on the ground floor, providing the ground floor proves to have been near enough to the ground so that they do not suffer any loss afterwards. The banking house has the fact continually in mind that by giving its better customers a chance to participate, it strengthens its hold on them. The choice of individuals, however, has one or two other effects. In the first place, it has a distinct effect on the borrowing capacity of the syndicate. Lenders are not nearly so free to lend money on the strength of individual subscriptions in syndicates, as they are on the underwritings of well-known and established

Copyright, 1908, by
President and Fellows of Harvard College,
Boston.

ONE TASK which Gay was spared, in that hectic spring and summer of 1908, was fundraising. This remained Professor Taussig's burden. His most significant success had come in January, when the General Education Board of New York, founded in 1902 by John D. Rockefeller, had agreed to give $12,500 per year—or half the subscription money needed—provided that Harvard could raise the balance elsewhere. While Taussig had done most of the groundwork on the proposal, it was Eliot who had made the formal approach to the Board on December 13, 1907:

"I have received many assurances from business men that young men who had received the training described in the accompanying memo would quickly make themselves highly useful in the great business organizations of the country—the incorporated institutions of finance, transportation, mining, and manufacturing." While Harvard wanted to start the school "forthwith," continued Eliot, the necessary funds weren't likely to "flow freely during the next few years. Under these circumstances, I am instructed to ask temporary aid from the General Education Board."

**John D. Rockefeller established the General Education Board in 1902 to support experiments in education.**

**In December, 1907, Taussig began his informal contacts with John D. Rockefeller's General Education Board. Dr. Joseph Warren, a member of the Law School faculty, supplied a list of the Board's members to Taussig.**

**The General Education Board, circa 1910, from a biography of John D. Rockefeller. The Board subscribed to the Business School drive in part to facilitate Harvard's President Eliot's election to their ranks.**

**Two original subscribers to the Harvard Business School: Allston Burr, Boston stockbroker; and George F. Baker, Jr., New York banker. Both contributed one hundred dollars a year for five years.**

By lucky coincidence, the General Education Board was at that precise point in time considering President Eliot as a possible member of the Board. (In January, Eliot met with a member of the Board for five and a half hours, and no mention was made of Harvard's application for funds.) While the Board—at Rockefeller's direction—rarely gave money for operating expenses, preferring instead to endow educational ventures, in this case its members decided to facilitate Eliot's election by approving the request, citing the experimental nature of the project.

Securing the Board's support was a solid success for Taussig, but, after a year of solicitation, he had grown tired of the fundraiser's job. "Needless to say," he wrote to Eliot on March 21, "I shall appreciate any aid in raising this money; not less, in view of my having secured virtually all that has already been got." But by May, Eliot had only bad news: the Corporation had voted not to contribute any further funds to the project until—and unless—the subscription drive was completed. Taussig had just learned of this unwelcome development when he received a telephone call from Higginson, requesting a meeting.

The meeting occurred the next day. "Major Higginson," recalled Taussig, "went at once to the root of the matter, and asked whether I had received the communication from the Corporation about the funds for the Business School. Hardly waiting for a reply, he went on in some such words as these: 'Go to President Eliot tomorrow morning and tell him that a donor

whose name you are not at liberty to state, but whose financial ability you can guarantee, has underwritten the entire sum still remaining to be raised on the estimated annual requirements for the Business School.'"

Taussig forwarded the good news in a letter to Eliot the following day. "This does not mean that I expect the money to be obtained in this way, but only that we are on sure ground. My hope is still to secure the entire sum needed without calling upon the guarantor." By July, Taussig had secured pledges of $11,600 per year. His "guarantor," he told Eliot, was therefore liable for $900 per year. "I should prefer not to call on the guarantor now," he continued. "I shall do some more begging in the autumn." It was for Taussig a miserable summer: he was simultaneously teaching summer school; attempting to finish his long-overdue book, *Principles of Economics*; coping with personal financial reverses; and nursing his wife, who had contracted tuberculosis. Nevertheless, he managed by the fall to complete the subscription drive without resorting to Higginson's pledge.

Higginson appreciated Taussig's efforts; through this process, they established a friendship which lasted until Higginson's death in 1919. Higginson particularly appreciated Taussig's discretion: the "guarantor" who kept the Business School alive at a crucial juncture retained his anonymity. "People get so sick of my meddling with matters that they don't like to hear my name," Higginson wrote to Taussig in July, "and the President is one of them. I am a kind of nurse, and nobody likes nurses unless they are young and pretty."

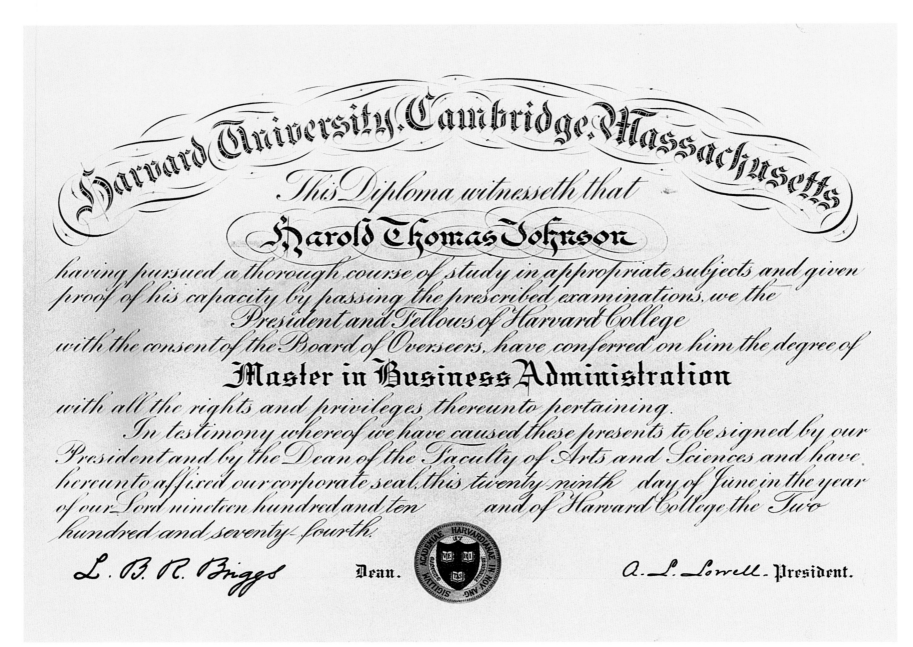

Harvard University, Cambridge, Massachusetts

This Diploma witnesseth that

Harold Thomas Johnson

having pursued a thorough course of study in appropriate subjects and given proof of his capacity by passing the prescribed examinations, we the President and Fellows of Harvard College with the consent of the Board of Overseers, have conferred on him the degree of

Master in Business Administration

with all the rights and privileges thereunto pertaining.

In testimony whereof we have caused these presents to be signed by our President and by the Dean of the Faculty of Arts and Sciences and have hereunto affixed our corporate seal, this twenty-ninth day of June in the year of our Lord nineteen hundred and ten and of Harvard College the Two hundred and seventy-fourth.

L. B. R. Briggs        Dean.        A. L. Lowell, President.

The diploma of Harold T. Johnson, a member of the School's first graduating class. Although Edwin Gay was nominally the dean of the Business School, the dean of the Faculty of Arts and Sciences signed HBS diplomas during the School's five-year trial period.

Ralph Bradley, MBA '10, shared the School's interest in railroading: after graduation, he worked briefly as a fireman on the Springfield division of the Wabash Railroad.

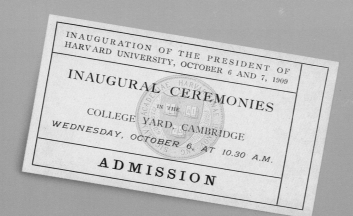

INAUGURATION OF THE PRESIDENT OF
HARVARD UNIVERSITY, OCTOBER 6 AND 7, 1909

INAUGURAL CEREMONIES

COLLEGE YARD, CAMBRIDGE
WEDNESDAY, OCTOBER 6, AT 10.30 A.M.

ADMISSION

President Eliot (front, center) and Professor Lowell (to Eliot's left): their two presidencies spanned 64 years, and brought Harvard to the forefront of American higher education.

## Passing the torch

In October, 1908, Charles Eliot informed the Corporation that he would resign the presidency of Harvard University the following May. His forty-year tenure remains the longest in Harvard's history.

Professor F. W. Taussig wrote to Eliot in November on the subject of Eliot's successor:

"On the whole, my candidate is Lawrence Lowell. I wish he were ten years younger, and I should not be sorry if he were not a Brahmin-born. But he has qualities of the highest order. He is an experienced and successful teacher; he has academic training and academic interests; he is a distinguished scholar, an able man of affairs, a devoted son of the

University; he is known to the alumni and to the public; he has ideas and ideals; he has great nervous vigor and endurance. I do not agree with him upon all matters of academic policy, and have thrashed some of them out with him. I always respect his judgement and admire his spirit. I do not think we can have a better chief."

Lowell, who had taught under Eliot for twelve years, succeeded him on May 19, 1909. He served as Harvard's president until 1933, giving the Harvard Business School —which he had helped bring into being—nearly a quarter-century of strong administrative support.

**Funds and a curriculum were not enough: the Business School needed students, as well. A. Lawrence Lowell and others made informal recruiting efforts among Harvard's graduating class, and advertisements for the new School were placed in national periodicals.**

**The 1908–1909 Harvard treasurer's report reflects the modest scale of Harvard's experiment in business education. The**   **School showed a surplus of just over $4000 on an income of $33,000. In terms of its income, it ranked far below most other Harvard graduate schools.**

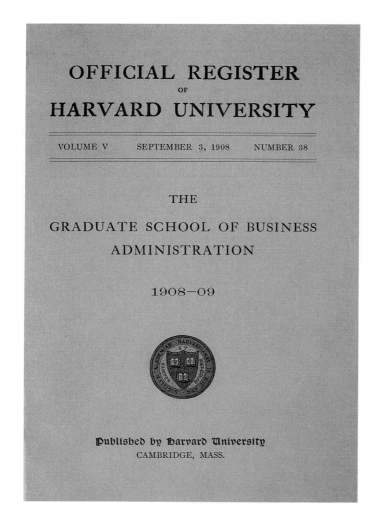

OFFICIAL REGISTER
OF
HARVARD UNIVERSITY

VOLUME V      SEPTEMBER 3, 1908      NUMBER 38

THE

GRADUATE SCHOOL OF BUSINESS

ADMINISTRATION

1908–09

Published by Harvard University
CAMBRIDGE, MASS.

BY THE FALL OF 1908, the new business school was ready. It had a faculty of fifteen, including its dean. It had a new degree — the "Master in Business Administration," the first Harvard degree not to be conferred in Latin. ("The use of plain English," Gay wrote to Eliot, "seems not inappropriate to our new School of Business.") It had a course of study — at least for the first year — which would lead to that degree, outlined for prospective students in its brand-new course catalogue.

And — thanks in part to Lawrence Lowell's efforts to drum up local interest in the project — it had students: in the first semester, 24 regular students and 35 "special" students, taking one or more courses. (In the second semester, nine more regular students enrolled, along with twelve new special students.) For the first time anywhere, a group of students would assemble exclusively for *graduate* business studies. Not surprisingly, more than half of these prospective students were Harvard College graduates. While three of each four students were from Massachusetts, students representing ten other states, and two foreign countries, were also enrolled.

The new school also had a committed dean, who, despite a painful appendicitis attack in September, postponed his surgery until after the School opened on the first of October. ("No gardener," he wrote two years later, "ever tended a fragile plant more carefully than I did, to keep an eye on all the details of our infant School.") And while the School had only a five-year lease on life, Dean Gay was already dedicated to finding the means to carry on the experiment beyond 1913.

The School had the active support of Harvard's President Eliot, and of Professor Lawrence Lowell, who would succeed Eliot in the presidency the following year. Eliot and Lowell collaborated on a name for the experiment: the new school would be, they agreed, a *Graduate* School of Business *Administration*. There had not previously been a graduate school of business — indeed, it seems that no institution had yet called itself a "school of business." The addition of the word "administration" was a further distinction, which would take on unanticipated significance in years to come.

"And so," concluded business historian N. S. B. Gras some 35 years later, "a school with a good name was launched, as an alternative to something else, and launched upon the world with only a half crown in its pocket. What better start could be provided — a good name and honest poverty?"

**The first product of the
delicate experiment: the
Harvard Business School's
Class of 1910.**

# Chapter Two    *A Simple Scientific Endeavor*

IN HIS ELEVEN YEARS as dean of the Harvard
Business School, Edwin Gay faced a formidable
array of challenges. Foremost among these was
a question of invention: What *was* a graduate
school of business administration? What sort of
intellectual capital should it attempt to generate?
What sort of graduate should it hope to produce?

Gay and his small faculty solicited opinions
on these basic questions from both industry and
academia. The contradictory answers they heard,
early in the course of their decade of experimentation, led them to several important conclusions.
The "profession" of business that they intended
to serve, they realized, was far from a final definition. The structures that had helped to codify
and reinforce more established professions—
structures such as journals, professional societies,
and codes of ethics, for example—simply did
not exist for business.

Furthermore, with the increasingly rapid
pace of change and diversification that then characterized business, it appeared that the profession might never be clearly defined. What the

Members of the faculty, posing for the 1911 class picture. Left to right: Cherington, Cunningham, Moors, Gay, Schaub, Cole, and Sprague.

Overleaf:
Edwin Gay in his University Hall office, 1908.

Harvard Business School needed to invent, it seemed, was a wholly new educational structure, able to respond to changing realities and to redefine itself over time.

But a commitment to flexibility was only the means to an end. Skeptics in both the business and academic communities wanted more: they wanted a clear statement of the principles that would guide the profession —and, by extension, the School. If there were no clear principles, they argued, then there could be no profession, as such; if there was no profession, there was no need for a graduate school of business administration.

"I am constantly being told by business men that we cannot teach 'business,'" Gay confessed in a June, 1909, letter to economist W. E. Rappard, whom he was trying to persuade to join the Business School faculty. "I heartily agree with them; we do not try to teach business in the sense in which business men ordinarily understand their routine methods, or in the sense in which you speak of teaching young men to be 'money makers,' or 'to get the better of their competitors.' We believe that there is science in business, and it is the task of studying and developing that science in which we are primarily interested. It is our aim to give our young business men the breadth of horizon, as well as the equipment of information and grasp of principles, which will enable them, as you say, to be better citizens and men of culture, as well as broader men of business."

A year later, Gay wrote again to the skeptical Rappard: "I am convinced that there is a scientific method involved and underlying the art of business and that this science, which is a branch of Applied Economics, is to be investigated and ought to be investigated in a Business School such as ours. This was my belief when I undertook this work and it has only been strengthened by my experience of the last two years.

"There is at present little available literature in the new fields which I am indicating. I shall be glad, however, to send you an article by Mr. [Frederick Winslow] Taylor of Philadelphia which will indicate one branch of the work which is being done along this line.

"Our work in the Business School is undoubtedly professional in character, just as the work in the Law School is professional and utilitarian in character, but I believe that we shall have the impetus of a simple scientific endeavor."

THE THEORY UNDERLYING the School's "scientific endeavor," in 1910, was indeed simple. Gay hypothesized that the art of business consisted of two major functions: production and distribution. In part to distinguish his new school from existing schools of economics, he called those basic functions "manufacturing" and "marketing." In this framework, all other business specialties—banking, insurance, and transportation, for example—were activities which supported either manufacturing or marketing.

For Gay, the School's role was to discover and teach the principles that underlay the fields of manufacturing and marketing. In the process, the School would help to define the profession of business, both by providing it with scientifically derived information and by training qualified managers for its ranks. But how much intellectual territory could a faculty of fifteen, with no precedents to build upon and an operating budget of $29,000 a year, expect to cover, and cover well enough to justify the School's continued existence?

In 1908, President Eliot had predicted that the School would prove its worth to the business commu-nity within five years, and thereby ensure its survival. Gay did not agree: the strongest evidence in support of the School, he believed, would be the exceptional subsequent success on the part of its graduates. But at least a decade would be required for this kind of evidence to materialize.

As Gay looked ahead from 1908, he saw that two processes had to occur simultaneously. A curriculum had to be devised, which could be relied upon to produce the business leaders of the 1920s and beyond; and at the same time, the School needed to define territories in which it could make a clear and significant contribution to business theory—and practice—in the short run. The two processes were closely linked: because no texts or lectures existed for a graduate school of business, business theory had to be developed in a way that would inform the curriculum. Where were those territories which would provide new materials for teaching—territories significant enough to warrant the attention of business, yet manageable enough to be comprehended by the scarce resources of the Harvard Business School?

John Moors (shown at right with his wife), lecturer on investments from 1908 to 1917, was impatient with the "deficiencies in English composition of even the regular students of the School," according to the minutes of a 1911 faculty meeting.

"When I opened the first papers," Moors recalled of his initial grading experiences at the School, "I was appalled, not by the ignorance of the class on financial matters, but by its ignorance of the first principles of English composition and even of spelling. I, therefore, converted myself promptly into a teacher of elementary English."

The faculty at first declined to grade HBS students on the quality of their English, but pressure from disgruntled employers of HBS graduates eventually made such a step necessary. When grading on composition skills was first introduced—in the Marketing reports, beginning in 1914—four-fifths of the students "failed to reach the passing grade in English," according to Dean Gay's annual report.

The faculty also voted in 1914 to refuse a degree to any student who could not attain a passing grade in English by the middle of his second year.

F. W. Taylor, father of scientific management, inspecting concrete work: scientific management was applied to numerous industrial settings.

Wallace Sabine, renowned acoustics expert and dean of Harvard's Graduate School of Applied Science, introduced Edwin Gay to Taylorism. Later, Sabine and Taylor established a fund to provide books on scientific management for the Business School library.

They were not, Gay concluded, in the manufacturing field. For one thing, manufacturing was too large, complex, and changeable. Furthermore, there was already an impressive body of knowledge on this topic. It had been developed, for the most part, by a small but growing group of mechanical engineers; they called their field "scientific management," and they were the disciples of the founder of scientific management, Frederick W. Taylor.

Taylor was an 1874 graduate of the Phillips Exeter Academy, who, because of failing eyesight, had declined to attend Harvard after passing the College's entrance examinations. Instead, Taylor found work as an apprentice to a journeyman machinist near his home in Philadelphia. He distinguished himself as a machinist, engineer, and inventor, and eventually rose to the position of chief engineer at the Philadelphia-based Midvale Steel Company. His apprenticeship began in the 1870s, a period of prolonged economic depression, during which American manufacturers faced the problem of excess capacity. One of their responses to this problem was to de-emphasize technological improvements—which had been the engineer's principal responsibility up to that point—and to concentrate instead on organizational improvements aimed at enhancing profitability without expanding production.

Taylor proved adept at meeting this new priority. While at Midvale, he developed a novel approach to efficiency and productivity in manufacturing. He proposed that manufacturers should determine scientifically what workers ought to be able to accomplish, given the available equipment and materials. (This involved using time-and-motion studies to break down each task into its component parts.) With this information in hand, the manufacturer should then prescribe productivity levels. Workers who exceeded those standards would receive bonuses; those who failed to meet the standards would be penalized.

It was a controversial system, often bitterly opposed by the workers it sought to inspire and reward. "Taylorism," as it soon came to be called, was also opposed by shop foremen, who correctly interpreted it as an assault on their powerful positions as "inside contractors." Yet scientific management could, in the right circumstances, generate dramatic results: at Taylor's

Midvale "laboratory," for example, productivity doubled. In 1893, Taylor went into business for himself as a "consulting engineer," and his reputation in manufacturing circles grew. But the process of converting an existing company to scientific management was never painless. Hired in 1898 to reorganize the management structure of Bethlehem Steel, for example, Taylor was fired in 1901 by the company's president.

This experience marked the end of Taylor's career as a paid consultant. Financially independent, Taylor decided in 1901 to stop taking payment for proselytizing on behalf of scientific management. In his mind, his system had evolved into more than simply a cost-cutting technique. Visitors to Boxly, the immaculately manicured Taylor estate in north Philadelphia, soon learned from Taylor that his system's most important attribute was its supposedly salutary effect on the workman's character. "Character comes first," said Taylor, "common sense second, and intellectual training third."

It was to Boxly that Edwin Gay and Wallace C. Sabine traveled in May, 1908. Sabine was the dean of Harvard's Graduate School of Applied Science, which had been established in 1906, and it was he who had urged Gay to include scientific management in the Business School's curriculum. The two deans spoke at length with Taylor, and toured several local manufacturing firms that had adopted the Taylor system. Sabine was evidently impressed: upon his return to Cambridge, he wrote Taylor an effusive letter, telling the engineer-turned-consultant that he was "on the track of the only reasonable solution of a great sociological problem."

Gay, for his part, was more circumspect, seeing several problems with embracing Taylorism at Harvard. For one thing, the self-taught Taylor believed that even an undergraduate education was detrimental in manufacturing. Two months before the Boxly visit, for example, Taylor had informed the New York chapter of the Harvard Engineering Society that he had "ceased to hire any young college graduates until they [had] been 'dehorned' by some other employer." In conversations with his associates, Taylor was openly skeptical about Harvard in general, and about Harvard's graduate school of business in particular.

Nevertheless, Taylorism represented concrete evidence that there might indeed be a science underlying the practice of business, at least on the manufacturing side. Gay decided, in effect, to cede that territory to Taylor: he would incorporate scientific management in the Business School curriculum, and meanwhile invest the School's limited resources for research elsewhere. He initiated a correspondence with Taylor, and won a grudging agreement from the engineer to lecture at the School in the spring of 1909.

The administrators of Harvard's business school never overcame Taylor's initial skepticism, although the founder of scientific management returned to lecture to business students every year until his death in 1915. Taylor considered the bachelor's degree an irrelevant prerequisite for admission to a school of business: Why not, he once asked the Dean sarcastically, require that the matriculating students be doctors, or athletes?

"I have no doubt that a great deal of good will come from your school," he wrote Gay in 1913, "but I very much doubt whether most of the men who graduate from this school will ever become men capable of scientific management. Many of them may ultimately become good managers."

After each Taylor lecture, the School drew up a check in payment for his services; Taylor—like many other HBS lecturers—returned the checks.

THE PRELIMINARY ANNOUNCEMENT of the Harvard Business School, mailed in the spring of 1908 to generate public enthusiasm for the project, had little impact on the world of business. One of the announcements, however, arrived on the desk of Arch W. Shaw, a Chicago-based publisher of magazines and books. The outline of Harvard's new school prompted Shaw to write to both President Eliot and Dean Gay and express his support for the venture.

The completion of Harvard's stadium at Soldiers Field led to increased traffic across the Charles River, and the existing wooden drawbridge connecting Boylston Street in Cambridge and North Harvard Street in Boston was soon outmoded. In 1904, the Massachusetts legislature passed an act ordering Cambridge and Boston to replace the bridge with a more suitable structure, at a cost not to exceed $120,000.

After six years and little progress toward a new bridge, the legislature empowered the Metropolitan Park Commission to replace bridges over the Charles if and when funds became available. In 1911, Larz Anderson, a member of Harvard's Class of 1888, informed the Commission that he would finance the construction of a new bridge to Soldiers Field in memory of his father. Because the Charles was considered a navigable waterway as far west as the Watertown Arsenal, the federal government specified that the bridge had to leave a clear height of twelve feet above the water in the main ship channel.

Construction began in 1912. The photographic record suggests that it was a disruptive process for the coal merchants and farmers who occupied the southern bank of the Charles, east of the bridge.

The flagship publication of the A. W. Shaw Company was *System*—"the magazine for management." Under Shaw's direction, *System* attempted to take a practical approach to business. It was a successful magazine, and it grew steadily in size and influence during Shaw's tenure as editor. (In 1927, *System* was purchased by McGraw-Hill, and renamed *Business Week*.) But *System*, as Shaw saw it, faced a difficult question: how to uncover the principles that must underlie the evolving practice of business. It was a question that Shaw himself had faced in 1906, when he had helped Northwestern University design an undergraduate business curriculum. Now the question was raised again by Harvard's new experiment in graduate education.

"I think you will understand from our conversation," he wrote to Gay in August of 1909, "how thoroughly I believe in teaching the principles of business. I also feel that there is an almost equally important field in the gathering of this concrete information and furnishing it to men actually in business for themselves, or hoping some day to be."

Three months later, in another letter, he elaborated: "At this particular stage in the development of business it seems to me that it is the function of *System*, at least, to distribute as widely as possible the concrete, or as we call it, the 'how' information of business from which generalizations may be made later and definite principles determined."

Frederick W. Taylor: engineer, inventor, and reformer.

# A particular system of management

Edwin Gay's visit to Frederick W. Taylor's estate and model factories, in May of 1908, led eventually to the father of scientific management's first lectures at Harvard, in April and May of 1909.

At Gay's urging, Taylor spoke to the class from notes, rather than reading a prepared text. (Taylor had argued in vain that he could "go much faster" by simply reading.) Taylor — who liberally salted his discourse with off-color phrases — raced through his lecture notes, and still was able to allow only scant time for questions at the end of the class.

Two months later, at the nearby Watertown Arsenal, just west of Boston, Taylor's "management of the future" was to begin a very public trial. Arsenals at that time were manufacturers, as well as repositories,

of munitions. Congress, impatient with the low productivity of the arsenals, had begun awarding munitions contracts to private manufacturers. The Army responded by seeking new ways to increase its productivity, and in 1908 the commander of the Watertown Arsenal — generally considered the worst facility in the Army's arsenal system — was instructed to install a program of scientific management.

This work began in June of 1909 under the direction of Carl G. Barth, Taylor's most trusted lieutenant. Barth, a soft-spoken Norwegian, first standardized all machines and tools at the arsenal, and then established standard work tasks and an incentive wage system. By exceeding the established productivity levels, workmen could earn bonuses exceeding one-third of a day's wages.

Initially the system worked well at Watertown, and it was quickly adopted at other arsenals around the country.

In 1911, however, Barth attempted to install scientific management in the arsenal's foundry, and the foundry molders rebelled against Barth's time-and-motion studies. A short-lived but well-publicized strike ensued, which led directly to a congressional investigation sponsored by the "House Committee on the Taylor and Other Systems of Management."

At the Harvard Business School, meanwhile, Taylorism was receiving mixed notices. At the December, 1911, meeting of the School's Visiting Committee, chairman Howard Elliott suggested that Business 19 — The Practice of Scientific Management — might well benefit from a different name, "inasmuch as the phrase 'scientific management' tends to prejudice a considerable number of business men against a course, and even a curriculum, which includes the study of a particular system of management, whose advocates have made extravagant claims as to their efficiency in reducing the expenses of railroad operations, and so on."

But Dean Gay and the faculty were committed to an exploration of scientific management. In the fall of 1911, with Taylor's permission, they inaugurated a second-year laboratory course in scientific management at the Rindge Manual Training School in Cambridge. In Gay's eyes, the technical high school — which then had some 600 students — would not only help train his own students, but would also provide industry with significant numbers of technicians trained in Taylorism.

In 1913, Gay invited Taylor to join Harvard's faculty. "Could you by any possibility," he wrote to Taylor in May, "come here next year and join our staff in the Business School, taking charge of the advanced course in scientific management?"

Taylor declined, citing his wife's contentment in Philadelphia. And, he added pointedly, "I am conducting in Philadelphia here an even larger school for scientific management than the one which you have at Cambridge."

By 1914, the Business School faculty was prepared to drop scientific management from the first-year curriculum — a

move which reflected both student disinterest and mounting public sentiment against Taylorism. In June, Arch Shaw informed Gay that "the reaction against efficiency and the 'scientific' idea is already setting in. This is evidenced in our mail and it is hurting *System* because so many people think that we are linked up in some way with this 'efficiency' idea."

Taylor died in 1915, and therefore did not witness the decline of his movement's influence. (In 1916, for example, the "Army Bill" included provisions prohibiting time studies and bonus payments at government manufacturing facilities — restrictions which remained in effect until 1949.) Most American manufacturers who installed scientific management systems — even in Taylorism's heyday — did so only in moderation, in part because of the deficiencies of those systems. In addition to antagonizing labor, the efficiency systems also failed to assign interdepartmental authority adequately — a crucial prerequisite for the movement of materials from one area to the next.

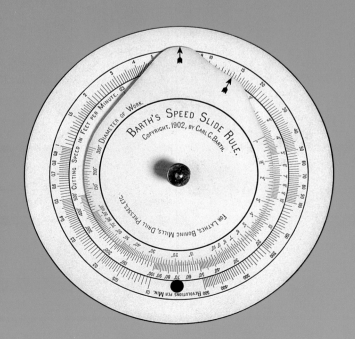

**Carl Barth's "Speed Slide Rule" — disparagingly referred to as "Barth's merry-go-round" — combined crude logarithmic tables with performance levels of specific machines to establish productivity norms.**

**The Rindge Manual Training School. In 1911, its 600 students began an experiment in Taylorism.**

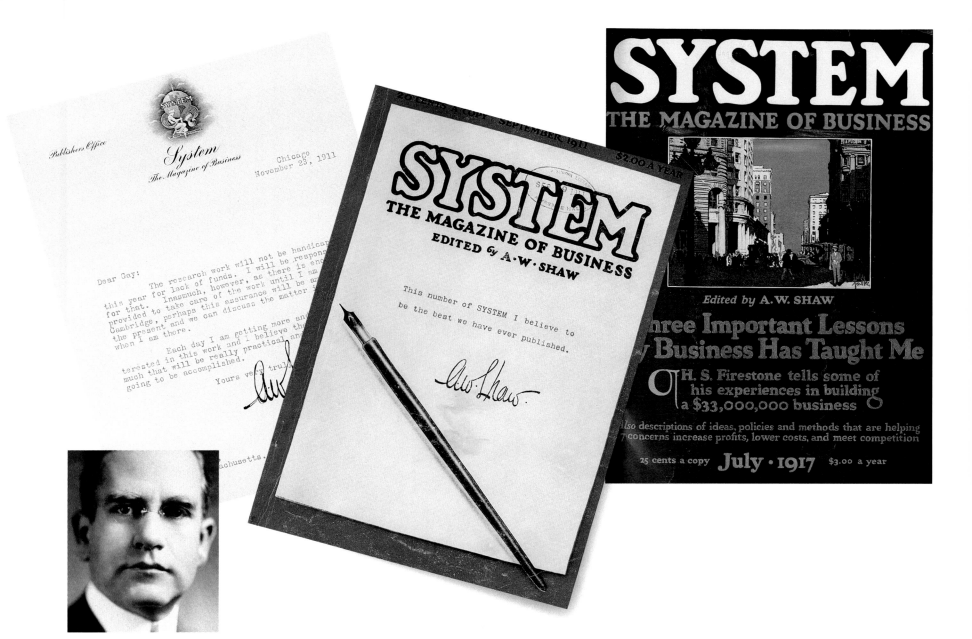

**Arch W. Shaw, founder of *System* magazine, underwriter of the Bureau of Business Research, and inventor of the Business Policy course.**

***System* had an attentive readership. When a Shaw editorial advocated the establishment of a federal "Bureau of Business Practice," the magazine received over 300 letters in response.**

**Edwin Gay, however, thought *System* had an unfortunate inclination toward "scrappiness." He congratulated Shaw when revisions in the magazine minimized that inclination.**

Shaw began to visit the School regularly in 1910, attending classes and talking with the faculty. He agreed with Gay's general division of business into the manufacturing and marketing functions (although he preferred the terms production and distribution), and thought that the School's research and curriculum could be built on that premise. And although he thought that the advocates of scientific management too often lost sight of larger questions—preoccupied as they were with the rituals and paraphernalia of time-and-motion studies—he was willing to follow their lead on the manufacturing side.

On an April afternoon in 1911, Shaw and Gay (who recollected the event years later) were crossing Harvard Yard together after a class meeting. As often happened, their conversation turned to scientific research on business topics. "What is needed," said Gay, "is a quantitative measurement for the marketing side of distribution."

Replied Shaw, "Why don't you get it?"

In his retelling of the event, Gay did not record his own response, but it almost certainly included a request for money. Within days, Shaw sent Gay a formal note:

"I wish to give for use in this School a fund which shall be applied for the purpose of investigation of business problems, primarily for the problem of distribution of products."

The fund, gratefully accepted by Gay, amounted to $2,200. It was an ample sum of money to investigate *some* aspect of distribution; now the question became, where to start? Gay and Shaw shared a conviction that the work they were about to begin would ultimately be taken over by some government agency. It therefore seemed logical to focus on a subject that hitherto had been ignored by government. They settled on the small retailer, convinced that the federal government—then preoccupied with "big" business—might eventually do for "little" business what the Agriculture Department was doing for farmers. By gathering information on agricultural techniques and crop yields from large numbers of farmers, the department had been able to provide individual farmers with standards of productivity. Could Harvard do the same for the small retailer—and simultaneously develop much-needed material for its curriculum?

**The Shoe Retailer, as well as other trade publications, lent welcome publicity and credibility to the Bureau's first field investigations.**

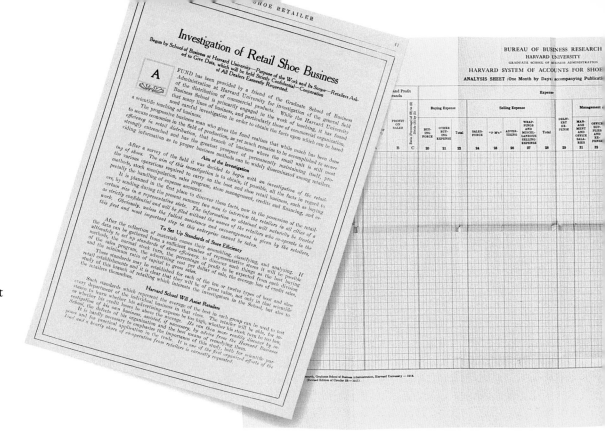

IN THE SUMMER OF 1911, Paul T. Cherington, Harvard Business School Instructor in Economic Resources of the United States, and Clarence B. Stoner, MBA '11, set off for the Midwest as representatives of the School's newly created "Bureau of Business Research." Their mission seemed modest: to establish definitively the costs of operating a retail shoe business. Yet it had great significance, for it was an approach that would come to typify research at the Harvard Business School. Rather than attempting to survey the entire field of marketing, for example, or the retail trade in general, these first business researchers would attempt to derive concrete, usable information within a well-defined area of inquiry. Given obvious limits on time and resources, Cherington and Stoner emphasized the *practical*: What could they discover that would be of immediate use in the curriculum? What form could their research take to persuade more retailers to cooperate with the School in the future? And, ultimately, in what ways could this approach to research help justify the School's continued existence at the end of its five-year trial?

The initial results were discouraging. Cherington and Stoner soon discovered that no two retailers kept exactly comparable records. Some included their own salaries in operating expenses, while others accounted for salaries separately. Some charged themselves rent for stores that they owned; others did not. The Bureau of Business Research—which at that point consisted of nothing more than its two investigators—decided to organize a committee of manufacturers and retailers, public accountants, and Harvard faculty members to establish a standard classification of accounts for retailers in the shoe industry.

The committee met intermittently during the academic year of 1911–1912, and by the summer of 1912, the standard classification system was available for use. As soon as it was ready, Selden O. Martin, a young faculty member recently back from a year's research in South America, used it to obtain information on the operating expenses of shoe stores in the East and Midwest. Over 130 stores were included in the survey. Martin visited most of them in person, explaining the purposes of the study, and overcoming through dogged persistence the merchants' reluctance to divulge what they considered proprietary information.

Some retailers refused to cooperate. "Why, damn it, man, you're asking for the guts of this business," complained one president of a New York department store. "That's exactly what I'm asking for," Martin replied. In this case, as in others, it later emerged that the executive actually was more embarrassed by the inadequacy of his accounting system than he was concerned about revealing trade secrets.

The fruits of Martin's efforts appeared in May of 1913—exactly coincident with the end of the School's five-year trial period—when the Bureau of Business Research issued its first bulletin: *Object and History of the Bureau with Some Preliminary Figures on the Retailing of Shoes*. The "object and history" section of the report said that the Bureau represented "an approach to the scientific study of business, which up to the present time has developed in the main in an empirical, rule-of-thumb fashion. There is in general a feeling that the time is now at hand for the business man to have more scientific information to aid him in meeting and solving his problems."

**The "Harvard System of Accounts for Shoe Retailers," first used in 1912, was not designed to replace existing accounting systems, but rather to generate standardized data for the Bureau. Many retailers, though, lacked an accounting system even as rudimentary as the Bureau's, and therefore adopted it for their own use.**

**The Cheringtons of HBS: when Paul T. Cherington (left) joined the HBS faculty in 1908, he established a family tradition. His son Paul W. (second from left) served on the School's faculty from 1950 to 1965, and his son Charles (front) served several decades on the faculty of the Harvard Graduate School of Public Administration.**

Month    Year

**Other Business Profits (or Losses)**

| | | REPAIRING | | HOSIERY | | | MISCELLANEOUS PROFITS AND LOSSES | | | | Total Other Net Profits (Loss in red) | Day |
|---|---|---|---|---|---|---|---|---|---|---|---|---|

The summary table from the first bulletin of the Bureau of Business Research. The Bureau discovered that the operating expenses of retail shoe stores ranged from 18 percent to 35 percent of net sales—a variation of nearly 100 percent in operating efficiency.

Retailers in the grocery trade, investigated subsequently, showed an even greater spread, with variations of up to 250 percent in operating efficiency.

**14**

The following table condenses the essential facts of the foregoing paragraphs:

### SUMMARY TABLE OF PERCENTAGES

| Item | Lowest percentage | Highest percentage | Percentage about which data centre (not an average) | Percentage about which a concentration is sufficient to indicate a realizable standard |
|---|---|---|---|---|
| Gross profit, including discounts .......... | 20 | 42 | Low grade 23–25 | |
| Total operating expense not including freight and cartage and interest ............. | 18 | 35 | High grade 30–33 Low grade 23 High grade 27 | Low grade 20 High grade 25 |
| Buying expense ...... | 0.8 | 1.8 | 1.1 | 1.0 |
| Salesforce............ | 5.0 | 10.3 | 8.0 | 7.0 |
| Advertising .......... | 0.0 | 8.8 | 2.0 | 1.5 |
| Deliveries ........... | 0.0 | 1.4 | 0.6 | 0.4 |
| Rent ................ | 1.8 | 14.6 | 5.0 | 3.0 |
| Interest ............. | 1.0 | 7.9 | 2.5 | 2.0 |
| Stock-turns ......... | 1.0 | 3.6 | 1.8 | 2.5 |
| Annual sales of average salesperson ........ | $5,000 | $16,500 | $10,000 | |

There were two reasons for publishing "preliminary figures": Dean Gay was anxious to have a research product in hand as soon as possible, and Martin—who was named director of the Bureau in 1913—wanted something tangible to show to the next round of shoe retailers. Immediately after the publication of the bulletin, Martin and four other "field agents" left Cambridge once again, soliciting data from additional shoe retailers. This time out they reported a perceptible difference: the first bulletin had been well received in trade publications, and retailers were now much more willing to cooperate. The Bureau's efforts were also commended in newspapers and other general interest publications, bringing the Harvard Business School to the attention of a much broader audience.

In all, some 10,000 shoe retailers were surveyed, and a series of bulletins on the shoe trade were issued. Following up in a different industry, the Bureau undertook in 1914 a study of operating expenses in the retail grocery trade, and eventually secured the cooperation of some 14,000 grocers. Wholesale shoe firms were included in the Bureau's research in 1915; wholesale grocers in 1916; retail general stores in 1917; retail hardware dealers in 1918; retail jewelers in 1919; and department and specialty stores in 1920.

Gay and Shaw had originally planned to carry the Bureau's research "backwards" from retailing to wholesaling, and eventually to manufacturing—thereby establishing scientific principles of manufacturing that were independent of "scientific management." But because of constraints on the Bureau's activities, this goal was never achieved. Office space was one problem: in 1914, only a single room, six feet by fourteen feet, was available to the Bureau. This "alley," as it was called, located in Harvard's Lawrence Hall, housed all five of the Bureau's full-time researchers. In 1915, the Bureau took over a small adjoining classroom, and in 1916, a nearby kitchen and stable. Money proved a less tractable problem, since the Bureau's activities had to be funded out of the School's general revenues. Finally, during American participation in the First World War, mail solicitations replaced the activities of the field agents.

The Bureau's studies were ongoing, and published findings were used to encourage participation by more "cooperators." In the year following the publication of Bulletin #15, "Operating Accounts for Retail Jewelry Stores," 182 retail jewelers, with aggregate sales of $13,780,000, responded to the Bureau's requests for information.

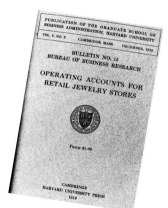

Lawrence Hall was the location of a Business School reading room, and also the headquarters of the Bureau of Business Research, which occupied the former kitchen and stable of the dean of the disbanded Lawrence Scientific School.

# The sweeping view

"The day must come," said the young economist, "when the impartial historian shall take his stand in the valley of the Mississippi and with a view sweeping from the Alleghenies to the Rockies present our history in its true perspective."

It was Commencement Day at Harvard in June of 1904, when Selden O. Martin—that day receiving his A.M. in economics—spoke as the representative of the graduate schools. In his address, he argued that Americans had too long been preoccupied with their East Coast, neglecting the contributions and opportunities of the western states.

Six years later, in October of 1910, Martin himself was afforded the "sweeping view." The continent he surveyed was not North America, but South America; and he traveled not as a historian or economist, but as a representative of Harvard's new Graduate School of Business Administration.

Martin, then 29 years old, had received his Ph.D. in economics in 1907. His faculty advisors included department chairman Edwin Gay. He spent several years in Washington at the Bureau of Corporations (forerunner of the Federal Trade Commission) as a special investigator, examining concentrations of economic power in the tobacco industry, in electricity generation, and other fields. In 1910 he had been released from a teaching obligation at Bowdoin College to help the Business School's Paul T. Cherington teach a new course, Economic Resources and Commercial Organization of Central and South America.

But this course—like many others at the School—sorely lacked teaching materials, other than those Cherington had gathered on his own summer "study tours" in the region. When the United Fruit Company's president, A. W. Preston, established a five-year traveling fellowship at the School to develop such materials, Martin seized the opportunity.

"I was sent to South America in October, 1910, to travel, to observe, and to interview," he later wrote of the journey. "An economic perspective of South America that was approximately correct was sought for." In the course of his explorations, Martin traveled some 26,000 miles, crossing the Andes six times, and visiting every South American country except Venezuela and the Guianas.

Martin's research, reflected his background in classical economics. Upon Martin's return to North America, however, he received a total immersion in a new approach to research: he joined an investigation of the retail shoe trade —then being mounted by the Bureau of Business Research—and obtained data on operating expenses from scores of retail and department stores. This new methodology had a clear impact on Martin's thinking, and when he published a summary of his South American research in 1913, his conclusions were somewhat unorthodox:

"What I have sought is to leave with you two ideas, one general, the other specific. One an economic perspective of

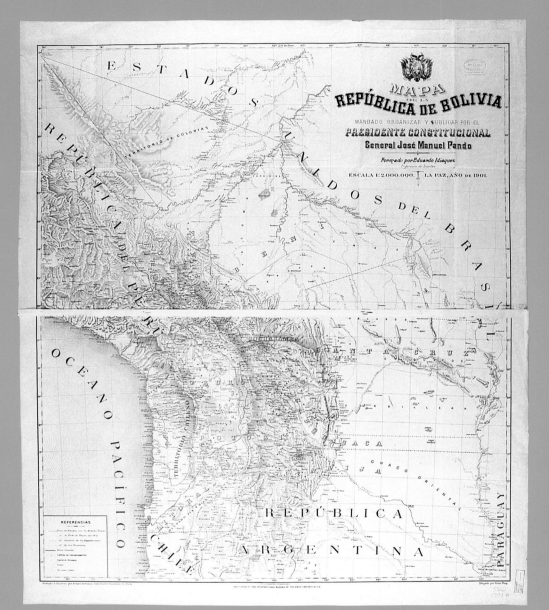

South America that I believe to be correct, and the other a concrete suggestion for our South American trade to establish an American department store in at least one city in South America, and preferably in four cities—as a potent stimulator of trade."

An economic perspective and a concrete suggestion: Martin's combination of ideas became a model for later HBS research.

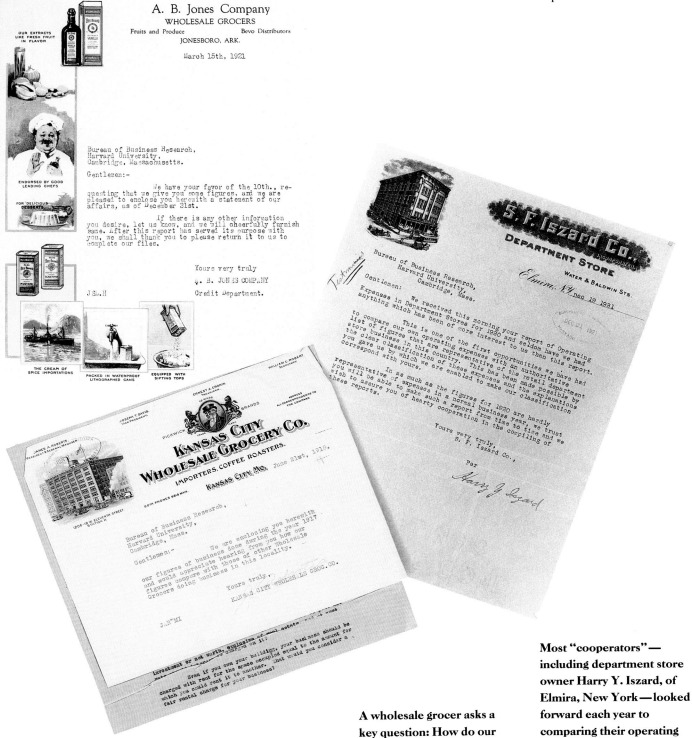

News from "cooperators" in the wholesale grocery business and the department store trade. The Bureau's original goal was to investigate various trades in two stages: first at the retailing level, and then at the wholesaling level. (A study of the manufacturing level was a more distant goal.) Because shoe wholesalers were a disappearing breed, the shoe trade did not lend itself to investigation beyond the retail level.

But in 1916, the Bureau began a study of the wholesale grocery trade; this developed into a ten-year collaborative effort with the National Association of Wholesale Grocers, and was the first industry study to encompass both retailing and wholesaling.

The Bureau did not attempt to prescribe operating techniques; rather, it sought to establish operating cost norms. Even so, many businessmen—including manufacturers—sought advice from the Bureau.

A wholesale grocer asks a key question: How do our figures compare with those of our competitors?

Most "cooperators"— including department store owner Harry Y. Iszard, of Elmira, New York—looked forward each year to comparing their operating expenses with industry norms.

Still, during the decade 1908–1918, the Bureau recorded some notable achievements. In the shoe investigation, the School's agents undertook the first organized research in the field of business administration. The Bureau had defined and satisfied a significant need of the business community. Within four months of the publication of the first bulletin concerning the retail grocery trade, for example, some 15,000 individual orders for the findings had been received. By 1920, in spite of resource constraints, the Bureau was compiling inventory and expense records for a group of American businesses with aggregate gross revenues of over $1.5 billion.

Most important, the Bureau established effective working relationships with thousands of retail and wholesale businesses. In the process, it earned for the Harvard Business School a reputation for integrity and competence. Business managers learned that operating-expense information—hitherto a jealously guarded secret—could be divulged with confidence, with the knowledge that the figures would be employed for the general good. In 1920, at the beginning of the Bureau's second decade of operation, this record of accomplishment allowed the Bureau's researchers to take on a significant new role: case collection.

IN AUGUST OF 1904 the novelist Henry James returned to his native America, temporarily ending a self-imposed exile of twenty years. After landing in New York, he spent one night in New Jersey with his publisher, George Harvey of Harper and Brothers, and Mark Twain; the next day he left for his brother William's summer home in New Hampshire. There he remained until the fall, when he journeyed to Boston to begin a ten-month tour of the United States.

He was stunned by what he found in Boston. The face of the city had been transformed by commerce, and the buildings that had once been dominant were now either dwarfed by their new neighbors, or absent entirely. Park Street Church, James discovered to his horror, was jeopardized by a proposed commercial development. He was pleased to find, in the course of a walking tour, that one of his former residences (on Ashburton Place) had survived — but when he returned a few weeks later, the house had been demolished. America was awash, it seemed, in a tide of materialism and impermanence. The stores were filled with standardized products, and, James observed, seemed

**Selling condiments:**
H.J. Heinz's first venture into food packaging — a horseradish and pickle concern founded in 1869 — folded after only six years. His second attempt was more successful: the H.J. Heinz Company's vinegar, pickles, catsup, and condiments line prospered after its founding in 1876.

Of 63 major firms in the food business in 1873, only Heinz survived the century. The famous "57 Varieties" slogan, which effectively caught the public's eye, was coined in 1896 — despite the fact that there were already over sixty "varieties" in the company's product line. By 1910, there were well over 200 varieties.

Selling dairy products: Gail Borden's first "condensed" food product—a meat biscuit—won a prize at the 1851 International Exhibition in London, but nearly bankrupted him. His second attempt, a sterile condensed milk bearing the "Eagle" brand name, also fared poorly at first, but was rescued from oblivion by the Union Army, which wanted milk for its men in the field.

Before the perfection of the condensing process, all milk products had to be sold within a few miles of their source. After Borden's discovery, however, milk products could safely be consumed on shipboard, in extreme heat, and at distances far from the producer. Borden netted $145,000 in 1864, and returned his profits to the business. As the first company to deliver milk in bottles, Borden also established itself as a purveyor of quality fresh dairy products, and expanded into animal feeds, soy products, and later, chemicals.

"to swarm, to bristle, to vociferate." Lingering at a corner of Boston Common, James failed to overhear a single English-speaking pedestrian in the passing throng.

"In the early American time, doubtless," he wrote, "individuals of value had to wait too much for things; but that is now made up by the way things are waiting for individuals of value."

James had, in fact, returned to an America undergoing a second industrial revolution. In his arch fashion, he correctly identified two key contributors to that revolution: American manufacturers, and the immigrant laborers who populated their factories.

The revolution had started in the 1870s, when manufacturers began to take advantage of the huge national markets created by the nation's new railroad and telegraph networks. Between 1860 and 1899, the value of American manufactured goods rose from $2 billion per year to $11 billion; annual steel production grew from 69,000 tons in 1870 to 10 million tons in 1899. Increasingly, companies both produced and distributed, and on a previously unimagined scale.

Production became mass production, and distribution became mass distribution.

A single business enterprise could make *and* sell a product, or line of products. "The visible hand of managerial direction," wrote Alfred Chandler, in his Pulitzer Prize-winning account of this process, "had replaced the invisible hand of market forces in coordinating the flow of goods from the suppliers of raw and semifinished materials to the retailer and ultimate customer."

One result of the emergence of the national (and in some cases multinational) firm was the torrent of standardized manufactured goods that so dismayed Henry James—first in his adopted home of Boston, and later in his native New York. (Wall Street he described as "the heaped industrial battlefield.") Another result was an unprecedented demand for professional executives, who were now needed to manage the integration of production and distribution. These managers now began to devise the systems and techniques that still dominate integrated companies today.

**Selling cereal:** a consortium of oat millers, worried by the specter of heightened competition and decreasing prices in the 1880s, banded together to form the Oatmeal Millers' Association. Aggressive marketing techniques developed by Henry Parsons Crowell, vice president and general manager of the Association's corporate offspring, the American Cereal Company, brought oats out of the feedbag and onto the breakfast table—as Quaker Oats—during two decades of remarkable growth.

Through hitherto unknown or underutilized advertising techniques—such as free samples, scientific endorsements, billboards, customer testimonials, box recipes, and package premiums (such as the 1893 booklet of poems pictured here), the "Quaker man" became one of the best-known trademarks of its time. Diversification into feed grains, baby cereals, and pet foods kept Quaker in the vanguard of the cereal business through a period of enormous economic change.

**Selling canned foods:** in 1868, brothers Arthur and Charles Libby joined Archibald McNeill in a modest $3,000 business venture—producing beef in barrels. By 1875, they had broken with several traditional meat-packing practices: they began curing beef with ice, and employing the refrigerated box, which for the first time enabled packers to ship fresh meats hundreds of miles from their plants. Company lore tells of Libby corned beef tins recovered from the battlefields of the Zulu Wars in 1884, and cans of Libby soup accompanying the Arctic expeditions of the same year. (Libby's advertising department depicted one of its products surviving a shipwreck.)

Not surprisingly, big business began to replace the railroads and robber barons as the focus of economic and ideological criticism. Theodore Roosevelt, succeeding the assassinated William McKinley as president in the fall of 1901, assured the nation that he would continue his genial predecessor's pro-business policies. The following February, however, his attorney general sued to dissolve the Northern Securities Company—a railroad holding company created by financier J. P. Morgan and railroad magnates Edward H. Harriman and James J. Hill—under the long-neglected provisions of the Sherman Antitrust Act.

The suit was successful, but it eventually proved more significant as symbolism than as economic policy. Roosevelt, although popularly considered a "trust-buster," was in fact a pragmatic and conservative Republican. He did not again tackle a business concern as large as Northern Securities, or a foe as formidable as Morgan. But with his orations against the "malefactors of great wealth," and in favor of a "moral regeneration of the business world," he did legitimize criticism of the American economic system.

In the early 20th century, the company branched into the fruit and vegetable canning business. It was a fortuitous move: Americans were then changing their diets from the traditional meat-and-potatoes regimen to lighter, more nutritious, and easier-to-prepare foods. Libby, McNeill and Libby's sales grew from an estimated $2 million in 1890 to roughly ten times that figure in 1920.

Selling soap: Procter & Gamble, started in 1837 by two brothers-in-law, exploited Cincinnati's by-products, manufacturing candles and soap from slaughterhouse wastes. A lucrative contract to supply the Union Army during the Civil War gave the company the resources to expand later in the nineteenth century.

"Ivory," the floating soap, was brought out in 1879 with a new marketing hook: a groove in the middle of the bar to enable the housewife to split it into two smaller cakes. The company expanded and diversified over the early decades of the new century: in 1891, net profits slightly exceeded $600,000; thirty years later, sales volume exceeded $105 million, with profits approaching $7.5 million.

Roosevelt's rhetoric and occasional interventions lent new authority to the reform movement then gathering momentum in America. Roosevelt disparaged the "muckraking" journalists, but they proudly adopted his label, and continued their exposés of corruption in business and government. Ida Tarbell's painstaking history of the Standard Oil Company established a new genre of critical analysis. Even John D. Rockefeller, founder of Standard Oil and the quintessential capitalist, contributed to the reform movement: in 1902, at the urging of his counselor, Frederick T. Gates, Rockefeller established the reform-minded General Education Board.

Reform dominated the American political and intellectual mainstream, until America's entry into the First World War. The 1912 presidential election was a four-way race between Democrat Woodrow Wilson, Republican William Howard Taft, Progressive Roosevelt, and Socialist Eugene Debs. Both Wilson and Roosevelt beat the conservative Taft; the combined vote for the candidates of reform totaled nearly 11 million, while Taft—representing the status quo—polled only 3.5 million.

BUT THE COMMERCIAL REVOLUTION that so appalled Henry James continued unabated. The year before James's return to America, a young Midwestern mechanic and tinkerer had gone into the automobile business. Henry Ford had long dreamed of mass-producing a lightweight and inexpensive car; in order to do so, though, he had first to build successful race cars. After accumulating some $28,000 in prize money, he established the Ford Motor Company, and set out to build a car for the masses.

In 1908, the Model T was ready. It was by far the most complicated product of the metalworking field, employing sophisticated machine tools, new metal alloys, and new approaches to plant design based on scientific management. At $845, the T began to create its own market, and Ford—by constantly refining his company's production and distribution techniques—continued to broaden that market. In six years he cut production time from twelve hours to two and a half hours, and then again—with the opening in 1914 of a new manufacturing facility—to an hour and a half.

This new facility featured the first fully automated assembly line, and promised to be so productive that Ford announced unprecedented wage increases—from an average of $2.40 for a nine-hour day to a minimum of $5.00 for an eight-hour day. Even so, the T continued to become cheaper: by 1924, it cost only $290. Production increased from 18,664 units in 1909 to 1,250,000 in 1920. The T was produced by the highest-paid industrial workforce in the country, and cost only half as much as its nearest competitors; Ford, nevertheless, made a huge personal fortune.

In 1895, there were four automobiles registered in the United States; by 1920, there were over eight million, a large percentage of them Model T's. The Ford Motor Company's success was an object lesson in mass production and distribution. Henry Ford had actually "invented" very little—in fact, he had borrowed heavily from the production techniques employed in Cyrus

**Henry Ford's Model T: a lesson in mass production and distribution. Left: the upholstering station. Center and right: mounting bodies on frames.**

McCormick's reaper works, and in Ransom Olds's short-lived automobile assembly line. What he had done was apply those techniques thoroughly and relentlessly, while also cultivating vast new markets. Manufacturers in his own industry, as well as others, soon followed Ford's lead.

Within the prewar decade, there was a vast array of manufactured products available to the consumer, some of them new, some of them newly affordable. Between 1900 and 1910, the nation's non-rural population grew by 40 percent, and this group—some 12 million people—consumed the products of industry and agriculture. Consumer-oriented magazines, such as Edward Bok's *Ladies' Home Journal*, began instructing new legions of consumers in the "good life." The journals proliferated and prospered as advertising revenues grew. (The *Saturday Evening Post* grew in circulation from 300,000 in 1902, with ad revenues of $360,000, to 2 million in 1922, with ad revenues of $28 million.) New forms of retail outlets, including the chain store, were developed for the distribution of consumer goods.

The Great Atlantic and Pacific Tea Company, for example, operated 200 A & P stores in 1900, 400 in 1912, and 11,000 in 1924.

Concealed within this overall growth were the very different circumstances faced by the principal players in the American economy prior to and during World War I. For each group, the stakes had grown higher. Business had to compete on a new level of sophistication and intensity; if it did so successfully, it reaped immense rewards. Labor, for its part, had to do battle—often literally—to share those rewards. (Few manufacturers emulated Ford's paternalistic approach; in fact, many denounced the automaker for driving up wage scales.) Government, which had created ample problems for itself with the financing and conduct of World War I, was drawn inexorably into managing the national economy, and into the struggle between business and labor.

THE TWO BEST Harvard Business School theses of 1916 —to which the faculty awarded the May Prizes, from a fund established by Price Waterhouse partner George O. May—neatly reflected the manufacturing and marketing issues of the day. First prize was taken by H. H. Gordon's "The Problem of the Used Car in the Automobile Industry," while second prize was earned by W. J. Keyes's "Should a Retail Grocer Buy Futures in Canned Goods?"

Since the School's founding, the faculty had required every second-year student to "submit a thesis dealing with some concrete problem in the business which he plans to enter and embodying the results and conclusions derived from his original investigation of actual business conditions." But only 207 of the 1,442 students who enrolled at the School in its first eleven years ever satisfied that requirement—because, for the most part, students stayed for only one year of Harvard's new experiment in business education, and then left to take jobs.

**Dean Gay was accustomed to receiving letters of withdrawal from the School, but William Harper's was nonetheless unusual. He thanked Gay for the "great privilege" of attending HBS, where he had developed a line of thought leading to his firm's construction of six new steamers.**

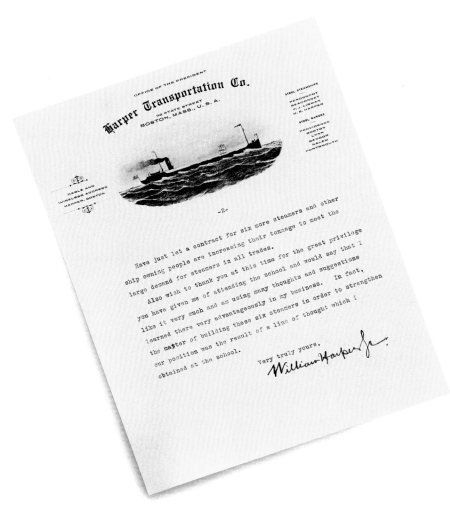

This alarming rate of attrition reflected several influences. First, in an era when many businessmen still thought a college education was a hindrance, one year of graduate business education was, presumably, less objectionable than two. In addition, Dean Gay insisted that students find useful employment, related to their chosen field of interest, in the summer between their first and second years. (In fact, the School often lent a hand in finding such employment.) Many students, having found a congenial working environment during the summer, simply elected to stay there.

For some students, it proved financially impossible to remain at Harvard, especially given the School's limited scholarship and loan funds. A number of students left to join or take over family businesses; later in the decade, many volunteered for service in the European war.

But many others, especially in the School's first half-dozen years, left because of dissatisfaction with their first-year studies, and because of the unimpressive reputation of the second-year curriculum. It was a period of experimentation, and many of the curricular innovations of the day—such as the thesis requirement, which was abandoned in 1922—proved unsatisfactory.

In the first few years of the School's existence, the curriculum was for the most part a combination of elements from undergraduate departments of economics and schools of commerce. Principles of Accounting was, effectively, the same course it had been before it was transplanted from the College to the Business School. Many courses were *descriptive* in nature, and were taught from the economist's perspective: Economic Resources of the United States, Commercial Organization and Methods, Banking, Railroad Organization and Finance, and so on. While these courses helped give students from a variety of undergraduate institutions a common intellectual ground, their vantage point was often not that of the administrator, but rather of the analytic "outsider."

There were exceptions. Commercial Contracts— which used mimeographed case material from the Law School as the basis for discussion—was clearly of a

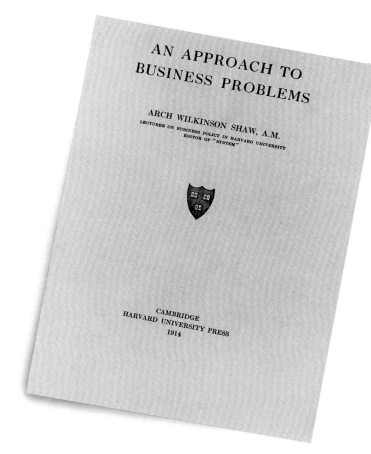

practical bent. Several of the first-year electives, such as Accounting Practice and Railroad Operation, attempted to teach business students to do a practical job. In general, though, even these courses were aimed at the department head or division supervisor, rather than the chief executive. When enrollment warranted a lecture format, the professor lectured; otherwise —as was usually the case—classes resembled informal graduate seminars.

The first turning point came early in 1911, when *System* publisher Arch Shaw complained to Dean Gay that the School's courses were too general and descriptive, and that its students "wouldn't recognize a problem if they saw one."

"If you know so much about it," Gay replied, "why don't you tackle it yourself?"

Shaw, who was then scheduled to return to his publishing duties in Chicago after a year at Harvard, could not resist the challenge. He and Gay agreed upon the concept of a required second-year course, to be called Business Policy and offered the following spring. Shaw would be the course head; his experiment would attempt to integrate the lessons of the first year by adopting the vantage point of the upper-level manager.

After observing the classroom techniques of the Law School's Samuel Williston and the Department of Economics' F. W. Taussig, Shaw decided to take a new approach to getting students to "recognize a problem." He secured the cooperation of fifteen senior managers, each of whom agreed to present a real problem to the class over the course of a week. In the first of three sessions, the businessman would explain his problem, and answer students' questions regarding it. In the second class meeting, two days later, students would hand in a written "problem analysis," with a recommended solution. In the third session, at the end of the week, the businessman would discuss the reports.

The approach was not without its pitfalls, as Gay recollected in 1927: "Since no case books had yet been collected, businessmen would be induced by the persuasion of Mr. A. W. Shaw to exhibit themselves and their troubles as clinical material—walking cases. . . . But suppose these eminent business practitioners from whom you asked a talk on Revelations insisted on filling

A forerunner to the case book: Arch Shaw's *An Approach to Business Problems*. While Harvard was printing an expanded version of Shaw's pamphlet as the first in a projected series of "Harvard Business Studies," A. W. Shaw Company was publishing Paul T. Cherington's study of the wool trade as the first in an "American Industry Series." Neither series, however, survived the First World War.

their allotted time with a discourse on Genesis? Then here was simply another kink to be straightened out."

One of the first businessmen to exhibit himself as a "walking case" to a Business Policy class was Walter H. Cottingham, president of the Sherwin-Williams Paint Company, who visited the School in the spring of 1912. Cottingham was evidently more anxious about his "lecture," to be presented the following day, than he was about a board meeting he would be attending immediately after the class session. Shaw, however, resolutely avoided discussing Cottingham's "lecture." A tour of the campus was followed by talks with professors and a dinner at the faculty club. Late in the evening, Cottingham brought up the question of the "lecture" once again, and finally Shaw responded.

"Why, you have just what we want in that briefcase of yours," said Shaw. "Why not lay your agenda before the class tomorrow?" Cottingham, apparently, went along with the suggestion.

Walter Cottingham, a "living case."

**Elizabeth Wilson (at right, circa 1950) eventually earned her Master's and Ph.D. degrees from Radcliffe, and was the first woman ever seated at an International Actuarial Congress.**

## Students and live interests

Two students who enrolled in the Harvard Business School in the fall of 1915 were deceived by appearances. Behind their rooms in Perkins Hall they discovered 32 tennis courts, and —being avid tennis players— they assumed that Business School students were not supposed to overtax themselves intellectually. But by January, according to one, they found themselves devoting nine hours a day to their studies.

In the preceding spring, the Business School's faculty had attempted to determine how much time the curriculum actually demanded of the students, including classroom hours, field work, required reading, and thesis preparation. Returns from a survey sent to all regular students suggested that they were spending between nine and ten hours per week per course. President Lowell responded "favorably" to these results, according to the minutes of a faculty meeting. But perhaps not favorably enough: Lowell then recommended further study to determine "the practicability of taking more than four courses a year."

The School's students were, for the most part, just out of college. Increasingly, during the years preceding World War I, they represented more diverse academic and geographic backgrounds. In 1914, for example, 29 percent of the incoming students were Harvard College graduates; the following fall, however, only 15 percent were Harvard College graduates. In its first year of operation, the School had students from 14 colleges in 12 states; by 1916, it had representatives from 72 colleges and 36 states.

All, of course, were men. It was not until after America's entry into the war that women expressed an interest in admission to the Business School. At that point—early in 1918—six Radcliffe students petitioned for permission to take courses related to the war effort. After considering the petition ("as a war measure so as to afford to women the higher business-education opportunities of the Business School"), the faculty voted against it.

The question arose again in October, 1919, when the faculty met to discuss "the crowded condition of the Business School library," and to consider the petition of one Elizabeth W. Wilson, Radcliffe graduate, to study life insurance at the Business School. "It was the general feeling," the faculty secretary recorded, "that since the School aims to prepare for executive positions, it could not at this time logically admit women, as executive positions in business are not ordinarily open to them."

Graduating MBAs of that era strongly preferred manufacturing, which attracted as many graduates as any other two fields together. Early returns on the "marketability" of the MBA degree were mixed. On the one hand, American Telephone and Telegraph had in 1911 placed an informal "standing order" for all available graduates. Price Waterhouse and Co., furthermore, had offered to pay graduates at the start twenty dollars a month more than they paid men who had had only a college training. On the other hand, as business conditions worsened, starting salaries declined consistently —from $2,144 in 1910 to $1,450 by the middle of the decade.

Impermanence was the principal characteristic of student life for most of the decade, with only a quarter of the School's enrolled students ever receiving a degree. Even the School's Visiting Committee had to conclude, in 1915, that the "best students" were not returning for a second year of study. Dean Gay, although several times maintaining that the School had "turned a corner" in this regard, continued to receive a steady stream of letters from withdrawing students.

But most alumni—whether graduates or not—expressed satisfaction with the education they had received. In 1914, the secretary of the Harvard Business School Association solicited frank comments on the value of the School from its alumni. The responses were generally positive. One former student called the School "a concentrated experience producer." The father of one graduate noted, "You have educated not only the son but also the father."

"To the school," wrote Bryant B. Glenny (MBA '11), in response to an inquiry from a New York businessman, "I am deeply indebted for the opportunity to make my choice of a life work intelligently, for the inspiration received from Dean Gay, the faculty, and lecturers; and for a knowledge of the theory of business, which I believe has been largely responsible for any success I have had since graduation. The value of the Case System, better known in connection with the curriculum of the Harvard Law School, has been of incalculable value to me, and has given me confidence in solving whatever problems have been put up to me.

"But perhaps the thing that I feel most grateful for is the vast field of live interests to which the School opened my eyes, and which I feel sure I should have largely overlooked, or at least, not have discovered for years, had I entered business at the end of my college course."

**The student population grew slowly but steadily in the School's first five years. Concealed in these statistics, however, was a serious imbalance: only 11 of the 88 "students doing full work" in 1912 were second-year students. The ratio of first-year to second-year students improved considerably in 1913, but the former still outnumbered the latter by more than two to one.**

### HARVARD UNIVERSITY
### THE GRADUATE SCHOOL OF BUSINESS ADMINISTRATION

The Graduate School of Business Administration was established in March, 1908, by votes of the President and Fellows and of the Board of Overseers of Harvard College.

**Aim**   It aims to give thorough and scientific training in the methods and principles of business organization and management.

**Growth**   The growth of the School during the five years of its existence is shown by the following table:—

| Year | Students doing full work | Special | Total | Colleges represented | States represented | Foreign countries |
|---|---|---|---|---|---|---|
| 1908–09 | 33 | 47 | 80 | 14 | 12 | 2 |
| 1909–10 | 50 | 41 | 91 | 19 | 16 | 5 |
| 1910–11 | 53 | 41 | 94 | 22 | 20 | 2 |
| 1911–12 | 65 | 32 | 97 | 25 | 21 | 4 |
| 1912–13 | 88 | 32 | 120 | 42 | 26 | 4 |

Like the other Harvard professional schools, the School of Business Administration is strictly a graduate department of the University. The requirement for admission as a regular student is the possession of a bachelor's degree from an approved college or scientific school. The privilege of taking special work has been opened to young business men, many of whom hold college degrees. Among the special students have been business men of large affairs.

The Class of 1912.
Only 8 of 43 members of the
first-year class received
MBAs.

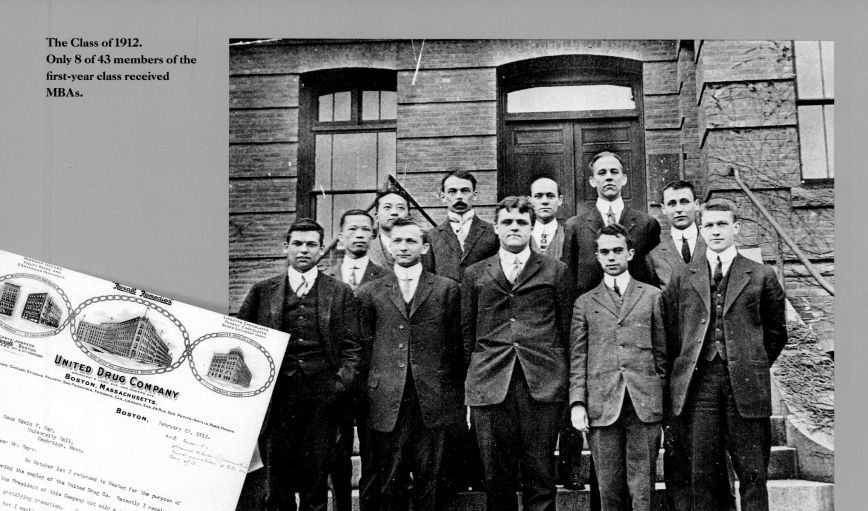

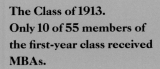

An unsolicited testimonial,
from a member of an early
class, concerning the
"practicability of the
Business School."

The Class of 1913.
Only 10 of 55 members of
the first-year class received
MBAs.

IN HIS INITIAL PLANNING for the Harvard Business School, during the summer of 1908, Dean Gay had considered at length the elusive relationship between the intent of his curriculum — the training of the professional administrator — and the teaching method most appropriate for achieving that goal. In the catalogue produced at the end of that summer, Gay stated that the School would employ "an analogous method [to the "case method" used in the Law School], emphasizing classroom discussion, supplemented by lectures and frequent reports, which may be called the *problem* method."

Gay sought to distinguish his "problem method" from the Law School's case method, but the Law School's experience was an instructive precedent. There, forty years earlier, Christopher Columbus Langdell, professor and dean, had instituted a radical approach to the teaching of law. In the first meeting of his Contracts course in 1870, Langdell — who felt that the proper way to study the law was to record numerous examples, and to derive general principles from those examples — declined to deliver a standard lecture.

Christopher Columbus Langdell, Harvard Law School professor and dean, and author of that school's case method.

Instead, he asked a surprised student to "state the case." He asked questions of a second student, and then a third. After a dozen or so questions, without having presented a formal analysis of the case, Langdell proceeded to lead a "discussion" of a second case.

The students reacted first with bewilderment, then with anger. They were not interested, they proclaimed, in hearing what their fellow students thought about a case; they wanted to learn the law. Attendance and enrollment in Langdell's classes plummeted. (Boston University's law school, which opened in 1872, was established in part to accommodate disaffected Harvard students.) But Langdell, and the "Langdell system," prevailed, at first because the dean had the unwavering support of Harvard's President Eliot, and subsequently because the Law School's graduates were soon achieving unprecedented professional success.

Gay knew that his own School's circumstances were necessarily different: most important, there was no established body of cases available to him. His faculty would simply have to employ a "problem method" whenever it seemed possible. In February, 1908, Gay asked Instructor Stuart Daggett, who was to begin teaching Railroad Accounting that fall, what "problem work" Daggett would be including in his course. Daggett replied that he intended to supply students with pertinent materials and ask them to work through a problem: "In the matter of claims specific cases will be made up, and the men asked to handle them in accordance with the freight claim rules, indicating the necessary statements to connections, and the liability of each road so far as determined by inter-railroad agreement."

Some faculty members, such as former Boston and Maine signalman J. O. Fagan, were confused by Gay's suggestion to "reserve certain points with which to initiate the discussion." Gay wrote in the fall of 1909 to Fagan — then about to begin his second year of instruction — and explained what he had in mind:

"I suggested the holding in reserve of one or two topics merely that you might thus find it easier to open the discussion. This, however, is of course left entirely to your own discretion. The only thing I am desirous of effecting by this arrangement is the development of active discussion between lecturers and students. It is unadvisable, in my opinion, to have a course made up only of lectures read from manuscript."

**"When, as a train master or superintendent, you inspect a freight station…": William Cunningham's Railroad Operation course emphasized operational skills, and often adopted the middle manager's perspective.**

In a 1938 Harvard Business School *Bulletin* article, William J. Cunningham, the railroad administrator turned professor, reminisced about the earliest days of the Business School's case method. "In the very beginning," he recalled, "we made an effort to follow the Law School practice of teaching by means of cases, but inasmuch as cases of the right kind were not available and the financial resources of the School would not permit the organization of a research staff to gather and prepare such cases, the case system was more a wish than a reality. With the small numbers of students in a class, however, the instructors as a rule conducted the courses more by general discussion than by lectures, and within the first two or three years a start had been made toward the collection of cases."

Class enrollments, as Cunningham suggests, may have encouraged informality, but they also limited the practicality of the case method. During his second week as a teacher, for example, Cunningham informed Gay that his course in Railroad Operation had experienced a 50 percent increase in enrollment: from two to three. Edgar J. Rich, instructor in Railroad Rate-Making, remarked that 100 percent of his class—that is, one student—was in the hospital with appendicitis.

Some instructors flatly declined to employ the "problem method." Regarding his Banking survey course, O. M. W. Sprague told Gay, "It does not seem to me regrettable that the case system cannot be adopted in this course. It is more suitable to many other courses in the School and exclusive absorption in case study in my opinion commonly breeds a very narrow type of mind."

But Gay continued his experiments with the case method. In 1912, he persuaded Melvin T. Copeland to return to Harvard to teach a new course in Business Statistics. (Copeland, then an instructor at New York University, had studied under Gay while earning his doctorate in economics at Harvard, and had subsequently spent one year on the Business School faculty.) Then, on the Monday night before school began in the fall of 1912, Gay gave Copeland an additional responsibility: he was to take one section of Paul Cherington's oversubscribed Commercial Organization and Methods course. Copeland was somewhat taken aback. He had never before taught the course, which was to begin in two days. In addition, Cherington was considered an

**1913-14**
**HARVARD UNIVERSITY**

**BUSINESS 28**
**RAILROAD OPERATION**
Assistant Professor CUNNINGHAM

1. A difference of opinion exists as to the fairness of the per diem rate for the use of freight cars. Some railroad officers believe that it should be fifty cents; others hold that the former rate of thirty-five cents is adequate. How would you proceed to test the reasonableness of the rate, and what figures would you use as the basis for your conclusions?

2. When, as a train master or superintendent, you inspect a freight station, what features of operation would you observe particularly, and on what other points would you make inquiries?

3. How would you summarize the advantages and disadvantages of very heavy freight trains? What are the several means or methods of increasing the train load, and what are the limitations of each?

4. Assume that a change in division terminals requires a new classification yard at a point where there is unlimited room and favorable topography. The normal movement is 1600 freight cars in each direction per day. Coal cars comprise one-half of the total, and the loaded coal cars must be weighed. There is also a steady movement of live stock and other perishable freight. With an allowance for an increase in traffic, draw a rough diagram showing the design of an ideal classification yard, with all auxiliary facilities, indicating the capacity of each unit in the group.

5. Enumerate the several daily reports (and their contents) which a superintendent should have in order to keep in close and constant touch with station, yard, and train operation.

6. Explain what is meant by "positive meet" in rules governing train movement. In what respects does this differ from the Standard Code of train rules?

**Melvin T. Copeland was brought to HBS from New York University to "keep the students talking."**

outstanding lecturer; the course's high enrollment was in part an expression of student interest in Cherington. Nevertheless, Copeland obtained Cherington's outline and assigned readings, and began teaching a section of the course.

"About ten days later, as I was coming from a meeting of the class," Copeland later recalled, "I met Dean Gay on the steps of University Hall in the Harvard Yard, where he had his office. He asked me how things were going, and since at the moment I was feeling optimistic I told him that I had found enough to talk about so far. 'Humph,' was Dean Gay's rejoinder, 'That isn't the question. Have you found enough to keep the students talking?'

"From that day on," said Copeland, "I did no more lecturing in Commercial Organization or in any other course. We had no case material and, in fact, little pertinent literature. We assigned readings in a variety of publications, and I attempted to carry on discussions which centered around those readings. It was hard going for both the instructor and the students, especially the students, but they took it as good sports."

There was strong support for the case method—or at least for *some* innovative teaching method—from another important quarter: the School's Visiting Committee. Like Harvard's other graduate schools, the Business School was observed regularly by a group of distinguished practitioners in its field of study. This group, appointed by the University's Board of Overseers, reported regularly to the Board on the School's activities. At its first meeting, on January 13, 1909, the six Visiting Committee members and eleven faculty members in attendance discussed "the desirable characteristics of young men entering business," and how to promote those characteristics.

"One very important question," commented one member of the Committee, "is, will the young man bend himself to the problem? Will he be able to grasp and handle a concrete proposition with good judgement?... It is, therefore, important to ask whether there is any difference in the method of instruction in the Business School from that which prevails in the College. In the College too much emphasis is laid on memorizing, although for business success quick and accurate judgement is more essential."

Seven years later, Donald Scott—a New York publisher and advisor to Gay—gave more specific recommendations in a letter to the chairman of the Visiting Committee:

"First: there should be a considerable extension of what in the Law School is called the 'case system' to the teaching of the Business School. The examinations papers"—which Gay had consistently encouraged Committee members to read—"seemed to show that in courses where this is most used there is a marked increase in the intelligent application of teaching to new problems; in fact, in many instances the students showed a breadth of judgement in their discussion of problems which was surprising. The Business School should not consist simply of more specialized courses in economics. It should endeavor to show the student the business world as it is today, and to point out the fundamental principles underlying all trades and commerce. ... To do this means less teaching of theory and more deduction of principles from actual examples. Discussion in the class-room should be encouraged even more than it is at present."

Gay himself was committed to discussion in the classroom whenever possible. "We are pushing as rapidly as is possible toward the discussion method of instruction," he wrote, "but this is attended with a number of difficulties. One of the chief difficulties is the obtaining of proper case material for discussion. Time and experience will, however, solve this difficulty."

**Donald Scott at Pirie Canyon, Utah, in 1934. After a distinguished career in publishing, Scott left the industry to take up anthropology, eventually heading Harvard's Peabody Museum.**

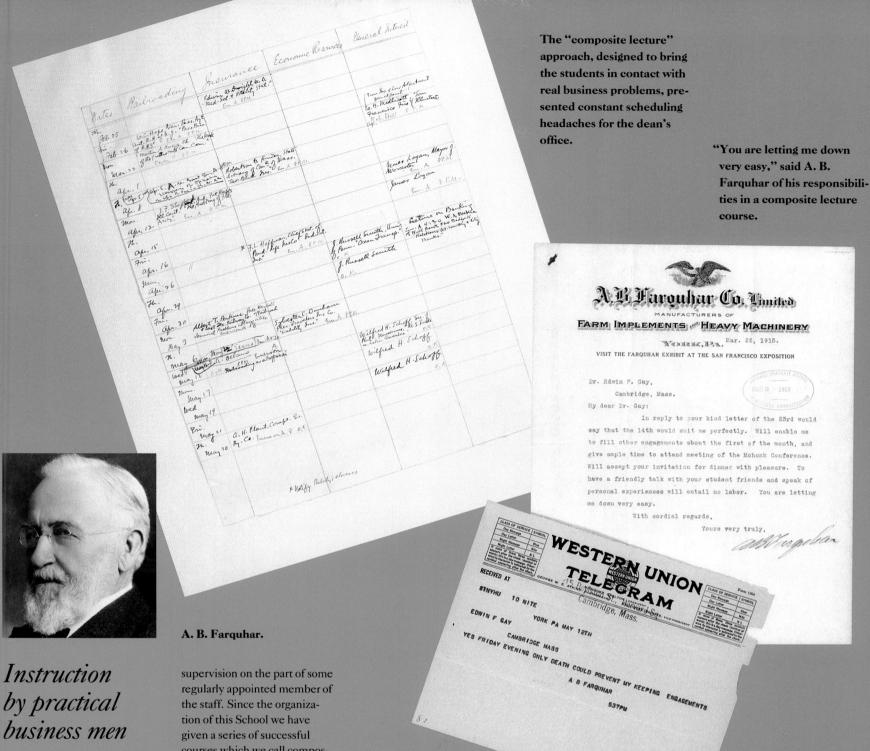

**A. B. Farquhar.**

## Instruction by practical business men

In addition to the lecture and "problem-method" teaching techniques, the Business School faculty in its early years devoted much effort to the development and maintenance of the "composite lecture course." The approach is described in a letter from Dean Gay to a representative of Washington University in St. Louis, who had asked if Gay favored instruction by "practical business men":

"Most certainly we do favor instruction by practical business men. But such instruction can only be made really effective by careful planning and supervision on the part of some regularly appointed member of the staff. Since the organization of this School we have given a series of successful courses which we call composite lecture courses, in which we have had the cooperation of a number of business men.

"The course is systematically outlined in considerable detail; the best and most available lecturers are picked for separate topics; each one is sent the whole outline of the course, and this with his own sub-topics is discussed with him in detail. A member of the staff takes charge of the course and all the lectures, organizes the work of instruction, discussion, and report work, and sets the examination paper. At the conclusion of the course the list of lecturers is carefully revised, and we find that where necessary to make changes in the lectures in order to avoid duplication or waste, the lecturers are very willing to receive suggestions and to adapt their work in accordance."

"Systematic outlines" and cooperative lecturers notwithstanding, the composite lecture system created serious pedagogical difficulties. "One of our problems," Gay confessed to a friend, "has been to knit special lectures into a continuous, effective whole." It also presented the dean's office — which coordinated the School's correspondence with prominent corporate executives — with a logistical nightmare. Many executives simply declined invitations to lecture; others accepted but canceled on short notice. Gay attempted to limit such last-minute cancelations with a steady stream of notes to scheduled lecturers.

One such reminder was sent in May of 1915 to A. B. Farquhar, the 77-year-old president of a York, Pennsylvania, farm-implements and heavy-machinery manufacturing firm. Could the Business School count on his appearance, Gay inquired?

A telegram arrived from Farquhar the following morning: "Yes Friday evening only death could prevent my keeping engagements."

BETWEEN 1908 AND 1914, with the introduction of Business Policy and an increased emphasis on the "problem" method, the School's curriculum gradually became less descriptive and more oriented toward administrative action. The 1914 course listings reflect several abrupt moves toward that goal. Commercial Organization—the subject of Gay's case method experiment—was divided into two courses: Marketing, and Foreign Trade Methods. While the latter remained essentially descriptive, Marketing had a new, *functional* orientation—the orientation of the administrator.

Similarly, Industrial Organization—which since 1908 had been taught at HBS by Frederick Taylor, Carl Barth, and other distinguished advocates of scientific management—was renamed Manufacturing in 1914. The Harvard faculty had come to think of the "engineer-as-reformer" as the quintessential outsider, whose prescriptions—while well intentioned—often led to extremely one-sided, anti-labor management systems. After the engineers were displaced from their primary position in the first-year curriculum, the needs of labor got what one observer called "a more friendly consideration" at Harvard.

**In 1915, the Committee on Course Planning prepared a "suggested program of courses" for first-year students. Although the outline organized HBS courses by industry, the School's curriculum was already reflecting a functional orientation.**

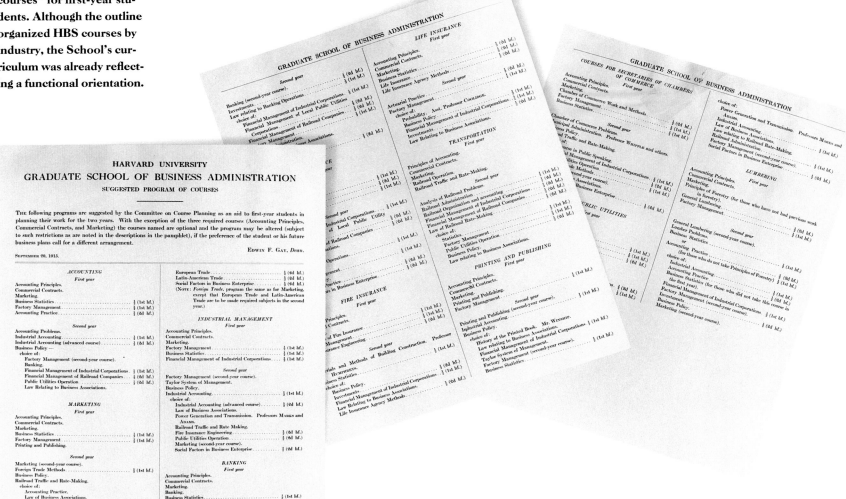

William McCormick, president of the McCormick spice company, thought that the U. S. Chamber of Commerce could serve as the link between government, industry, and academia.

Gay agreed with the spirit of McCormick's letter, saying that cooperative efforts would be essential "if the business men of the United States are to lift the standards, both technical and professional, which will be necessary with the probability of a developing competition in foreign trade."

Paul T. Cherington applied the lessons learned during the retail shoe trade investigation when he organized the Work and Methods of Trade Associations course, offered in 1913. With this questionnaire, he sought to "secure some data about commercial executive work which we find never have been brought together."

During this same period, and again culminating in 1914, the Business School conducted a number of experiments in industry-specific courses. To a certain extent, these courses were a pragmatic response to available resources: when Boston's Society of Printers offered in 1910 to support a course in printing techniques, the School gladly accepted the support— some $7,000. Similarly, when Boston retailer Edward A. Filene and the Boston Chamber of Commerce expressed their interest in a course of study for secretaries of chambers of commerce, the School inaugurated such a course. And, to a certain extent, these courses sustained themselves: in January, 1911, for example, the Technique of Printing course had only two MBA candidates enrolled, but nearly a dozen tuition-paying "special" students.

Courses oriented toward specific industries, and therefore toward specific technologies, had their pitfalls. As Visiting Committee member J. P. Morgan, Jr.,

warned at a November, 1910, meeting, "It would be unwise to adopt the methods of trade schools or technical schools." Gay responded that the faculty didn't intend to offer technical instruction; for that, he said, they would seek a closer relationship with Harvard's Graduate School of Applied Science.

Nonetheless, Gay and the faculty did feel an obligation to provide students with a strong technical background, in addition to the elusive principles of general administration. "We are not, of course, a trade school," Gay wrote in 1911 to L. C. Marshall, a friend who would soon inaugurate a business school at the University of Chicago, "and we find it necessary in training men for various lines of business that they shall have some notion of the technical side, and this experiment which we are trying with printing, if successful, will be followed by some other courses of general character for other leading lines of industry."

Saturday Evening Post 4/30/1910

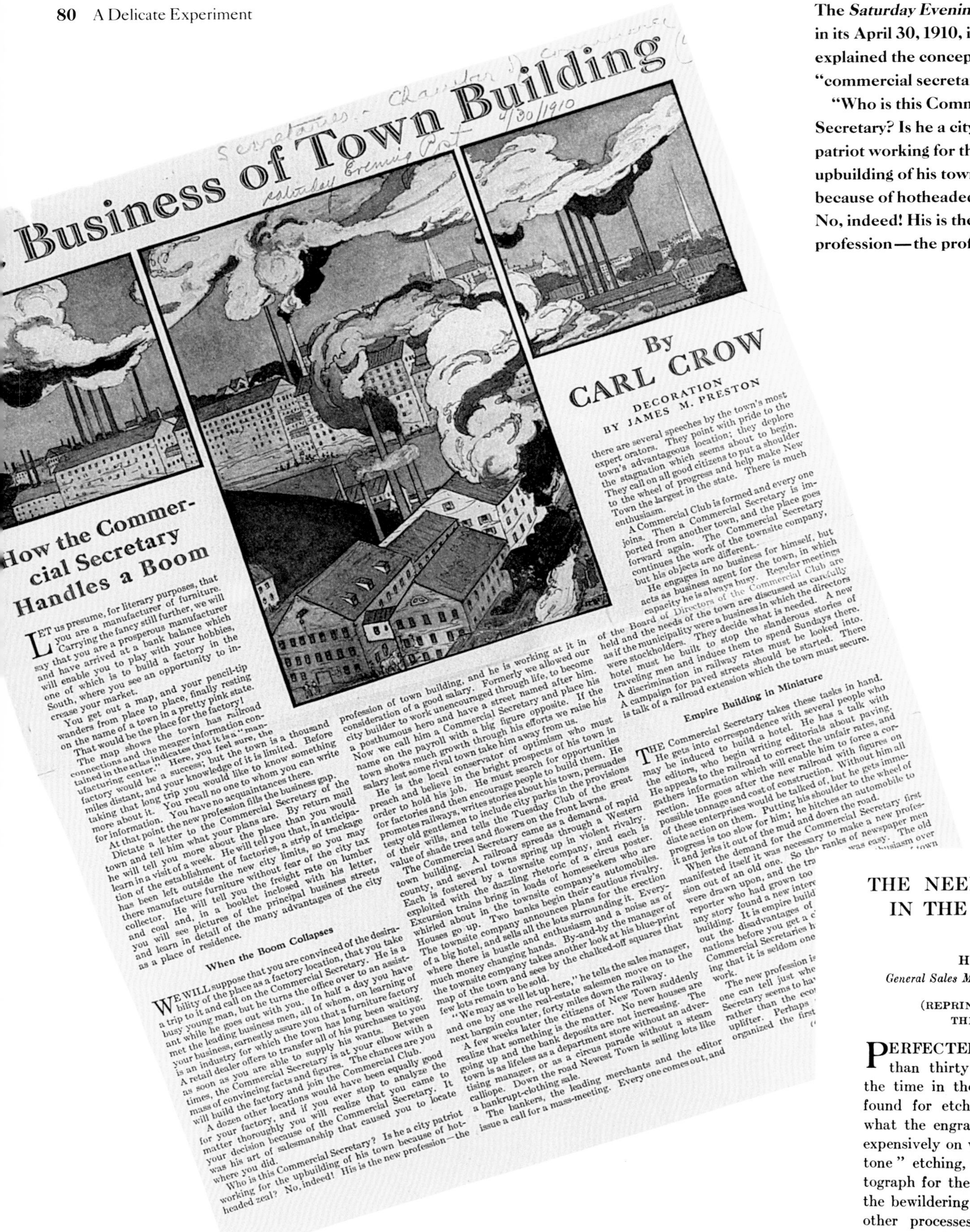

# Business of Town Building

## How the Commercial Secretary Handles a Boom

By CARL CROW

DECORATION BY JAMES M. PRESTON

LET us presume, for literary purposes, that you are a manufacturer of furniture. Carrying the fancy still further, we will say that you are a prosperous manufacturer and have arrived at a bank balance which will enable you to play with your hobbies, one of which is to build a factory in the South, where you see an opportunity to increase your market.

You get out a map, and your pencil-tip wanders from place to place, finally resting on the name of a town in a pretty pink state. That would be the place for the factory!

The map shows the town has railroad connections and the meager information contained in the atlas indicates that it is a "manufacturing center." Here, you feel sure, the factory would be a success; but the town is a thousand miles distant, and your knowledge of it is limited. Before taking that long trip you would like to know something more about it. You recall no one to whom you can write for information. You have no acquaintances there.

At that point the new profession fills the business gap. Dictate a letter to the Commercial Secretary of the town and tell him what your plans are. By return mail he will tell you more about the place than you would learn in a visit of a week. He will tell you that, in anticipation of the establishment of factories, a strip of trackage has been left outside the new city limits, so you may there manufacture furniture without fear of the city tax collector. He will tell you the freight rate on lumber and coal and, in a booklet inclosed with his letter, you will see pictures of the principal business streets and learn in detail of the many advantages of the city as a place of residence.

### When the Boom Collapses

WE WILL suppose that you are convinced of the desirability of the place as a factory location, that you take a trip to it and call on the Commercial Secretary. He is a busy young man, but he turns the office over to an assistant while he goes out with you. In half a day you have met the leading business men, all of whom, on learning of your business, earnestly assure you that a furniture factory is an industry for which the town has long been waiting. A retail dealer offers to transfer all of his purchases to you as soon as you are able to supply his wants. Between times, the Commercial Secretary is at your elbow with a mass of convincing facts and figures. The chances are you will build the factory and join the Commercial Club.

A dozen other locations would have been equally good for your factory, and if you ever stop to analyze the matter thoroughly you will realize that you came to your decision because of the Commercial Secretary. It was his art of salesmanship that caused you to locate where you did.

Who is this Commercial Secretary? Is he a city patriot working for the upbuilding of his town because of hotheaded zeal? No, indeed! His is the new profession—the profession of town building, and he is working at it in consideration of a good salary. Formerly we allowed our city builder to work unencouraged through life, to become a posthumous hero and have a street named after him. Now we call him a Commercial Secretary and place his name on the payroll with a big figure opposite. If the town shows much growth through his efforts we raise his salary lest some rival town take him away from us.

He is the local conservator of optimism who must preach and believe in the bright prospects of his town in order to hold his job. He must search for opportunities for factories and then encourage people to build them. He promotes railways, writes stories about his town, persuades testy old gentlemen to include city parks in the provisions of their wills, and tells the Tuesday Club of the great value of shade trees and flowers on the front lawns.

The Commercial Secretary came as a demand of rapid town building. A railroad spreads through a Western county, and several towns spring up in violent rivalry. Each is fostered by a townsite company, and each is exploited with the dazzling rhetoric of a circus poster. Excursion trains bring in loads of homeseekers who are whirled about in the townsite company's automobiles. Houses go up. Two banks begin their cautious rivalry. The townsite company announces plans for the erection of a big hotel, and sells all the lots surrounding it. Everywhere there is bustle and enthusiasm and a noise as of much money changing hands. By-and-by the manager of the townsite company takes another look at his blue-print map of the town and sees by the chalked-off squares that few lots remain to be sold.

"We may as well let up here," he tells the sales manager, and one by one the real-estate salesmen move on to the next bargain counter, forty miles down the railway.

A few weeks later the citizens of New Town suddenly realize that something is the matter. No new houses are going up and the bank deposits are not increasing. The town is as lifeless as a department store without an advertising manager, or as a circus parade without a steam calliope. Down the road Newest Town is selling lots like a bankrupt-clothing sale.

The bankers, the leading merchants and the editor issue a call for a mass-meeting. Every one comes out, and there are several speeches by the town's most expert orators. They point with pride to the town's advantageous location; they deplore the stagnation which seems about to begin. They call on all good citizens to put a shoulder to the wheel of progress and help make New Town the largest in the state. There is much enthusiasm.

A Commercial Club is formed and every one joins. Then a Commercial Secretary is imported from another town, and the place goes forward again. The Commercial Secretary continues the work of the townsite company, but his objects are different.

He engages in no business for himself, but acts as business agent for the town, in which capacity he is always busy. Regular meetings of the Board of Directors of the Commercial Club are held and the needs of the town are discussed as carefully as if the municipality were a business in which the directors were stockholders. They decide what is needed. A new hotel must be built to stop the slanderous stories of traveling men and induce them to spend Sundays there. A discrimination in railway rates must be looked into. A campaign for paved streets should be started. There is talk of a railroad extension which the town must secure.

### Empire Building in Miniature

THE Commercial Secretary takes these tasks in hand. He gets into correspondence with several people who may be induced to build a hotel. He has a talk with the editors, who begin writing editorials about paving. He appeals to the railroad to correct the unfair rates, and gathers information which will enable him to force a correction. He goes after the new railroad with figures on possible tonnage and cost of construction. Without him all of these enterprises would be talked of, but he gets immediate action on them. Putting his shoulder to the wheel of progress is too slow for him; he hitches an automobile to it and jerks it out of the mud and down the road.

When the demand for the Commercial Secretary first manifested itself it was necessary to make a new profession out of an old one. So the ...

The *Saturday Evening Post*, in its April 30, 1910, issue, explained the concept of the "commercial secretary":

"Who is this Commercial Secretary? Is he a city patriot working for the upbuilding of his town because of hotheaded zeal? No, indeed! His is the new profession—the profession of town building, and he is working at it in consideration of a good salary."

The salary was indeed good: the secretary of Boston's Chamber of Commerce was hired in 1910 at a salary of $15,000 a year. Business school professors, by comparison, were earning only several thousand dollars a year.

The School's interest in printing was in part a result of the explosive growth of that industry, in the first two decades of the twentieth century. As Herbert L. Baker's article suggests, periodicals and catalogues both derived from and sustained the flood of newly available consumer goods.

# THE NEED FOR TRAINED MEN IN THE PRINTING BUSINESS

BY

HERBERT L. BAKER

*General Sales Manager of the C. B. Cottrell and Sons Co.*

(REPRINTED, BY PERMISSION, FROM THE NATIONAL MAGAZINE)

PERFECTED MODERN PRINTING is less than thirty years old. It really dates from the time in the early eighties, when means were found for etching cheaply with acids on metal what the engraver had previously cut slowly and expensively on wood. Quickly followed the " half-tone " etching, which exactly reproduced the photograph for the first time in history. Then came the bewildering development of color printing and other processes innumerable. Along therewith came new inks, new papers, new machinery, in breath-taking succession. Rotary presses made possible fine illustrated magazines at a popular price, and a national periodical literature was born. With nationally circulated periodicals came nationwide demand for advertised articles. This made necessary thousands of catalogues showing goods not everywhere in stock. Printing received a tremendous impetus and increased until it now

1

The rationale for offering training in the lumber business, according to Harvard's Official Register of 1916, was the increasingly competitive nature of that industry.

The lumbering courses were offered jointly by HBS and Harvard's School of Forestry between 1914 and 1923. The program took advantage of available funds from the Gordon McKay bequest, and its students conducted experiments in the two-thousand-acre Harvard Forest.

Instruction in fire insurance fell victim, in 1916, to the emerging student preference for courses which emphasized administration. Only four students signed up for Fire Insurance Engineering when it was offered in the spring of 1917.

SUPPLEMENT TO

Official Register of Harvard University

VOLUME XIII    MARCH 27, 1916    NO. I, PART 10

*Training for the Lumber Business offered by the Harvard School of Business Administration in Coöperation with the Department of Forestry*

GENERAL STATEMENT

WITH the changes that have taken place in recent years, the lumber business has come to offer an attractive field for trained men. In the earlier days of the industry, when timberland was abundant and relatively cheap, lumbering was largely a business of speculation in stumpage, and the rise in the value of the timber often made up the bulk of the profit. Under such conditions the manufacture and distribution of the product did not require the highest efficiency of organization. Meanwhile the supply of timber has become greatly reduced, the business of handling it has become large and complicated, and the costs of labor, materials, and other factors, have gone up rapidly. The result has been that, deprived of the support of cheap stumpage, lumber companies are being compelled to operate on a narrow margin of profit. To secure this

A PRELIMINARY OUTLINE OF A COURSE OF LECTURES AND OF LABORATORY AND FIELD WORK

'ON

FIRE INSURANCE ENGINEERING

TO BE GIVEN IN THE

GRADUATE SCHOOL OF BUSINESS ADMINISTRATION

OF

HARVARD UNIVERSITY

The printing course, first offered in 1911, had been preceded by a course in fire insurance, as well as courses in railroading and banking. In 1914, a new array of specialized offerings appeared: in chamber of commerce and trade association work, in lumbering and forestry, and in public utilities operation. In 1916, water transportation was added to the curriculum. But a definite enrollment pattern soon emerged—students consistently favored the functional courses (and the "tool" courses, including accounting practice and business statistics) over both the theoretical and the industry-specific courses.

In a school with limited resources and an uncertain curriculum, student preferences had an immediate impact. "Voting with their feet," as the faculty later came to refer to it, was immediately established as a Business School tradition. Arch Shaw's Business Policy course was elected by some 70 percent of the eligible students the first time it was offered; the specialized courses, on the other hand, were generally underattended, particularly as better functional courses became available. For example: although Instructor W. B. Medlicott's fire insurance courses had been well subscribed until the fall of 1916, Gay in that

year informed Medlicott that the faculty had to "contemplate the fact that there will be no course this fall," because no students had signed up for it.

Melvin T. Copeland, in his history of the Harvard Business School, cites three reasons for this enrollment pattern. First, there were restrictive hiring and promotion policies within certain industries. (The seniority systems that dominated the railroads, for example, precluded rapid advancement through their ranks.) Second, business school students, then and now, sought to avoid limiting their employment possibilities by overly specialized courses of study. Third, many students simply found it more stimulating intellectually to solve problems in a variety of industries, rather than in just one.

"I suppose," wrote Arch Shaw to Gay in the spring of 1914, "in a hundred years from now when the work of the School is more specialized, we will have a professor of egg marketing, cabbage marketing, etc." In fact, specialization was then entering a short-lived heyday at the School. Only banking and transportation—the two fields that had been independently endowed through chaired professorships—survived much beyond the First World War.

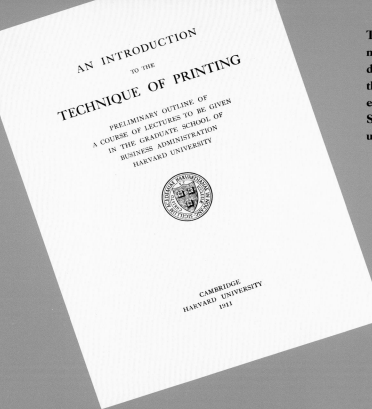

AN INTRODUCTION
TO THE
TECHNIQUE OF PRINTING

PRELIMINARY OUTLINE OF
A COURSE OF LECTURES TO BE GIVEN
IN THE GRADUATE SCHOOL OF
BUSINESS ADMINISTRATION
HARVARD UNIVERSITY

CAMBRIDGE
HARVARD UNIVERSITY
1911

**The printing course materials were elegantly designed and produced, but the courses—the most expensive offered by the School—were chronically undersubscribed.**

## Printing, the Press, and the Business School

A Pennsylvania printer, J. Horace McFarland, declared to a January, 1910, gathering of his peers among Boston's Society of Printers that printers should no longer be considered the "football of the publishers." He argued for more scientific and systematic research into the graphic arts, and particularly into the aesthetic aspects of printing, which were then enjoying a vogue.

Edwin Gay, Dean of the Harvard Business School, was invited to comment after McFarland's lecture. His response to McFarland's argument was generally favorable. "Our limited means will make it impossible for us to launch at once any elaborate scheme," Gay told the gathering. "We can commence with one or two courses and gradually enlarge it, as the numbers of students justify us in incurring greater expense."

With $7,000 of support from the Society of Printers, the Business School undertook to offer a course of instruction in the business of printing. A "History of the Printed Book" course was offered in 1910. (It was taught by a member of the Department of Fine Arts, whose salary was paid by the Business School.) In the same year, the Business School

offered an "Introduction to the Technique of Printing" to its first-year students, and in 1911 second-year students could elect to take Business Practice in Printing. Charles Chester Lane, Harvard's Publication Agent and Secretary of the Society of Printers, was put in charge of the courses.

For the printing courses, as for other sequences of courses, Dean Gay created an "Advisory Committee" of distinguished practitioners. The committees were intended to keep the curriculum in close touch with business realities, as well as to make friends for the School. But whereas most of the advisory committees proved relatively inactive, the Advisory Committee on Printing became actively involved in the School's—and the University's—affairs.

**The Society of Printers' appeal eventually produced over $7,000 to support the School's first experiments in printing education.**

In April of 1912, with Gay's encouragement, the Advisory Committee discussed a proposal to "erect and equip suitable buildings for a Harvard University Press in which the work involved in printing and publishing books shall be carried out, courses in printing conducted for students in the Business School, and an Institute of Graphic Arts maintained." This proposal, said a printing consultant in attendance at the meeting, would cost approximately $250,000 to realize.

Harvard University had long had a printing office, in one form or another, to produce routine publications. (In 1892, the University had created the position of "Publication Agent" to oversee these activities, which C. C. Lane had held before joining the HBS faculty.) But despite the existence of successful university presses at other institutions—including such Harvard "rivals" as Johns Hopkins, Yale, and Princeton—Harvard had cautiously refrained from setting up its own press. The Advisory Committee's vote brought the issue to a head, and in October of 1912 President Lowell authorized a fundraising drive to endow a "Harvard University Press."

The Business School's Dean worked diligently behind the scenes to establish the press. Gay, as a scholar, was particularly impressed with the products of the presses at Oxford and Cambridge universities, and felt that Harvard needed a publishing arm to disseminate the research of its growing faculty. But it had also occurred to Gay that a university press

AN APPEAL FOR THE SUPPORT OF A COURSE OF LECTURES ON PRINTING IN THE GRADUATE SCHOOL OF BUSINESS ADMINISTRATION OF HARVARD UNIVERSITY

IT is because we believe that you are interested in the promotion of good printing that this circular is addressed to you. It is to call your attention to the fact that for the first time in American education or in the history of American typography, a University has placed among its courses one upon Printing. In the Graduate School of Business Administration of Harvard University, a course of lectures has been given this year called *An Introduction to the Technique of Printing*. This course is offered for men who expect to enter upon the management of some portion of a printing business.

Besides the actual education which it gives in printing, the fact that Harvard College has considered the industry of sufficient importance to place it upon its list of subjects to be studied and investigated, is for printing itself an important step. The Committee has been assured that the lectures will later be printed in book form, thus preserving as a permanent contribution to the bibliography of printing, the information brought together.

It is planned to make provision for continuing the course for at least five years. The expense is between $2500 and $3000 annually. The Society of Printers, to some members of which the inception of the scheme is largely due, has felt that it is important to coöperate with the university authorities in the support of the course, and members of this Society have pledged an initial subscription of over $500 toward it.

Our purpose in addressing you now is to ask whether you

*A Keepsake*
*printed on the occasion of the*
*first meeting in*
*Randall Hall*
*of the Syndics of the*
*Harvard University Press*

*October 30, 1916*

**Randall Hall, first home of the Harvard University Press and the Harvard Business School's printing laboratory.**

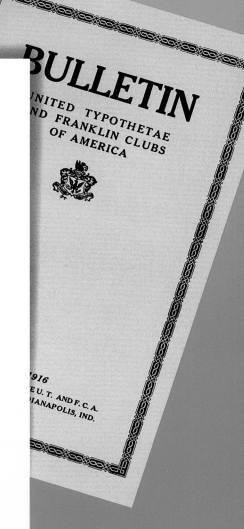

## EDUCATION FOR PRINTERS AT HARVARD UNIVERSITY

By Frederick W. Hamilton, National Apprentice Director

In the moving of Harvard University Press to its own building a great step forward has been taken in the development of the printing course in the School of Business Administration. Not only does this incident mark a new and larger era of fine printing at Harvard University as well as an increased opportunity for the production of scholarly work, but it also offers, through the close cooperation of the Press with the highly specialized courses in Printing and Publishing offered by the Graduate School of Business Administration, greater facilities for the training of men to fill executive positions in the printing industry. Mr. C. Chester Lane, the Director of the Press, is also a member of the Faculty of the School and in charge of the two courses. A laboratory and class room for the students has been established in the new quarters of the Press where many of the theories and problems discussed in lectures may be worked out practically not only under laboratory but also under shop conditions. The students in the courses in Printing and Publishing at Harvard University are thus offered a unique combination of study in a highly perfected university and also an opportunity for research in a practical printing and publishing plant.

The college year 1916–17 opens Oct. 1. Following is a sketch of the courses offered.

### FIRST YEAR COURSE

The first year course provides an introduction to the technique of printing. As a full course it is intended to give the student a fairly comprehensive knowledge of the various operations and processes involved in the manufacture of a book, to show him the reason for each step that is taken, and to give him an opportunity to apply in practice what he learns in the class room.

As a half-course, the first half-year is intended to acquaint the student with the various fundamental processes involved

**AT ATLANTIC CITY, NEW JERSEY, SEPTEMBER 12-13-14**

would require a printing plant; and a printing plant, in turn, could provide a laboratory for Business School students interested in printing and publishing.

Donald Scott—the treasurer of a New York publishing house, a member of the Advisory Committee, and later an influential member of the Business School's Visiting Committee—agreed, and further consented to head the fundraising drive for the press. Depressed business conditions prevented the raising of the endowment, but Robert Bacon, a Harvard benefactor and member of the Corporation, offered to subsidize any losses the press incurred. Late in 1912, Lowell and the Corporation agreed to establish the Harvard University Press.

"I must congratulate you and Lane on the Corporation's vote on Wednesday," Scott wrote to Gay on December 20. "All the credit for this belongs with you and Lane, who have worked for it so steadily and unselfishly."

Gay demurred, arguing that the credit belonged to Lane. (He was, however, soon named a charter member of the Press's Board of Syndics, at that time its only governing board. Scott, too, became active in the governance of the Press.) "I am delighted over the Corporation vote on Wednesday," Gay admitted, "since it enables us to make a definite start with the Harvard University press as an institution and indirectly to get funds necessary for a printing plant."

The Press and the Business School's printing courses moved together into Randall Hall, on the University's Cambridge campus, in 1916. Scott was still trying to secure an endowment for the Press. ("All such gifts are made necessarily from an individual's surplus funds," Scott pointed out in a letter to Gay, "and with the present low prices of all kinds of property, 'there ain't no surplus.'") Gay, meanwhile, was struggling to keep the printing courses going. Enrollments in the courses were flat, even as overall enrollment in the School increased. The printing courses, furthermore, were disproportionately expensive to the School, and the Society of Printers' financial support had terminated. In

April, Gay informed his printing Advisory Committee that the School could not support the course indefinitely: "We shall continue one more year, and during this time hope to interest a larger circle of those engaged in printing and publishing in our work in this field."

Support was indeed secured from a new source—the United Typothetae and Franklin Clubs of America, a printing-trades organization—but the School's declining enrollments as America entered World War I helped dispatch the printing courses.

The Harvard University Press, of course, met a happier fate, distinguishing itself in ensuing decades as a leading scholarly press.

**A 1916 article from the *Bulletin* of the United Typothetae and Franklin Clubs, praising the School's experiment in printing education.**

**Beginning in 1916, the United Typothetae partially underwrote the School's printing courses, and also assumed some responsibility for publicizing them.**

## THE INNER LIFE OF THIS STORE

ONE of the ideals of the Wanamaker business has always been the training of its employes to greater usefulness and self-development, and the organizations through which this is being accomplished daily have considerable interest for those concerned with modern educational, social or industrial conditions. Two schools, lower and higher—

The John Wanamaker Commercial Institute, and The American University of Trade and Applied Commerce— give the employe an admirable education in common branches, business courses, and a few college subjects, with strong additional features of physical training, military drill, and instrumental and vocal music. The younger boys and the girls attend school for several hours each day, and there are also evening classes for those older. Occupational training includes practical, technical courses in specific lines such as fi employe for his or her particular function in the business.

ALL this training is practically free, the occasional expense books and items for personal use being small, and no pay being lost for the time spent in school. Many boys and girls grow up in the business, getting their whole higher education while they are earning. Social clubs and entertainments add a healthy note of recreation, and matters of health and hygiene are carefully watched by a competent medical staff, whose services are free.

Interest in music is fostered by singing classes, an orchestra and a junior orchestra, the Wanamaker Chorus, and boys' and girls' drum and bugle corps. The latter are connected with the military organization of the boys in the Store—the six companies forming the "First Regiment, J. W. C. I.," drilled according to United States Army regulations. Athletic activity among the girls consists chiefly of basket ball and tennis matches. The athletic association of the boys and men, called the Meadowbrook Club, has grounds not far from the Store, on the east bank of the Schuylkill, at Twenty-third and Market Streets.

Such interests as these unite the employes of the Store in a movement whose results cannot help benefiting themselves and the business they serve. The unique and interesting nature of this "Store family," as it is often called, and the educational and social activities which grow under its endeavors, are foremost among the notable things that characterize the Wanamaker Store.

Philadelphia retailer John Wanamaker was an early advocate of human relations in business, offering educational and social activities to his "store family." Edwin Gay reviewed such programs in his short-lived Social Factors in Business Enterprise course.

John D. Rockefeller's *The Personal Relation in Industry*.

## Difficult subjects

When paper manufacturer F. W. Bird contributed $500 to the original subscription for the Business School, he took the opportunity to lobby for instruction in a "higher code of business morals." Professor A. Lawrence Lowell agreed— but suggested that such training should appear "an integral part of the principles that are explained or demonstrated."

Thus began a debate that continues to this day. What is the appropriate place in a business school curriculum for "business morals"—which in today's terminology might include both ethics and certain aspects of human resource management?

Dean Gay faced the question in the summer of 1908, as he drew up the School's initial curriculum. His decision to omit a course specifically devoted to ethical conduct caused some consternation among the School's supporters. Boston lawyer Frederick P. Fish, for one, argued strongly in favor of ethical instruction, and particularly in the field of corporate finance. But Gay held firm.

"I decided not to have any courses on Business Ethics in the Business School," he explained, "but I have tried to choose our lecturers with reference to their standards in conduct of business. I believe with you that we should give some occasional lectures which seek to give our students some light on what is at present a very perplexing and not wholly

solved problem. The difficulty is to find lecturers who can handle this theme in the proper spirit, at once practical and elevating, without being 'preachy.'"

Several months later, Seth T. Gano, personal secretary to financier Henry Lee Higginson, asked Gay for any available information on the history of business ethics. Gay responded ruefully that he had been intending to ask Gano the same question: "I am naturally interested in the topic, particularly as I am to give a talk on business ethics here [at Harvard] in March. I have been unable so far to obtain much information of value on the subject."

In their 1915 report, the School's Visiting Committee cited "the increasing attention being given to the vital human

relationships in business," and suggested that the faculty devote more attention to the topic. The following year, Gay did so: he and three other professors—and thirteen interested businessmen—offered Social Factors in Business Enterprise. Though 22 students signed up, Gay decided that the principles of Social Factors ought to be taught in the required Business Policy course; Social Factors was therefore not repeated.

Boston lawyer Galen L. Stone—who had helped organize the School's second subscription drive—entered the debate in March of 1917, when he sent Gay a pamphlet by John D. Rockefeller entitled *The Personal Relation in Industry*. This, said Stone, paraphrasing Rockefeller, would be an "important part of college

courses which aim to fit men for business life."

"Realizing its fundamental importance," Gay responded, "we have had this topic in mind in the Business School and last year I undertook to give a course which we first planned to name 'The Personal Factors in Business,' but then decided, since a number of other points had to be taken up, to change the title to 'Social Factors in Business Enterprise.'... This year, in order to reach a larger number of students, the main subject matter of the course has been included in the second-year course named Business Policy.

"I find it is an extremely difficult subject to teach. It is one thing to recognize its importance, and another thing to analyze it and to see its various applications."

ENDOWMENT AND SURVIVAL were themes very much on the minds of Edwin Gay and his counselors. Professor Taussig's subscription drive had provided adequate funds for a five-year trial period, after which—according to President Eliot—the School would be able to count on the business community for support.

Gay was not so confident. As early as 1909, in the first year of the School's operation, he contemplated a $100,000 drive for a Business School building. He also began accumulating a surplus account: between 1908 and 1913, he managed to save $19,500. But because tuition was fixed at $150—the same fee charged by both the College and the Graduate School of Arts and Sciences—additional income could be derived only from increases in enrollment and gifts to endowment.

A few early gifts were earmarked for specific purposes. A. W. Preston, president of United Fruit, established a five-year traveling research fellowship, which funded research in Central and South America. In 1910, four donors contributed $850 for a student loan fund. (Dean Gay had called this the "most immediate need" of the School at a 1910 Visiting Committee meeting; legend has it that this prompted J. P. Morgan, Jr., to establish the loan fund by passing Gay several $100 bills under the table.) And, in 1911, Arch Shaw contributed the money needed to establish the Bureau of Business Research.

Early in 1911, Gay approached A. Lawrence Lowell, Harvard's newly inaugurated president, with a plan for a $1 million endowment drive. Lowell was not enthusiastic: like his predecessor, he thought the School could be made financially secure without a University-sponsored appeal. He particularly disapproved of Gay's plan to ask Rockefeller's General Education Board—which was then providing half of the School's non-tuition income—for $300,000 in endowment funds. Lowell decided to consult his predecessor, Charles Eliot, on the matter. Eliot was at that point well placed to render an opinion: he was a member of both the General Education Board and of the Business School's Visiting Committee.

"Money does not come as easily as is often supposed," Lowell wrote to Eliot in March of 1911. He implied that Gay's projected expenses seemed excessive. "Of course," he continued, "Professor Gay is distressed at my doubting the wisdom of raising such an endowment, and I should like very much to have your views on the matter."

In this context, Eliot was equivocal. He was now more in touch with the School's needs than Lowell, in part because there was an additional administrative unit—the Graduate School of Arts and Sciences, where the Business School was then lodged—between Lowell and Gay. (It was not until 1913, when the Business School gained administrative autonomy, that Lowell began to attend the School's faculty meetings.) Eliot suggested that Gay's expense projections might well be correct. The School, Eliot pointed out, would have to have a "disproportionate number of professors ... since to hold them in the service of the University it will be necessary to make them professors earlier than in other departments, just as we have had to do with the Law School."

Eliot also implied that the General Education Board might well prove helpful. "The officers of that Board are perfectly aware that they have done a great deal more for several American colleges and universities than they have done for Harvard. They have given, for

Harvard President A. Lawrence Lowell leads a commencement procession. As president, Lowell had little contact with the Business School until it gained administrative independence in 1913. He confessed, at that point, that he was pleasantly surprised at the quality of work being done at the School, and was particularly impressed by the Bureau of Business Research.

instance, a million dollars to Yale, and two hundred fifty thousand dollars to Johns Hopkins."

Eliot's opinion also reached Lowell by a more circuitous route. The Business School's Visiting Committee had appointed Eliot chairman of a subcommittee on the School's condition and needs. The subcommittee reported in April that "measures should be taken to raise an adequate endowment for the School"—a recommendation that the larger committee passed along to the Board of Overseers. Lowell, in his 1911 President's Report, concluded that the School had "proved its value, and deserves to be put on a permanent foundation."

"It looks to me as though we should be able to raise the money," Gay wrote to his wife in June. (He had previously confessed to her that it aroused his "'sporting' blood" to tackle the job.) "People seem interested. But all I am doing now is to scatter seed and prepare the way."

The relationship between Gay and Lowell, already somewhat distant, soured early in 1912, the casualty of a dispute over fundraising. Gay had been assured by a member of the General Education Board that the Board would respond favorably to a request for endowment from the Business School. Lowell, however, planned to approach the Board for other University needs, including buildings for freshmen dormitories, the new library, and the chemistry department. The dispute grew more heated, and Lowell apparently asked for Gay's resignation—which Gay declined to submit.

"I find I was premature in thinking that Dean Gay intended to resign at the end of next year," Lowell informed the Corporation on March 25, 1912. "He intends to resign when he has got the program of his school carried out, and that is likely to be two years."

The General Education Board, in any case, did not prove sympathetic to the School a second time. (A request in 1914 for funds to support the Bureau of Business Research was also turned down.) "The money," wrote Board member Jerome Greene to Gay in March, 1912, "has got to be raised and will be raised in other quarters."

The first good endowment-related news came in April, 1912, when Edmund Cogswell Converse, president of Bankers Trust, gave $125,000 establishing a pro-

fessorship to "give instruction and conduct or promote investigations in the subject of banking and finance." Thomas Lamont, then a member of J.P. Morgan & Co., had persuaded Converse to make the gift. "It is the first endowment that we have had for the Business School," wrote Lowell to Converse, acknowledging the gift, "and we have been, as you know, somewhat worried as to whether we should be able to get an endowment for that School which would be worthy of its object and its success."

The School's Visiting Committee met early the following month, and, after praising Lamont's achievement, established three fundraising committees—in Boston, New York, and "the West." Each group was charged with raising $125,000 for an endowed professorship. It was informally agreed that the "western committee," based in Chicago, would seek support for a chair in railroading.

A second gift arrived unexpectedly in April, 1912. Jesse Isidor Straus, a member of the Harvard College Class of 1893, informed Lowell that he and his brothers Percy and Herbert were interested in establishing a Business School fellowship in their father's name. (Isidor Straus had built Macy's into the world's largest department store.) Lowell asked the Strauses to meet with Lamont in New York; at that meeting, Lamont persuaded Jesse Straus that the School's most pressing need was endowment funds. The Straus brothers agreed to redirect their gift to that purpose.

While a single lunch in April at Boston's Exchange Club netted pledges of $25,000 as "a nest egg toward the Boston fund," progress soon came to a halt. The New York and Western committees could report little success. ("At present," Gay wrote to Arch Shaw in June, "I am not likely to be invited to visit any western centers of affluence within the near future.") After its encouraging start, the Boston drive also stalled: in January, 1913, a Boston businessman and Harvard graduate informed Gay that Harvard's local supporters were more inclined to contribute to the freshmen dormitories and the Harvard Club. It was soon clear that for the near future the School would incur an operating deficit, and its Dean would be responsible for making up the shortfall.

After serving as secretary of the Harvard Corporation, Jerome D. Greene—an organizer of the Tuesday Evening Club—became general manager of the Rockefeller Institute for Medical Research. "The situation is far from pleasing to me," Greene wrote to Dean Gay in January of 1912, concerning the General Education Board's decision not to endow the Harvard Business School, "and in my opinion shows a very imperfect understanding of the epoch-making character of what you have accomplished during the last five years."

Thomas W. Lamont played a key role in establishing links between HBS and the New York financial community; he also secured the School's first two endowed professorships.

**The Business School's endowment-seekers— Edwin Gay, Howard Elliott, and Thomas Lamont—posing for news photographers at Harvard in 1915.**

**One 1912 lunch in Boston generated some $25,000 in endowment pledges. But by 1913, funds had dried up: "Boston has been rather severely hit by 'hard times' in business," as Dean Gay wrote to a young protégé.**

**James J. Hill, chairman of the board of the Great Northern Railway, declined Edwin Gay's 1909 invitation to speak at the Business School. Six years later, Hill doubled the endowment of an HBS professorship in his name.**

Gay did so until the spring of 1915, when a group of Business School supporters, mostly Bostonians, subscribed to a fund to underwrite the School's deficits. A number of these donors—including Arthur T. Lyman and Walter C. Baylies—had also contributed to the School's original subscription drive.

But the most significant news that year again came from New York. In June, a group of New York businessmen established a chair honoring railroad magnate James J. Hill. (The two largest gifts to the fund came from George F. Baker, president of New York's First National Bank, and financier Arthur C. James. Baker's son, George Jr., also contributed.) This development was itself welcome news, but equally momentous was Hill's own decision, in October, to double the chair's endowment. According to the terms of the gift, funds not spent on transportation-related studies could be applied to the School's general needs.

In both cases, as in the securing of the Converse chair, Thomas Lamont played a key role. "Your tele-

phone call this morning brought a great flash of joy into this office," Lowell wrote Lamont on October 13, "and I wish you could have seen Gay's delight when I ran downstairs and told him. Both the gift and the liberality of its terms are just what we need. I have no doubt that in a few years Transportation will absorb all the income from the two hundred and fifty thousand, but at the moment it is a great advantage to be able to use a part of it for the general needs of the School."

After the second Boston subscription drive, and with the creation of the Hill chair, Gay was able to concentrate his fundraising activities less on immediate needs and more on long-term endowment. The need remained critical. Although the endowment principal had grown from nothing to over $450,000, the endowment in 1917 still produced an income of only $20,492— significantly less than the tuition income of $34,705. With relatively fixed expenses, the School remained vulnerable to declines in enrollment.

As a part of the fund to be raised in Boston as a gift for capital for the general purposes of the Graduate School of Business Administration, I promise to pay to the President and Fellows of Harvard College

## A *social pioneer and promoter*

"Dark of hair and eyes, compact of frame, brisk but never brusque," a newspaperman described Edwin Gay in October of 1918, "he would harmonize with and function perfectly, atmospherically and otherwise, in a factory or a bank. Lecturing to classes has given him style, vigor, and readiness as a conversationalist."

The Harvard Business School represented, in Gay's phrase, a "simple scientific endeavor." Gay's war service in Washington was, by contrast, an increasingly complex scientific endeavor: after serving on Arch Shaw's Commercial Economy Board, he became director of the Division of Planning and Statistics of the U. S. Shipping Board. (There, according to a newspaper caption-writer, he was "fighting the Hun with high velocities composed of facts.") By the end of the war he had served— "brilliantly," according to one observer—in a number of positions, culminating in the directorship of the Central Bureau of Planning and Statistics.

Throughout this period, and also during his years at the Business School, Gay cultivated a group of highly loyal advisors and aides. Several of his wartime associates followed him to his next position: the editorship of the New York *Evening Post*, offered to him by banker and diplomat Thomas W. Lamont. While in New York, Gay also served as the first secretary-treasurer of the Council on Foreign Relations, and helped launch the quarterly *Foreign Affairs*. But the

*Post* collapsed after five years, and in the fall of 1924 Gay returned to the Harvard faculty —this time in the Department of Economics, where he remained until his retirement in 1936.

Gay's career is most often described in terms of dualities. He was, in Melvin Copeland's analysis, a "social pioneer and promoter" who could not resolve the conflicts between those roles. Gay's biographer, Herbert Heaton, called Gay a "scholar in action."

Business historian N. S. B. Gras agreed, but also pointed out a streak of simple bad luck. "His decision to resign from the School, however," wrote Gras, "really came at a time when students were ready to pour into the School after the War and when the prosperity of the country would have made the raising of money easier than in the past; and his entry into the high-class newspaper

business came at a time when America was turning away from literary newspapers to tabloids."

Toward the end of his life, Gay concluded that his decision to accept the deanship of Harvard's business school had been a serious mistake—the first in a series of distractions that had limited his career as a scholar, and kept him from completing even a single book. But he remained proud of his work on behalf of the School.

"Whatever may be said about the inadequacies of the early years of the School," he wrote to his friend Arch Shaw in 1944, "I don't think it can be ... said that [we] failed in laying the foundations well and truly.... The School made a new departure in business education by emphasizing the two fundamental functions of industrial management and commercial organization, or marketing, with chief emphasis upon the latter."

**The Sunday Star Magazine.**

*Features* · *Fiction*

SUNDAY, OCTOBER 6, 1918.

## An Important War Work of Forty Scientists

Power of One Man in Washington, Though Nowhere to Be Found in an Act of Congress, Is Prodigious—He May Alter the Trade Currents of Europe and South America.

The Matter of Transportation When America Entered the War. How the Shipping Board Is Fighting the Hun, and Even More Is Required Than a Big Building Program.

BY JAMES B. MORROW.

THE FEARLESS CREW OF AN AMERICAN MERCHANT SHIP. MUCH HAS BEEN DONE BY THESE MEN TO-WARD DRIVING BUS PIRATES FROM THE SEAS.

DR. EDWIN F. GAY.

**Gay (above, second from right) in Pasadena in the late 1930s. He resigned from the Harvard faculty in 1936 to study at the Huntington Library, San Marino, California.**

The Harvard Regiment on the steps of Widener Library. The regiment — which included Business School students — was trained, in part, by six French officers brought to America for that purpose.

As a result of the war, enrollments declined in every department of the University except the Medical School. Total University registration fell from 4,708 in 1916 to 2,840 in 1917; Business School enrollment dropped from 205 to 75.

A certificate from the School's World War I quartermaster program.

THIS VULNERABILITY was starkly demonstrated in the academic year 1917–1918, when total enrollment dropped precipitously — from 232, in the preceding year, to 97. By the fall of 1918, the School's tuition-paying population had plunged to 32 students: 18 first-years, six second-years, one "unclassified," and seven "specials."

The reason, of course, was the Great War, which America entered in April of 1917. Most of Harvard's normal activities were soon suspended; war duty called away not only the majority of Harvard's students, but many of its administrators and faculty members as well.

War was declared on April 6; on the preceding day, Melvin Copeland — then the director of the Bureau of Business Research — had been called to Washington to serve as secretary of the Commercial Economy Board of the National Council of Defense. The Board (which later evolved into the Conservation Division of the War Industries Board) was chaired by Arch Shaw, and was responsible for establishing standardization to reduce waste in war-related industries. One Division directive, for example, ordered a reduction in the number of front and rear gears for farm wagons from 1,764 to 16.

Copeland proved to be only a vanguard: eventually, all but three members of the Business School faculty left Cambridge to join the war effort. Edwin Gay also served on Shaw's Commercial Economy Board, and soon began an extended leave of absence from Harvard. His direct involvement in the Business School's activities ceased, for the most part, late in 1917. Lincoln Schaub, professor and former Secretary of the School, was then appointed acting dean.

Those who stayed behind worked overtime, even given the much-diminished student population. The School had established a "Committee on Military Preparation" early in 1916, which had recommended the inauguration of a "commissary course." Four days after war was declared, the School inaugurated a tuition-free course for military supply officers, in addition to the MBA curriculum. The course was taught in June, and again in early 1918.

The School's war-related efforts were, on balance, unsuccessful. The military supply courses were hastily conceived and underattended, and the war ended before they could be much improved. The most important benefits of the School's World War I experience, in fact, may well have been internal. For one thing, it was clearly demonstrated that a school without buildings and with only a minimal endowment was in the best of times vulnerable. Furthermore, the School was forced once again to define what it intended to achieve, and also to show how that intention related to an urgent national need.

In April, 1918, a survey of first-year students revealed that ten, at most, planned to return. A faculty committee — comprising Professors Sprague, Schaub, and Cole — was asked to review the School's activities in the face of this emergency. In their report, presented at the next faculty meeting, the three professors recommended that most of the existing curriculum be dropped, and that new courses be devised to attract "men of maturity and business experience to a one-year course of intensive training whereby they may be fitted for direct and immediate war service." The point would be, in other words, to fit men for a specialized function.

The faculty agreed, in ensuing meetings, that it should concentrate its resources on a one-year curriculum designed to graduate such "trained specialists." But it also reaffirmed that, in ordinary circumstances, the Harvard Business School sought to train *generalists* — and although a student might desire training in a specialized field, he would nevertheless be required to become familiar with "the general aspects of business."

"The purpose of the School is not to teach rules and methods and specific facts about business," the faculty declared — summarizing the lessons of a decade — "but to train men who have initiative and intellectual capacity in such fashion that they can analyze business problems and make decisions on the strength of knowledge and experience."

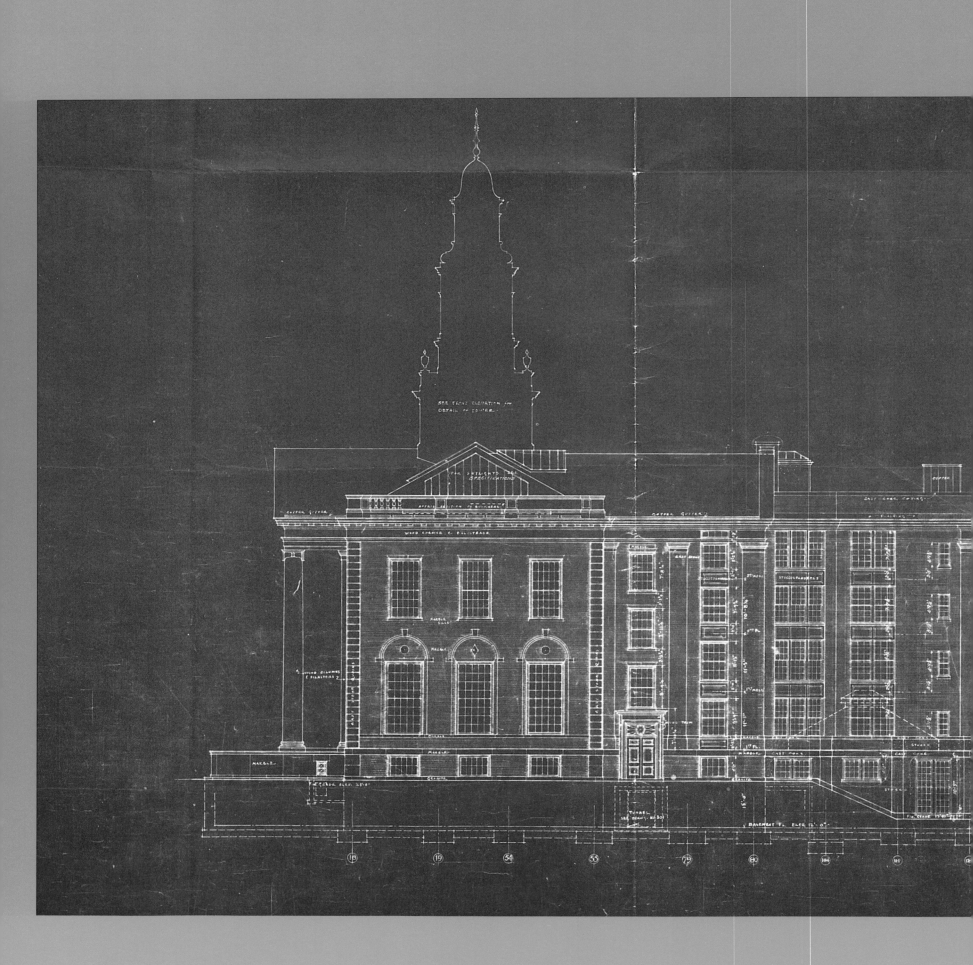

"LIKE OTHER DEPARTMENTS of the University," wrote New York dry goods manufacturer Thomas Slocum in August of 1919, "the Business School was shot to pieces by the war. When the smoke cleared away, they found a loss [for the previous academic year] of $4,000, which was much better than had been anticipated in view of the conditions."

Slocum, an influential member of the School's Visiting Committee, had agreed to raise $2,000 among the School's supporters in New York. He was sympathetic toward Acting Dean Lincoln Schaub: the School's deficit had been incurred even though Schaub, in Dean Edwin Gay's absence, had reduced the School's annual expenditures by more than 20 percent—from $76,000 to $60,000. To help close the remaining gap, Slocum was seeking $100 contributions from nineteen fellow New Yorkers—including, in the case of this letter, Thomas W. Lamont.

But Slocum had to work carefully, as he confessed to Lamont. Harvard University was then in the midst of a $15-million endowment campaign, and the University's various schools and departments were under orders not to compete

**Thomas W. Lamont began his second decade of service to HBS with a contribution to a fund to retire the School's First World War–era debts. He later helped secure George Baker's gift of the campus, and subsequently contributed to the fund to landscape that campus.**

with this campaign. "At the same time," Slocum argued, "those who believe in the Business School, and who have been pleased by the success resulting from its eleven years of existence, wish to see it start in fresh again without handicap." And, he might have added, the School was obligated to make up its $4,000 debt to the University.

Lamont, then a partner at J. P. Morgan & Company, knew the circumstances of both the School and the University only too well. He had responded to similar calls from the Business School in 1912 and 1915, and had been instrumental in establishing the School's Converse and Hill professorships at those critical junctures. He had recently made a substantial personal commitment, to be paid over three years, to the University's endowment drive. And while he readily subscribed to Slocum's quiet campaign, he sent along with his check an expression of impatience regarding the School's chronic financial difficulties:

"I do hope," he wrote to Slocum on August 10, "that we can get the [Business School's] endowment fund under way in the near future, so as to avoid these individual calls."

Meanwhile, in Cambridge, Harvard's President Lowell was experiencing impatience of a different sort. Unlike Lamont, he was not particularly concerned about the School's annual deficits. "The fact is," he wrote to a friend and advisor, "that the other departments of the University have to run on their income. This School has been started on an entirely different basis, that of spending more than it has with an obligation on the Dean to raise the balance. It has worked well." Nevertheless, there were recurrent difficulties between Lowell and Gay, in part arising from their very different administrative styles. In the previous year, for example, Gay had ignored Lowell's informal recommendation to suspend the School's operations; a month into the 1918-1919 school year, however—facing the substantial deficits that would soon result from the inadequate enrollment—Gay attempted to reverse his position. At that point, Lowell said in no uncertain terms that the University had committed itself to keeping the School open.

When Gay announced his intention to leave the deanship in August, 1919, therefore, Harvard's president carefully considered his alternatives. He saw no compelling successor to Gay among the remaining Business School faculty members. Preliminary indications were that the returning veterans would fully restore university enrollments—although the Business School's entrance requirement of a bachelor's degree might delay its own recovery by several years. Lowell sensed that it was an opportune moment to push the School in a new direction, and he already had in mind a candidate for the task. At the October 7, 1919, Business School faculty meeting, he introduced the School to its new dean: Wallace Brett Donham.

Donham may well have struck the faculty as an unlikely choice. Cherubic in appearance, and, except for his abundant energy, unprepossessing in manner, Donham was a Boston banker trained at the Harvard Law School. He had achieved some minor public repute as the court-appointed receiver for the troubled Bay State Elevated Railway Company between 1917 and 1919; in that capacity, he had kept several thousand disgruntled streetcar workers on the job throughout the war period. In April of 1919, public trustees took over the operation of the Bay State, and Donham was preparing to return to his positions as vice president and chief legal officer of the Old Colony Trust Company.

It was then that Donham received an unexpected call from his former patron and teacher, A. Lawrence Lowell. "A more complete shake-up of one's life would be hard to conceive," Donham later wrote of his transformation from banker to dean.

From Lowell's viewpoint, this was entirely appropriate: in appointing Donham, the president hoped for a comparable "shake-up" in the life of the School. He further expected from Donham a marked improvement in the quality of the School's management. Lowell knew Donham to be a formidable fundraiser, as demonstrated by his efforts on behalf of Harvard College. If anyone could solve the School's chronic financial woes —without working at cross-purposes with the University, of course—it was Wallace Donham.

**A. Lawrence Lowell,** **as "alert, conversational,**
**described by his cousin,** **sympathetic, [and] demo-**
**Bishop William Lawrence,** **cratic in conviction, though**
**not always in manner."**

AT THE SAME TIME, however, there was another shake-up in the making. Unexpectedly, it was not Harvard College, but Harvard's professional schools that were swamped with students in the postwar summer and fall of 1919. The Medical School, lacking sufficient teachers and laboratory equipment, broke tradition by turning down scores of qualified applicants. The Law and Business schools — considered by University authorities to be expandable according to demand — now had to accommodate their largest first-year classes ever. Both schools were forced for the first time to consider dividing their entering classes into sections, a step which would necessitate a dramatic increase in their permanent teaching staffs.

For the Business School, the reversal of fortunes was particularly abrupt. On June 11, 1919, Lowell, Acting Dean Lincoln Schaub, and five other faculty members voted to award MBAs to that year's graduating class — four students. Four months later, the School's enrollment was 412, almost double the previous high, which had been attained in the fall of 1916. The largest first-year class before the war numbered 142; the class entering in the fall of 1919 exceeded 300. Similarly huge increases were reported from undergraduate schools of business across the country, which suggested to Harvard's administration that a structural change was occurring in higher education. Business, it seemed, was

gaining students at the expense of the older professions, with the apparent exception of law.

Harvard faced an immediate problem: where to educate this new population of students? "For the Law School," wrote President Lowell in his 1919 report to the Board of Overseers, "the question of more room could be solved by adding to Langdell Hall, as soon as possible, the second wing contemplated in the original design. For the Business School the problem is more difficult. During the experimental years, which certainly ought now to be regarded as at an end, the School has occupied such quarters as could be spared in Lawrence Hall, and a couple of rooms, with a space in the stack, at the Widener Library. The time has now come when, if its work is to be properly done, it must have a building of its own."

Dean Donham agreed. A month into his tenure, he inaugurated a drive to solve the problem. He began by soliciting comments from the faculty, and soon established a "Building Committee of the Faculty." He submitted his own recommendations to the Building Committee on January 13, 1920 — three months after assuming the deanship — and outlined an "architectural problem" to Charles W. Killam, a friend on the faculty of Harvard's Graduate School of Design.

The proposed "Business School Building," he told Killam, should have a good location with room to expand. It should somehow convey a "colonial atmosphere in a brick building, but with architectural effect subordinated, if and where necessary, to a utilitarian point of view." Its exterior walls should be "independent of interior partitions," to ensure future flexibility, and there should be a "business-like character and aspect to the interior arrangements of the building."

Meanwhile, the Dean was cautiously investigating ways to finance his evolving construction plans. Early in 1920, he asked Joseph Warren, an acquaintance on the Law School faculty, for advice about raising money for a building. Warren recommended drawing up some architectural plans — a task which Killam's architecture students undertook in February — and developing a large mailing list. "It seems to me," commented Warren, "that you have a good cause, and one that ought to appeal to a class of individuals who have the money to help."

## Hazards to academic precedent

George Edwin Donham, country dentist, served the three southeastern Massachusetts towns of Abington, Whitman, and Rockland in the later decades of the 1800s. Every third Sunday night, he hitched up his horse and buggy and left his hometown of Rockland for a week of dentistry in Abington. This was followed by a week in Whitman, at the end of which Donham made the long drive home to see his family and attend to his Rockland practice.

Donham was determined to provide his three children with a college education—a difficult task, even for the most hard-working of country dentists—and he invested most of his limited resources in the stock market to generate more income. In 1893, disaster struck: a financial panic wiped out his holdings.

For Wallace Brett Donham, then a student at the Rockland public high school, the family's financial reversal had serious consequences. When he

enrolled in Harvard College in the fall of 1895, Donham was compelled to live at home and travel to and from Cambridge daily—some fifty miles—rather than rent a dormitory room. His older brother and sister, who had by then completed their educations, paid his tuition and travel expenses. Given the family's difficult circumstances, Donham completed his undergraduate education in three years. Although he graduated with the Harvard Class of 1898, he nevertheless considered himself a member of the Class of 1899, with whom he had entered the College.

A. Lawrence Lowell, then a professor in the Department of Government, had been impressed with Donham's energy and sense of purpose. He served on Donham's oral exams committee, when Donham presented himself for a degree with honors in government. In the spring of 1898, according to Donham family lore, Lowell asked his young protégé—who was soon to graduate *summa cum laude*—what he planned to do next.

"I'd like to go to law school," Donham replied, "but I can't afford it, so I suppose I'll have to teach."

"Nonsense," Lowell said, in his accustomed imperious manner. "I will lend you $2,000 without interest if you will attend the Law School. Interest will begin after you get out of school." Donham accepted the offer, and during his first two years at the Law School he served as Lowell's teaching assistant in Government 1. Upon receiving his law degree, Donham was again approached by Lowell, who wanted to learn his plans.

"Well," said Donham, "I want you to be the first to know that I'm engaged to be married. But we'll wait until after I've paid off my debt to you, and I have my feet under me."

"Nonsense," Lowell replied. "I don't believe in long engagements. If you'll get married forthwith, I will forget the debt."

Admitted to the Massachusetts bar in 1901, the newly married Donham began his legal career in Boston's Old Colony Trust Company. "Starting in the Legal Department," he later recalled, "with the great asset of having no authority and therefore being readily accepted by my new associates at all levels, I gradually drifted into administrative work." When one of his superiors

became physically incapacitated, Donham gradually took over that man's workload of various corporate reorganizations. In 1906, he was elected a vice president of the Old Colony.

Donham's first decade in banking—during which he increasingly immersed himself in corporate restructuring, and practiced little law—coincided with a period of consolidation in the Massachusetts street railway industry. Electric street railways, both interurban and intraurban, had gone through a period of explosive growth and overbuilding in the 1890s; consolidations followed inevitably in the early years of the twentieth century. Between 1910 and 1920, new factors combined to promote a wave of bankruptcies in the industry: soaring wages and materials costs, obsolete rolling stock, competition from "jitneys" (gypsy cabs) and private automobiles, and erratic state regulation.

In December of 1917, the Bay State Street Railway Company, comprising over 1,000 miles of track and serving most of the major industries in eastern Massachusetts, went into receivership. Wallace Donham, the court-appointed receiver, was entrusted with significant responsibilities: to rationalize the company's operations, and to ensure that strikes by the company's well-organized work force did not disrupt war-related industries. He succeeded on both fronts. Between late 1917 and the spring of 1919, he abandoned 270 miles of underutilized and poorly maintained track. Nevertheless, upon his resignation from the receiver's post in May, 1919, the railway workers' union awarded him a sterling silver table clock, in recognition of his efforts on behalf of the Bay State's work force.

Harvard's President Lowell, meanwhile, was faced with the prospect of replacing HBS Dean Edwin Gay. Naturally, he thought of Wallace Donham. In discussing the possibility with Donham, Lowell found that his former protégé had ideas remarkably similar to his own about what a professional school should be. "He felt that it should have its own atmosphere, its own temperament, its own standards, its own loyalties," Lowell commented at a dinner in Donham's honor in 1939. "I knew, of course, that it would make some people uncomfortable, but the business of education is making people uncomfortable. In any case, I have not heard anyone say that the project did not succeed."

Donham accepted President Lowell's offer of the Business School deanship, in the summer of 1919, for several reasons. One was certainly loyalty to his friend and benefactor of two decades earlier. Another was the apparent opportunity to become a "specialist," as Donham saw it: to conduct research and further qualify himself as an authority in the field of labor relations. And, finally, he was attracted to the challenge of recasting and firmly establishing an institution whose potential seemed limitless.

Except for the impossibility of developing a field of academic expertise—which was entirely precluded by administrative demands—Donham found no substantive disappointments in his new job. "The only complaint the most captious critic of the job could make," he wrote in 1924, "is that it offers more constructive opportunities for accomplishment than should be laid on any one man's doorstep."

Like the school he guided, Donham's disregard for orthodoxies —as well as his impetuous manner—did indeed make some of his contemporaries uncomfortable. But even in the most traditional of academic circles, there were observers who grasped the significance of Donham's appointment. In a 1924 letter to a Boston banker, Dartmouth's President Ernest Hopkins confessed that he was "intrigued by the fact that Harvard University should be willing to accept the hazards to academic precedent and scholastic conventions of introducing into one of their schools a man as direct in his thinking and as forceful in his personality as Donham is."

**S. Agnes Donham helped pay for her younger brother Wallace's college education.**

**A Bay State Street Railway trolley in Post Office Square, Boston, in August of 1914. This car made an experimental run to New York City, testing a proposed daily route which was never instituted.**

In fact, Donham had in mind a number of prospects who might well support his cause. A larger problem existed, however: the $15-million Harvard Endowment Fund drive, then only four-fifths completed. The Corporation, recognizing the financial difficulties of the University's junior faculty, had voted a 20 percent raise in all teaching salaries, effective January 1, 1920. It had done so even without the necessary endowment funds in hand, thereby ensuring that the previous year's record deficit of $161,000 would at least double. To the fiscal conservatives who ran Harvard, this was a necessary evil, to be tolerated only until the endowment campaign and receipts from increased tuition and enrollment could right the income statement. All in all, it was not a propitious moment for the Business School dean to propose—as he did in the spring of 1920—an independent fundraising drive.

"I find that [Harvard treasurer C. F.] Adams feels very strongly that we must not let Donham loose on a big campaign of his own this year," a member of the Corporation reported to Lowell in April, "because of its effect on the minds of the alumni and the Endowment

**A School portrait, 1920, on the steps of Widener. In the preceding spring, Harvard had conferred a total of four MBA degrees; in the following spring it would confer 122 MBAs.**

Fund workers, and also because if we let Donham loose we have got to let the other fellows [deans] loose, too, which will make more trouble still with the minds of the alumni."

By the end of the academic year, President Lowell's implicit prediction—that the quality of education offered by the Business School would suffer because of limited facilities—had proven true. It was, as Wallace Donham noted flatly in his first Dean's Report, a year of "social disintegration to a lamentable extent." Classes were too large; furthermore, the first-year class had outgrown its dorms and the informal social mechanisms available to Business School students. "The School," said Donham, reiterating Lowell's conclusion of the previous year, "must be equipped with an adequate building and an enlarged staff." For the first time, Donham articulated publicly his vision of an expanded Business School, with a total enrollment of a thousand students and an endowment sufficient to offset the School's annual deficit of approximately $50,000.

The entering class in the fall of 1920 was slightly smaller than that of the previous year, but because of a substantial increase in the size of the second-year

A map from the early 1920s, prepared by the HBS dean's office, emphasizing the School's widely scattered quarters.

Objects Doubly Advanced   97

population, conditions grew even more cramped. "Our physical equipment is hopelessly inadequate," wrote Donham the following spring. "The School is scattered all over the Cambridge buildings of the University without proper administrative quarters, professors' studies, classrooms, laboratory facilities, library and reading room quarters, or dormitories." Donham was increasingly preoccupied by the dormitory question: "The living problem is more difficult to solve for our men than for the students in most other departments because our men are here for two years only, and therefore, are not inclined to go to the expense of furnishing their own rooms. It is peculiarly difficult to knit the men into a coordinated social unit under present conditions."

It was a problem with some unexpected manifestations. During the preceding fall, for example, disaffected Business School students had established a tradition of cheering noisily for the visiting teams at Harvard's football games — a practice which President Lowell found irritating. When Harvard's comptroller offered in January of 1921 to set aside for Business School students two floors of the University's Perkins

Hall dormitory, Donham was quick to accept: "If, with a dormitory, we could organize club tables I think we should succeed in giving the men in the Business School a bit more Business School spirit and along with it we would be able to inculcate some Harvard spirit."

The School's problems in a related area were mounting. In the fall of 1920, tuition across the University had been increased from $200 to $250. In the spring of 1921, Donham calculated that at that rate, the Business School was losing $150 per student. An increase in enrollment was a physical impossibility. (In fact, the faculty voted in March to limit the fall, 1921, entering class to 300 students.) Donham therefore concluded that he needed either an additional $1 million in endowment, or another tuition increase, this time to $400. Given the larger University context, only the latter course was open to him, and he duly requested the increase.

For the first time, the Corporation allowed one of its graduate schools to raise its tuition above that of the College. (Lowell, among others, accepted Donham's argument that Business School students should not enjoy a subsidized education; furthermore, he was still reluctant to "let Donham loose" on an endowment campaign.) Even so, the School was forced to admit 35 students at mid-year, in an attempt to reduce its deficit. This compounded the other standing problem: no additional space was made available for this new group of students. Circumstances grew even more difficult in the fall of 1921, when an unexpectedly high percentage of returning second-year students forced the scheduling of classes as early as 8 a.m., and as late as 7 p.m. Almost every department of the University, furthermore, experienced record enrollments that fall — including the

The Staplers (at left, 1922) were a fraternal group of Business School students organized "for the purpose of promoting interest in and the interchange of ideas concerning modern business problems." It provided some cohesion to the scattered HBS community.

The completion in 1912 of
the subway to Harvard
Square (under construction,
facing page, in 1909)
reduced travel time
to Boston from 25 minutes
to 8 minutes.

departments from which the Business School was borrowing classroom and office space. Looking ahead to
the following fall, Donham realized that he would soon
be without any office space at all for four of his fifteen
professors, or for any of his thirteen instructors.

There were ways, of course, for the Business
School to carve out more office space for itself. Donham
described one of them to the dean of the School of
Education: "It occurs to me that you might get some
relief in the same way we have, — by moving our offices
into spaces that were formerly used for other purposes."
The conversion of classrooms to offices, for example,
had achieved this end — although classes had conse-
quently been dispersed even further afield. "I realize
the difficulty of having classes meet all over the University," Donham continued, "but it seems to be one of the
necessities so far as we are concerned."

Much more difficult was the problem of dormitory
accommodations. In the winter of 1922, Donham and
his assistants analyzed the Cambridge housing situation
and arrived at some sobering conclusions. Since 1913,
the four large Cambridge-based departments of the
University — the College, the Law and Business
schools, and the Graduate School of Arts and Sciences
— had grown by over 1,300 students. The professional
schools had grown from 1,271 students to 2,028 — yet
the University was providing no more housing than it
had in 1913. As a result, as Donham stated in his 1922
Dean's Report, only about two Business School
students in nine could be accommodated in the
University's dormitories.

It was evident to the Business School administration that the city of Cambridge had changed radically
in a decade. The arrival of the subway in 1912 had
hastened Cambridge's transition from suburb to city.
Cambridge was now as accessible as Boston, and — in
addition to the new ranks of Harvard students — many
students from other Boston-area schools were being
drawn to the residential sections of Cambridge.

Furthermore, the departure of much of the student
population during the First World War had driven many
of Cambridge's private dormitories out of business.
While Harvard had purchased a number of these to
serve as University dormitories, the majority had simply
been converted by their owners to apartments. Such
conversions had, in fact, entirely offset the rooms
gained from Harvard's new freshman dormitories. It
seemed clear, furthermore, that in the postwar economic climate, no new private dormitories would be
built.

The four large Cambridge-based departments of
the University, Donham concluded, needed 1,600 additional dormitory rooms. His institution alone needed

**Harvard's comptroller sug-
gested in January, 1921, that
the Business School might
reserve half of Perkins Hall.
Dean Donham readily
accepted. To the Dean's
chagrin, the comptroller
then qualified his offer:
"[We] do not want you to
count on more than the
equivalent of two floors,"
he wrote, "and I cannot
absolutely promise that."**

some 350: "The Business School, being the only foot-free department in Cambridge, should be lifted bodily out of its existing surroundings and developed as an entity. The development of Business School dormitories for at least 350 men should precede the construction of class-rooms and administrative buildings if both cannot be accomplished together. I am so convinced of the importance of this whole matter that if we were offered the choice between the two types of buildings I should personally not hesitate a moment to choose the dormitories."

President Emeritus Charles W. Eliot—then 88 years old, and more than a decade into his retirement—read Donham's report with interest. "I notice that you attach importance to getting a dormitory or several dormitories for the students of the School," he wrote to Donham in November of 1922. "Is not such a gift one that ought to come from a single individual, or from a family having monumental or memorial purposes in view? Have you any such person or family in sight? Possibly I could help toward getting such a gift or gifts."

"I attach much importance to a dormitory or dormitories for men in this School," Donham replied. "Without this, particularly with our lack of centralized administrative and teaching space, the faculty feel the great difficulty of developing the professional spirit without which we are hardly justified in having such a school. I am sure you recognize how much harder it is to build up a professional attitude toward business than it is to build up a knowledge of the ethics and practices of law or medicine. Dormitories would help us immensely in accomplishing this result."

Donham agreed that a gift of the dormitories ought to come from the sort of donor that Eliot described, but, "unfortunately I have no such person or family in sight. One attractive possibility," he wrote, "arises out of the fact that the net income from such a dormitory or dormitories could by the terms of the gift be used to develop business research of which there is the greatest need. I have made sufficient investigation to be confident that we can earn six per cent on the investment in dormitories. Such a gift, therefore, could be made to do most effective work in two directions. If you can help in any way toward this vital accomplishment, I should be deeply appreciative, as would all members of our faculty."

IN FACT, Donham did have such a person in mind, if not in sight. That person was George F. Baker, the 81-year-old chairman of the First National Bank of New York. Reputed to be one of the richest men in America, Baker had achieved a near legendary stature in his own lifetime. With J. Pierpont Morgan and James Stillman, he had marshaled the resources in New York's financial community to overcome the severe Panic of 1907. In addition to directing the activities of the First National Bank, Baker had held directorships in more than forty banks and corporations, and had been influential in the organization or operation of nearly thirty railroads.

An intensely private man, Baker had first come to the attention of the public in the congressional hearings of 1912, which attempted to determine whether a "Money Trust"—allegedly headed by Morgan, Stillman, and Baker—was responsible for the cyclical panics and other fluctuations of the American economy. Over the following decade, he made a series of charitable gifts which kept him in the public eye: to the 1917 Red Cross War Fund campaign, for example, Baker contributed $1 million; he repeated that gift the following year.

**George Baker, the "Sphinx of Wall Street," and pet Peggy.**

## "*Everyone should reduce his talk*"

In the early 1920s, George F. Baker's fortune was variously estimated to be between $100 million and $300 million. These were figures he dismissed among friends as wildly exaggerated: "I'm not a twentieth as rich as people think!"

Born in Troy, New York, he worked after graduation from high school as a clerk in the New York State Banking Department in Albany from 1856 to 1863, at which time he moved to New York and became an original shareholder in the newly organized First National Bank of New York. He began his career with the bank as a paying teller, then became Cashier, and finally — as of September, 1877 — President. Under his leadership, the First National Bank acted as a conservative and steadying influence on the volatile American economy of the late nineteenth and early twentieth centuries. Through the Panics of '73, '93, '01, and '07, the First National Bank consistently met its obligations to its customers. As a result of this reliability, Baker was fond of saying, his bank's money was worth one percent more than any other bank's money.

Throughout his life, Baker maintained an extremely low public profile, in part due to shyness, but also because he felt that business people should be seen, if necessary, but not heard. Like his friend J. P. Morgan, however, Baker was called to testify publicly before the 1912 congressional hearings investigating the fabled "Money Trust." Baker's testimony at the hearings (proceedings which took a generally hostile stance toward both Baker and Morgan) suggested that there was, indeed, an inordinate concentration of power in the hands of New York's bankers — but that in his own case, that power was in capable hands.

His testimony was apparently quite persuasive. An editorial in the *New York Sun* commented: "The Pujo subcommittee is indebted to [subcommittee counsel] Mr. Samuel Untermeyer for exhibiting to it, in the person of Mr. George Fisher Baker, that type of financial ability and integrity which it is highly desirable that the legislative mind should study and comprehend.

"There have been several generations of such bankers in this town. They have done perhaps more than any other factor to make the metropolis what it is to-day. The honorable traditions of the past have been kept alive by a succession of New York bankers up to the present time, firmly establishing American credit in the eyes of the world, and immeasurably promoting the national prosperity, which depends on credit, as credit in turn rests upon individual character."

The second act, or series of incidents, that established Baker in the national consciousness was a number of gifts to charitable, educational, and medical institutions. Most of his numerous earlier gifts had been made anonymously, but as they increased in size and visibility, anonymity became impossible to maintain. In 1912, he contributed a large sum to effect closer ties between New York Hospital and Cornell Medical College; in 1916, he gave a group of residence halls to Cornell, and gave Regnault's *Salome* to the Metropolitan Museum. In 1919, he gave Cornell a new chemistry laboratory, and in the following year purchased the land for Columbia's new football stadium. Several months later, he had the unique experience, while attending the Cornell-Columbia football game at the new site, of having both sides of the stadium stand and cheer him.

In 1923, in response to a plea from a young reporter — who had been promised a job if she could obtain an interview with the reclusive Baker — he granted the second interview of his life. "Business men of America should reduce their talk two-thirds," he said in response to an early question. "Everyone should reduce his talk. There is rarely ever a reason good enough for anybody to talk." He paused, and then added, "Those are the first words I have spoken to a newspaper reporter since 1863."

The Morgans, senior and junior, arriving to testify at the Pujo hearings in December, 1912. The investigating committee's counsel asked Morgan to confirm that commercial credit was based on money or property.

"No, sir," replied Morgan, "the first thing is character."

Testifying later, George Baker made the same point: "There would not be much business done if it was not done on confidence."

George F. Baker (right) with fellow Great Northern Railroad directors James J. Hill (center) and Charles Steele.

While Baker himself had no direct ties to Harvard, his son, George Jr., did. The younger Baker was a member of the Harvard College Class of 1899, and a classmate of Wallace Donham. As a result of Thomas Lamont's relationship with George F. Baker and the First National Bank, the younger Baker—who had joined his father at the First National—was among the original subscribers to Harvard's new Business School in 1908. When Lamont sought subscribers to the James J. Hill Professorship in 1915, he went first to George F. Baker, Hill's friend and business associate. Two years later, the two Bakers made a substantial contribution to the Harvard Endowment Fund, a gift which in 1919 was used to endow the George Fisher Baker Professorship of Economics.

It was a history with which the Business School's Dean was evidently familiar by February of 1922. Following the advice and example of other Harvard fundraisers, and building upon the suggestions of his faculty and Harvard's architecture students, Donham had engaged Boston architect Harold Kellogg early in 1921 to prepare sketches and a model of "proposed buildings for the Business School," including an admin-

istration building and several dormitories. The model was shown to the School's Visiting Committee—which included New York, New Haven, and Hartford Railroad president Howard Elliott—on January 9, 1922.

Three weeks later, Donham sent Elliott a letter that would help Elliott put the model—or photographs of it—to a new use: "The Dean's report of which I am sending you a couple of copies contains, I think, most of the information which you will need in talking with Mr. Baker. The principal need of the School, as you know, is for a group of buildings."

Elliott broached the subject of the Business School to Baker in late February. They met in Brunswick, Georgia, at the Jekyl Island Club, the "resort of the 100 millionaires" which Baker had helped to organize in the 1880s. "I found him interested in the School," Elliott reported to Donham on March 16, "but whether he is interested enough to become a 'backer,' I do not know.

"I made a brief memo for him which I gave him, together with a copy of the [dean's] report and the photographs of the three buildings. . . . The reference [in the memo] to President Eliot was put in because Mr. Baker seems to be quite an admirer of his. Bishop

George F. Baker, Jr., his father's trusted aide and representative, eventually succeeded George F. Baker as chairman of the First National Bank of New York.

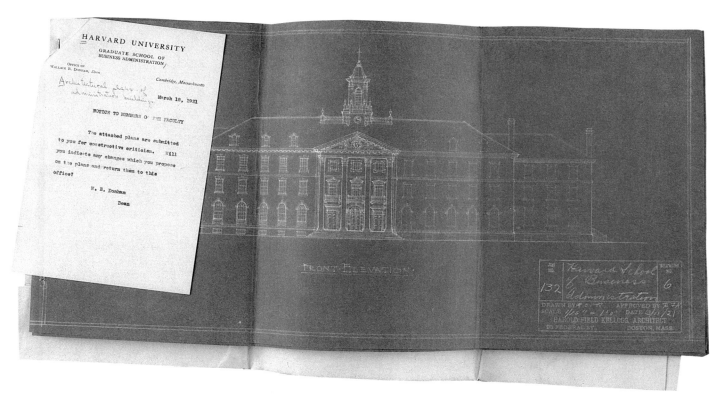

Architect Harold Kellogg prepared an elevation in 1921 of an HBS administration building, and the sketch was then circulated to the HBS faculty with a Donham memo attached. Baker Library—designed five years later—bore a strong resemblance to this plan.

**"Ignorant as I was of chemistry, art, and even business,"** wrote Bishop William Lawrence in his memoirs, **"I found myself broadcasting and speaking upon these subjects with the utmost confidence. The truth is that if one can cram under the right coaches, learn the salient points, and set them forth in clear and untechnical language, he may speak more effectively than an expert. He has the enthusiasm of a recent convert, and is not hampered by the exactness of expression and the conditions and exceptions which often clog the flow of an expert's exposition."**

A member of Harvard's Class of 1871, Bishop Lawrence was A. Lawrence Lowell's first cousin once removed. Although Lawrence came from a family of successful Boston merchants, he himself had been drawn to the ministry. Ordained in the Episcopal Church in 1875, he served first in Lawrence, Massachusetts — named for his grandfather, who founded that city's textile mills — and later in Cambridge. He was elected bishop of the Diocese of Massachusetts in 1893.

While rising to positions of prominence in his church, Lawrence maintained an active affiliation with Harvard. He was appointed "Preacher to the University" in 1888, although he concluded that he was not particularly effective in that role: "I was too familiar a person in Cambridge; and the students were naturally drawn by men of greater intellectual power and eloquence as well as of greater distinction." From 1899 to 1908, he was vice president of the Harvard Alumni Association; he was an Overseer of the University from 1894 to 1906, and again from 1907 through 1913. In 1913 he was elected a Fellow and Member of the Harvard Corporation.

Throughout this period, he served various causes as an unparalleled fundraiser. He first experienced his "invigorating avocation" as an undergraduate, when he raised substantial sums to support the Hasty Pudding Club's theatrical productions. In 1904 he headed a drive for $2.5 million to increase Harvard College teachers' salaries; in 1914, he helped raise $2 million for Wellesley College when its main building burned to the ground. Between 1915 and 1917, he collected over $8.5 million in a national drive to create and endow an Episcopal Church pension fund. After the First World War, he raised $1 million to endow Cambridge's Episcopal Theological School.

Lawrence happened to be at Jekyl Island also and he thought it was wise to stress the fact that the School was started by President Eliot.

"About all I can say now is that I have planted some seed, but I cannot tell whether it will grow or not. Mr. Baker made a suggestion that he thought dormitories ought to be built on a business basis and that money could be raised for that purpose if it could be shown that the investment was reasonably safe. This suggestion indicated perhaps that he was not taken by the idea of creating some of the buildings himself, although as already stated, he may feel disposed to do something later on."

Bishop William Lawrence, Elliott's informal fundraising advisor at the Jekyl Island Club, knew that subject intimately. The following year, he published an *Atlantic* article — entitled "An Invigorating Avocation" — describing his approach to fundraising. "You strike what is called a deep pool," he wrote. "No fish rises, and you go back to camp depressed. You cast into a shallow and almost hopeless pool, and come away with big game. You have all the fun of the gambler, and do not gamble."

**Wellesley College, after a disastrous fire in 1914. Bishop William Lawrence headed a $2-million drive to expand the school's facilities and replace this gutted structure.**

## Dangerous radicals

On Halloween, 1921, the Harvard Club on Boston's Commonwealth Avenue was the setting of an acrimonious meeting between seven manufacturers and seven HBS professors. The principal subject of the meeting was "union labor teaching," and its proper place in the Business School curriculum. The reason for the attendance of the manufacturers—who included F. C. Hood, president of the Hood Rubber Company—was the fact that for the second year in a row, Mr. Robert Fechner was lecturing HBS students on the subject of labor relations.

Fechner, who also lectured at Brown and Dartmouth, was the general vice president of the International Association of Machinists (IAM). He had been active in the successful 1901 movement for the nine-hour workday, and again in the 1915 movement for the eight-hour workday. Like Wallace Donham at the Bay State Street Railway, Fechner had helped resolve labor disputes in defense-related industries during World War I. At Donham's request, the IAM had granted Fechner a leave to teach at the three schools.

One of the manufacturers at the Harvard Club meeting stated, with seeming amiability, that he saw no reason why union organizers should not be presented to the students. But why not go all the way, he inquired neutrally—why not present the International Workers of the World as well? (The "Wobblies," as the IWW's members were known, were perceived by industrialists in the early 1920s as a serious threat to the established order.)

Dean Donham, in attendance at the meeting, answered that the Business School "drew the line somewhere."

"We draw the line a little closer than you do," rejoined the manufacturer.

Hood recounted this exchange in a letter to Howard Elliott, a fellow member of the School's Visiting Committee. "The fact is, Mr. Elliott," he wrote, "I do not think I have exaggerated this condition and I do not think Dean Donham realizes the facts or the teachings or the results, and I do not think he understands the employment relation of a factory.

"As a receiver of a street railway, he dealt with a group of union labor men, and other than that he has not been an employer.

"The fundamental difference between Dean Donham and his group of professors and the fundamental viewpoint of the manager of industry lies in one simple statement— theories or observation or some experience are entirely different from the experiences of manufacturers who have put their own money into an institution and realize the necessity of productive efficiency and scientific and human management."

Elliott found himself somewhere between the positions defined by the manufacturers and the professors. Himself a capitalist and railroad president, Elliott likened socialists to rattlesnakes. ("A prudent man does not let a rattlesnake bite him, even if he is fortunate enough to have the whiskey necessary to save himself," he wrote in a letter mailed a week before the Harvard Club meeting. "He kills the rattlesnake if he can.") But Elliott was a confidant of both Deans Gay and Donham, and understood better than some of his peers in the business world— and on the Visiting Committee —the attitude of open exploration in academia.

In spite of his misgivings on this subject, Elliott willingly approached George F. Baker three months later on the subject of support for the School. In November of 1923, however, Fechner again became an issue in the minds of Elliott and others. This time there was a direct tie to the economic fortunes of the School. "I am wondering," Elliott wrote to Donham, "whether you have come to any conclusion about this [Fechner] matter. We had a lunch here a day or two ago about this business [of HBS endowment] and I want to help all I can in getting the money. As I explained to you, there is some feeling among the people with whom I go that Harvard is a little too sympathetic with certain tendencies that so-called business men do not believe in. I believe it would help the general situation if we were in a position to say that a man like Mr. Fechner was not employed by the College."

In response—although Fechner was then nearing the end of his three-year appointment as visiting lecturer— Donham restated the position he had first outlined in 1921: "I personally believe that it is not only safe but wise to have college graduates who are about to undertake administrative responsibility in business come in contact with the labor point of view, as presented by men like Mr. Fechner. I have not the slightest fear that these men will be thrown off their feet by the type of instruction that we are giving, and I believe that contacts of this sort are absolutely essential if they are to be trained for business. Certainly in my experience here at the School it is far more likely that we shall create dangerous radicals by avoiding the point of view of organized labor than by having them listen to Mr. Fechner. . . .

"We are not ex cathedra laying down the law about business and the way it must be done; we are not trying to put these men in leading strings and control their opinions; we are not endeavoring to prevent them from thinking and to keep them from having a basis on which to think for themselves. On the contrary, everything that we are doing is intended to have exactly the opposite effect. We are trying to give them the basis for sane thought and independent thought and we are stimulating this thought as much as possible. Underlying our whole policy is an abiding faith in the sanity of our type of young men."

It may have been the bishop's self-confident article in the September, 1923, *Atlantic*—as well as his informal advice to Howard Elliott the preceding winter—that prompted Dean Donham to seek Lawrence's help. They met in November, and had what Lawrence described as a "most interesting" talk.

"I believe that you have a proposition which will appeal and which can be carried through," the bishop wrote to Donham after that meeting. The proposition, which Donham had previously described to his faculty, was a sweeping one: a $5-million campaign to build and endow a new Business School.

"Since then," Lawrence went on, "I have had a short telephone talk with the President. Of course he is sympathetic: there is, however, before the University today, as you well know, the question of the campaign for chemical laboratories, towards which half a million has been promised and which has the organized support of the alumni." Harvard's chemistry department was indeed in a woeful state. Its laboratories were so crowded, according to department faculty members, that experiments took twice as long to perform as would otherwise be necessary. This, in the eyes of the Corporation, was the University's most pressing need.

"The President tells me," Lawrence concluded, "that Mr. Mallinckrodt, the Chairman of that campaign, is to be in Cambridge within a few days, and he is going to talk with him, and no doubt you and the President will have a talk also."

IN HIS ENSUING TALKS WITH LOWELL, Donham reiterated the point that both men had already made publicly: the Business School, as then accommodated, could not function properly. Its facilities were, in Donham's words, "thoroughly inadequate." Its department heads were now located in six different buildings. Only two classrooms were available for the exclusive use of the School—basement rooms in Lawrence Hall and the Harvard Union—both of which had been used previously for storage. The School shared nine additional classrooms with other departments, but might lose any of them on short notice.

The fact that the Business School's first-year enrollment in the fall of 1923 was the largest ever—in part reflecting the recent graduation from college of many World War I veterans—only exacerbated the over-

Overcrowding in Boylston Hall: the Harvard Corporation felt that the chemistry department, in 1924, had the most serious difficulties deriving from space and equipment shortages. The Business School's needs could not be addressed unless a solution to chemistry's problems was forthcoming.

Edward Mallinckrodt, Jr., informal head of the chemistry drive, felt that a gift to the campaign from the Morgan family would "set the yardstick to the size of gifts all along the line." He recommended to Wallace Donham that the campaigners ask Morgan partner Thomas Lamont to approach J. P. Morgan, Jr. Events took a different course—although Lamont was indeed enlisted in the campaign.

crowded conditions. Chester N. Greenough, dean of the College, summarized the situation in a letter to Donham the following fall:

"In a certain sense, the Business School is our guest: that is to say, we were here first; we have admitted it to University Hall, to the Library, and to some of our classrooms. It has grown astonishingly and has deserved to grow, for it has been served with great enthusiasm and its policy has been soundly devised and attractively made known to the public. Therefore we are now in the position of a crowded family in a small house. It is emphatically the duty of the College, as the older branch of the family, to be hospitable, or at least decently courteous, under physical arrangements which are as inconvenient to you as they are to us." Greenough's note, while unfailingly courteous in tone, effectively conveyed the College's discomfort in its role as "host."

President Lowell was, of course, aware of the difficulties created by the success of the Business School, but he and other members of the Corporation were still reluctant to "turn Donham loose" — particularly in combination with Bishop Lawrence. One impediment was the $3-million chemistry campaign, which was already under way. (The Mallinckrodts to whom Lawrence had referred had contributed $500,000 to the cause.) The Department of Fine Arts, furthermore, had recently won permission to launch its own $2-million drive to build a new museum.

Harvard's governing boards also suspected that funds would be hard to come by. The $15-million Harvard Endowment Fund drive, officially terminated several years earlier, had fallen over a million dollars short of its goal, and much of the pledged money had

not yet been received. It appeared that for the time being, Harvard's alumni had given all that they were inclined to give.

In December of 1923, Donham asked the Corporation to consider a new approach: combining his proposed $5-million Business School drive with the existing chemistry and fine arts campaigns. The expanded drive could be described as an effort to extend Harvard's service to the nation — which would enable Harvard to seek support from prominent citizens who were not Harvard alumni. The drive should be headed, said Donham, by Bishop Lawrence, who in his efforts on behalf of his church's pension fund had already led a national campaign almost as ambitious in scope.

On Christmas Eve, 1923, the Corporation agreed to the plan, appointing Lawrence as chairman and Donham as executive chairman of a "Committee to Extend the Service of Harvard University." Donham was voted a de facto leave of absence from his administrative responsibilities. The Corporation further agreed to "protect" the Business School's budget for the duration of the campaign — although Donham would eventually have to make up any deficits that were incurred in his absence.

The Corporation also attempted to suggest priorities to its newly appointed committee. Since the chemistry department's needs were deemed the most pressing, these were to be addressed first. Then the Business School's problems were to be solved — a priority established in part by "the relief which will be furnished to other Departments of the University by the removal of this School to new buildings" — and last, those of the fine arts department.

**Consolidation of the School's staff and administrative offices, as Wallace Donham stated in his 1923 dean's report, "would now require a building approximately three times as large as the new building at 36 Quincy Street."**

**The new building (left, from a *Harvard Alumni Bulletin*) cost some $21,000, and required the removal of the University's paint and carpentry shops.**

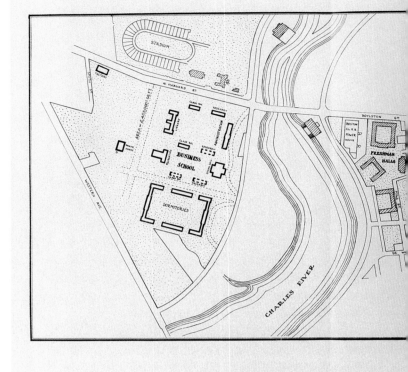

Lawrence and Donham ignored this advice, and proceeded on all fronts simultaneously. They decided to announce the campaign publicly on March 20th, 1924 — President Emeritus Eliot's ninetieth birthday — and they set out to secure by that date close to half of the money needed by each of the three departments. They were most concerned about their obligations to the chemistry department: previous uncoordinated solicitation had spoiled the most promising prospects. The two fundraisers were therefore disinclined to begin by pursuing support for chemistry alone. "If we did not have this job to do," wrote Donham of the chemistry campaign, "the whole thing would be easy. With this job to do, the whole thing is very hard."

The Business School, on the other hand, went into the campaign with several advantages. First, the members of the Corporation — particularly Lowell and Lawrence — recognized the School's needs. Second, Donham and his faculty had spent nearly three years defining those needs, to the point of commissioning models and sketches of a proposed campus. Third, the School enjoyed a "broad background of interest" in the business community, in large part because of the success of the Bureau of Business Research. The fact that the Business School was the only exclusively *graduate* school of business administration in the country had an appeal to potential donors. So did the fact that the School was charging the full cost of its teaching programs to its students. And finally, as Donham noted, "it was not difficult to prove that the Business School already was exercising considerable influence in business education."

THE BISHOP AND THE DEAN wasted little time. In the first week of January, 1924, they paid a visit to the First National Bank of New York. Donham — who had informed Lawrence about Howard Elliott's earlier conversation with George F. Baker — waited downstairs while Lawrence talked briefly with Baker in the chairman's office. Lawrence and Baker knew each other

The fine arts campaign was ably represented by Professor Paul Sachs. A member of Harvard's Class of 1900, he spent ten years as a partner with Goldman, Sachs in New York. In 1914, he joined Harvard's faculty as an assistant professor at the Fogg Museum, of which he became associate director in 1923.

Sachs and Donham often traveled to and from New York together during the course of the $10-million campaign, dividing between them the prospects with whom they hoped to meet.

socially from Jekyl Island; Baker, furthermore, retained an admiration for Boston's Brahmins from his childhood days in Dedham, Massachusetts. (By coincidence, Lawrence's father had rented and later sold a house in Dedham to Baker's grandfather.)

"I started in with telling him," Lawrence informed Thomas Lamont the following week, "that he and I were in the same boat, he having been in the banking business for fifty years, and I being saturated with business through my father and two grandfathers. He immediately recalled a business adage of either my grandfather or great-uncle which he said he had often used.

"The point that I tried to make was that with the enormous development of business, and the hundreds of thousands of business men, small and great, a definite forward step had got to be made in sustaining the ethical standards of himself, and those of other days; and that the one spot from which that influence was to come, at all events at first, was the Graduate Business School of Harvard University."

While the Corporation had suggested that the chemistry department's needs be addressed first, Lawrence mentioned neither chemistry nor fine arts to Baker. Instead, he proposed that Baker contribute $1 million for a Business School building. Baker was cordial but noncommittal: he said he would speak with his son, George Jr., about the matter.

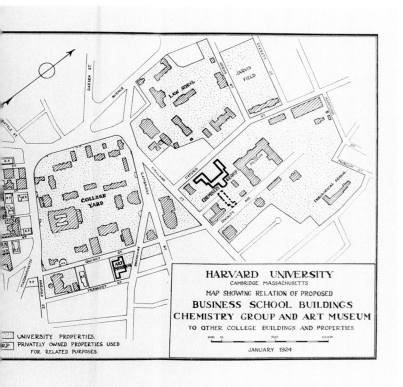

HARVARD UNIVERSITY
CAMBRIDGE MASSACHUSETTS
MAP SHOWING RELATION OF PROPOSED
BUSINESS SCHOOL BUILDINGS
CHEMISTRY GROUP AND ART MUSEUM
TO OTHER COLLEGE BUILDINGS AND PROPERTIES

JANUARY 1924

New York public relations consultant Ivy Ledbetter Lee, advisor to the Rockefellers, contributed his services—and a much-needed New York base of operations—to Harvard's campaigners. Lee was also friendly with George F. Baker, among other Harvard prospects.

Proposed Chemistry Laboratory for Harvard University.

**The proposed Business School, fine arts, and chemistry buildings in the larger University context. This site plan—prepared for use in the $10-million campaign—includes a Business School "factory" (above, upper left), intended to provide practical training to HBS students.**

**Solutions: new buildings for chemistry, the Business School, and fine arts (from a campaign brochure). Acquisitions through the mid-1920s had rendered McKim, Mead & White's original Fogg Museum increasingly inadequate for the storage and exhibition of Harvard's fine arts collection.**

**Harvard Economics Professor C. J. Bullock was the first incumbent of the George F. Baker chair in economics, established in 1919. He and his family became close friends of the Bakers, often visiting them at their Tuxedo, New York, mansion.**

**In January, 1924, Bullock wrote to Baker in support of Bishop Lawrence's recent solicitation. "I am glad to do this," he wrote, "because that School is doing a very remarkable pioneer work in raising standards of business instruction in the United States, and is doing it with a plant which is painfully inadequate. . . ."**

Baker took the same position when Thomas Lamont, his former lieutenant now working for J. P. Morgan, called on him at his house the following week. "Of course you know, Mr. Baker," said Lamont, "that the Bishop and, in fact, the whole Harvard community have their eye on you in connection with this important matter."

"Oh yes, I realize that," replied Baker, and then said no more on the subject. Lamont had to take comfort in the fact, as he subsequently informed Lawrence, that Baker "certainly didn't turn the idea down."

These two interviews immediately preceded Baker's departure for his winter vacation at Jekyl Island. January was the beginning of the short Jekyl "season," and it was not surprising, therefore, that Lawrence turned up at Jekyl shortly after Baker. Lawrence was reluctant to broach the subject of the Business School in that setting, however. "I am a guest here," he wrote Lamont, "and he is here for rest. My instinct is that I should say nothing to him on the subject unless he speaks to me."

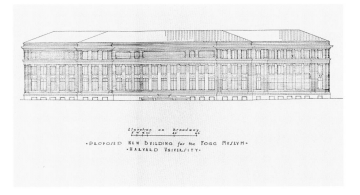

PROPOSED NEW BUILDING for the FOGG MUSEUM HARVARD UNIVERSITY.

But Lawrence had a keen sense of the timing and momentum of the fundraising campaigns he directed, and he was aware that unless Baker's contribution came soon, it would come too late to be announced at the formal inauguration of the campaign on March 20. The bishop had with him ample ammunition: a carefully composed letter, three pages long, written by Charles Eliot in support of the Business School; a statement by Donham; and various sketches and other supporting material. "It is barely possible," Lawrence suggested in a letter to Lamont, "that you may think it well to write Mr. Baker here, reminding him of your talk and suggesting that he talk to me, and if he does not, that shows that he wants no talk down here."

Lamont wrote the letter, and it produced the desired effect. Baker asked Bishop Lawrence to stop by his room in the Jekyl clubhouse. The elderly banker—whose well-publicized gifts had secured for him an unending and unwelcome stream of pleas for financial assistance—confessed that he was indeed interested in the Business School. However, he told Lawrence, he

**George Whitney of J. P. Morgan.**

had obligations; if he decided to contribute to the School, he said, he would have to "save up some money for it."

Baker again said that he would consult his son, and that he would also speak with his acquaintances in business who knew most about the School: Thomas Lamont and George Whitney — both partners in J. P. Morgan & Company — and AT&T president Walter Gifford. All three had served on the School's Visiting Committee.

This was welcome news to Lawrence. "I told him not to hurry," Lawrence recounted in a letter to Lamont, "to think it over and especially to talk to these four men who as business men could tell him more than I could." It was a promising group of advisors for the School's cause: Lamont was, in effect, a fellow campaigner, and Whitney and Gifford had been thoroughly coached on the subject of the Business School. In fact, at Donham's request Gifford had visited George F. Baker, Jr., during the preceding week, trying (as Lawrence phrased it) to "get him right on one or two points."

At that juncture, it appeared that the younger Baker — by then almost the only unknown factor in Bishop Lawrence's equation — had become a supporter of the School. This represented a significant change in the thinking of George Jr., then vice chairman of the First National Bank. In a 1920 interview with Wallace Donham, he had expressed his thoroughgoing skepticism toward his former Harvard classmate's efforts: "Donham," he had said, "not only am I not interested in what you are doing, but I positively disbelieve in it."

That statement was "rather a challenge," Donham later recalled. "I fell into the habit of going in to see him every few months." Within the year, the younger Baker was a convert. "I have changed my mind," he told Donham during one of their talks. "I think that the Business School is doing a real job, and I am interested in it."

**The Jekyl Island Club, circa 1900.**

**AT&T's Walter Gifford, in a 1950 photograph. Gifford and Whitney — both friends of HBS — were consulted by George F. Baker en route to his momentous decision.**

IN LATE FEBRUARY, Harvard's Department of Building and Grounds found a bargain price on 3,000 yards of fill, and began work on the swampy site across the Charles River, formerly intended for a relocated Massachusetts Institute of Technology, and now reserved for the new Business School campus. "It was evident," wrote the department superintendent to President Lowell, "that much of the land is at marsh level. The marsh ground should not be under drained until after it has been filled and had a chance to settle, so that no mistake could be made by filling the marsh."

This work was progressing faster than the work of the Committee to Extend the Service of Harvard University. Lawrence and Donham had hoped to have pledges of nearly $5 million in hand by President Emeritus Eliot's ninetieth birthday on March 20. Instead, they had approximately $1.25 million. For the Business School, they had secured endowment pledges of only $250,000: $100,000 from Price, Waterhouse, & Co., in honor of economist Sir Arthur Lowe Dickinson; $100,000 from the investment banking firm of Goldman, Sachs & Company, in recognition of the need for businessmen trained "not so much in the technical details as in the habit of analysis"; and $50,000 from the School's old friend Arch Shaw. Most heartening was a commitment from the three Straus brothers for the second in their series of gifts to the School: a dormitory in memory of their father, Isidor, the retailing genius who had died in the *Titanic* disaster.

But no word was heard from George Baker, who remained in Georgia until the end of March. Some confusion existed in the mind of both Baker and his son concerning what Bishop Lawrence was hoping to secure. In early April, George Jr. told Thomas Lamont that it appeared as if the bishop wanted one dormitory each from his father and J. P. Morgan, at a cost of around $300,000 apiece.

Through Lamont, Lawrence clarified the point: "[Harvard treasurer C. F.] Adams and I feel that with the prestige of Mr. Baker and the respect for him as the leader of business in this country a gift of one million dollars at this time would practically ensure the success of the campaign." In a subsequent telegram, he added: "Success of campaign depends so much upon Mr. Baker that in case you feel I can be of any help do not hesitate to telephone me."

In mid-April, the campaign experienced what Lawrence considered a close brush with calamity. While he was dictating another in his series of strategy letters to Lamont, his secretary took a call from a *Boston Traveler* reporter. Was it true, the reporter wanted to know, that the wealthy banker George F. Baker had just agreed to contribute $1 million to Harvard's fund drive?

Lawrence cut the conversation short. Baker was then in Boston for an AT&T board meeting, and had at Lawrence's urging driven by the site of the proposed campus. (Lawrence described it as "a pretty bad looking spot, but not so bad as the site of the Freshman Dormitories when I was in college.") Also at Lawrence's suggestion, Baker had visited the Harvard Medical School to see the buildings given by J. P. Morgan in memory of his father.

Subsequently, Lawrence and Baker had, indeed, met at the Somerset Hotel to discuss a $1-million contribution. Lawrence guessed that a hotel employee had eavesdropped on part of that discussion, and relayed it to the newspaper. This lent new urgency to the situation. "Mr. Baker has now had several weeks to think of the matter," Lawrence dictated, returning to the point of his letter, "and while no one would want to press him, I believe that he has reached a point where he is ready to make a decision, and every day that goes by is of importance, not only to the campaign, but also in connection with this mistaken report getting into the papers."

The climax of the drama, which came the following week, is best told by Lawrence himself:

"On going to New York on Monday, April 21, to talk about the campaign to a drawing room of ladies at Mrs. Harold Pratt's, I received word that Mr. Baker would call on me at my daughter's, Mrs. Lansing Reed's, at six o'clock. Promptly on the hour he came, alone. . . . He evidently had something on his mind, however, and I was a bit keyed up.

"After a few minutes of general talk he said, 'Bishop, since you talked with me about the Harvard Business School, I have been thinking things over; I have read all the documents carefully. For a time I was interested in the proposition that you put before me. But as I have thought it over again, I have lost interest in the idea of giving a million dollars, and I am not going to do it. And I don't care to give a half a million, either.'"

Baker then described a longstanding dream — the construction of a bridge over the Hudson River, roughly where the George Washington Bridge now stands — and explained that War Department interference had so far made the bridge impractical. Lawrence waited in suspense, suspecting that Baker would not have arranged their meeting only to turn him down outright.

"'We might be able to get the bridge now'" — Baker continued — "'but as you have been talking to me and I have been thinking, I have decided that the Business School might be a better object to give my money to. I have no interest in the Chemistry or the Art; but if by giving five million dollars I could have the privilege of building the whole School, I should like to do it. I have consulted my heirs. If it were one of several such schools, or an old story, I shouldn't care to do it. But my life has been given to business, and I should like to found the first Graduate School to give a new start to better business standards. It may not be the right kind of pride, but I should like to feel that my descendants could point to the Harvard Graduate School and know that I had done it.

"'But I want to do it alone, and you have other buildings pledged. Can I do it? Will the Corporation let me?'"

Even Lawrence, accustomed as he was to fundraising successes, was stunned. He assured Baker that Harvard would welcome such a gift, and that his condition would be acceptable. He then suggested that Baker's name should somehow be incorporated in the name of the School, which evidently pleased Baker. (Ultimately, the School's formal name became the "Graduate School of Business Administration, George F. Baker Foundation.")

"'You prepare a little letter for me to sign,'" the banker concluded, "'and if you want to bring it down this evening, I will be at home. I was going out to Howard Carter's lecture on the Egypt discoveries, but I will stay at home.'"

It was an electrifying turn of events. Lawrence, who had intended to withhold the news until his return from New York the following day, finally couldn't contain himself: he got off the train in New Haven and sent a telegram to President Lowell. Lowell waited to hear his cousin's firsthand account of the event and then wrote to Baker, thanking him for his "great gift" to the Business School. "You have done a vast service to a new form of education," wrote Lowell, "working for better preparation and higher standards in business education."

Among the campaigners, there was unrestrained celebration. "Such a splendid climax!" wrote Dean Donham to Bishop Lawrence. "In no other way, I believe, could the profession of business have been so lifted as you and Mr. Baker have lifted it. . . . From my standpoint you have brought to fulfillment in a few short months a dream which it took four years to dream."

In the following weeks, Lawrence and Lamont each attributed the campaign's great success to the other's efforts. "This ends a very happy chapter for Harvard," said Lamont in a letter to Lawrence, "the responsibility and credit for which belong to you." Lawrence, though, refused to take full credit: "Your friendship with the Bakers," he replied, "was an essential part."

But perhaps the most significant voice in the chorus of celebration which followed the announcement of the gift was that of George Baker, Jr. His modest letter to Bishop Lawrence, two days after the event, suggests most clearly how the gift was secured:

"I do not know whether Donham ever told you of some talks I had with him over a year ago on this very subject. I made some suggestions which I thought would be helpful in presenting the proposition to anyone, and particularly to my father. The thing all came

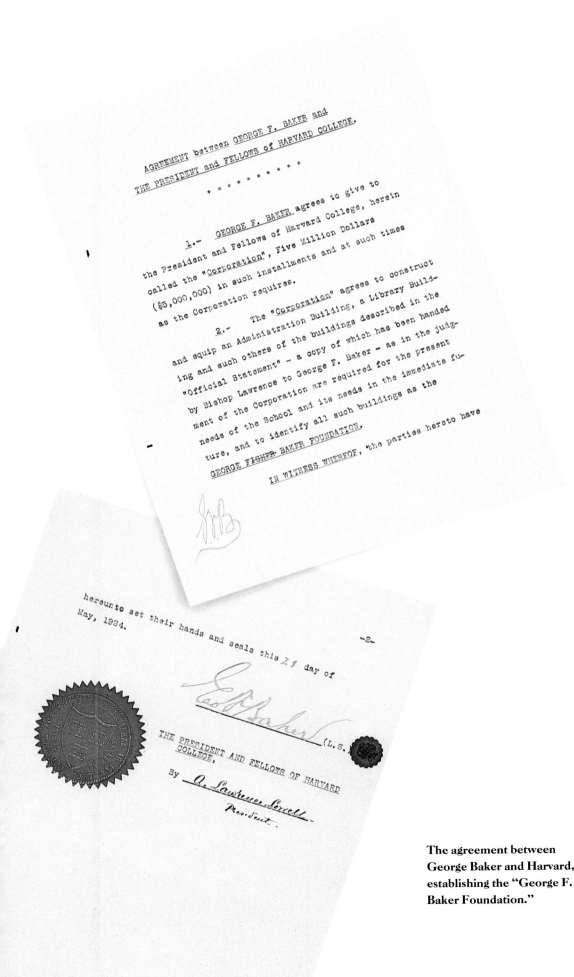

**The agreement between George Baker and Harvard, establishing the "George F. Baker Foundation."**

around very nicely, and you handled it so well, that when the time came for the final decision and Father and I discussed the matter at length, it was not very difficult for him to arrive at the conclusion which he did."

PUBLIC ANNOUNCEMENT OF THE GIFT was delayed until June 2, 1924, after Baker had left on his annual cruise to Europe. The Business School faculty, apprised of the benefaction several days earlier, sent a message of thanks to Baker on board the boat. "I was working on the Cape when the announcement came out in the papers," Donham wrote to the younger Baker on June 5, "but they tell me the effect on the School was perfectly amazing." Of the prior announcement he reported, "One of the professors said it was the first time he had ever seen a faculty speechless."

The *New York Times*'s news summary of the following Sunday, referring to the senior Baker's first paying job, observed wryly that "this has been a notable year for grocery boys." The *Times* suggested that support for business schools was long overdue in a nation "made great by commerce." The Harvard Business School, the account continued, "is a cornerstone of sixteen years' endurance, the foundation of an arch that is binding the academic to the practical." If the concept of the business school needed any further endorsement, the *Times* reporter concluded, "that endorsement had been supplied by the endowment of Mr. Baker, looked upon as one of the most hard-headed and sure-footed leaders in American affairs."

Donham's "work on the Cape" in early June included the redirection of several gifts from the Business School to other parts of the University. (The larger campaign was not completed until the following March, when the last gifts for chemistry were secured.) Later in the month, and certainly long before he had ever expected to, Donham took up the task of designing and building a campus. On June 20, he and President Lowell asked architecture professor Charles W. Killam — who four years earlier had helped Donham develop his first rough building plans — to serve as professional advisor to the project. The first step would be to hold a competition to select an architect.

The Straus brothers: Jesse, Percy, and Herbert.

## *About the Straus dormitory*

The Straus brothers were all Harvard men: Jesse was a member of the Class of '93; Percy, the Class of '97; and Herbert, the Class of '03. Like their father Isidor—the retailing genius who built Macy's into the world's largest department store—they were also businessmen. After Isidor and his wife died in the sinking of the *Titanic*, their three sons decided in 1912 to establish a Business School scholarship in their memory. Through Thomas Lamont, President Lowell suggested that the School needed endowment funds more than scholarships, and the Strauses redirected their gift accordingly.

When the Committee to Extend the Service of Harvard announced its $10-million campaign in the spring of 1924, the Strauses responded with a pledge of $300,000 for the construction of a dormitory on the Business School's proposed new campus. Three months later, George Baker's gift of the entire campus was announced, and those who had previously pledged buildings were released from their commitments. Nevertheless, as Jesse Straus informed Lowell in June, 1924, the Straus family wanted to make a gift "as nearly like the original plan as possible." He proposed that the Strauses provide for a college dormitory in Harvard Yard, the net income from which would be used to support a "Straus Professorship or Professorships" at the Business School.

The gift was gratefully accepted, since the School— then, as twelve years earlier —badly needed money for faculty salaries and research initiatives. But the gift created an unwieldy administrative situation, since both the College and the Business School had an interest in the new dormitory. "In accordance with the instructions of the Corporation," Lowell informed Donham in a June 20 letter which hints at some of these administrative difficulties,

"I write this to you about the Straus dormitory. A dormitory in the Yard such as we propose would have to be three stories in height, and that means a slightly, but not much, greater cost per room than if it were five stories in height. On the other hand, the rooms will average a somewhat better price than if the building were higher. We cannot guarantee what the net rent of the building will be; but we will be as economical in building as is consistent with the type of building the Messrs Straus would want to bear their father's name, and we shall let the rooms for as large a rent as possible. I may add that the Colonial or Georgian type of architecture which we use is one that is very far from involving any extravagance in ornament."

In other words, the Business School would own the building, and have the benefit of the income it generated, but would have scant influence on its design, construction, or use. This point was illustrated when Straus Hall opened in the fall of 1926, and Jesse Straus's son Robert—then beginning his senior year at the College— applied unsuccessfully for a room in the new dormitory. Jesse Straus appealed to Dean Donham for assistance, but Donham was able only to repeat to Straus what the College authorities had already told him: that Straus Hall was reserved for underclassmen.

In 1927, when the School sought to appoint the first incumbent to the Straus professorship, the combined income from Straus Hall and the family's 1912 gift was not adequate to attract to Harvard N. S. B. Gras, the eminent economic historian with whom both Dean Donham and Jesse Straus had become impressed. The Straus family therefore agreed to provide an additional $3,500 annually to create and fund the "Isidor Straus Professorship in Business History," to which Gras was subsequently appointed. At the end of 1930, the three brothers capitalized this annual giving by making a gift to the Business School of $70,000.

The rental income from Straus Hall continued to fund the Straus professorship for over fifty years. Gras was succeeded in the chair in 1957 by Ralph W. Hidy, who was in turn succeeded by Alfred D. Chandler, Jr., in 1971.

By 1981, however, both the College and the Business School were seeking ways to alter the financial arrangement supporting the Straus chair. Questions had arisen about the appropriateness of including certain charges in determining the net income of the building; furthermore, it was unclear who would finance the major capital improvements that the building would eventually need. With the assent of the Straus family, therefore, the Business School transferred ownership of Straus Hall to the Faculty of Arts and Sciences on June 30, 1982, in return for Harvard endowment units valued at $750,000. Consistent with the original intent of Jesse, Percy, and Herbert Straus, these funds are now used to support the Isidor Straus Professorship of Business History.

**Straus Hall: supporting business history.**

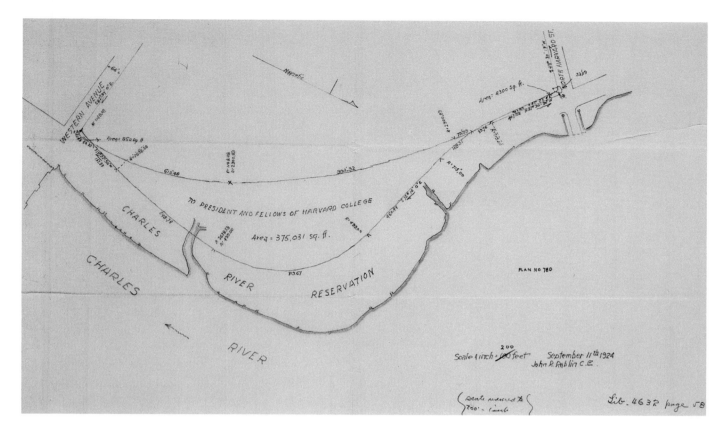

Architecture had been very much on the minds of the Bakers, according to Thomas Lamont. At a New York luncheon in late May, the elder Baker had asked that Harvard conduct a thorough search for an architect.

"Tom," he had said, "you don't know how much my heart is in this whole matter. We mustn't let any chance slip up in having the most adequate and beautiful buildings across the river there, consistent with the useful purpose of the School. If the money that I have promised is not sufficient, I'd rather give even more and be certain that we had just the right architectural result. I cannot tell you how strongly I feel on this."

In spite of this offer — received only indirectly, if at all — Harvard's administrators were soon finding themselves in an uncomfortable position. They did not intend to ask Baker for more money for buildings when construction had yet to begin. Yet even with Baker's generous gift, Harvard would not be able to construct the elaborate campus described in the campaign literature. Those plans had included, in addition to dormitories and classrooms adequate for a thousand students, a research building, a recreation building, a separate power plant, and an experimental factory building. Nevertheless, at Killam's suggestion, Donham and Lowell decided to ask competing architects for a complete set of plans for the campus. If and when economies proved necessary — as they almost certainly would — whole buildings could be deferred.

Economy was therefore very much on the minds of Donham, Killam, and architecture student Harry J. Korslund as they set about to create an informal design studio at Donham's summer home in Chatham, Massachusetts. Beginning in early July, they carved a drafting room, an office, and a dormitory out of the corners of Donham's garage. Their principal task was to adapt the American Institute of Architects' standard competition form to the specifics of the job at hand.

A second priority was to "pre-design" certain aspects of the campus, in advance of the competition. This was in part an economy measure: the School needed to guarantee, for example, low maintenance costs and an adequate rate of return on its dormitories. But Donham also had other goals in mind. As Killam later recalled it, the Dean wanted the School's buildings to reflect "the definite ambition of the faculty to help the students to be something more than money-makers." In other words, there was to be an inspirational component to the architecture at Soldiers Field. "Should not a student lead a simple life?" asked Killam. "Not a bare one, not an ugly one, but a life of plain living and high thinking in surroundings of quiet good taste?"

The designers on Cape Cod felt the lack of adequate precedents for what they were attempting to do. There were few lessons to be learned from the School's nomadic existence up to that point, and certainly no other school of business had ever been "lifted bodily" out of its parent university. Furthermore, the widespread publicity attending Baker's gift had created high expectations for the School, and those expectations focused on the new campus. "Only in recent years," editorialized the *New York Times* in August, "have business men begun to see that [beauty and utility] may not only be combined but that beauty of surroundings actually possesses a utilitarian value. The Harvard Business School should be able by its structures to embody this truth for many who otherwise would fail to grasp it."

**"It would be very well,"** President Lowell directed Dean Donham on June 24, 1924, **"if you would see someone whom you know on the Metropolitan Park Commission and find out if there is any probability of their being willing to put the park line nearer the river, and sell to the University the land between such a line and the present road. . . . It is of very distinct value to the University."**

The Park Commission agreed to sell just over 375,000 square feet of land to Harvard on three conditions: first, that the University would pay six cents a square foot for the land; second, that it would reimburse the Commission for an estimated $27,000 worth of fill already deposited there; and third, that it would pay an estimated $9,000 for the extra 400 feet of Soldiers Field Drive — then under construction — that would result from the adjustment.

Lowell agreed to these terms, and title to the land (outlined above in a map accompanying the deed) was transferred on October 16, 1924. The University paid a total of $57,401.86 for just over 375,000 square feet of land, thereby substantially expanding the Business School's "front lawn."

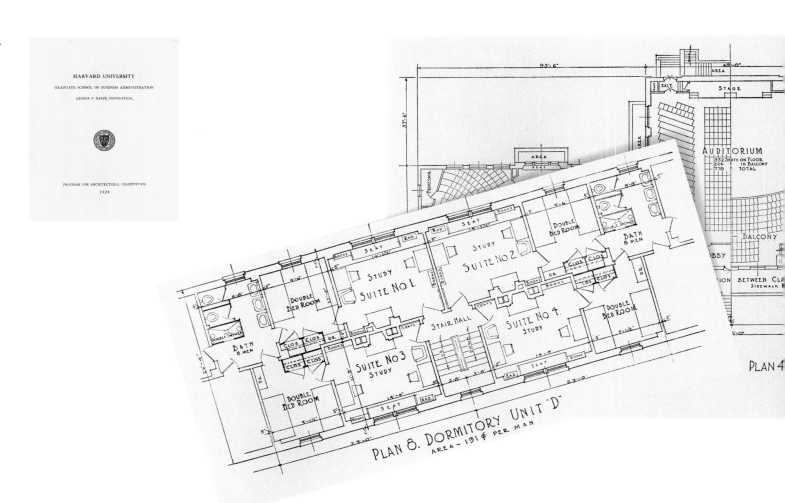

Even while relaxing on Cape Cod, President Lowell kept in close touch with the progress of the HBS campus. Dean Donham's Chatham house — design headquarters in the summer of '24 — was only thirty miles further out on the Cape.

Donham was particularly aware of the dangers in casting ideas in stone. "This is a pretty active time with us here," he wrote in October to the dean of Ohio State University's School of Business, "as we are right in the midst of the determination of policies which are affected by the type of buildings we build. When once determined, it is going to be awfully difficult to change them. In other words, the responsibility of spending $5,000,000 on buildings with the knowledge that inanimate objects exercise a tremendous degree of control on future policies and that this particular group of inanimate objects is likely to continue to exist for centuries makes a problem that should be absorbing all my time."

The library was a case in point. In Donham's tenure the Business School library — a section of the stacks on the top floor of Widener — had grown far beyond its capacity. Newly acquired collections remained in unopened boxes, and a number of staff members had had no desks for several years. This was not a precedent to be built upon; therefore, librarian Charles C. Eaton visited several dozen university and public libraries in search of design ideas. He also drew on his previous experience in industry in making his final recommendations: an orderly routing of books and readers through the library, a minimal use of interior bearing walls and utility shafts, adequate natural light, and a delivery desk on the ground floor — to avoid, as had not been avoided in Widener, the "common bad practice of mountain climbing."

In the dormitory plans, economy (and not the hoped-for inspirational component) eventually led to a configuration of four two-man suites sharing a bath. The dormitories, as built, provided only limited closet space, and no through ventilation. In the end, "mountain climbing" in the library was not completely avoided. Because the separate classroom building was one of the first to be omitted, the library had to be modified to accommodate instruction. The classrooms themselves, however, were protected from the drive for economy: they retained their scheme of curved rows of desks and tiered floors, first sketched out in that summer of designing on the Cape.

Dean Donham's and Professor Killam's summer of designing on Cape Cod led to a very specific architectural outline for those firms competing in Harvard's competition.

"This study," Killam later concluded, "led to the construction of dormitories that earned a better return on their cost and could be more economically maintained than more extravagantly planned buildings."

As a result of his investigation of 25 libraries, as well as his consulting work for General Electric, HBS librarian Charles C. Eaton argued for an orderly routing of books and readers through the new HBS library.

In 1920, Harvard treasurer Charles F. Adams opposed "letting Donham loose" on a campaign for a new Business School campus; four years later, however, he worked closely with Dean Donham to select an architect to design the new campus.

THE ARCHITECTURAL COMPETITION, announced publicly in August, attracted some two hundred proposals. Of these, 49 included the required drawings, and Harvard's treasurer C. F. Adams and Dean Donham checked the references of each of these firms. The first round of the competition, judged by Adams, Donham, and three architects, resulted in invitations to six firms to compete in the finals. There, they would vie on an equal footing with six other firms specifically invited by Harvard. (These companies included five that had previously done work for the University, and one that had worked for George F. Baker.)

The lessons learned from the first stage of the competition were applied to the second. Donham and Killam, for example, decided to ask for two dining halls in this second round, an arrangement which might provide more intimacy than the single large dining hall specified in the first round. President Lowell — who knew firsthand the difficulties of acquiring land for the University, and the resentment that often arose when Harvard took new land off the tax rolls — stated that many of the proposals used the Soldiers Field site wastefully. The twelve firms in the final competition

were given from November 15, 1924, until the following January 5 to revise their drawings, based on these and other observations.

The Bakers, meanwhile, were becoming increasingly involved in the life of the School. The elder Baker accepted an invitation to a Business School Club dinner in his honor; the dinner was scheduled to coincide with his November 18 trip to Boston for the American Telephone Company's board meeting. At the dinner, following a series of speeches by students and faculty praising Baker's generosity and foresight, the banker himself rose to speak briefly.

"I want to thank you for this tremendous greeting," Baker began, his cheeks flushing. He quickly fell victim to stage fright, which always plagued him when he was called upon to speak publicly. But he struggled on: "I hope that in this great college of business administration, from which I hope there may graduate some of the greatest men in the world, they will teach them so to conduct themselves as to gain the respect of their fellows and also to keep up their standards of integrity, for thereby they may gain for themselves the greatest happiness that life can bestow."

Lowell on lecture rooms in the library: "Are three of these needed? Are so many likely to be used at the same time? Should they not be on the ground floor near the entrance or a separate entrance?"

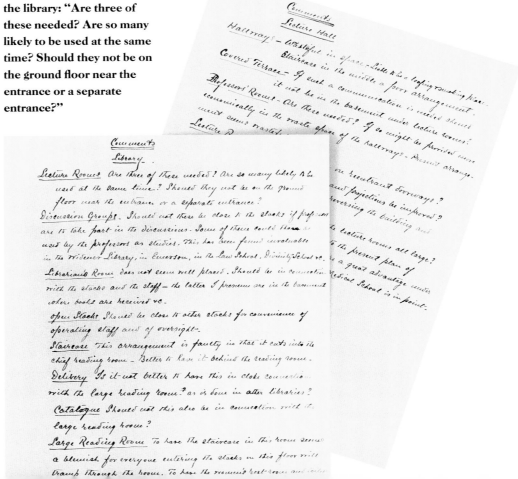

SECOND FLOOR PLAN
...OM BUILDING WITH AUDITORIUM
...RD BUSINESS SCHOOL
...FOR ARCH'L PROGRAM
...S W. KILLAM, ADVISER.

The following morning, Donham recounted the event in a letter to Baker's son. "Everybody here was perfectly delighted with the general effect and everything that happened at last night's dinner," he wrote. "I think it is impossible to characterize the influence that your father's simplicity and dignity will have on the future of the School. . . . Mr. Lowell came down to my office this morning to say what a wonderfully effective, dignified, and impressive talk he felt your father made."

In that same week, the senior Baker sent Harvard the first payment toward the foundation that would bear his name: a check for $50,000, which enabled Donham to purchase, among other things, an inventory of furniture which was then available at a good price. By coincidence, the funds arrived just as the President and Fellows of Harvard were considering some difficult questions being posed by the Business School's dean. Donham was then reluctantly requesting yet another tuition increase, and for unexpected reasons.

It appeared, Donham had told the Corporation in September, that George Baker thought he was giving his $5 million exclusively for buildings. The goal of the campaign had been different in a significant way, Donham reminded the Corporation: he and Lawrence had sought only $4 million for immediate construction, and an additional $1 million for much-needed endowment, which would allow the School to increase faculty salaries. The $4 million would be used to build the educational plant for 1,000 students, but construction of up to half of the dormitory buildings would be postponed until it was clear that the income from $1 million worth of additional dormitories could at least equal the income from that same $1 million invested as endowment.

Now, Donham told the Corporation, the School was in a bind. Baker had said several times, "I want to get my first look at these buildings"—*all* the buildings—"from not too far above." The younger Baker, furthermore, had said emphatically that money should not be reserved for endowment except for a reasonable margin on building costs, and that in urging his father to make the gift, he had had buildings in mind. Yet, from Donham's viewpoint, additional endowment funds would be difficult to raise elsewhere, given the widespread publicity generated by Baker's gift and the public announcement that the School's needs had been met.

In the near term, the School could meet its financial problems by raising tuition. Over the long run, however, the outlook was bleak: if faculty salaries could not be increased, the School would certainly deteriorate. Baker's handsome new campus, now in the planning stages, would be distinguished more by its buildings than by quality of education.

At a series of meetings at Baker's New York townhouse in early December, 1924, Donham explained these difficulties to Baker and his son. Would the Bakers agree to a postponement of some of the dormitories, he asked, until those dormitories were needed? The senior Baker agreed readily that the needs of the School should determine the construction sequence, although he was very anxious to see the campus completed. On one point he was adamant: "I do not wish the construction of these buildings to be made conditional either on getting further money," he said, "or on a demonstration of earning capacity which would make these buildings a part of the endowment of the School."

"Father," added George Jr., "I am very glad you made that statement. It is exactly my view. One of the things I have had in mind from the start is that it will house practically the entire School, and I don't want to see that result delayed because the dormitories cannot earn money, or until the School has further endowment. The primary object of your gift, Father, has always been in my mind to build a plant for this School which would be adequate, and include the whole thing."

This ended the meeting—an unsatisfactory conclusion, since Donham still lacked the flexibility he needed. But the Dean and the younger Baker continued their conversation as they rode downtown together.

From the Harvard Class of 1899's 25th reunion picture. Classmate #116 (center, left) is Wallace B. Donham, HBS dean; classmate #97 (seated on the ground) is First National Bank vice-chairman George F. Baker, Jr.

The revised agreement between Harvard University and the Bakers, whereby George, Jr. joined in the Baker Foundation gift, and Harvard received an infusion of money not specifically allocated to building expenses.

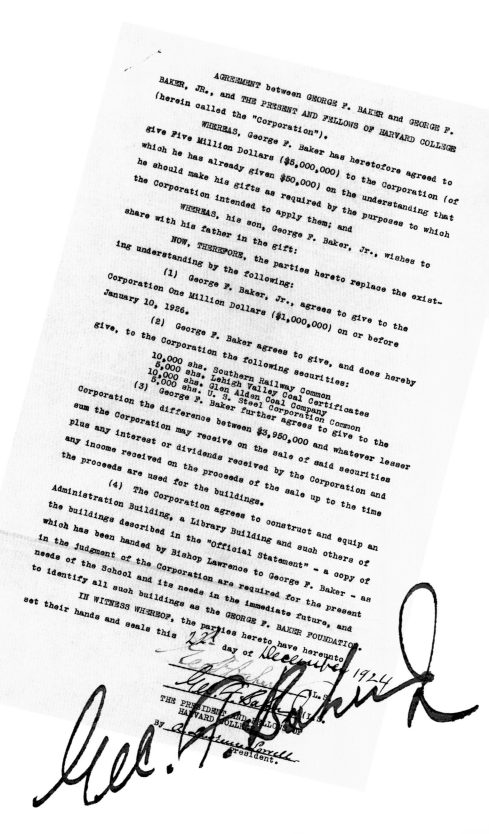

By now on very friendly terms, the former classmates spoke frankly. Baker made it clear that he understood the School's financial difficulties, particularly since his father's gift had effectively ended the flow of contributions. "If you decide that the School does not need all of the dormitories immediately," he told Donham, "while I should regret your doing so, I have no objection to your writing my father a letter which asks him when he intended to pay in the million which the Bishop refers to as not being needed immediately for construction.

"I should want, if you wrote such a letter, to have my father told it was entirely a question of what his original intention had been, and not a question of whether he would do it. If he says his original intention was to pay in whatever money was to be used for endowment after the buildings were completed, I think the University ought to stand on the statement."

Within two weeks, however, a new solution—evidently of George Baker, Jr.'s design—was arrived at, and spelled out in an agreement signed by Harvard and the Bakers on December 22. Under the terms of this revised agreement, the elder Baker would give to Harvard securities worth approximately $4 million. In addition, George Jr. would now "share with his father in the gift," contributing $1 million within the next thirteen months.

This change was significant for three reasons. First, the Business School's financial crisis was eased considerably, as a substantial sum not specifically devoted to construction expenses would now be in hand. Second, George Baker, Jr., declared himself a committed friend of the School, with a considerable personal investment in its fortunes. And, finally, George Baker, Sr., found himself in an unaccustomed position: being responsible for a smaller contribution than he had originally elected to give.

Egerton Swartwout,
Architect
New York

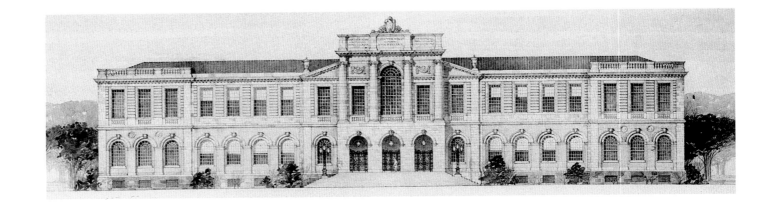

Egerton Swartwout,
Architect
New York

Parker, Thomas & Rice,
Architects
Boston

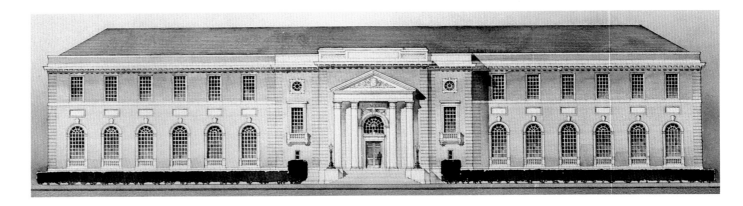

Competing to design the Business School. Harvard's administrators spent approximately $40,000 planning for and conducting their architectural competition — one of the most thorough such competitions held, up to that point — and concluded that it had been money well spent.

Furthermore, architectural advisor Killam recalled, "a number of the unsuccessful competitors wrote praising the fairness of the unusual competition."

**Ludlow & Peabody and
Harold F. Kellogg,
Associated Architects
New York and Boston**

**Raymond M. Hood,
Architect
New York**

**McKim, Mead & White,
Architects
New York**

The undersigned jury has the honor to report, in accordance with Section 12 of the Program of Competition for the Graduate School of Business Administration, Harvard University, George F. Baker Foundation as follows:

A careful examination of the twelve sets of drawings submitted resulted in the unanimous decision that the drawings Number 10 exhibited the best evidence of the ability of their author to carry the design and execution of the school group to a successful conclusion.

Upon motion, the jury unanimously voted to award the commission as architects of the buildings to the author of the drawings Number 10.

The envelopes were thereupon opened and Messrs. McKim, Mead & White of New York were discovered to be the appointed architects.

OF RECORD
JAN 12 1924·5

---

**"Drawings number 10" were selected unanimously by President Lowell, treasurer Adams, George Baker, and three architects. The drawings proved to be the work of McKim, Mead & White.**

THE ARCHITECT FOR THE CAMPUS was blind-selected on January 10, 1925, by a panel consisting of the senior Baker, President Lowell, Dean Donham, and three distinguished architects. There was unanimous agreement that "Drawings number 10" were the most successful. They depicted a straightforward group of buildings with the desired "semidomestic" character. They recognized the bend in the Charles, reflecting it in their designs of curved buildings and roads, and trapezoidal courtyards. The fan-shaped building group depicted in the drawings afforded views both out of and into the campus, with the library building serving as the focal point. In keeping with Baker's expressed wish, the campus had a central and visually dominant feature: the library façade and bell tower.

The winning architects were McKim, Mead & White, a prominent New York firm whose previous work had included the Morgan Library in New York, the Boston Public Library, and numerous Harvard buildings. They immediately set to work preparing working drawings for the contractor, since the University had made it clear that it expected the dormitories to

be ready for occupancy in the fall of 1926 — only a year and a half away. This would increase the likelihood that the 84-year-old Baker would live to see the completed campus; it would also provide the Business School with an estimated $100,000 in dormitory rental income for the 1926–1927 academic year.

As the architects developed the needed drawings and specifications, Harvard's President and Fellows continued to refine their expectations for the Business School campus. In February, 1925, Lowell informed Donham of the outcome of a recent discussion: "The Corporation was decidedly of opinion that building a special chapel for the School was not necessary or wise. Grave doubt was expressed also about placing the class room [building] on the street" — North Harvard Street — "where the noise is sure to be considerable, and may become worse. Also there was some doubt whether it would not be better to have the building for research in close connection with the library."

To Donham's dismay, the Corporation was not persuaded that Business School students should gain practical experience in an on-campus model factory.

Transforming the marsh: preliminary work at the site of the Business School's new campus, three weeks before the official groundbreaking in June, 1925.

Objects Doubly Advanced  **121**

"They were clearly of the opinion," Lowell reported, "that factories on the School grounds would be undesirable."

In April, the University hired the firm of Frederick Law Olmsted, designers of New York's Central Park and Boston's "Emerald Necklace" park system, to landscape the campus. The following month, the Hegeman-Harris Company, a New York contracting firm specializing in "monumental" buildings, was engaged on a cost-plus-fixed-fee basis, allowing building foundations to be laid before finished working drawings were available. And, on the morning of June 2, 1925, according to the Harvard Business School *Bulletin*, "Dean Donham moved a lever. There followed a hissing of steam and a grinding of meshing gears. An anxious crowd followed the deliberate movement of the long crane as it dipped downward. With a huge gulp the steam-shovel swallowed its first scoopful of earth on the site of the new Business School."

Donham and architectural advisor Killam were responsible for most of the day-to-day supervision of McKim, Mead & White and Hegeman-Harris. The Corporation had specified that instead of the usual arrangement—under which the architect supervised the contractor on the client's behalf—Harvard would consider both firms to be its expert advisors, and on an equal footing with each other. This was designed to afford the University greater control over the project, but its immediate practical consequence was that Donham's de facto leave of absence for fundraising purposes now became a leave for construction supervision.

Perhaps inevitably, given the breakneck pace of the project and the overlapping functions of design and construction, tensions arose: among the various subcontractors, between the contractor and the architect, and between the architect and the University. At an October, 1925, meeting of the principals, Lowell, Donham, and Killam tried to remedy the situation. Hegeman-Harris, they made it clear, would be expected to supply more and better cost estimates in the future. Decisions had been made, said Killam, without Harvard's participation; this would not be acceptable in the future.

Dean Donham breaks new ground: June 2, 1925. Construction: June 2, 1925 to October, 1926. During 1926, the Business School administration telephoned the New York offices of contractors Hegeman-Harris approximately 250 times a month.

AIRPLANE VIEW OF HARVARD STADIUM, CAMBRIDGE, MASS.

Lowell emphasized that he wanted someone in Cambridge who was competent to conduct the "give and take" necessary for decision making. "Such minor questions," he concluded, "probably could be settled in about fifteen minutes, where they now require matters of weeks."

The discussion then turned to cost cutting. Much of the remaining ornamentation on the buildings— already curtailed — was now eliminated. Copper was to be cut out of the plans entirely. Design work on the research and recreation buildings was halted. This last decision was in keeping with Baker's expressed wish: rather than economize unwisely on all the buildings, he had suggested, Harvard should omit certain buildings entirely.

"From my standpoint," wrote Donham in a February, 1926, letter to George Baker, Jr., "the inability to build the whole group immediately within the $5,000,000 in no way releases us from the duty of carrying out your father's expressed desire to have the whole plant built as part of his foundation, and what follows in this letter is my personal plan for carrying out his wish to the last detail." Harvard, said Donham, would build the entire dormitory group, as well as the library, the administration building, the classroom building, and the Dean's House. ("I should omit the Dean's House," commented Donham, "if your father had not several times expressed his desire to have it included.")

Building the entire dormitory group was an idea to which Donham had only recently subscribed. He was now persuaded that this would be a good idea. With the Corporation's approval, he would put all dormitory receipts into a special building fund, to be applied against construction expenses until the entire campus was completed — a process which might take up to ten years. The problem with this approach, Donham noted, was that the dormitory income had been intended to support the School's research.

"On the other hand," he continued, "for several years we have financed research without such an assured income, and if necessary I am confident we can continue to do this. A still better way to solve the problem is by building up our endowment, and I have for the last two months been working in this direction. If we can secure about ten professorships endowed at $200,000 apiece, or a smaller number with a larger endowment, this will give us an income comparable with what we expect from the dormitories."

Donham was, at that point, confident that several such professorships would be forthcoming within the next few months. "In the early days," he elaborated, "before the School had demonstrated its ability to do its job and before it had the tremendous asset of your father's backing, it obtained two such professorships, named for Mr. E. C. Converse and Mr. James J. Hill. What was possible then, appears possible now on a larger scale."

Baker Library's bell tower was intended to be one of three on the campus, but economies forced the elimination of proposed towers on the river dormitories.

Throughout the design and construction phases, the concept of the Business School dormitories continued to evolve. In February, 1925, Bishop Lawrence made a suggestion to Dean Donham: "I wonder if the Business School cannot set the precedent of doing away with that horrible word 'dormitory,' which sounds as if students did nothing but sleep there; and smacks of a hotel annex—why not West Hall? East Hall?"

Donham agreed, and took further steps to emphasize that the School was constructing *residence* halls. Rather than the single dining room originally planned, for example, Donham insisted on including serving kitchens and dining rooms in each of the six halls, which were connected to a central kitchen by an extensive tunnel system.

Construction of the new campus was slowed first by the extreme sogginess of the site, particularly on its northeastern perimeter. Subsequently, because all of the buildings were constructed on roughly the same schedule, each of the building trades in turn was in short supply: carpenters, then plumbers, then plasterers. The problem was compounded by the fact that the Hotel Statler in downtown Boston was then under construction—as were the new fine arts and chemistry buildings, also being erected by HBS contractor Hegeman-Harris.

## Cutting corners

Harvard's President Lowell assigned himself a personal responsibility for the proper construction of the Business School. (His attention to the School's affairs was remarkable in its comprehensiveness. According to the faculty minutes of 1922, he was accustomed to reviewing, each spring, the academic records of every HBS student whose grades were "above or slightly below Distinction, and those whose grades were below the passing mark, or whose work was incomplete.") He now included the Soldiers Field site in his morning constitutional, ascertaining firsthand how the work was progressing, and subsequently making his opinions known. In June of 1925, for example, he objected to McKim, Mead & White's design for dormitory fireplaces: two feet, four inches wide was

inadequate, he said; fireplaces needed to be no less than three feet wide. In the same month, Lowell advised Donham on the relative merits of various flooring materials.

"Wasteful of space," the president wrote to Donham of a McKim, Mead & White design for a hallway. "Liable to be a loafing and smoking place." Early in 1926, he gave mixed reviews to Donham's furniture selections, approving of a certain colonial table but noting that "the other pieces of Colonial furniture seem to me rather flimsy, and on the whole not strong enough for their purpose."

Lowell was distressed by the conflicting goals of economy and beauty. It was clear even before construction started that corners would have to be cut, sometimes with esthetic conse-

quences. This became literally true when it came to the quoins, or cornerpieces, on the dormitories. Stone was prohibitively expensive, and Harvard had reluctantly agreed to the use of concrete. Then McKim, Mead & White made a further suggestion, which elicited from Lowell a wry objection: "Professor Killam tells me that you want to paint the quoins white, to look like wood, to which he objects. . . . Personally, imitation stone is rather repugnant to me, but imitation stone painted to look like wood reminds me of the German during the war who was lamenting the fact that they might have to eat rat, when his friend said that it wasn't rat he objected to but rat substitute."

As was generally the case, Lowell's decision was not contested: the quoins were left unpainted.

2323-2

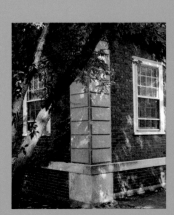

**Leaving imitation stone unpainted.**

Lowell, promulgator of the grand plan, was also a master of detail. On one inspection tour of the new HBS campus, he espied an

unacceptable color on a freshly painted wall. To the painter's astonishment, the diminutive Lowell strode across the room, clambered up a convenient ladder, and scrawled "NO—A.L.L." on the offending wall.

In May, 1925, Mrs. F. E. Heard—Secretary of the School—traveled to New York City to begin selecting furnishings and equipment for the new campus. Her first stop was Macy's, where Herbert Straus gave her suggestions about possible vendors. It cost roughly $15,000 to equip each dormitory with beds, chairs (left), desks, tables, and bookcases. Dining hall equipment and furniture cost, all told, an additional $17,500.

As usual, President Lowell made his opinions known on the subject. Regarding a particular table design, he commented, "It could be improved by having the supports near the floor run diagonally between the legs instead of in a square, and having a leaf for magazines, etc."

IN OCTOBER, 1926 — almost exactly sixteen months after ground was broken — 521 Business School students, and 275 students from other Harvard departments, moved into the School's new dormitories. (The buildings now had names: Baker, to whom the honor of naming the buildings had been assigned, had in turn honored various secretaries of the Treasury with memorial dormitories.) Work on Mellon Hall, on the swampiest part of the Soldiers Field site, had fallen behind, and the building was not completed until November. Two floors in Gallatin Hall were reserved for faculty offices until the administration building (named by Baker for his friend, J. P. Morgan) could be completed. Like Morgan Hall, Baker Library — so called at Donham's insistence — was not yet completed; both were finished in February of 1927. Against the odds, however, the dormitories had been finished in time for the fall semester, providing University housing for all Business School students who wanted it, and supplying to the School a welcome infusion of rental income. It had been a close finish: the plaster in the dormitories was barely dry; and faculty members had been pressed into service the day before the students' arrival, helping to prepare the rooms for occupancy.

The Bakers were pleased with the progress of the campus. They had both grown personally fond of Dean Donham, who had faithfully executed their wishes throughout the design and construction stages. The elder Baker, through Donham, was still urging the University to erect bell towers atop the dormitories facing the river — a design element included in the original plans, but later dropped as a cost-saving measure. (He also pressed Donham on the Dean's House, both directly and through his son: "He [is] very anxious," wrote George Jr. of his father, "to see you settled right there with the School.") In December, the Bakers asked Donham to arrange for a dedication ceremony for the new buildings, to be held sometime in the spring, after the projected completion of Morgan Hall and Baker Library.

Meanwhile, Donham was finding himself in a familiar circumstance: the gradual resolution of one major problem — the securing and construction of a campus — coincided with the onset of another. His letter to George Baker, Jr., in the previous February

On December 30, 1926, the eight children of Rhode Island Senator Nelson W. Aldrich donated his collection of publications on banking and finance to Baker Library. With George Baker's permission, they also decorated and furnished a room to house the collection in Baker Library, then under construction.

The "Aldrich Library of Finance" was installed the following spring. It remained a separate collection until the early 1970s, when it was assimilated into the larger Baker collection. At that time, the Aldrich room was made available for recreational reading by HBS students.

had hinted that the School, lacking endowment, was still overly dependent on tuition and other fees. The steady rise in tuition had reflected increases in every aspect of the School's operation. The cost of instruction, for example, had increased 128 percent between 1920 and 1927; the cost of administration was up 312 percent; research, 532 percent; and student health (including, for the first time, a School physician's salary), 932 percent.

Faculty salaries, as noted earlier, had not kept pace with those outside academia. The $2 million of needed endowment that Donham had described to the younger Baker was required, in part, to keep teachers on the faculty in the face of lucrative offers from the business world. In February, 1926, the problem was still somewhat hypothetical; but by January of 1927, as Donham reported in a confidential memorandum to his Visiting Committee, circumstances had changed for the worse.

"This problem," he wrote, "while not quite new, has become suddenly acute. It has perhaps the gravest significance of all our problems, because it threatens to destroy our foundations. . . . Today, the most burdensome care of the Dean is that of keeping the services of our most effective men, in direct competition with the business world."

Outside consulting, Donham noted, was one problem: "During the last year there has been an astonishing increase in the demand from great business houses ready to pay liberally for part-time services of our teaching and research staff." In fact, the faculty had set up a committee to investigate this problem over a year earlier, and it appeared that the guidelines it had recommended were beginning to work to good effect.

"The other aspect of the difficulty is more alarming," Donham continued. "It comes in the form of flattering offers made to our men by business interests bidding for their full time. On the whole, it is remarkable that they resist these offers to the extent that they do. Such offers frequently involve the doubling, trebling, or quadrupling of salaries, besides other inducements."

Within the previous year, the Dean noted, the School had "lost to business" Professors Dillon, Edwards, Hettinger, and Starch. Academia was also proving predatory: "Professor Jackson, who was loaned by us temporarily to Stanford University, has been asked to stay there at nearly double his present salary, and the chancellor of one university recently expressed a willingness to pay $20,000 salary to a man, preferably from our faculty, who could organize and develop his business school." This was substantially more than anyone on the HBS faculty, including Donham, was then being paid.

Consulting, in Donham's summary, represented a partial solution, if controlled adequately. Tuition increases, applied to salaries, might be considered,

George F. Baker, junior and senior, on June 24, 1926, following the elder Baker's receipt of an honorary doctorate of laws from Harvard. President Lowell cited Baker as "a great banker, whose labors have not clogged his sensibility, whose power has not dimmed his magnanimity, whose position has not impaired his simplicity."

"were it not for the fact that the Business School tuition is already the highest charged by any university school in the country." The only real solution, he concluded, was to build up the School's endowment: "The income of a fund of $2,000,000 would save the School from what may be considered its greatest danger."

The Visiting Committee, it can be assumed, agreed with Donham's assessment of the gravity of the problem. What neither the Committee nor Donham knew was that the elusive solution was close at hand.

"I have never been accused of a lack of nerve," the Dean wrote to L. E. Phillips, the vice president and general manager of Phillips Petroleum on January 28, "although these omissions have not been uniformly complimentary. I have a problem on my hands now as to which I am turning every stone and you are one of them, although I say quite frankly that I shall not be surprised if I don't succeed in turning this particular stone."

Donham enclosed a copy of his memorandum to the Visiting Committee, and added a few pertinent statistics. The School's maximum pay, reached only after fifteen years of service, was $8,000. Fully 40 percent of the faculty had received offers of "shockingly good" business positions in the past few months, and several had resolved to take them.

"Last week," Donham continued, "I was fortunate enough to convince one of our friends, whom I have been trying to interest in the School for several years, that this situation was of great importance to the future of the School. He was good enough to offer me (I tell it to you in confidence) one million dollars if I could match it immediately."

The friend of the School to whom Donham had promised a temporary anonymity was George F. Baker, who was now prepared to contribute $1 million to the School's endowment. ("You make life very much worth living," Donham had written in response to Baker's conditional offer.) And while the Dean was not able to "turn over the particular stone" of L. E. Phillips, he soon had good news to report to Baker:

"It gives me a great deal of pleasure to wire you last night that we had been able to comply with your condition of a million to enable us to put in an adequate salary scale in the School by matching it with another. I am not at liberty at the moment to give you the name of the other donor, and I have not disclosed your name to him."

Dedication of the Weeks Bridge, May 16, 1927. The bridge provided both symbolic and functional links between the Business School and the University.

## Minimizing the separation

In their initial discussions of the campus to be erected on the Soldiers Field site, HBS administrators contemplated separate heating systems for each building. Harvard's Inspector of Buildings and Grounds, Walter S. Burke, advised against that approach, and in favor of a central heating system. Burke's case was persuasive, and the Committee to Extend the National Service of Harvard University included a Business School power plant in its plans.

But the same arguments of efficiency and economy could be made, on a larger scale, for tying the Soldiers Field site into the Boston Elevated Railway's power station, located on Memorial Drive in Cambridge, and then serving the University's main campus. If steam and electricity could be piped across the river, the new Business School campus would share in the University's relatively low utility rates. Two problems presented them-

selves, however. First, Boston's Edison Electric Illuminating Company, which would ordinarily service the site, would have to agree to the arrangement. Second, a means would have to be devised for getting the utilities across the river.

Dean Donham approached Edison Electric in the spring of 1925, hoping to secure permission for the plan. He argued that by allowing HBS to take power from Cambridge, Edison Electric could avoid having to generate new electrical capacity for the Allston area. Edison's administrators were extremely reluctant to set such a precedent, but finally agreed, reasoning that the utility could in this way support the School's research and teaching in public utilities management.

The second challenge—spanning the Charles—was more formidable. Donham quickly settled on the idea of a footbridge. ("It was obviously easier to obtain money for a memorial bridge than a memorial tunnel," recalled architectural advisor Killam.) A bridge with one end at the foot of De Wolfe Street in Cambridge, and the other at the southeastern tip of the Soldiers Field site, would also serve another important purpose. "It is the

desire of the Faculty to minimize as much as possible the separation of the School from other parts of the University," Donham noted in his 1925 report to the president. "The proposal for a footbridge . . . . is therefore of great interest to us."

The Massachusetts legislature had by then approved the footbridge proposal. It remained for Harvard's administrators to find sponsors for the bridge—a difficult task, made more difficult by the publicity afforded George Baker's $5-million gift. It was not until the following October, in fact, that Donham was able to announce to the Corporation that he had found a group of backers for the bridge. These were thirteen friends and former business associates of John W. Weeks, who was then retiring as President Harding's secretary of war. (Weeks had previously been a partner in the brokerage firm of Hornblower & Weeks; the mayor of Newton, Massachusetts; a U. S. representative; and a U. S. senator.) The Weeks group had agreed to pay up to $200,000 for a footbridge in his honor.

In January, 1926, Harvard's President Lowell asked McKim, Mead & White for a

status report on the Soldiers Field campus, then in its seventh month of construction. Barring any unanticipated labor difficulties, the project's chief architect replied, the dormitory complex would be largely completed by the September 30th deadline.

"There is one part of the construction that is troubling us a great deal," McKim, Mead & White's representative warned Lowell in the last week of January. "The buildings cannot be used until such time as service connections are made across the proposed [Weeks] bridge over the Charles River. We understand that the exact location of the bridge is still undecided and that no appointment has been made for the consulting engineer to design the layout." The contractor, furthermore, would need sufficient time after the completion of the bridge "to insure the proper service connections for both heating and electricity with the Business School group."

The news was distressing to Lowell, who then contacted the mayors of both Cambridge and Boston, as well as the relevant state and Metropolitan District Commission authorities, seeking their help in

speeding up the project. As a result, the bridge was soon under construction, and was dedicated on schedule, in May of 1927. The dedication ceremony had a distinctly military flavor: the Army, Navy, Marine Corps, and National Guard were represented by regiments on both ends of the bridge; an Air Corps squadron patrolled above; and small Navy vessels were anchored in the Charles.

By this time, of course, the bridge had been in use for nearly eight months: as a steam tunnel and electrical conduit. At Lowell's instruction, Buildings and Grounds' Burke had rigged up a temporary pipe across the unfinished footbridge in September of 1926, to provide steam to heat—and dry the plaster in—the Business School's new dormitories.

"I feel perfectly certain after talking with Mr. Burke and the builders," Donham informed Lowell on September 9, "that the heat will be on in all the buildings several days before the earliest arrivals of students. The builders feel that if this is done, the plaster, which is already drying out rapidly under the natural circulation of air they are keeping up, will be in good condition for men to live in."

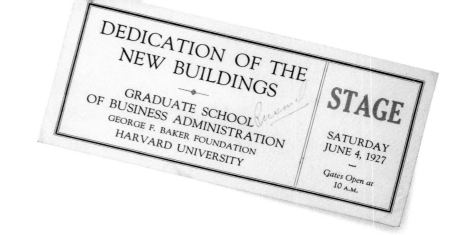

The other donor to whom Donham referred was William Ziegler, head of the Royal Baking Powder Company. Early in the $10-million campaign, Ziegler had offered $135,000 for a building in memory of his father, founder of Royal Baking Powder and a self-styled arctic explorer. George F. Baker's gift of the entire campus had foreclosed that possibility, but Ziegler had remained interested in supporting the School. In the summer of 1926, he had offered to pay $10,000 a year for two years to expand the School's research and teaching in international relationships; he had also informed Donham that he intended eventually to endow this work on a permanent basis, with a gift of up to $500,000.

Donham was careful to give credit where credit was due — particularly since Donald K. David, the young assistant dean who had successfully cultivated Ziegler — had earlier impressed Baker. "One thing which I am very glad to write you," Donham concluded, "is that in securing this gift Mr. David had worked with me, and that the final accomplishment is largely the result of his efforts."

On March 3, 1927 — four days before the Business School conducted the first classes held on its new campus — Donham summed up the recent course of events to George Baker, Jr. "Your father made me personally very happy," he wrote, "by telling me that this additional gift was largely on the basis of personal fondness for me, and if I ever wanted anyone to be fond of me I have wanted your father to be. It is impossible to tell you in a few words how critical a situation in the School is solved by this gift."

ON THE MORNING OF JUNE 4, 1927, four thousand people were gathered in the courtyard in front of the Harvard Business School's new library. The campus being dedicated that morning actually was not quite complete. Construction had not begun on the Dean's House; work on the four planned "instructors' houses" had been halted after their foundations had been laid; the rear extensions on Baker Library were still in the planning stage; and the top floor of Morgan Hall remained a shell. A temporary fence along the rear perimeter of the site screened from view acres of marsh that had yet to be filled.

Inside the main court, the bare look of the new buildings had been softened by parallel rows of newly planted trees, stretching from the library toward the river. For the occasion of the dedication, the effect of the trees had been reinforced by a small thicket of potted plants, which lined the base of the temporary platforms in front of the library.

**Dean Donham addressing the dedication assembly. In the week following the ceremony, the dean of Harvard's Graduate School of Education — a friend of Donham's — teased his fellow administrator: "I ought to have sent you from this School on Saturday a bunch of flowers or a case of whiskey or a potted elm tree or a check for another million dollars."**

**An aerial view of the dedication exercises. The land to the east of the campus (at left in photograph) still remained to be filled, and a gangplank connected the campus with the Weeks Bridge (not pictured).**

Just inside the library entrance, a freshly cast bronze tablet had been hung on the otherwise bare walls of the main hall. The inscription on the tablet had been composed by President Lowell: "This group of buildings dedicated on June 4, 1927, and an endowment therefor were given by George Fisher Baker, banker and philanthropist, to promote knowledge and integrity in the art of finance, industry, and commerce, objects doubly advanced by his generous gift and by his lifelong example."

Bishop Lawrence opened the dedication ceremonies with an invocation, and gave a short speech on behalf of George F. Baker, who was seated behind him on the platform. Baker, now 87 years old, had fallen ill earlier in the spring, and some doubt had arisen as to whether he would be able to attend the ceremonies. By April, he had recovered enough to attend American Telephone's board meeting in Boston; on that same occasion, he had also spent a contemplative half-hour sitting by himself in Baker Library's cavernous reading room.

**George F. Baker and Dean Donham at the dedication.**

**As part of the dedication celebrations, the HBS campus was illuminated at night. President Lowell, pleased with the effect, later arranged to illuminate similarly the bell towers of the River Houses — the undergraduate residential complex on the Cambridge side of the Charles which Lowell built following the completion of the new Business School campus.**

As a result of that April visit, Dean Donham had grown confident that Baker would be able to attend the dedication. Donham's own circumstances, however, had taken two unexpected turns for the worse: his wife had been gravely injured in a car accident in late February, and he himself had been confined to his house for two weeks in April, suffering from fatigue and a debilitating renal condition. While he would soon suffer a serious relapse, on this day in June he was able to serve as host to the School's patron.

After a stirring address by Owen D. Young — the chairman of the General Electric Company, often mentioned as a potential Presidential candidate — George F. Baker stood and approached the podium, where President Lowell was waiting. In the hours preceding the ceremony, Baker had appeared decidedly feeble, declining to move from the uncomfortable antique chair he had first come upon. Now, though, distinguished by his black frock coat, white vest, and muttonchop whiskers, he walked steadily.

"Mr. President and Fellows," Baker began, "ladies and gentlemen. First, I want to thank you for this kind

and ever-to-be-remembered reception. These buildings have turned out so unexpectedly fine that I must extend congratulations to you. I hope and believe that this school is to be the standard for all others, but it must be remembered always that the standard of excellence which must be maintained comes not simply from the outside of the buildings, but from the work and training on the inside."

By now, both stage fright and the emotions of the moment had caught up with Baker. His eyes filled with tears, and his voice faltered: "Mr. President, it gives me great pleasure to present to you the keys to these buildings."

There followed a sustained round of applause, and it was several minutes before Lowell was able to respond. "Mr. Baker," Lowell finally rejoined, "I hope that your happiness may be commensurate with the privilege which you have provided for generation after generation of young men, seeking to enter on the career which you yourself have adorned."

The Dean's House, a project of particular interest to George F. Baker, was completed in 1929, on the outskirts of the campus. The Olmsted landscaping plan for the building was made possible by a gift from the HBS Visiting Committee.

## Planting and settling

Although the Olmsted firm was hired in April of 1925 to landscape the Business School's new campus, much of the landscaping work was deferred for several years. Lack of money and an unsettled terrain were the chief obstacles.

"The [Olmsted] plans call eventually for a total of $18,000," as Visiting Committee member N. Penrose Hallowell informed Thomas Lamont in April, 1928, "but because two of the eastern quads are still settling, they cannot be planted for probably two years, so $10,000 is all that is needed now. If you have seen the buildings recently you appreciate how badly planting is needed." Hallowell then solicited Lamont's support for a fund to address the problem.

Four months later, Dean Donham—just returned from a European vacation— informed President Lowell of a pleasant surprise he had received. "The Visiting Committee of the Business School, past and present," he wrote, "with a few other friends of the School have just sent me quite unexpectedly a check for $10,000 for planting on the School grounds."

EARLY IN HIS FIRST WEEK as Dean of the Harvard Business School, Wallace B. Donham asked marketing professor Melvin T. Copeland to join him in his University Hall office for a conference. Donham quickly got to the point: he understood that Copeland planned to produce a textbook for the first-year Marketing course. The Dean argued against that plan, and proposed instead that Copeland produce a "problem book."

Copeland heard out Donham's arguments with some misgivings. He was becoming re-acquainted, after his war service in Washington, with the rapid changes in assignment that seemed to characterize his work at Harvard. Acting Dean Schaub had made an urgent request in January of that year—1919—that Copeland come back from Washington to teach Business Policy to returning war veterans. Copeland was then suffering from pneumonia, which had followed a bout with a virulent and pandemic flu virus, and he later recalled that he had been "too ill to say anything but 'yes.'" Upon his return, he had been given an even larger responsibility: marketing authority Paul T. Cherington had resigned from the faculty, and Copeland, his

William Cunningham
embodied a Business School
faculty ideal: the able practi-
tioner turned competent
teacher. Dean Donham, like
Dean Gay before him, rarely
found both attributes in one
person.

**Overleaf:**
**Donald K. David (left)**
**and Melvin T. Copeland**
**(second from left), at**
**a 1921 comptrollers' con-**
**ference. As HBS faculty**
**members, both made key**
**contributions in the 1920s**
**to the development of the**
**case method.**

former assistant, had been left in sole charge of the School's Marketing course. The course lacked an adequate textbook, and Copeland had decided to produce one to supplement his lectures. Now the new Dean, only recently installed, was suggesting a radical departure.

Donham had reasons, of course, for selecting his Marketing professor for the proposed "problem book" experiment. With seven years of experience at the Business School, Copeland was a relatively senior member of the faculty; yet, compared with his faculty peers, he was also relatively flexible in his approach to teaching. He had tried to follow Dean Gay's 1912 dictum—to "keep the students talking"—and his approach to marketing "problems" seemed promising to Donham. In the week before his conference with Donham, for example, Copeland had asked his students to consider the case of a New England department store faced with the question of when in the market cycle to buy silk piece-goods. "Make a report to the President of this store," the assignment concluded, "advising him as to the policy which you believe that he should follow. State reasons concisely for your conclusions."

These problems elicited *written* responses, however, and Donham was proposing to transform the problems into case studies suitable for classroom discussion. In using the word "problems" to describe what he had in mind, the Dean hoped to distinguish business cases from those used in law schools.

Again, Donham had ample reason for experimenting with a new teaching technique. Business School students—already annoyed by their cramped physical circumstances—were beginning to voice complaints about the curriculum's seeming lack of relevance, and the inadequate teaching skills of certain professors. Students had taken to stamping their feet during lectures they considered boring or irrelevant, and faculty lore suggests that students were particularly unhappy with Professor Copeland's own dry lecturing style.

Donham had concluded that the first objection was valid: with the notable exceptions of finance professor O. M. W. Sprague and railroad expert William J. Cunningham, the faculty and curriculum were, indeed, weak on practical information. Perhaps a variation on the "case method" that had informed and enlivened his

own law school education could be devised to solve the problem. Without a doubt, students encountering a modified case method would be forced to become "more active mentally," as he later put it — more actively engaged in the learning process. At the same time, the discussion method might help the School's weaker teachers become more effective.

Copeland agreed to take on the assignment, in spite of his other pressing obligations, and in spite of the seemingly unrealistic deadline for the project. The Dean wanted the "problem book" available for use in the fall of 1920, which meant that the manuscript had to go to the printer within six months.

"I wrote all the cases myself while running the courses in Marketing and Business Policy and serving as the Director of the Bureau of Business Research," Copeland later recalled. "The material for the cases was obtained from a variety of sources. Some grew directly out of the work of the Bureau. Others were situations that I had run across, either as an agent of the Bureau or in the course of the Bureau's correspondence. Still others had come to my attention during the period that I was working in Washington from April, 1917, to December, 1918. Others were obtained, in substance, from published articles or books, and a very few were obtained directly from business men for that particular purpose."

With Copeland at work on his compilation of problems, Donham began engaging the rest of the faculty in a broad discussion of the School's course content and methods. At the first faculty meeting following his discussion with Copeland, Donham outlined a plan to extend the scope of the Bureau of Business Research, and asked faculty members to provide him with a list of "concrete problems which justify investigation and report by the Bureau." He also noted that he could find no record, official or unofficial, of what was being taught in the School's courses, and argued that there should be a means of documenting the questions that were considered in class. Without such a record, he said, there could be no continuity, and each new instructor in the expanding School would have to begin his teaching from scratch.

Wallace Donham's periodic lectures to HBS students usually reflected his experiences with the Bay State Street Railway. Cecil E. Fraser, a member of the MBA Class of 1921 and later an HBS faculty member, took notes on Donham's

September 29, 1920, lecture, in which the Dean suggested that "labor must have some hand in management, in so much as it affects them."

In fact, it was in part Donham's dissatisfaction with lectures, and also with existing approaches to labor problems, which led to a new "case method" of teaching.

Toward the same end, Donham organized a series of informal faculty dinners. In advance of these meetings, individual faculty members were asked to prepare descriptions of their courses, to be shared with and discussed by their peers. Drawing on the substance of these discussions, on talks with President Lowell, and on his own experience, Donham next prepared a lengthy memorandum, which he circulated to the faculty in early 1920. The memorandum, divided into eight sections, effectively defined the new Dean's conception of the School.

"How," Donham asked his faculty rhetorically, "can we state the aims of the School?" His answer was twofold. First, the School would equip the student for business by providing a background of facts and principles, and by "giving the student training for practice in dealing with business problems." Second, it would "fit the student into business and society." The latter objective necessitated instruction in both the "relation of the individual to his business opportunity," and the "relation of businessmen to society."

In this first section of his memorandum, Donham was not describing a School substantially different from that headed by his predecessor. In the next two sections, however—on the "Method of Instruction" and the design of specific courses—sharp distinctions began to emerge. Donham proposed that the important fields of business be divided "not on an individual specialized business basis (such as steel, paper, etc.) but by subject matter, such as Marketing, Factory Management, Employment Management, etc." He proposed further that instruction be "based in large part on specific facts or problems stated in varied forms as they present themselves to the businessman. The student should be required in each course to investigate facts, to sort undigested material, to state problems, to analyze problems, to reach conclusions and to present the subject matter and his decision orally and in writing as he will be required to do in business."

Donham argued that all business could be divided into two categories: the routine and the unusual. The routine tasks of business should be learned on the job —although the student of business needed to be made aware of the "practically universal opportunity" to improve upon existing business routines. "Generally speaking," the Dean continued, "all business not of a

The Public Utilities faculty group, in the later 1920s. Except for transportation and banking, which had the sustaining benefit of endowed professorships, Public Utility Management was the only area of specialized teaching to flourish during Dean Donham's tenure, principally because it enjoyed substantial industry support.

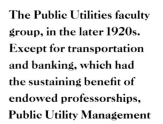

In April, 1922, Dean Donham asked Harvard Law School Dean Edward H. Warren (above) for advice on compiling case books. "A fire must be kindled in the student's mind," responded Warren. "There is no use in trying to set fire first to some great log; you have to set fire to some kindling and then let the fire spread to bigger things."

routine nature presents itself in the form of problems." He identified four categories of such problems: a mass of unorganized material, a specific problem in need of solution, a request from subordinates for a particular action, and an order from a superior needing implementation.

"Cannot a systematic effort be made to enrich the problem content of the various courses," Donham asked, "by getting regularly from industry problems which are current and illustrative? Cannot the Dean's office be of value to the staff in this way? It appears to me that it should be possible to work out such contacts with industry that we might in a comparatively short time get several hundred problems in each field."

By favoring a *functional* course orientation, Donham was in one sense only formally recognizing the curricular change that a preponderance of Business School students had effected, over the previous decade, through their course selections. On the other hand, he was going against a powerful external trend — the trend toward industry specialization. The School's entry in the 1919–20 Harvard University catalogue, for example, affirmed that the aim of the School was "to give to each individual student a practical and specialized professional training suitable to the particular business which he plans to enter." In November of 1919, the Business School faculty had declared itself willing to work with the American Pulp and Paper Association to develop specialized training in that field. Now, only two months later, the Dean was asking the faculty — some of them authorities in printing, insurance, and so on — to abandon specialized training.

It was not a merely academic question. Industry groups like the American Pulp and Paper Association willingly subsidized the courses they called forth. And some students, at least, were still demanding the specialized training that Harvard's catalogue promised. The typical student, Donham wrote in the fall of 1920, "wished in far too many cases to make himself into a narrow specialist." It might also have been argued that the trend in the business education "industry" was running in the other direction. When the Wharton School established its MBA program in 1921, for example, it did so in the interest of specialization: its new MBA candidates were to acquire superior "technical equipment" by taking 10 of their 28 courses, as well as writing a thesis, in a specialized field of study.

Within a month, Donham had won a partial victory. The function-oriented Factory Management and Finance courses joined Accounting and Marketing as required first-year courses. Business Policy, the integrative second-year course, was also made a required subject. According to the faculty minutes, however, the changes were made in part "to allow concentration to a greater extent than is now possible," by enabling students to take specialized electives earlier. The nine study groups established by the faculty — Accounting, Actuarial Training, Banking, Business Statistics, Foreign Trade, Industrial Management, Lumbering, Marketing, and Transportation — reflected a similar ambivalence on the subject of specialization.

MARKETING PROBLEMS

BY
MELVIN THOMAS COPELAND, Ph.D.
PROFESSOR OF MARKETING
DIRECTOR OF BUREAU OF BUSINESS RESEARCH
GRADUATE SCHOOL OF BUSINESS ADMINISTRATION,
HARVARD UNIVERSITY

NEW YORK   A. W. SHAW COMPANY
CHICAGO

**Melvin Copeland (right) wrote the first business "case book" for his Marketing course. When the Harvard University Press declined to publish the projected series of HBS case books, publisher A.W. Shaw willingly took on the task.**

The subject of teaching *method*, discussed at length in Donham's sweeping memorandum, was never brought to a formal vote by the faculty. There was, after all, nothing more tangible to evaluate than the Dean's concept, since Melvin Copeland's experiment was still several months from completion. (Donham had a clear gift for making the speculative seem concrete, however. In March of 1920, the faculty voted in favor of seeking a commercial publisher to produce the projected series of "problem books," since the Harvard University Press had declined to do so without a Business School subsidy.)

Furthermore, the Dean had chosen not to force the issue. On the contrary, he had made it clear that not all faculty members would be expected to conform to his new model, since not all courses would prove equally amenable to a problem-method approach. As he noted in his first report to President Lowell, produced in the summer of 1920, "Indeed, at the present moment we fail to see how several courses may be so treated and we shall always have certain advantages from a diversity of methods at the School."

Melvin Copeland, meanwhile, had to develop the prototype on which the Dean's concept might stand or fall. Copeland had organized his problem book on the basis of his Marketing course outline of 1915, which began with the consumer's point of view ("because every student was a consumer") and proceeded into retailing and other marketing areas. By June of 1920, the manuscript was ready to go to the printer. It consisted of 216 relatively short problems, for the most part not readily distinguishable from the written-assignment "problems" from which they had been derived.

At the first meeting of the Marketing class in September, 1920, Copeland outlined a "method of analysis" that he wanted his students to use in pondering the material in the School's first problem book — the recently-published *Marketing Problems*:

- Crystallize the problem.

- Break it up into constituent parts.

- What questions must be decided?

- List factors for and against each question of policy decided.

- Avoid one-sided analysis and snap judgements.

- Harmonize decisions on the constituent problems and reach a final conclusion.

- The conclusion is less important than the analysis but a conclusion must be reached.

- Differences of opinion are welcome.

- Distinguish between questions of fact and questions of policy. It is in the latter that we are interested.

- A policy once established furnishes a precedent. It sets up rules which can be carried out by subordinates. Hence our job is to study policies, for we are approaching the subject from the standpoint of the business executive, and not from that of a clerk.

The class—which included future faculty members Winslow A. Hosmer, Charles I. Gragg, and Carl N. Schmalz—responded enthusiastically to the innovative course, in spite of the many "deficiencies" that Copeland later attributed to it.

Even before student reaction to the "problem method" experiment could be assessed, however, Donham approached Copeland with a new experiment in mind. Alvan Simonds, a member of Donham's college class, had contributed $5,000 in unrestricted funds to the School. Donham wanted the Bureau of Business Research, under Copeland's direction, to use the money to research and produce "problems." Copeland readily agreed, and two young members of the Bureau's staff, Richard Lennihan and Clinton P. Biddle, were assigned to the task.

Lennihan had been Copeland's assistant at the War Industries Board in Washington, and had followed Copeland to Harvard in 1919; Biddle was a 1920 graduate of the School, who had joined the Bureau staff shortly after graduation. Together, they began gathering material on labor relations, a field of particular interest to Donham. By June, 1921, the Dean was satisfied that the approach was workable, and Donald K. David, another recent graduate of the School, was hired to begin problem research in retail store management. (This was a subject suggested, in part, by the Bureau's extensive statistical research in the retail field.) In addition, several students between their first and second years were hired for the summer, allowing an expansion of the research into the banking, industrial management, and sales management fields.

By October of 1921, some $25,000 had been spent on these projects, as well as on similar efforts by individual faculty members. Donham likened these costs to capital expenditures in industry, which could not be fairly charged to current students in the form of tuition fees. He therefore took personal responsibility for raising the needed funds among supporters in the business community. And while fundraising for case research proved a difficult task, it was facilitated by evidence of solid progress. The research effort had produced immediate results: there were now in print four additional "case books"—as they were beginning to be called—with another expected shortly. Some 90,000 mimeographed pages of case material had been prepared for distribution to students between November, 1920, and July of the following year.

The second case book, following Copeland's *Marketing Problems*, was *The Law in Business Problems*, by Professor Lincoln Schaub and Harvard Law School teaching fellow Nathan Isaacs. Schaub had needed little prompting to adopt Donham's "problem method," having used mimeographed Law School cases to teach the Business School's law-oriented courses before the war. Schaub and Isaacs, though, collaborated to produce a case book very different from its antecedents in the law field—using, as it did, particular business subjects as organizing themes for the discussion of related law doctrines.

*The Law in Business Problems* also presented the reader with a novel blend of text and case material. Case material was introduced gradually, until the end of

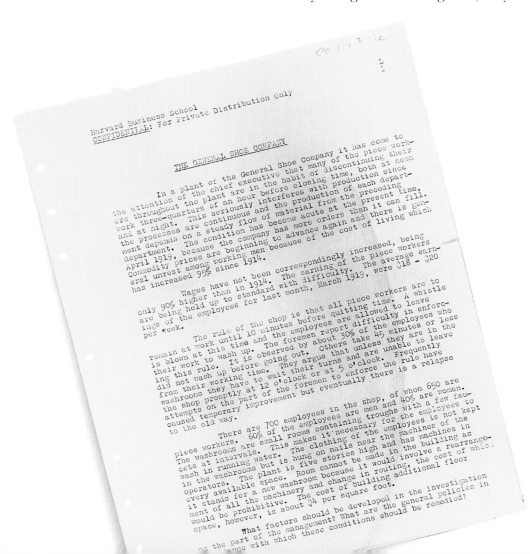

Leon C. Marshall, a founder of the University of Chicago's School of Commerce and Administration, also helped to found the Association of Collegiate Schools of Business in 1917.

Malcolm McNair —holder of a Harvard College master's degree in English — was an early example of an HBS instructor and research assistant who eventually became a faculty member. In Dean Donham's tenure, there was still no formal academic training available for teachers of business.

the book became a case book with only minor interruptions by the authors. For Schaub and Isaacs, the pedagogical advantages of this approach outweighed its commercial disadvantages. "The authors realized that this arrangement would spoil the symmetry of the book and probably puzzle reviewers," Isaacs later recalled, "but they were determined to shape the work for the practical needs of an actual student body."

In his 1921 report to President Lowell, Dean Donham reflected on the differences between law cases and business cases. The compiler of the law case book, he wrote, focused on precedent and the "legal method of thought." This focus was achieved at the expense of the *facts* of the case, which were usually summarized in a brief statement or in a finding of a court or jury. In business cases, on the other hand, precedent had no authority, but "every fact of business which can be brought in is an asset to the student, giving him a broader foundation for executive judgement." Business cases, furthermore, contained no "decisions" comparable to opinions of the court; nor could they contain the reasoning by which a business decision had been reached.

"These differences," Donham continued, "caused us some concern in the beginning, and in practice they clearly impose on the teacher of business a definite obligation to finish the class-room discussion of each case with a clean cut summary of the reasons and analogies which appeal to him as most important for its solution."

While Donham constantly emphasized facts, he did so for methodological reasons. Every case, he noted, must have "the atmosphere and detail of reality." It was facts, meticulously recorded by firsthand observation, that would recreate the reality of business for the student, and enable him to enhance his "executive judgement." Reality, therefore, was to be brought to the classroom, and Donham was searching in particular for the reality of *decision making*. The specific facts of individual cases—and the solutions suggested by students—represented secondary concerns.

Method, in other words, overshadowed content. When the recently organized Association of Collegiate Schools of Business (ACSB) proposed to focus its 1921

meeting on the appropriate content of a business curriculum, Donham protested to L. C. Marshall, Edwin Gay's friend who now headed the University of Chicago's School of Commerce and Administration. "You know I have a perfect mania on the subject," Donham wrote, "but I should really like to see more of method and less of content on the program. To me, method is so much more important than content that there is no comparison."

Donham tried and failed to win over the ACSB delegates to his point of view. His failure in this instance, however, was mitigated by his gradual success at converting the members of his own faculty. Throughout the early 1920s, the Dean sponsored a series of faculty lunches which focused on the problems of collecting and using cases. "Some members of the faculty," recalled Copeland, "welcomed enthusiastically the innovation which the Dean was sponsoring. The attitudes of other members ranged all the way from lukewarmness to covert hostility."

A 1924 innovation by Copeland's Marketing staff sharpened one aspect of the debate. In the previous year, Copeland had taught both sections of the first-year Marketing course. But when the growing student population necessitated a third section in the fall of 1924, Copeland assigned that section to Malcolm P. McNair, a young instructor and member of the Bureau's research staff. Copeland and McNair taught the course following the same outline, using the same cases, and assigning the same reports and exams. At times, they took over each other's classes. "The case system," Copeland concluded, "made possible the handling of a large class in manageable sections that would amount, in my judgement, to a system of interchangeable parts so far as the instructors are concerned. . . . This sort of thing would obviously be wholly impossible under a lecture system."

Donham later greatly expanded the concept of faculty interchangeability: not only would professors be expected to substitute for their peers within an area of specialization, but they would also be asked to teach in fields entirely outside of their own expertise. Even the limited version of "interchangeability" suggested by the 1924 experiment, however, raised strong objections.

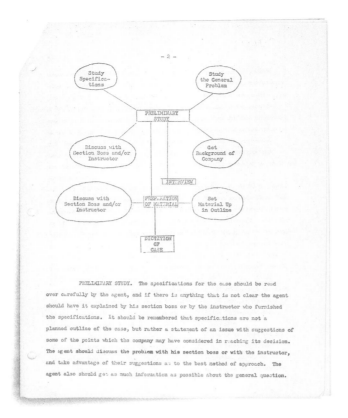

PRELIMINARY STUDY. The specifications for the case should be read over carefully by the agent, and if there is anything that is not clear the agent should have it explained by his section boss or by the instructor who furnished the specifications. It should be remembered that specifications are not a planned outline of the case, but rather a statement of an issue with suggestions of some of the points which the company may have considered in reaching its decision. The agent should discuss the problem with his section boss or with the instructor, and take advantage of their suggestions as to the best method of approach. The agent also should get as much information as possible about the general question.

**A Bureau of Business Research case-writing "flow chart" from the early 1920s suggests a budding organizational problem: the professor, the presumed generator of the case, is nowhere mentioned.**

At least one faculty member resigned in protest; others decided simply to ignore the case method. But Donham was, by all accounts, persuasive. He also had an important advantage presented by circumstance. The faculty was expanding rapidly—from 15 in 1919 to 24 in 1923—and the Dean was evidently careful to appoint new faculty members who would be sympathetic to his goals. By 1923, he was able to report to President Lowell that two-thirds of the School's courses were taught by the case system.

Once again, student enrollment patterns were helping to determine the direction of the School. Polished lecturers such as O. M. W. Sprague continued to enjoy large and attentive audiences, but students were drifting away from the faculty's less stimulating lecturers and toward case-oriented courses. "I want to tell you," Dean Donham wrote to a New York supporter in 1922, "that in my experience the last two years lead me to believe much more strongly in what we are doing along this [case-method] line than I had any conception I could believe in it. The results of the duplication of the method in the School have been astonishingly satisfactory. Among other things, there is a decided tendency in the School to elect the courses where the case system has been developed in preference to those where it has not been developed."

Melvin Copeland was involved in another controversy growing out of the case method, this time in his capacity as Director of the Bureau of Business Research. Donham had anticipated that the case-collection process would be a temporary endeavor— perhaps of two or three years' duration—which would largely cease after enough cases had been collected.

Given that assumption, and given the existing resources of the Bureau, it seemed sensible to centralize the seemingly finite task of case collection under Copeland's supervision.

Trouble arose when this theory was put into practice, however. To employ the Bureau, a faculty member had to prepare a course outline and case specifications. These specifications were turned over to a "research supervisor," who, after identifying a businessman who had faced the issues in question, assigned a case writer. But this sequence assumed that the instructor already knew all the issues in need of investigation in a given course, and could suggest the cases that best illustrated those issues. Given the relatively uninformed state of business education and the novelty of the case method, this was rarely true.

Confronted with what they considered to be inadequate case specifications, the Bureau's researchers were at times critical of their faculty collaborators. "The way in which the Bureau's work for [Business Policy] is now being handled is most unsatisfactory," one supervisor complained to Copeland about a course administered by Professor Neil Borden. At that time, the course was a composite of case material and lectures by visiting businessmen. "Some material has been collected by our agents in emergency. Mr. Borden has given the agent a general idea of what the lecturer is planning to talk about, but no specifications as to the principles that he would like to have brought out."

The Bureau's role in case collection was presumed to relieve pressure on faculty members, but in fact it often created burdensome new responsibilities. One professor argued in the spring of 1924 that while the field agents did indeed spare him the task of "running around from plant to plant," the preparation of the course outline took inordinate amounts of time. "The activities of the field agents," Copeland noted with some pride, exerted a "continuous pressure on [the professor], which makes his load far from light."

## Unsung heroes

Except for staff lists, scant record remains of the hundreds of HBS staff members who made possible the administration of an increasingly complex institution in the decades before the Second World War. Several individuals do stand out, however, in the memory of those who lived through that period.

Fancha Eaton Heard—"Mother Heard" to Dean Donham's assistants, whom she dubbed the "Baby Deans"—exercised great authority in the School's administration. Widowed at a young age, Heard had worked for Donham at the Old Colony Trust Company and moved with him to his new post at the Business School. In addition to supervising day-to-day operations, such as the secretarial pool, admissions correspondence,

and the planning of social functions, Heard assumed numerous special responsibilities. In 1926, for example, she selected and arranged for the purchase of $122,000 worth of furnishings for the new campus. She served as the first Secretary of the School, a title created to recognize her wide-ranging activities.

The second Secretary of the School, Mary Elizabeth Osgood, was a 1909 graduate of Simmons College who joined the staff of the Bureau of Business Research in 1912. The following year, Bureau director Selden Martin singled her out for praise in his report to the Dean: "The statistics on [research] results, which I regard as distinctly important, were supplied by our secretary,

Miss Osgood. That they could be supplied without a well-nigh prohibitive amount of work is due to the efficient and comprehensive filing system she has maintained, and in good part designed, and her attention has been confined by no means solely to filing nor to routine work."

Osgood served as the School's first woman grader of written reports, and she was named Assistant Secretary of the School in 1926. Her 25th anniversary at the School was celebrated in June, 1937, with the production of a three-act skit based on her career; Dean Donham and Bureau Director Melvin Copeland played themselves in the production. In 1941, Osgood succeeded Heard as Secretary of the School.

HBS professor and historian Melvin Copeland cites the particular loyalty and dedication of the Baker Library staff: "The Library personnel, it should be noted, has included not a few of the women who have contributed so loyally and effectively to the development of

the School. Among them were Mrs. Grace Bowser, head of the Acquisitions Department for over 25 years; Mrs. Anna E. Spang, who held several positions, most recently serving as head of the Circulation Department; Miss Mildred Holt, the first Curator of the Corporation Records Collection; Miss Etta Philbrook, the genial and helpful Supervisor of the Reading Room; and Mrs. Stella Kerr, who during her nearly 30 years of responsibility for the Circulation Desk made hosts of grateful friends among both students and faculty."

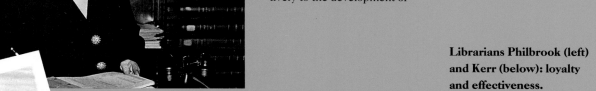

**Librarians Philbrook (left) and Kerr (below): loyalty and effectiveness.**

**Mary E. Osgood**

**Fancha Eaton Heard, circa 1914, with horse and sons.**

In addition to its new case-writing tasks, the Bureau of Business Research continued to conduct its cost studies, particularly in the retailing field. Members of the Bureau staff attended a Chicago shoe retailers' convention in 1923 to publicize the Bureau's work (right), and posed for a group picture (far right). BBR Director Melvin Copeland (center, seated) and Assistant Director Malcolm McNair (to Copeland's right) headed the delegation.

Dean Donham had come to his Harvard post with a deep distaste for academic departmentalization, and the growing autonomy of the Bureau of Business Research—and the frictions which attended that autonomy—contradicted his vision of the School. Happily, the problem reached a crisis stage only after the Bureau had completed the bulk of the initial case collection. By the summer of 1925, its two dozen agents had produced over 5,000 cases, each averaging several pages in length. At that point, therefore, the Dean moved swiftly to decentralize the case-collection function, a step which strained his relations with Bureau Director Copeland. In December, the Bureau began dismantling its case-research apparatus— "as fast as it is practical to do so," noted one internal memorandum, "with fairness to each individual in the organization." Case writing was subsequently controlled by the individual faculty member with a specific need.

In one sense, the Bureau's highly structured approach to case research reflected the inclinations of its director. Melvin Copeland was an economist trained in the scientific method; and, as he once explained to a faculty protégé, his peers regarded him as dogmatic. This perception had arisen, he said, because he used his working hypotheses persistently, in diagnosis and prescription, until he found practical evidence that they were inadequate to explain the business situation at hand. In his capacity as Director of the Bureau, he expected a comparable rigor from his faculty colleagues.

In a larger sense, however, the Bureau's approach reflected the meager intellectual underpinnings of the Harvard Business School. As late as 1922, the faculty ended a long evening of discussion by concluding that it should consider itself a faculty of applied economics,

with incidental responsibilities toward law and engineering. The Business School, in other words, would adopt classical economic theory as its intellectual foundation, and seek to provide a bridge between that theory and its practical applications. Over the following three years, the case researchers who were sent out by the School were actually seeking facts to illustrate established principles of economics. These principles, and their supporting cases, would comprise the heart of the Business School's curriculum.

Applied economics was a bridge that could also serve the business community—at least as Donham envisioned the approach. The 1920–22 depression, he noted in his 1921 report, had demonstrated that businessmen suffered from "a lamentable lack of knowledge of the broad economic background of business and how it affects their own affairs." The Dean concluded that the School should create, in its faculty, a group of men capable of making economics useful to businessmen.

Several experiments were begun as preliminary steps toward these goals. It was clear to Donham and others on the faculty, for example, that a common terminology was a prerequisite to any credible "science" of business; toward that end, a short-lived "Committee on Terminology" was created. An experiment of more significance and duration was the *Harvard Business Reports*, a publication first described in Donham's 1922 report. "Case books, like textbooks, should be built on precedents, including the solutions," he asserted. "Business itself, as well as the case system for its proper development, needs something like the court reporter who systematically records numerous cases for current publication."

While the Bureau's statistical research began to be widely imitated by various industry groups in the 1920s, a cartoon from the 1929 HBS student yearbook suggested that retailers still had something to learn from Harvard.

Even after faculty commentaries were included in the *Harvard Business Reports*, the publication failed to find a broad audience. Just over 9,000 copies of the eight volumes appearing before 1931 were sold; the series was discontinued the following year.

Law cases, Donham noted, were reported in the sequence in which they occurred; it was only in retrospect, through use of elaborate indices and digests of those cases, that legal theory was deduced and applied. Something similar was needed in the field of business. "We have, therefore, in preparation a volume intended to be the first of a series to be published under the name of 'Harvard Business Reports.' This series will be designed to help develop the theory of business."

This proved not to be the "easy and inevitable" job that Donham hoped it would be. He himself complicated the task by insisting—as he noted in the first issue of the quarterly *Harvard Business Review*, published in October of 1922—that cases included in the *Reports* were to retain their individual flavor, conveying the individuality and vitality of the situations they described. It was a full three years before the first volume of the *Reports* actually appeared, by which time the Dean's expectations for the series had diminished. Perhaps, Donham noted modestly in 1925, the *Reports* might be "useful in the formulation of principles in the developing profession of business."

The most durable experiment of all, from this period of experimentation with applied economics, was the *Harvard Business Review*. Donham's prospectus for the School's quarterly magazine, included in his 1922 report, is equally a prospectus for the School as it was then conceived: "We confidently hope to aid in developing the theory of business," he wrote, "through the serious discussion of the underlying principles of industry and commerce. The *Review* should serve as a medium for pointing out the relation between fundamental economic theory as it is worked out by the economist and the everyday experience and problems of the executive in business."

# Publishing the Review

The *Harvard Business Review* had its roots in a March 10, 1917, memorandum written by Professor Melvin Copeland. "The purpose of the magazine will be to publish contributions on subjects of business administration," Copeland proposed. "The point of view will be that of the School—the promotion of scientific business management."

Copeland outlined a magazine that would include theoretical pieces, as well as articles based on individual cases "which illustrate principles of general applicability." President Lowell then appointed a faculty committee of five "to work out a definite plan for a Business School journal," to be completed by the end of the academic year.

All planning for the journal, however, was postponed in the face of the Great War. The discussion was not revived until the spring of 1921, when a group of students argued in a letter to Dean Donham that such a vehicle would promote student spirit and scholastic achievement. The journal could also help promulgate the Business School's research, the students noted, and "if creditable, it would conceivably add to the prestige of the Business School among business men."

The faculty took up the matter again that fall, and in November voted to undertake, if financially feasible, "the publication of a Business School Review, the faculty to assume responsibility for the leading articles, with miscellaneous articles under student editorial control." Dean Donham was authorized to continue his informal discussions on the subject with Chicago publisher and former HBS instructor Arch Shaw.

Although the students had seized the postwar initiative, the School's faculty and administrators elected not to delegate control of the magazine to the students. The quality of editorial content—and not the "promotion of student spirit" —was soon established as the magazine's overriding objective. Neil H. Borden, one of the School's assistant deans, was appointed editor-in-chief. "The paper is intended to be the highest type of business journal that we can make it," wrote Assistant Dean Donald David, "and is for use by the student and the business man. It is not a school paper."

Quality, it seemed, would not only reflect well on the School, but might also prove profitable. Publisher Shaw suggested that a monthly *Review* (to be initiated after a trial year on a quarterly schedule) might well generate $30,000 to subsidize the School's research activities. "With this as a nucleus," he wrote to Donham in the spring of 1922, "and with the added contributions from trade associations and others interested in the particular type of research that may be current at the time, it would seem to me that all the funds necessary for the extension of the research and problem work could be met."

Donham argued vigorously in favor of a prestigious appearance for the magazine—"I really feel very strongly that we should not issue any publication unless it distinguishes itself for quality in every way" —while Shaw emphasized commercial realities. The Dean, for example, held out for an annual subscription price of five dollars. This was very high by the standards of the time, but no higher than the model Donham had in mind: the economics department's *Quarterly Journal of Economics.* Shaw conceded on this point (but only after declaring that it would "break [his] heart") and also agreed to Donham's design for the magazine's cover.

The negotiations also established, once and for all, how the School would describe its teaching method. Shaw wanted to refer to the method in an advertising circular, but didn't know which term was currently in favor—the "case method" or the "problem method"? In April, Assistant Dean David informed Shaw that the School had settled on the former term. "We shall use that term," Shaw responded in a letter to Donham, "and are sending David some pages from our new catalog for your approval. Personally, I have been rather inclined toward the problem method, but you know a great deal more about it than I do."

After sending out his promotional brochure, Shaw was soon reminded that having the name "Harvard" on a product was not an unmixed blessing. A Cleveland roofing manufacturer, for example, emphatically declined to subscribe to the new magazine. "It would seem to me," he wrote, "after going over the data in question, that Harvard University would like to get some of my money, but at the same time does not seem to care very much for my son's society. Under the circumstances, I will have to ask you to kindly excuse me from having anything to do with anything that comes from Harvard."

In the second week of October, 1922, Shaw sent Donham the second copy of the *Review* to come off the press, having kept the first for himself. His clients at the Business School were generally pleased with the results. Less satisfying, though, was the subsequent progress of the *Review.* The magazine made a small profit in its first year—$468.29—but then entered two long decades of annual losses, made up by Shaw's company. Several factors worked against the *Review:* the relatively uninformed state of business theory, the ambiguous mission of the magazine (which still bore some resemblance to a law school journal), and the noncommercial approach imposed by the School upon its publisher. On the other hand, the magazine benefited greatly from the labor and affection of Professor Harry R. Tosdal, the *Review's* second editor, who served from 1922 to 1939. Assisted by Ruth Norton, Tosdal spent literally thousands of hours shaping the magazine's content and editorial policies.

To the outside world, the *Review* spoke for the School, and little distinction was made between the two entities. Indeed, in its early issues, most articles were written by HBS faculty members. Gradually, more articles came from beyond the confines of the School—a 1931 tally, for example, showed that 63 *Review* articles to that date had been written by HBS professors, while 216 had been contributed by outside sources—but to people outside the Business School community, the difference remained unclear.

This close identification with the School was a serious concern, of course, only when something went wrong—as was the case in July, 1930, when the *Review* published R. Minturn Sedgwick's "Investment Advice." Sedgwick, a graduate of the School then employed by an independent investment counseling firm in Boston, suggested that the advice of many investment companies was not wholly impartial. This was at times due to the fact that investment counselors were not paid adequately for their services, according to Sedgwick; at other times, he wrote, they were in a condition of "subservience to some larger organization having different and frequently opposed objects and interests."

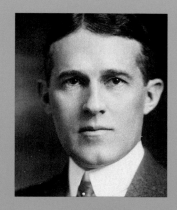

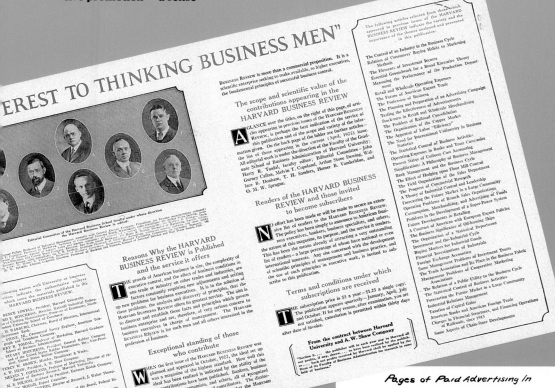

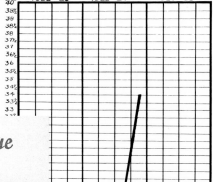

This imputation of a conflict of interest raised the hackles of N. Penrose Hallowell, an influential member of the School's Visiting Committee and a partner with Lee, Higginson & Co. Hallowell protested to Donham that the *Review* should restrict itself to publishing the "best thinking on the subject," and not the slanted analysis of someone "trying to build up his business by damning the other fellow."

"Your banking friends around the street are, to put it mildly, considerably annoyed," Hallowell further informed the Dean, "and I am afraid that this article has done the school considerable harm among those who have been most active in its support."

Donham chose not to contest the issue. "Of course, the blame is entirely on me," he wrote in response, "as I take the responsibility for everything that goes on and anything that goes into the *Review*. . . . The only alibi I can think of is to ask, did you ever put out an issue of securities that turned sour? This isn't much of an alibi, I know."

The magazine's Student Review Board, in charge of student contributions, presented other problems. It performed erratically, dependent as it was on the talents and commitment of its chairman. The board was further hindered by the fact that the MBA program was only two years in length, which effectively precluded the continuity afforded to law reviews by students in three-year programs. "[The board] has failed miserably this year," an administrator informed Donham in 1931, "due largely to their irresponsibility and the decentralization of faculty control." One distinguished student, Stanley F. Teele, thought so little of the board that he declined to serve when elected to it. The board was eventually abolished in 1937.

Like most School activities, the *Review* suffered staff curtailments and budget cuts throughout the Depression period, and showed small losses each year. Subscriptions continued the decline begun in the mid-1920s: from a 1923 high of 5,200 to a low, in 1942, of 2,000. In 1943, however, the magazine made a $500 profit—its first since 1923—suggesting once again that if produced and marketed effectively, the *Review* could support itself, and perhaps provide a source of revenue to the School.

The scene on Wall Street, shortly after noon on September 11, 1920.

With its November 2, 1920, coverage of the Harding-Cox election returns, KDKA Radio in Pittsburgh began a new era in communications, and foreshadowed the birth of entirely new industries.

IN 1919, SOME FOUR MILLION American workers struck against their employers. Seattle became the scene of the nation's first general strike, and Boston experienced a walkout by its entire police force. Three days of looting ensued, ending only when Massachusetts Governor Calvin Coolidge sent in the State Guard to reestablish order. Coolidge also sent a terse telegram to Samuel Gompers, head of the American Federation of Labor: "There is no right to strike against the public safety by anybody, anywhere, any time."

The public applauded Coolidge's decisive action, which established his national reputation. Labor agitation seemed a short step from Bolshevism, and a worker uprising—variously labeled Bolshevik, communist, socialist, or syndicalist—seemed a real possibility to many in postwar America. Bombs were mailed to J. P. Morgan, John D. Rockefeller, and Supreme Court Justice Oliver Wendell Holmes, among others; one such package blew up the Washington townhouse of Attorney General A. Mitchell Palmer. On September 11, 1920, a huge bomb exploded outside J. P. Morgan's offices on Wall Street, killing 38 people and causing over $2 million in property damage.

Before the war, organized labor had opposed large-scale immigration on the grounds that it undercut the already depressed wage structure. On the same grounds, the business community had generally supported immigration. Now, however, employers' associations joined labor in a successful drive for restrictive immigration policies. Business also supported a protectionist trade policy, and the temporary trade barriers set up to counter the severe depression of 1920 evolved into the highest tariff structure in peacetime history. Several

key industries benefited greatly from these tariffs, and the prosperity of the ensuing decade was often attributed to them.

The depression of 1920–22, although harsh, still did not push wages back down to their prewar levels. More important, the strong recovery which followed it initiated a prolonged suspension of the "business cycle" of booms and recessions. By the mid-1920s, the Coolidge administration was speculating publicly that the business cycle had been broken permanently, and that the American economy would thenceforth be characterized by steady growth.

The rapid social change, the boisterousness, and the sheer exuberance of the 1920s are recalled in such appellations as the "Roaring Twenties" and the "Lawless Decade." In a general rebellion against the stuffiness and moralism of the prewar period, the nation embraced cigarettes, bobbed hair, and Freudianism, and winked at flagrant violations of Prohibition. Other nicknames speak more specifically to the heady economic times of the Twenties: the "Seven Fat Years," the "Entrepreneurial Riot." Between 1922 and 1929, the nation's agricultural and industrial production increased by more than 30 percent, and productivity rose more than 20 percent. Annual automobile production increased from 1.9 million in 1920 to 4.8 million in 1929, and electricity generation doubled. Entirely new industries flourished: for example, the first regularly scheduled radio broadcasts began in Pittsburgh late in 1920. By 1929, some 10 million radios were in use.

The consolidation of American business—a subject of bitter controversy in the prewar decades—accelerated during and after the war with little significant opposition. In 1920, the Supreme Court ruled against the proposed dissolution of United States Steel, and the holding company soon came to dominate the American economic structure, particularly in the railroad, banking, and power-generation industries. By 1930, fifteen companies had assets of over $1 billion, and oligopolies gradually replaced monopolies in such key industries as oil, chemical, steel, automobiles, tobacco, and appliances.

Service industries, such as advertising, also prospered in the changed economic climate. Price competition was generally considered unethical; competition, by general consent, took place in the arena of product quality. This notion, combined with tax-code revisions early in the decade, infused the advertising industry with unprecedented amounts of cash. The total volume of advertising grew from $1.5 billion in 1918 to $3 billion in 1920. The J. Walter Thompson agency—which soon emerged as the industry leader—increased its billings from $3 million in 1916 to $37.5 million in 1929.

In 1922, the Thompson agency demonstrated its growing interest in the new field of demographic studies by creating a research department. Paul T. Cherington, formerly the Harvard Business School's chief marketing authority, was appointed Director of Research. "Consumption is no longer a thing of needs, but a matter of choices freely exercised," Cherington wrote in an industry journal. "The consumer's dollar is not a coin wholly mortgaged to the necessary task of providing a bare living. It has in it a generous segment to be spent at the consumer's own option as to what he will buy, and when he will buy, and where."

The consumer's dollar, however, was soon mortgaged to those same discretionary purchases. By 1925, three-quarters of all automobiles were purchased on installment plans. Financing plans facilitated all major types of consumer purchases, including furniture and appliances. Like the increasingly popular "balloon" mortgage, the trend reflected consumer confidence; it also made more serious the consequences of any unexpected interruption in household income.

The combination of consumer confidence and disposable income also contributed, beginning in the middle of the decade, to a series of speculative manias. The great Florida land boom of 1925 was followed by an uncontrolled explosion in stock prices. The Standard Statistics Index of common stock prices stood at 100 in 1926; it rose to 148 in June of 1928; to 191 in June of 1929; and to 216 three months later. Banks lent huge sums to brokers to finance margin stock purchases; the total committed to such loans was $3.5 billion in mid-1927, and $8 billion in September of 1929.

The Republican administration in Washington was not inclined to intervene. At least up to 1927, the increase in stock prices could be justified on the basis of business expansion and profits. In any case, public opinion ran strongly against government intervention. The Federal Reserve was even criticized for its efforts—generally acknowledged as ineffectual—to use banking regulation as a weapon against stock-price inflation. Roy Young, governor of the Federal Reserve, was once observed laughing at the stock prices emerging from his ticker. "What I am laughing at," Young explained, "is that I am sitting here trying to keep 120 million people from doing what they want to do!"

Young, like Cherington before him, overstated the relevance of his activities to the majority of Americans. While the average worker experienced real gains in personal income during the 1920s, 60 percent of American families still earned less than $2,000 in 1929, and one in five earned less than $1,000. Still, a loaf of bread cost only five cents, and a sense of prosperity and optimism abounded. "We in America today are nearer to the final triumph over poverty than ever before in the history of any land," declared presidential candidate Herbert Hoover in a 1928 campaign speech. Hoover's overwhelming electoral victory in November, 1928, led to a new surge in stock market prices.

Secretary of the Treasury Andrew Mellon had suggested earlier in the year that "prudent investors" might begin favoring bonds over stocks. Few heeded his caution, however. In the ten months following Hoover's election, U. S. Steel stock doubled in price, General Electric tripled, and RCA quintupled.

**The J. Walter Thompson agency's research department, headed by former HBS professor Paul T. Cherington, pioneered the application of statistical techniques to market research. Cherington, in particular, sought to devise questionnaires which would "secure the truthful answers with a minimum of distortion due to self-consciousness."**

The "Oriental Friends" of the Harvard Business School, a student group which flourished briefly in the 1920s, reflected the relatively large number of Oriental students who attended the School during and just after World War I. The presence of an international contingent of HBS students, however small, suggested to Dean Donham (seated, center) that the Business School's growing influence would soon extend outside America.

THE GROWTH of "our business civilization" — as historian James Truslow Adams described the American culture of the 1920s — was reflected in the growth and successes of Harvard's business school over the same decade. George F. Baker's gift of the School's new buildings in 1924 was only the most visible of such successes. The School's student population more than doubled between 1919 and 1926. In 1919 only 40 percent of the students completing the first year returned for the second year; by 1925, 73 percent were returning. This was due in part to the development of better techniques for screening candidates for admission, in part to a stronger second-year program, and in part to the School's growing reputation in the business world.

Placement statistics from the 1920s illustrate the School's increasingly strong position. The 120 members of the MBA Class of 1921 entered the job market in the worst of the business depression, but only five were unplaced a year later. Over 300 firms, as well as 59 colleges and universities, attempted to recruit among the 168 members of the Class of 1923. The School had "no difficulty placing our men in a chosen field of industry," the Dean wrote that year. "Our problem of placement has changed to the problem of satisfying reasonable requests of employers who have been using our men in the past." In the spring of 1923, for example, more than 60 firms sought students interested in marketing careers, though only 25 members of the class declared themselves interested and available.

Indeed, the growing demand for the School's graduates soon created a new problem: firms seemed willing to pay too much to Harvard's MBAs. Since the School's founding, its supporters had emphasized that a business school could only prepare its graduates for a

Despite the 1920–22 depression, HBS graduates' starting salaries in 1922 approached the record levels set during the 1919 boom. This led apprehensive School administrators to suggest that employers curtail starting salaries for those recent graduates without previous experience in their field.

| | | | | | | | | | 60% of Graduates Reporting | | | | | | | | |
|---|---|---|---|---|---|---|---|---|---|---|---|---|---|---|---|---|---|
| Class | Salary Upon Graduation | Salary 1 Yr. Out | Salary 2 Yrs. Out | Salary 3 Yrs. Out | Salary 4 Yrs. Out | Salary 5 Yrs. Out | Salary 6 Yrs. Out | Salary 7 Yrs. Out | Salary 8 Yrs. Out | Salary 9 Yrs. Out | Salary 10 Yrs. Out | Salary 11 Yrs. Out | Salary 12 Yrs. Out | Salary 13 Yrs. Out | Salary 14 Yrs. Out | Salary 15 Yrs. Out | Salary 16 Yrs. Out |
| 1910 | 660 | $1,022 | $1,297 | $1,683 | $1,970 | $2,670 | $2,993 | $3,810 | $4,550 | $5,125 | $6,250 | $8,075 | $10,488 | $14,000 | $18,600 | $21,200 | $20,800 |
| 1911 | 782 | 1,216 | 1,875 | 2,540 | 4,560 | 5,680 | 6,220 | 7,880 | | 9,375 | 11,400 | 15,600 | 16,400 | 15,100 | 17,600 | 17,600 | |
| 1912 | | 1,500 | 2,000 | 3,200 | 4,200 | 5,250 | 6,500 | 5,500 | 7,500 | 6,500 | 7,000 | 9,250 | 9,750 | 14,500 | 17,000 | | |
| 1913 | 1,000 | 1,000 | 2,000 | 2,700 | 3,250 | 3,883 | 5,800 | 9,500 | 9,500 | 9,500 | 13,500 | 15,000 | 11,733 | 11,867 | | | |
| 1914 | 1,183 | 1,621 | 1,759 | 2,014 | 2,247 | 3,170 | 3,480 | 3,929 | 4,236 | 4,935 | 5,190 | 6,202 | 6,720 | | | | |
| 1915 | 1,748 | 2,150 | 2,975 | 3,612 | 3,788 | 4,750 | 5,614 | 5,500 | 5,657 | 6,057 | 6,807 | 6,475 | | | | | |
| 1916 | 1,096 | 1,519 | 2,294 | 2,934 | 4,070 | 4,052 | 5,212 | 6,014 | 6,126 | 6,560 | | | | | | | |
| 1917 | 1,620 | 2,340 | 2,957 | 3,367 | 3,785 | 3,683 | 4,311 | 4,544 | 5,110 | 5,546 | | | | | | | |
| 1918 | 1,973 | 2,100 | 2,430 | 2,884 | 3,314 | 3,571 | 3,762 | 4,309 | 5,102 | | | | | | | | |
| 1919 | 2,033 | 2,436 | 2,740 | 3,100 | 3,580 | 3,980 | 4,180 | 4,440 | | | | | | | | | |
| 1920 | | 2,131 | 2,370 | 2,988 | 3,674 | 4,057 | 4,709 | | | | | | | | | | |
| 1921 | 1,663 | 1,933 | 2,397 | 2,757 | 3,315 | 3,983 | | | | | | | | | | | |
| 1922 | 1,891 | 2,284 | 2,669 | 3,247 | 3,859 | | | | | | | | | | | | |
| 1923 | 1,760 | 2,227 | 2,814 | 3,451 | | | | | | | | | | | | | |
| 1924 | 1,758 | 2,258 | 2,871 | | | | | | | | | | | | | | |
| 1925 | 2,000 | 2,483 | | | | | | | | | | | | | | | |
| 1926 | 1,938 | | | | | | | | | | | | | | | | |

12½% of reports

87½% of reports

concentrated "apprenticeship"; it could not produce business leaders overnight. By 1923, the School's administrators—apprehensive that the institution would be blamed for the salaries its graduates were beginning to command—were suggesting that employers impose "a limitation on salaries" paid to MBAs with little or no practical experience.

In one sense, the School prospered during the 1920s simply because business prospered. At the same time, however, there could be no question that the policies adopted by the School had begun to gain recognition and acceptance in influential business circles. The case method made a rapid transition from an experiment in pedagogy to a strong selling point. It was the case method, according to a story told by J. P. Morgan, that convinced George F. Baker in 1924 that "the Business School was being established on the right basis and being run on the right lines."

Most surprising, and no doubt gratifying to Dean Donham, was the gradual acceptance of the case method by other undergraduate and professional schools. In 1921, as noted, the Association of Collegiate Schools of Business had been decidedly cool toward Donham's "mania" for method; four years later, that organization chose method as the focus of its annual meeting and asked Donham to speak in support of the case method.

Donham declined. "It would be preferable to have someone other than myself lead the discussion," he explained to a Columbia University business professor, "because I am too controversial a character on the subject." Instead, he suggested that Donald K. David— one of the School's first case researchers, and by 1925 an assistant professor—speak in his place. The suggestion was accepted, and David (with two other Business School faculty members) traveled to Columbus, Ohio, in the first week of May to argue on behalf of the case method.

"We believe the case system is a method which promotes activity on the part of the student most nearly analogous to the task of the business executive," David told the ACSB gathering. The best possible business education, he suggested, might be to serve as assistant to a top-level businessman and observe "the way the executive mind works." But there are few such positions, and the businessman is often too preoccupied to be an effective teacher.

The executive, said David, goes through four processes in making a business decision. First, he analyzes a situation. Second, he looks for relevant precedents and principles. Third, he weighs the relative importance of principles, and, finally, he arrives at a decision. The student of the case method, David continued, follows the same four steps. Furthermore, the case method arouses great interest in class discussions. "As a first stage of learning," he said, "we think that is tremendously important. Getting the class into a receptive frame of mind where the men in it will think and think clearly, as to the principles which are involved, is of utmost importance."

The case method was proving useful not only to students and teachers, David said, but also to alumni. "In the larger cities of the country," he explained, "there are alumni groups of the Business School that have gathered together and have asked us for cases which they can discuss. . . . I think it is the duty of the schools to try to furnish some intellectual stimulus which these men can use."

**Donald K. David was a 1916 graduate of the University of Idaho, and a 1919 graduate of the Harvard Business School. Acting HBS Dean Lincoln Schaub informed President Lowell in August, 1919, that "Mr. David has this summer completed all requirements for our degree of MBA, and is a man whose record in this school has been exceptionally good."**

**As a newly appointed Instructor in Retail and Wholesale Management, David soon proved useful to both Melvin Copeland and Wallace Donham. When the dean of the Suffolk Law School publicly criticized the Harvard Law School's case method as "a waste of precious time and energy" in 1924, Assistant Professor David sent a copy of the broadside to Dean Donham. "This will interest you," he advised the Dean.**

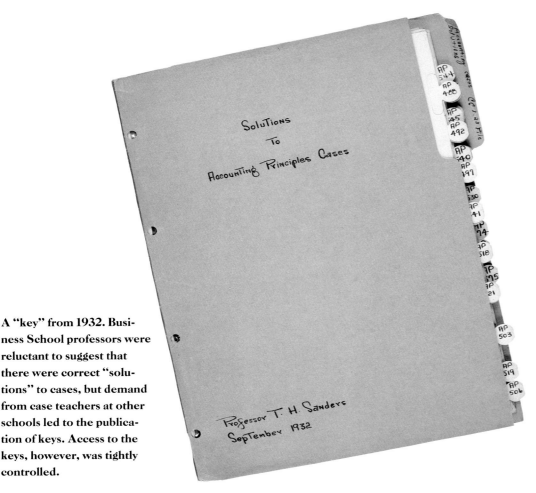

**A "key" from 1932. Business School professors were reluctant to suggest that there were correct "solutions" to cases, but demand from case teachers at other schools led to the publication of keys. Access to the keys, however, was tightly controlled.**

But the case method was not without its problems, as David was careful to point out. Aside from the most obvious difficulty—that of procuring cases—there was the troublesome question of case "keys." What material should be provided to the instructor to help him guide the discussion of a particular case? "We have tried to put out keys to the various case books," he noted, "which would suggest topics for discussion, but would not give absolute answers. It is extremely difficult, and extremely unwise from our point of view, to give a definite answer to most of these cases, because in our own minds, there is no definite answer." Nevertheless, teachers were using the keys in this fashion—"a very bad thing," said David.

"Many people believe," he continued, "that the case method is slower in covering prescribed topics in the teaching of content. To that point, I agree. To that point, I think, Dean Donham disagrees. But I am not much bothered by this, because I am convinced that the case method is more inclusive and—when applied to a course as a whole—is faster than any other method."

David also noted that undergraduate institutions, in particular, had difficulty in adopting Harvard's case method and materials. Their students were less mature than those in a graduate business school, and, in most cases, did not benefit from the sustained immersion in the case method provided by Harvard.

"I hope you have gathered from what I say," David concluded, "that we are not at all satisfied that the material which we introduced in Cambridge, and which we are using, is anywhere near perfection. We know it isn't. We welcome very much suggestions as to how that can be improved for your use, if you care to use it, because we feel that it is the best way to teach business."

Teachers at other institutions, including many of those represented at the Columbus meeting, were agreeing in increasing numbers. In 1923—three years after the publication of Melvin Copeland's *Marketing Problems*—106 American colleges and universities were using one or more Harvard case books. By the time Donald David addressed the ACSB in 1925, at least 217 schools were doing so. (There was also good evidence, according to Donham, that certain business schools were making use of mimeographed cases "without obtaining them from the School and in some cases without giving credit to the School.")

Harvard's delegates to the Columbus convention reported back to their faculty colleagues the following week. The outstanding characteristic of the meeting, they said, was the "interest exhibited by delegates in the case method of teaching." But even the institutions most interested in case teaching didn't seem to understand the method fully, or have instructors competent to employ it. Those that employed the case method often failed to use it in enough courses for it to be effective. "It was the impression of those attending the meeting," according to the faculty minutes, "that other schools of business were looking to this institution to assume a leadership role in developing methods of teaching business."

Dean Donham then advocated two steps. First, he said, there should be "a digesting and organizing of the case material collected by the Bureau to date." This would cost an estimated $75,000. Second, the School should organize a summer school for teachers. The program, which would begin the following year, would be

Henry W. Holmes, Dean of Harvard's Graduate School of Education, asked Dean Donham to describe the case method at an Ed School seminar in December, 1924. "The meeting was very inspiring," Holmes later wrote to Donham. "In a month or so I will ask you to make another missionary effort for me."

designed to provide instructors from other schools with "a true appreciation of the case method," and instruct them how to use it.

Donham's first proposal was not simply an outgrowth of the ACSB meeting and ensuing discussions; rather, it reflected the Harvard faculty's growing awareness of the deficiencies of some existing cases. The oldest ones were particularly suspect. By the Dean's own reckoning, as many as a quarter of the approximately 5,000 cases produced to that date were already obsolete.

Other assessments of existing case material had reached the School through the A.W. Shaw Company, publisher of the case books. The reviews were generally favorable when the case books had been used in advanced courses; they were less so when employed in introductory courses. A number of complaints focused on a perceived lack of facts. "In many cases," wrote a faculty member at the Agricultural College of Utah, "there is not enough information given to furnish the basis for careful judgement. That is, there is not as much information as the ordinary executive would have in making business decisions."

A junior faculty member at the University of Iowa commented: "The very frequent answer I get from a student when I ask him for his decision on a certain case is, 'I don't think that we have facts enough,' and I have to agree with him." This same instructor concluded that while the case book's author could probably teach the material effectively, he himself couldn't — "largely because of my lack of experience and ability in that field . . . . In conclusion, I would say that that particular course has been just about the hardest thing to teach that I have ever tackled."

The faculty authorized both of Donham's proposed initiatives, and the Dean—although then very much preoccupied with designing the new campus — secured an anonymous $75,000 gift to support the case indexing and upgrading project. ("You really are a wonder," General Electric's President Gerard Swope wrote to Donham regarding this fundraising success. "I wish you could come and help me on some of my financial jobs as ably as you help your own institution.") The summer school for instructors, however, never materialized: it was first postponed and later cancelled, a casualty of more pressing demands on faculty time.

SINCE DONHAM'S UNSUCCESSFUL EFFORT at the 1921 meeting of the Association of Collegiate Schools of Business, the Harvard Business School's administrators had been committed to disseminating the case method. Although schools across the country had developed case-oriented courses, mostly using Harvard materials, none had reoriented its curriculum in a thoroughgoing way. Without such a commitment, Harvard's case-method advocates felt, the method could not succeed.

When Stanford University decided in 1925 to establish the nation's second exclusively graduate school of business, Donham perceived an unusual opportunity. With President Lowell's blessing, he took a three-week leave from his Harvard duties to travel to Palo Alto and lend his support. "My trip to Stanford is unfortunately not a vacation," he explained to George F. Baker, Jr., who had inquired about his proposed absence. "It is rather an obligation as Dean of the School to help them start their business instruction right."

The original Stanford Business School building. Eliot Mears, a Harvard Business School administrator during Edwin Gay's deanship, was an early member of the Stanford faculty, and strengthened ties between the two institutions during the early 1930s.

J. Hugh Jackson was a highly respected accounting professor at Harvard. His appointment as dean of the Stanford Business School in 1932, according to some, reflected that institution's rekindled interest in adopting HBS methods.

Stanford further requested the temporary services of J. Hugh Jackson, since 1920 a professor of accounting at Harvard. Donham supported the proposed year's leave of absence in a letter to President Lowell: "I am very desirous of assisting this new school to start with the highest possible standards." The following year, Jackson resigned from the Harvard faculty to accept a Stanford professorship—and in 1932 he was named the Stanford Business School's second dean.

Part of the motivation for building the Soldiers Field campus in the mid-1920s was the sense—shared by Lowell and Donham, among others—that Harvard's professional schools should be equipped to accept all qualified applicants. In the three years following the completion of the new campus, this was the case; but by 1930, the Harvard Business School was again oversubscribed. The demand for case-method instruction continued to grow, in spite of the rapid unraveling of

the national economy, but no additional schools were then inclined to join Harvard and Stanford in offering a novel brand of graduate business education. Stanford, not surprisingly, was not yet educating sufficient numbers of students to alleviate the problem.

"In view of the number of students who continue to come to the School from the Pacific Coast," a Harvard faculty committee on enrollment noted in November of 1930, "and in light of other information, it does not appear that the Stanford Business School is likely to attract enough more students in the near future to relieve appreciably the pressure on the Harvard Business School."

Perhaps the clearest indication of the optimistic mood which prevailed at the School—even as the economic depression deepened—is contained in the final report of the faculty committee on enrollment, submitted in April of 1931. The committee stated again that Harvard could expect no significant help from other universities in meeting the unfilled demand for case-oriented business education. Expanding the size or number of sections in the School, at least as it was then organized, seemed unrealistic.

The committee noted one final alternative: to create "another unit of instruction of approximately the same size as the present School." This new institution, presumably adjacent to Soldiers Field, would have its own faculty and buildings, and would be headed by an associate dean responsible to Donham. "Such a new unit should not be permitted to be any drain whatsoever on the resources of the present School. This probably would call for a new endowment of at least $10,000,000."

The committee recommended against this alternative, citing the more pressing need to resolve longstanding difficulties with the curriculum. The notion of duplicating the Soldiers Field campus originated with Donham, who had strong opinions about the appropriate size of a faculty and a campus. He wanted all members of his faculty to know each other and learn from each other, and to resist the academic inclination toward departmentalization. As he explained to his associates on more than one occasion, he would rather see a second school built than allow the one he had just completed to become too large.

J. Hugh Jackson gave much credit to Wallace Donham for the publication, in 1929, of Jackson's *Auditing Problems*.

# AUDITING PROBLEMS

### A COMPREHENSIVE STUDY IN PRINCIPLES AND PROCEDURE

By

## J. HUGH JACKSON

r of Accounting, Graduate School of Business, Stanford
y; Certified Public Accountant (California, Massachu-
Wisconsin); Member, American Institute of Accountants

LD PRESS COMPANY
NEW YORK

To Dear Wallace B. Donham whose inspiration and guidance are largely responsible for the preparation of this book.
Hugh Jackson

Georges Doriot (front row, second from left) at the 1926 International Congress of Accountants, in Amsterdam. Doriot had intended to attend MIT as a graduate student, but was steered to HBS by President Lowell. His presence on the HBS faculty led to a number of international initiatives.

## An adoption of American methods

In 1930, demand for a Harvard Business School education again exceeded supply, as it had before the construction of the Soldiers Field campus. Exacerbating the problem was the growing number of qualified applicants from overseas— many of whom the School reluctantly had to turn down. One heartening turn of events in 1930, therefore, was the establishment of a school in Paris patterned closely on the Harvard Business School.

The Centre de Preparation aux Affaires was the eventual result of a series of conversations between Georges F. Doriot of the HBS faculty and officials of the Paris Chambre de Commerce. Other alternatives—including the creation of a French school in New York, and the establishment of an all-French section at Soldiers Field—were contemplated and discarded. When the Paris alternative was decided upon, Doriot translated a number of Harvard cases for use at the new school, and otherwise shaped its development. "It is plain that this new school will have a great social significance, both from a national and international point of view," Doriot wrote. "Its establishment marks not only an advance in the development of the excellent French Chambres de Commerce, but an adoption of American methods."

Dean Donham spoke at the Centre's dedication ceremonies, and was cited by the president of France as an Officier de Legion d'Honneur—a rare honor for a foreigner. On his return trip, he stopped in England to meet with officials of the London School of Economics, which was then in the process of organizing a new "Department of Business." As a result of these and later discussions, Harvard's Professor Malcolm McNair was in residence in London the following fall to assist the new department during its first term. From these heady experiences, it seemed that the Harvard Business School was now serving as a model not only for business education in America, but also in Europe.

The last HBS class picture—of the Class of 1927—on the steps of Widener. Within three years, the HBS student body had again outgrown its facilities, until the Depression began to affect enrollment.

But it was Donham who also ruled out such a large-scale expansion. Only his personal initiative had made possible the creation of the Soldiers Field campus and the raising of most of the existing School's endowment. In the process, he had severely overtaxed his own physical resources, and had nearly died from a heart attack in June of 1927. Even after several years on a reduced schedule, he was not inclined to mount a drive for a new campus. In the face of the deepening depression, furthermore, finding resources four times as large as the existing endowment—which in 1931 barely exceeded $2.5 million—seemed an impossible goal.

TO THE HARVARD BUSINESS SCHOOL, the 1920s presented two indisputable realities: the immediate success of a means, and a continuing struggle to agree on a conceptual end. The gradual acceptance of the case method by other educators, as well as the School's own growing reputation, validated Wallace Donham's innovative approach to business education. But the School's conception of itself—as a school of applied economics, devoted to the practical illustration of known economic principles—was dissolving with equal rapidity. "The facts of concrete situations," Donham later recalled, "refused to stay within the concepts of our economists, who were thinking in terms of applied economics. In spite of the fact that our reporters were trying to ignore non-economic factors, non-economic facts persisted in coming into situations. By so doing, they forced us to recognize that problems faced by men of affairs—either public or private —can almost never be treated as problems in applied economics.

"On the other hand, we were impressed with the pervasive nature of human problems as they ran through the concrete reported cases, even though we were not seeking descriptive treatment of the human situations and indeed did not know how to report the facts."

Another set of perceptions added urgency to the resolution of this basic problem, at least in Donham's mind. First, and most important, was his conviction that the industrialized nations of the West were facing a crisis—social, economic, and spiritual—of unprecedented dimensions. This apocalyptic perception was shared by many intellectuals in the decades between the two world wars: that something at the core of Western society was unraveling. Many observers, including Wallace Donham, attributed that unraveling to the ascent of science and industry, and the concomitant decline of religion.

Donham had been impressed by his reading of British philosopher Alfred North Whitehead, who joined the Harvard University faculty in the fall of 1924 after retiring from the University of London. In *Science and the Modern World*, published shortly after his arrival at Harvard, Whitehead addressed many of the very issues that were then preoccupying the Dean of the Business School. In the interests of both science and religion, Whitehead had argued, society needed to recognize the dangers inherent in scientific materialism, and guard against the misapplication of technologies. "It may be," wrote Whitehead, "that civilization will never recover from the bad climate which enveloped the introduction of machinery."

Donham, building upon this thesis and a series of Saturday afternoon discussions with Whitehead, concluded that science had been elevated to a position of false authority. In its industrial applications, science had accelerated the rate of change to such a degree that events now seemed out of control—and yet, society persisted in turning to science for answers. This, as Donham saw it, was futile. The scientific community, as he noted in a 1926 address to Harvard students, had "let loose on the world powerful and revolutionary forces which were from the start and are now and always will be outside the control of the scientific group."

The problems created by scientific materialism were human problems. Society had once turned to the legal profession for its "wise counsellors" in these matters; but the law had lost its independent professional status, to a very large extent, by allowing itself to be transformed in the late 19th century into a servant of industry. Because religion was not likely to be reinstated to its position of moral authority, and because science and law could not lay claim to such authority, it fell to the business community to face what Donham saw as the critical social problem: the "control of the consequences of scientific development."

"I realize," he told the Harvard students in his 1926 address, "that there can be a very good superficial case made out at the moment to support the thesis that there are no great dangers facing our organized society. We are in a wave of conservatism, a reactionary wave which is at the moment very impressive"—resulting, he said, from the Russian revolution, the unsettled condition of Europe, and a general war-weariness. But those who perceived the impending crisis "should be

**Alfred North Whitehead was invited by Harvard's President Lowell —traveling in Great Britain at the time of Whitehead's retirement—to join the Harvard faculty.**

very grateful that these slowing-down forces are so strongly in operation at the moment, and we may well use every particle of energy that we have in the effort to build up intellectual and social points of view and ethical standards."

In the question-and-answer period which followed, a student asked Donham how he reconciled this "social point of view" with the profit motive. It was, the Dean admitted, a difficult question: "intelligent selfishness" —the stance of the enlightened capitalist of the early 20th century—was of only limited usefulness. "Getting control of all these forces is not a simple problem," he concluded. "It took two centuries for the English-speaking part of the race to get control of credits, of bills, mortgages, notes and so forth, to the point that they ceased to be weapons of oppression of the most serious sort, and the results of the industrial revolution are far more complicated. We face the necessity of socializing the results of science."

In Donham's mind, therefore, the School faced a formidable challenge. Even as the institution's intellectual underpinnings—as a "school of applied economics, with incidental responsibilities toward law and engineering"—were proving inadequate, the School's faculty had to join with the business community in an effort to "socialize the results of science." Without such an effort, society itself might collapse. Characteristically, the School's administrators devised a series of long-term initiatives which might, when taken as a whole, lead to a new foundation: first for the Business School, later for the business person with the "social point of view."

"The objective of our research," Donham later commented of this period, "changed from the collection of materials for the illustration of known principles into the ascertainment of new principles." This was, again, an imposing task. The social sciences, including economics, seemed to lack not only the requisite knowledge, but also the means to derive that knowledge.

"We are left with no expansion of wisdom," Whitehead had written, "and with greater need of it." To Donham he wrote privately, "Time is short."

George Woodbridge contributed his services to several key HBS initiatives. "To serve with you," he inscribed the accompanying photograph, requested by Dean Donham, "was a daily growing privilege."

The Harvard Law School library, in Langdell Hall, was the model that Donham had in mind for the Business School's new library.

"When the case system was introduced to the Business School," noted an HBS administrator in 1924, "Dean Donham quickly recognized the need of developing a library as both an instrument of training and of use by the faculty and the students. He felt that this was imperatively required under the method of teaching men to look for fundamental principles."

THIS "GREATER NEED" focused new attention on the Business School's library. Dean Donham was exaggerating somewhat when he suggested, in his 1924 report to President Lowell, that the Business School library had not been worth discussing before George F. Baker's gift of the new campus. In fact, since the inauguration of the case system Donham had considered an upgrading of the library a prerequisite to the effective training of both faculty and students. "He felt," noted a fellow administrator, "that this was imperatively required under the method of teaching men to look for fundamental principles."

There were two ways to build a library, as an internal memorandum noted. The first was to buy only selected items, and only when they were needed; this would result in a small library of much-used material. The second was "to sweep in with a dragnet everything that seems to be within our field," creating a much larger and eclectic collection. "With the development of the case system of teaching in the School," the memorandum continued, "the second method has seemed to the library, up to this point, the only logical course to

pursue. Our students have been trained to get information on nearly every conceivable subject of business, and the questions they ask are so diverse and heterogeneous that they can only be answered from a very large collection of books and documents."

The library's "dragnet" approach, then, was originally adopted to meet the case-related needs of the School in its "applied economics" phase. But the dragnet approach only increased in importance as the intellectual conception of the School broadened in the mid-1920s. Fortuitously, the new facility of Baker Library made possible an even broader acquisitions policy. "Absolute completeness, however unattainable, rather than mere adequacy for every-day needs, must be the basis of its purchasing policy," Donham wrote. "In short, the new library is asking for and receiving on a wholesale scale much of the very same ephemeral matter that our researchers have been bringing in in small lots for specific cases."

The rationale for the expanded library—and indeed, for much of the expanded Business School underwritten by George F. Baker—came from the fertile mind of George Woodbridge, a former journalist and life insurance agent who had joined Donham's administrative staff in 1922 to help in the planned fundraising campaign. "Uncle George," Donham was fond of explaining, "could come up with a hundred ideas in an hour; the challenge was to sort through them and find the good ones." Woodbridge had, in fact, made three key contributions to the 1924 campaign. First, he had persuaded Donham to raise his sights for the Business School's part of the campaign: from $1 million to $5 million. Second, he had suggested to Donham that he enlist Bishop William Lawrence in the campaign. Third, he had written an account of the Business School for the campaign "case book." Woodbridge's account was such a detailed rationale and exegesis that it was promptly dubbed "the Bible" by fellow campaign workers.

In connection with his work on "the Bible," Woodbridge sent a memorandum in mid-July of 1924 to the senior members of the Business School faculty. He needed their help, he wrote them, in demonstrating the need for a "great business library," comparable to the Harvard Law School's library, which he termed "literally the greatest and most complete law library in

FROM
THE BUSINESS
HISTORICAL
SOCIETY INC

1925

THE GIFT OF

**Charles H. Taylor, newspaperman and amateur business historian, argued against listing supporting industries on the Business Historical Society's letterhead. He lobbied, instead, for a more generic image: "It seems to me," he wrote to Dean Donham, "that [Atlas] would cover business from the beginning of the world."**

the world," and one that attracted scholars from around the globe. What could the Business School's library attempt which might earn it a similar stature?

One response came from finance professor Arthur S. Dewing, who suggested that the library "should, perhaps above all else, collect ephemeral pamphlets, reports, statistical data, and the like, which are created in the course of business operations and are destroyed as soon as the occasion which brought them into existence has passed." In fact, Dewing and his fellow finance professors had already cast their own "dragnet," collecting annual reports, mortgage documents, committee reports, brokers' circulars, and stock exchange listing sheets of the major railroad, industrial, and public utility corporations.

Melvin Copeland, for his part, suggested "the assembling in the library of a large quantity of historical source material. . . . I should like to see the library make a determined effort on a large scale to procure records and documents of various sorts that are now in the hands of individuals or corporations." This source material was in jeopardy, Copeland argued, and "the longer we delay in seeking such records, the harder it will be to secure them."

Business historical data, he continued, could serve "as a strong attraction to men of scholarly instincts who desire to come to the Harvard Business School for advanced study." He also hoped that it might prove feasible "to reconstruct a substantial number of cases from these old documents and reports in order that we may provide our students with a real historical perspective, and perhaps eventually include in the School's curriculum one or more courses on business history."

COPELAND'S SUGGESTION closely resembled one that Woodbridge had made to Donham the previous year. Over lunch at Boston's Parker House, Woodbridge had outlined his latest plan for the Business School. Why not, Woodbridge asked, establish an "Institute of Business" at Harvard, which would take a historical approach to business? He argued that in the wake of the World War and the 1920–22 depression, the public had lost respect for business, and businessmen had even lost some measure of respect for themselves. "The historical interest," he said, "could be awakened and used as a means to attain the desired respect."

Now, in response to Woodbridge's 1924 memorandum, two senior faculty members were proposing something very much like the "Institute of Business." With Donham's blessing, therefore, Woodbridge organized an informal group of local businessmen into a "Committee on the Development of the Harvard Business Library." This group—which included *Boston Globe* treasurer Charles H. Taylor, once described as an "incorrigible collector" of business records and artifacts—determined that there was a pressing need to gather and preserve business records, and to support research based on those records.

This discussion group gradually expanded to include interested Business School faculty members and supporters from other parts of the country—because, as Woodbridge emphasized, the point was to create a *national* society, which would support a national business library. In September of 1924, at a meeting in New York, the group approved a plan for a "Business Historical Society," which would ask the Harvard Business School to house its collections and assign to Business School librarian Charles C. Eaton the task of cataloguing them. Either the Society or the Business School could sever the relationship upon a year's notice; however, the Society's accumulated materials would in any case remain in Harvard's care. Donham promptly agreed to the plan.

The Business Historical Society was well endowed in its early years. In addition to income derived from membership fees, the Society received a $10,000 gift from the heirs of Charles A. Moore, a founder of the American Civic Association. A year after the founding of the Society, Donham reported to his faculty that the

In 1925, while HBS Dean Donham was engaged in the University's $10 million fund drive, he was "excused" by the Harvard Corporation for deficits incurred by the

School. All such deficits, however—including those incurred by the library in book acquisitions—had to be made up.

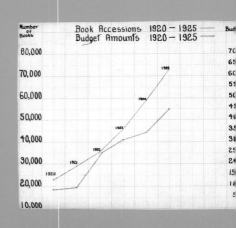

## The broadest and most complete library

**The Business School's new library had to give students and faculty access to the yield of a "dragnet." How would the eclectic collection be catalogued?**

Cecil Ross, superintendent of the Business School's "Special Library" in 1920, pointed out the obvious in a letter to the School's new dean. The facility —in assigned quarters on the top floor of Widener Library, in Harvard Yard—was over-crowded, and the demands placed upon it were increasing rapidly. For example, there were seats available for fewer than half of the School's students. "Our greatest service to Harvard College Library, it seems to me," Ross concluded, "is to relieve it, not to reform it."

Ross's successor, the acquisitive Charles C. Eaton, shared Wallace Donham's opinion that the Business School's library should be all-encompassing. This attitude may also have reflected the influence of Dean

Donham's predecessor, Edwin F. Gay, who had occasionally prevailed upon businesses to forward their unwanted records to the Business School. Eaton was at times the unwitting beneficiary of Gay's efforts. In mid-1921, for example, Eaton came upon a dozen boxes of records in the basement of Widener pertaining to the Slater Mills, a defunct Rhode Island cotton factory.

"Some years ago," Gay wrote in response to an inquiry from Eaton, "I learned they were about to destroy the account books and suggested that they be placed on deposit in the Harvard Library. . . . It is rather tedious going through them, but they furnish valuable information not merely on business methods and conditions but regarding prices and wages."

Gay had learned of the records from Arthur H. Cole, a graduate student in the economics department who discovered the threatened records in a wool shed. With Gay's encouragement, Cole arranged to have the records sent to Harvard, and in this way the School became the custodian of an historically significant collection—the records of the nation's first cotton manufacturing firm.

In the summer of 1922, Eaton and his staff undertook to reclassify the library's collection. This work was begun in part to reflect the School's changed curriculum, in part to check the overworked library staff's tendency to classify large numbers of new books as "general," and in part to make the best use of limited floor space. During that summer, some 2,600 books were reclassified (and over 10,000 file cards changed as a result), including all the books on marketing, production, statistics, and business education. Eaton estimated that the project would take eight full summers, if 2,000 hours of work were invested annually.

The plan was never carried out. Over the ensuing seven years, Eaton greatly augmented the collection; in the process, however, he also earned the displeasure of Dean Donham and other faculty members because of his some-times overzealous collecting. "I think we really ought to stop buying books, except as they are needed for the courses and except as we are given absolutely new money for buying books, for the immediate future," Donham wrote to Eaton in September, 1927.

"I know perfectly well that this is a good time to buy and that there are a lot of good things on the market, but I am also convinced that we haven't any money to buy them unless we have some more gifts." In 1929, Eaton was—in all but title—replaced as librarian by Arthur H. Cole, formerly of Harvard's economics department.

One of Eaton's last major initiatives as Business School librarian was to hire William A. Cutter, who was engaged in 1927 to devise a definitive classification system for Baker Library. The library then faced the forbidding task of unpacking and placing on its new shelves—according to some rational system—thousands of books, many of which were as yet uncatalogued. By all accounts, the 1922 classification scheme was inadequate to the task. The three existing systems of library classification —the Library of Congress, Dewey, and Cutter Expansive systems—had all been devised before the development of "business literature," and were equally inadequate.

Dean Donham expressed some frustration when comparing legal libraries and business libraries. The law student, he said to a 1927 meeting of his library staff, had the benefit of extraordinarily good indices and digests, affording ready access to all phases of legal material. But business "possessed no satisfactory analysis, and has perforce limped along when it should be running." To help address the problem, Donham secured a five-year gift from an anonymous donor to underwrite Cutter's activities.

Cole (left) and Clark in the stacks.

Cutter was the nephew of Charles A. Cutter, and had helped his uncle devise the eponymous Cutter Expansive system. A series of "guidance" conferences with Business School faculty members proved fruitless, and Cutter was soon inventing a new business classification system singlehandedly. He settled on a literal system linked to the Library of Congress's in certain broad areas, and—most important—established business *function* as its primary basis of analysis and elaboration. (This latter decision was in part a result of Arthur Cole's influence, after 1929.) The new system went to the printer in December of 1931, and the library staff was simultaneously trained to implement it. It was then estimated that reclassifying Baker's 125,000 bound volumes and monographs would cost some $90,000.

At this juncture, however, the five-year reclassification grant expired, just as the Depression began to force deep cuts in the library budget. "I cannot find present funds to place in the extension and completion of the business classification," Donham informed Cutter in the summer of 1932, "and I cannot, of course, make commitment for payment in the future."

Librarian Cole's primary task in the Depression years was to rationalize Baker's collecting policy. Cole had to take into account changing business conditions, the larger Harvard library system, and changing student demands. As time and resources allowed, he and his staff sorted through the manuscripts and records accumulated in the "euphoric twenties," as Cole referred to the decade preceding his own tenure. By the mid-1930s, institutions in other regions and with other areas of specialization were eager to take over collections originally acquired by the Business School's library, and many such collections were assigned to repositories in San Francisco, St. Louis, Baltimore, New Haven, and elsewhere.

The library experienced several deep budget cuts in the Depression years: from $175,000 in 1931 to $106,000 in 1932; and from $103,000 in 1934 to $66,000 in 1935. Donham's approach in both budgetary crises was to cut the research budget until instruction began to suffer, and then to make any additional needed economies at the expense of the library budget. The library staff was also cut, from a 1930 high of 74 employees to approximately half that number within the decade. In his October, 1935, report, however, Cole observed that the recent curtailment of the library staff had not unduly affected its morale or its operations. "I am happy also to make formal record of the growing recognition of Baker Library as a notable institution in the library world," Cole noted. "Of course, this is a development which reaches back many years, and is the result of contributions by a great number of individuals."

"While much remains to be accomplished," Cole concluded, "it is the hope of the School that the day is not far distant when the broad public recognition already achieved by the Harvard College and Harvard Law Libraries will not be withheld from that of the Harvard Business School."

Aside from restoring adequate funding levels, much of what remained to be accomplished was conceptual in nature. As early as 1928, Donham had told a staff meeting that Baker Library should be developed as soon as possible into an active reference tool for students and faculty. This was the main point of the classification effort, and remained Donham's goal for the library throughout the Depression years. It seemed, however, that the library was losing relevance to the MBA curriculum— based as that curriculum was on case studies—even as it was gaining stature among business historians and other scholars.

Donham made a final effort to resolve this dilemma before retiring from the deanship. In 1940, he agreed to hire Donald T. Clark, an experienced library administrator, as Cole's assistant and presumed successor. Donham stipulated, however, that Clark should obtain an MBA at the School's expense. This experience, Donham reasoned, would help Cole and Clark in an overriding postwar task—namely, the effort to reshape the library and mold it into an important part of the MBA experience.

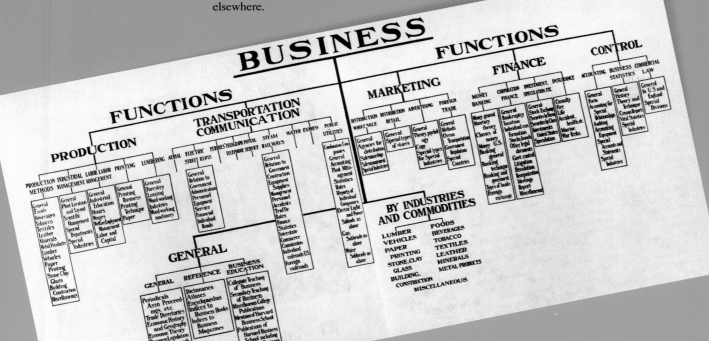

**Librarian Cutter decided to follow the example of the HBS curriculum, and organized Baker Library according to business function. The classification system was subsequently adopted by libraries across the country.**

A "real tin dinner pail" (left), contributed to the business historical collection by Charles H. Taylor; and an English patent issued in 1868 to Amos Holbrook, the "first and true inventor . . . [of] a machine for sewing books."

Society had spent some $8,000 acquiring over 45,000 books and pamphlets. Librarian Eaton, furthermore, was conducting his own dragnet, and had increased the library's historical holdings by over 50 percent. A huge collection of historical material—destined for ultimate deposit in the School's new library, then under construction—began to accumulate.

The completion of Baker Library in 1927 only underscored, in Eaton's mind, the importance of "absolute completeness." He pursued pertinent materials with zeal and determination. To the dismay of some on the Business School faculty, he also greatly broadened the definition of "pertinent," acquiring stoves, tools, and other artifacts. One unsuccessful pursuit—of the papers of railroad magnate and Business School patron James J. Hill—illustrates his approach and suggests some of the obstacles he encountered. In November of 1926, Eaton suggested to Professor Norman S. B. Gras (then a professor of economic history at the University of Minnesota, with personal ties to the Hill family, and also under consideration for a Harvard Business School appointment) that Harvard's new library would be the most appropriate repository for the Hill papers.

Hill's son Louis was not persuaded. "His point is clear," Gras subsequently wrote to Eaton. "So long as many of the chief actors in his father's affairs still live, he is unwilling to have anyone even read the letter files. . . . There is nothing to do but wait for the major collection, or a chance to get it."

Eaton responded that he sympathized fully with Louis Hill's point of view, but wondered if Gras had emphasized enough the security of Baker Library's specially-designed vaults. "Would it be wise to call Mr. Hill's attention to our facilities," he inquired, "or had we better wait, always with the understanding that there is a risk of losing by fire, rats, or thieves, something which could in this way be preserved?"

While the Hill papers were not successfully lured to Harvard, Gras himself was. His appointment, confirmed in February of 1927, was seen by Donham as a means to an important end. While Eaton, Donham, and the founders of the Business Historical Society all shared the conviction that the written records of business ought to be preserved, there was no clear consensus about how to use such records. Melvin Copeland had suggested that cases might be derived from the

collections, but no faculty members seemed inclined to take that step. Perhaps Gras — who at Minnesota had been teaching an economic history course which he described as "edging over to business history" — could provide an answer.

One precondition of Gras's appointment suggests what Donham had in mind. In accepting Harvard's terms, Gras agreed that he would serve as managing editor of a projected "business history quarterly," under the direction of former Business School Dean Edwin Gay, who had returned from his foray into business to join the Harvard economics faculty in the fall of 1924. The quarterly, as Donham envisioned it, would serve two purposes: it would bring Gay back into an active relationship with the School, and perhaps suggest ways in which the ever-growing historical collection could be put to a practical use.

The *Journal of Economic and Business History*, however, failed to accomplish either goal. Launched in 1928, its publication was suspended in 1932 after only four issues. The adverse economic circumstances of 1932 were only one reason for the failure; there was also, Gras later noted, "a fatal duality in the make-up of the *Journal*, as indicated in the title. There were two subjects represented, two horses to ride at the same time." Editor Gay, feeling that business history was still "immature," declined to publish any articles on the subject, and eventually resigned over a dispute on this point.

Gras, though, made contributions in two other areas. First, he conceived and organized the *Harvard Studies in Business History*, a series of monographs which collectively represent the first stage in the development of the field of business history. The series (which eventually included sixteen titles) examined the inner workings of individual businesses in minute detail. Gras's own account of the First National Bank of Boston, for example, included 205 pages of text and 550 pages of supporting material. These studies, and others patterned after them, helped set the stage for the analytical and synthesizing works that would follow in the field of business history.

The School's first "professor of business history" also took the first difficult steps toward integrating his subject into the Business School's curriculum. In September of 1927 Gras offered an early morning class in business history as part of the required second-year Business Policy course. "From the beginning," he recalled, "cases were used, not grudgingly but rather extensively." The first six such cases dealt with medieval situations, reflecting Gras's own area of expertise; eventually, these were eliminated in favor of more modern cases. A Business History elective was first offered in the following year, and in spite of its seeming irrelevance to contemporary issues — "not the sort of study that a *real* business man would be interested in," as Gras paraphrased his critics — the course enjoyed consistently high enrollments.

Gras explained the success of the course in terms of its contribution to the case method. The School had by then abandoned the unworkable conceptual model of applied economics, and had set out to develop its own theory—"which we were obviously too inexperienced yet to formulate," Gras noted. But in its rigid insistence on the *facts* of a given case, as a means of avoiding ungrounded theory, the School risked missing those crucial elements which did not emerge from business records. In short, said Gras, the case method was still "in danger of losing its human background" by failing to take into consideration such critical factors as public opinion, the influence of labor, and similarly elusive elements.

Business History, however, succeeded because it addressed these very issues. "It was clearly putting business into human culture," Gras contended in his 1942 memoirs, and students perceived and supported that effort.

"Putting business into human culture"—or, put another way, recognizing human culture within business—was perhaps Wallace Donham's central goal for

the Harvard Business School. This was the business "theory" that the School was in search of, by means of case research and the library's massive "dragnet"; this was the knowledge that would enable the business community, the emerging leaders of industrial society, to socialize the results of science.

But case research alone, Donham and his fellows realized, was not proving sufficient to the task of generating intellectual capital. The failure of the *Harvard Business Reports*—the publication designed to serve as an index and codification of the "principles of business"—emphasized this point in the mid-1920s. At an October, 1925, faculty meeting, for example, Donham urged faculty members to submit better analyses with the cases they contributed to the *Reports*, since "mere presentation of the cases without analysis probably means that business men will not get great value from the reports." At the next meeting, however, several senior faculty members rebelled. "It was suggested," the faculty secretary recorded, "that commentaries might be limited to mere suggestions, pointing out the significance of the case. Professor Sprague supported the point of view that most of the cases were mere weighing of factors, and that the applying of so-called principles drawn from any one case to another was dangerous because a slight change of circumstances might shift the weight of the factors."

Sprague's point was valid; Donham had himself often said that business cases allowed for more than one "solution." On the other hand, the Dean felt strongly that more than "mere suggestions" would be needed by the business leaders of an imperiled industrial civilization. This was not a recent perception: as early as 1922, Donham had decided that basic business research—in addition to case research—had to be conducted. "On the other hand," he had noted in his report to President Lowell that year, "it is a slow and difficult task to finance new and untried lines of business research. The business man is peculiarly skeptical of such efforts. We need, therefore, a continuous income through endowment which can be used to start new studies."

**George Elton Mayo, industrial researcher, philosopher, and "blithe spirit," in the words of a protégé.**

In the summer of 1925, therefore—in the midst of designing the School's architectural competition—Donham began assembling an innovative research initiative. Perhaps as a result of several provocative articles in *Harper's* magazine, and almost certainly in response to the recommendation of Harvard biochemist Lawrence J. Henderson, Donham sought out George Elton Mayo, whose reflections on the dangers to industrial civilization closely resembled his own.

Mayo, an Australian scholar and philosopher, had combined a variety of clinical and practical experiences to forge a new discipline: industrial sociology. He was then conducting industrial research in Philadelphia, where in the previous two years he had won the support of Joseph Willits, head of the Wharton School's Industrial Research Department. John D. Rockefeller, Jr., had personally underwritten Mayo's studies, which between 1922 and 1924 focused on the psychological and physiological aspects of factory work. While much of this research was inconclusive, Mayo had enjoyed one conspicuous success. The Philadelphia-based Continental Mills, like most of their competitors in the textile business, were experiencing the twin evils of high turnover and low productivity. Mayo correctly attributed these problems to the monotony and fatigue associated with textile mill work, and suggested a regular schedule of breaks for relaxation. Productivity rose 30 percent, and the Australian researcher won the respect of both workers and management.

Donham first met and exchanged views with Mayo in the summer of 1925; they met again in November when Mayo addressed a meeting of the Boston Chamber of Commerce. By the end of the month, the process of mutual examination was complete, and Donham asked Mayo if he would consider joining the School's faculty and initiating a program in industrial research. Mayo was then considering a similar offer from McGill University, but was inclined—if Donham could win President Lowell's approval—to accept a Harvard appointment.

To Donham, it seemed a rare opportunity. Here was a researcher with strong credentials willing to initiate the basic research that was so badly needed. (The spectre of social collapse, furthermore, was no longer a vision held by Donham alone. Boston merchant

**General Electric's Owen D. Young, an influential member of the School's Visiting Committee in the 1920s, gave behind-the-scenes support to many of Dean Donham's educational experiments.**

A. Lincoln Filene, a longtime supporter of the School, was now lobbying actively for an expansion of the School's work in "industrial relations.") Also significant, from the Dean's point of view, was the fact that Mayo brought with him his own funding. The Laura Spelman Rockefeller Foundation had agreed to support Mayo's research for four years.

"The objective," Donham wrote to President Lowell in mid-December, 1925, "would be a fundamental study of human relations in industry, in which [Medical School] Dean Edsall, [Boston Psychopathic Hospital director] Dr. Campbell, and Dr. Henderson have all told me that they and their scientific associates would be glad to cooperate."

Lowell was not convinced, however, and three months of delicate negotiations followed—an anxious period for Donham, who faced the clear prospect of losing Mayo to McGill. From Filene, Donham sought and secured a pledge of funds to cover any Mayo-related expenses not covered by the Rockefellers. From General Electric's President Owen D. Young, Donham won assurances that General Electric and other companies would replace any Rockefeller funds that were lost

**A. Lincoln Filene invited the HBS faculty to his country house in Lincoln, Massachusetts, in April of 1925—"to play golf in the afternoon," Dean Donham noted in a letter to President Lowell, "dine with him, and in the evening discuss the problem of instruction in Industrial Relations."**

L. J. Henderson, relaxing
at his Vermont retreat.
Mercurial, autocratic, and
brilliant, Henderson found a
congenial spirit in Elton
Mayo.

Physician Elmer Southard
headed the Boston Psycho-
pathic Hospital until his
death in 1920. His research
in the field of neuropatholo-
gies — known to biochemist
L. J. Henderson, among
others — was often cited as a
precedent for Elton Mayo's
investigations.

as a result of the delays at Harvard. He reminded Lowell of Lowell's own public statements that the subject of
human relations in industry was one of the most important in the whole field of business, and one which the
School had to investigate and teach.

Lowell continued to say no: "I resolved long ago
that I would never recommend to the Corporation to
undertake any work on an agreement for temporary
payment, unless prepared to recommend that it should
be permanently continued; because experience showed
that practically it could not be given up when the gift
came to an end." He also cautioned Donham that the
Rockefellers seemed to consider the Mayo grant as
"seed money," which would encourage Harvard to
establish "an enduring study" of the subject of industrial relations. This tacit precondition, he said flatly,
was unacceptable to the Corporation.

In March of 1926, Donham was finally able to
report to Lowell that all concerned, including Mayo,
understood the project to be "definitely experimental,"
and not demanding of any forward commitment or
endowment, either from Harvard or the Rockefellers.
On March 30, Lowell informed Donham that the Corporation had agreed to the plan, and in the first week of
June, Mayo was officially appointed — without tenure
— as the School's first "Associate Professor of Industrial
Research."

Mayo's was a unique position. He was not expected
to teach, although the institution which now employed
him particularly emphasized teaching skills. He had a
generous salary and ample research funding, two
advantages not shared by others on the Business School
faculty. Perhaps most curious of all, to Mayo's new colleagues, was his vaguely defined field of inquiry. The
Dean obviously had great expectations for "industrial
research," but how could someone like the elusive
Mayo — who seemed to thrive in the interstices
between established disciplines — possibly meet those
expectations?

THE HARVARD PROFESSOR whose intellectual and
administrative circumstances most resembled those of
Elton Mayo was Dr. Lawrence J. ("L. J.") Henderson,
a graduate of the Medical School and a member of its
faculty since 1919. A blood chemist of international reputation, Henderson had been the first to enunciate the

concept of acid-base equilibrium in the body. Like
Mayo, he felt the impulse to broaden his work across
the intellectual boundaries of academic disciplines —
an impulse which at times required him, like Mayo, to
assemble a disparate intellectual peer group.

In the mid-1920s, Henderson was becoming
absorbed by the writings of Vilfredo Pareto, an Italian
economist of the late nineteenth century who examined the ways in which societies accommodated
change. Pareto posited that social systems are by nature
hostile to change, but — provided that the degree of
change is not radical — will adapt themselves as necessary. Henderson was greatly enamored of Pareto's theory, and attempted to correlate it with his own research.
Could social systems be likened to the human body,
he wondered; and could homeostasis — the living
organism's tendency toward chemical equilibrium —
be likened to societal equilibrium?

In Wallace Donham and Elton Mayo, Henderson
found his strongest Harvard supporters. Each of the
three — dean, industrial researcher, and biochemist —
had independently arrived at similar conclusions about
the questions that had to be answered if social degener-
ation were to be avoided. Henderson and Mayo, furthermore, had both adopted the methods of the medical sciences to answer those questions; and Donham,
no longer confident of the methodologies of law and
economics, was open to conversion. All agreed that new
knowledge in the realms of psychology and physiology
was needed, and that firsthand observation, conducted
with precision over extended periods of time, was the
best way to proceed.

Their discussions in late 1926 and early 1927 led directly to an experiment significant in the history of the Business School: the Harvard Fatigue Laboratory. Its origins are outlined in a January, 1927, letter from Mayo to Donham. Mayo had begun looking for local firms that would cooperate with his investigations, but in the meantime he was working with the School physician, Dr. Fabyan Packard, to establish why certain Business School students were failing in their studies.

"Dr. Packard and I feel," Mayo wrote Donham, "that our joint work with students, my special work in industry, and his special work in medicine, require certain physiological laboratory facilities; it is of this laboratory equipment that I wish to write to you." Mayo cited two cases of students who were having difficulties with course work: neither of the students seemed to have any physical disabilities, and yet they both exhibited organic symptoms. The point, Mayo emphasized, was that so little was known. "It is unfortunately true," he wrote, "that at the present time there is nowhere any competent investigation of the physiological changes induced in the human organism by the conditions of its daily work."

There *was* one related research activity that showed promise, Mayo noted — that of L. J. Henderson and his colleagues, who had made important discoveries concerning the relationships between posture, exertion, and blood chemistry. "If it were made possible for a competent physiologist to apply any of these methods to the investigation of industrial situations," suggested Mayo, "there could not fail to be an immense enlightenment as to the merit and defect of common industrial procedures." He would be eager, he noted, to work with researchers of such stature, and emphasized that "human biological investigations of the sort that is contemplated are nowhere in existence; it would be highly appropriate that the laboratories of the Graduate Business School should house the first unit of such an inquiry."

Mayo concluded his comments with a call for integration: "Psychology, psychiatry, and medicine have at present achieved far too little for humanity in industrial situations. This is because each study has hitherto been condemned to a solitary approach to a highly complex problem."

Donham was convinced; and so, in turn, were the trustees of the Laura Spelman Rockefeller Memorial, who within the year made two supplementary grants. One (for $35,000) was to equip the proposed "Fatigue Laboratory" — under the direction of L. J. Henderson — for which space had been set aside in the basement of the Business School's Morgan Hall. The second grant ($30,000 a year for four years) was made to expand the Business School's industrial research program into the realm of physiology. In 1930, the Rockefeller Foundation recognized the close collaborative relationship between Mayo and Henderson by combining their separate grants, and allocating $125,000 a year for seven years to a joint study of "industrial hazards." It was a princely sum of money in those times: the annual cost of the rest of the Business School faculty's research, including case studies, rarely exceeded $200,000.

Henderson welcomed the opportunity to pursue his research agenda without interference from the more traditional departments at Harvard. The Fatigue Laboratory's agenda, as he saw it, was a continuation and expansion of his earlier researches into acid-base balance, gas exchange in the respiratory cycle, and most

Originally housed in
cramped basement quarters
at the north end of Morgan
Hall (above, left), the
Fatigue Laboratory was
expanded in December,
1941, to facilitate war-
related research. A $10,000

gift from John A. Hartford,
president of the Great
Atlantic and Pacific Tea
Company, financed a one-
story addition at the rear
of Morgan which housed a
low-pressure chamber and
a cold room.

recently the physiology of exercise. He also intended to continue an investigation begun in England during the World War by the Health of Munitions Workers Committee. That study had attempted to correlate working conditions with productivity rates and industrial accidents, and had concluded that "oxygen debt" in the blood might be the cause of such accidents. Oxygen debt was seen as one cause of fatigue—a phenomenon then only vaguely understood—and it was this aspect of the English study which suggested the name for the Harvard Fatigue Laboratory.

Under the day-to-day supervision of School of Public Health Professor D. Bruce Dill, with intermittent guidance from Henderson, the Fatigue Laboratory's small staff set out to establish the constants of human blood chemistry, and how those constants might relate to industrial settings. Business School students and other volunteers ran on a specially designed treadmill in the Laboratory's cramped basement quarters, while their respiration and blood chemistry were closely monitored.

At high points in the Laboratory's activities, visitors observed at their own risk: on more than one occasion, they were mistaken for research subjects and pressed into service. One compliant Welsh philosopher permitted measurements of his metabolism and sat still for an arterial puncture; but when the Laboratory's zealous staffers attempted to weigh him, he fainted, smashing a quantity of nearby glassware. "I am terribly sorry [he] should have had this curious experience," Henderson commented in a letter, "though I am bound to say that I think he was strikingly slow in making his business known."

What the Laboratory researchers determined in their first several years of work was that there were large differences in blood chemistry between individuals. "Oxygen debt," and similar gas measurements, proved not to be a particularly useful foundation for industrial research. Furthermore, as Donham noted in his 1932 report to President Lowell, such considerations seemed more pertinent to athletics than to industry, "with its diminishing number of tasks requiring heavy muscular exertion." But given the ample resources the Laboratory enjoyed, Henderson decided to broaden the scope of its activities. Between 1929 and 1940, researchers on some twenty field studies investigated the human body's ability to adapt and acclimatize to extreme

Workers at the Youngstown Sheet and Tube Co. (below, circa 1930) were the subjects and beneficiaries of a 1934 Fatigue Lab study on the causes of cramps among mill workers. "There is certainly a thrill," Dean Donham reported to a Rockefeller Foundation official afterwards, "in scientific work which comes through as this appears to have done."

On the executive treadmill: research in the Fatigue Laboratory.

With the approach of the Second World War, the Laboratory redirected its research efforts with military applications in mind. In 1941, for example, the Fatigue Laboratory studied the effects of simulated desert conditions on volunteers from a local army base, as well as the psychological problems connected with high-altitude flight.

environmental conditions—dry and wet heat, dry and wet cold, and high altitudes.

The most successful of these field studies was conducted in the summers of 1932 and 1934. At the site of the half-finished Boulder Dam, the Fatigue Laboratory's researchers concluded in 1932 that the problems of construction workers at the site—including cramps, heat prostration, and even death—were a result of salt loss through sweat. It appeared that the human body had not retained the instinct, common in other animals, to increase salt intake during periods of heavy exertion. This finding was confirmed in the steel mills of Youngstown, Ohio, which in 1934 suffered through one of the hottest summers on record. The Fatigue Laboratory's practical recommendation that workers increase their salt intake prompted an effusive letter from the Health Officer of the Youngstown Sheet and Tube Company.

"The prospect of death during hot weather, due to heat exhaustion and cramps, has been an ever-present nightmare for many years," he wrote. "You have shown us how to handle them in such a way that the fears which have beset us in the past can be banished and put away forever.... You can well be proud of the part you have played in making life a little more secure, of rendering homes more happy by the elimination of the terrible cloud which had hung over them before you began your work here."

While the Fatigue Laboratory remained largely outside the mainstream of the Harvard Business School, its existence illustrates the atmosphere of tolerance and intellectual curiosity which was then beginning to emerge at the School—attributes which later came to typify the institution's faculty and research. The presence of barking dogs and treadmills in the basement of Morgan Hall was the source of some amusement for faculty members not directly involved in the industrial research program; many of these same professors, however, took pride in the willingness of their institution to support such work.

One professor of manufacturing, for example, delighted in taking visiting faculty members from other business schools on a tour of the Fatigue Laboratory. "Of course," he would say matter-of-factly, as his guest surveyed the impressive array of laboratory apparatus and white-coated researchers, "*all* business schools of the first rank have facilities like these."

## Ethics, Edward Bok, and adversity

Instruction in business ethics had been an issue since the School's founding. Harvard President A. Lawrence Lowell had argued against a separate course on the subject, suggesting that students should instead encounter ethical questions in all their courses. Edwin Gay contemplated such a course in his original curriculum for the School, but concluded that it would be very difficult to teach.

Early in his tenure as dean, Wallace Donham decided that such a course could and should be taught. In his 1922 report to Lowell, he noted that instruction in business ethics was "much on the minds" of his faculty, and that the case method seemed to be the only sure means to that end. The professionalization of business demanded "a collection of cases on this subject and adequate class-room instruction to give it proper emphasis."

By 1924, however, Donham was not so confident. In a March interview with the Boston *Globe*, he suggested that business as a profession was barely out of the "frontier stage," and that while some aspects of business, such as banking, had developed clear codes of conduct, the wide variety of business activities hindered the formulation of an effective, all-encompassing ethical code.

As was true of other subjects investigated by the School's field agents, business ethics had proved immensely complicated. "Imagine you are employed by an automobile plant which is experimenting with four-wheel brakes," Donham suggested to the *Globe* reporter. "Suppose a friend in a rival establishment catches you unprepared and suddenly inquires point-blank: 'Is your concern experimenting with four-wheel brakes?'

"Now, I'm not suggesting what your answer should be, but I do suggest that you have many conflicting obligations to consider when you reply. . . . Obviously, even so simple a problem requires some thought."

While the School grappled with ethics in the curriculum, developments in the outside world took an unexpected turn. In June of 1923, Ellery Sedgwick—editor of the *Atlantic Monthly*, and a member of Harvard's Board of Overseers—approached Donham with a novel plan. Sedgwick said he represented an anonymous donor who wished to establish a series of advertising awards. In part, said Sedgwick, the prospective donor wanted to recognize forceful writing and design. But in equal measure, according to Sedgwick, the donor wanted to encourage truth and accuracy in advertising.

The prospective benefactor, it soon emerged, was Edward Bok, retired editor of the *Ladies' Home Journal.* The experience of winning a Pulitzer prize for his autobiography had inspired Bok to create several awards programs of his own, as a means of "serving notice on the younger mind that other achievements than the accumulation of wealth or the striving for commercial power are adjudged worthy of recognition in the world." Like many at the Business School, Bok was distressed by the then-prevalent "legacy of the P. T. Barnum theory of advertising," which seemed to cast much of the broader business community in a disreputable light.

HBS Professor Neil Borden and others worked with Bok to devise a "Harvard Advertising Awards" program, which would recognize not only effective campaigns, but also innovative marketing research. "It was agreed," Borden later recalled, "that the announcements should stress the importance we both placed upon integrity of statement in order to give what stimulus we could to improved standards of integrity and veracity."

The first nine awards—soon known simply as "the Bok awards"—were announced in 1925. Reaction was mixed, at first, but the awards program gradually achieved national recognition, and both reflected and contributed to improved ethical standards in advertising. In 1930, the Bok awards were taken over by a private foundation, but were discontinued the following year when that organization experienced financial difficulties.

"These awards were started and maintained from the standpoint of the School," Donham wrote to English scholar Graham Wallas in 1931, "solely with the idea of bringing into public discussion some of the ethical dilemmas which are involved in advertising, and raising the level of both integrity and research in this field." The Dean saw this effort as of largely symbolic importance. A much more substantive development, in his analysis, was the rise of the large corporation. "The history of every profession contains plenty of evidence," Donham suggested to Wallas, "that it will be practically impossible to get great groups of men acting from pure altruism. The hope for ethical progress lies, as I see it, in tying the institutional point of view into current business policies, and it is for this reason that the big, stable companies in this country have been most influential in building up ethical standards."

But the School, nevertheless, had a role to play; and in recognition of this fact, the faculty had in 1928 authorized a second-year elective in Business Ethics. Carl F. Taeusch, who held a doctorate in philosophy from Harvard, was hired from the State University of Iowa to conduct this first formal experiment in the teaching of business ethics. "Although moral fiber can scarcely be created in the student," Donham wrote of the course in his 1929 report to Lowell, "the more common ethical dilemmas of business can be presented to him while he has time for deliberate consideration free from the pressure of circumstance." Taeusch's course, however, remained more theoretical than practical, and never won sufficient student support. Even Donham's strong advocacy for the experiment could not save the course, which was discontinued in 1935.

"It is the opinion of those who remember Dr. Taeusch's course on ethics," wrote one observer many years later, "that it was unsuccessful because it was perceived as

**On one occasion, the entries in the Bok competition were displayed in the Baker Library reading room.**

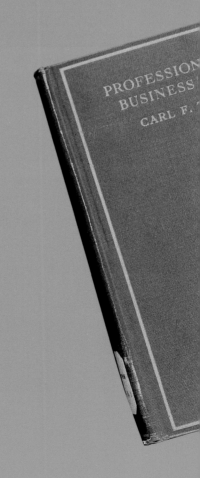

'Sunday School talk.' Indeed, that effort and another in the middle Thirties appear to have set back the desire to tackle the subject at all."

Events in the world of affairs had, in fact, bypassed Taeusch's modest efforts. "There was a steady improvement in ethical standards [in business] up to something like the year 1926," Donham wrote in a 1934 letter to a critic of the School, reflecting on the lessons of a decade. The effects of the Depression, and federal responses to the economic crisis, were by then lending a new urgency to the quest for ethical standards. "I think from 1926 to 1929 a good many business men, like an even larger percentage of the rest of the community, were swept off their

feet by a sudden apparent expansion in the wealth of the nation, and [contributed to] a temporary reduction in ethical standards.

"Since the crash in the fall of 1929 I think there has been an even more rapid improvement in ethical standards in business than in the period preceding 1926. Adversity has at least this advantage."

By a curious historical coincidence, another Bok—Derek, grandson of Edward, and president of Harvard fifty years later—also raised the issue of ethics and their proper place in the Business School curriculum. "While Cummins Engine Company has actually hired a moral philosopher to participate in many aspects of corporate planning," wrote Bok in his 1977–78 report to Harvard's Board of Overseers,

"few business schools, if any, have yet seen fit to appoint a professor of comparable background to serve on their faculties." Bok was evidently unaware of Carl Taeusch's unhappy experience in precisely that role; he nevertheless correctly identified a long-standing inability on the part of Harvard's business school—and other schools in the field—to teach ethics effectively.

"Desire outruns performance," Wallace Donham concluded in 1933, "all along the line."

**Edward Bok: publisher, author, and promoter of business ethics.**

**A 1927 HBS dinner honoring Bok, seated with Dean Donham at rear, near the fireplace.**

**Carl Taeusch wrote *Professional and Business Ethics* while still at the State University of Iowa.**

**Joseph P. Kennedy supported and helped organize a Business Policy experiment: a study of the American film industry.**

WHILE HENDERSON'S FATIGUE LABORATORY made steady progress in its own arcane field, Elton Mayo—the other principal figure in the School's industrial researches—could point to no clear evidence of success in his own work. "Our main problem," as Mayo's secretary and research assistant Emily Osborne wrote to Donham in 1928, "is to gain the confidence and cooperation of leaders in industry." While this was not a new problem for Mayo, he was finding it especially difficult to interest New England's manufacturers in his proposed research. "We have been unable to work in any plant," Osborne noted, "where we have received the confidence and cooperation of the management and heads of departments." In several cases, Mayo had begun his work only to discover that the firm's management expected him to implement a "scientific management" plan; in others, the deterioration of the firm's financial position had undercut his work.

Donham, hoping to direct Mayo's activities into a promising quarter, had asked him early in 1927 to study and report on the motion picture industry. The Dean was on friendly terms with Joseph P. Kennedy, then head of the Moving Picture Corporation; with the help of Kennedy and others, the School was about to mount a month-long experiment in the Business Policy course, consisting of lectures and discussions led by leaders in the film industry. Donham was intrigued by the fact that the founders of an important industry were still alive and available for study. But Mayo's report harshly condemned the studio system, which struck Mayo as irresponsible and unable to learn from its mistakes.

The Dean was undeterred, and arranged for Mayo to address a group of influential industrialists at the New York Harvard Club in October of that year. The success of that address, which concerned the benefits that psychology might provide to industry, led to closer ties with several advisors to John D. Rockefeller, Jr., and to a friendship with Rockefeller himself. A more important outcome of the Harvard Club lunch, however, was a connection with a firm that would eventually extend the "confidence and cooperation" that Mayo was seeking.

In the audience that day was T. K. Stevenson, personnel director of the Western Electric Company. Stevenson was evidently impressed with Mayo's speech, for in March of 1928, he sought the Business School professor's assistance. Could Mayo help, he asked, in interpreting the confusing data then emerging from a company-sponsored research project at Western Electric's Hawthorne Works?

This manufacturing facility, located on the outskirts of Cicero, Illinois, then employed over 40,000 workers, who manufactured most of the telephones made in America. The huge plant also produced cables, rod and wire components, relays and switching gear, and teletype apparatus for its parent company, American Telephone and Telegraph. Hawthorne, a city within a city, included restaurants, stores, and athletic facilities.

Since 1924, Western Electric, in collaboration with the National Academy of Sciences, had been studying worker productivity. The early experiments, which attempted to correlate lighting conditions to productivity, had led only to confusion. At one point, the test group had shown no productivity changes in response to different amounts of light, while the control group—with unchanged illumination—showed steady gains in productivity. Later, the test group had achieved steady productivity gains in response to less and less light, until the machinery they were operating was barely visible. The researchers had been able to conclude only that lighting had a minor impact on productivity, and that other more important factors had not been controlled.

In an attempt to determine and control these elusive factors, the Western Electric researchers had set up a special facility, later known as the "Relay Assembly Test Room," in April of 1927. Five workers had agreed to assemble telephone relays under conditions of close scientific observation, but without formal company supervision. Facts about the assemblers themselves, including their backgrounds, physical health, and attitudes toward work, were studied extensively. Their output was first determined under normal working conditions; it was then measured again when the workers were transferred to the Test Room. At staged intervals, changes were introduced into the working environment: pay incentives, various rest schedules, shorter work weeks, and so on.

Callan (far left) and
Ebersole: the aphorism
and the unstated opinion.

Sanders in the classroom.

The catlike Dewing.

Cabot (far left) and Doriot:
purposefully rustic and
infuriating.

## Urbane
## lightning

"I find myself remembering
with pleasure," wrote an anonymous HBS alumnus in a 1935
HBS *Bulletin* class note, "such
matters as the stimulating
paucity of stated opinion in
Professor Ebersole's class;
Doriot's studied technique of
infuriating students into positive brilliance; Dewing grin-
ning catlike behind his great
black whiskers and reaching

slyly out to give the student-
mouse one more poke with his
paw; the synthetic rusticity of
Cabot's approach, metaphor in
hand, to disembowel regulatory
stupidity at one stroke; 'Old
Faithful' Callan spouting an
aphorism a minute to lie and
gleam like pearls before the
swine; and Professor Sanders'
tranquil lightning flickering
urbanely among the control
accounts."

The Hawthorne Works, in
Cicero, Illinois, proved to be
Elton Mayo's long-sought
industrial laboratory.

The Relay Assembly Test
Room: what factors deter-
mined worker productivity?

Taken as a whole, the productivity of the workers again rose consistently. A return to the original working conditions reduced productivity somewhat, but not to the levels originally recorded. Only the most extreme changes in environment seemed to have a negative impact on the aggregate output of the observed workers. Most confusing, though, were the data that emerged for individuals: two of the workers showed similarly steady increases in productivity; two others shared a pattern of alternately high and low productivity; and the fifth increased her already high level of productivity after a vacation and maintained her new level.

The task that personnel director Stevenson proposed for Mayo was to search for correlations between individual physical differences among the test subjects and their respective productivity levels. Mayo accepted the assignment, and visited the Hawthorne Works in April with two assistants. Reflecting Henderson's influence—who in turn reflected Pareto's influence—Mayo hypothesized that the worker who enjoyed "organic equilibrium" would prove to be the most productive.

Following the established Fatigue Laboratory procedures, Mayo and his assistants measured the blood pressures of the five workers, and found preliminary evidence to support his hypothesis. The most productive worker, he informed a Rockefeller Foundation official, was the one "who achieved an organic equilibrium—and kept it."

In fact, this correlation soon proved false. The correlation that *did* seem promising to the Hawthorne researchers, though, was the one which apparently existed between supervision and productivity. Throughout the studies, the Test Room workers' comments had suggested the importance of their relative autonomy, and of the sympathetic attention they were receiving from their observers. In the fall of 1928, therefore, Western Electric decided to expand the study to include the impact of different supervisors. Early in 1929, the company proposed to broaden the research still further, informing Mayo that the company's new Industrial Research Division would, over the course of the next two years, interview every plant employee—at a total cost of $200,000. The interviews, it was

**Mayo and Roethlisberger developed an emotionally charged and productive relationship. Mayo served as a father figure and mentor for the younger Roethlisberger, and helped him through various personal crises; and it was Roethlisberger's efforts to summarize the Western Electric research that brought the lessons of Hawthorne to a broader public.**

**"I had to get a visible, tangible product," Roethlisberger later recalled, "that Mayo could show for his labors, whether anyone read it or not."**

hoped, would produce information from the workers' point of view, and suggest new approaches to supervision.

For Mayo, this was an unexpected opportunity, and it proved to be the one that he had been searching for. Although he was held in great esteem by the middle managers with whom he had worked at Hawthorne, his personal contributions to the Hawthorne studies up to that point had been limited. He had commented constructively on the research which had predated his involvement, and participated intermittently in the more recent Test Room experiments. He had, in addition, been the most effective advocate of the research in influential industrial circles. Now, however, he sought an important responsibility in the research effort: shaping the approach of the company's interviewers.

Mayo proposed an indirect approach. Rather than interrogation, Mayo argued for sympathetic listening—much like the attention enjoyed by the Test Room workers. According to Mayo's biographer, the approach was in part borrowed from child psychologist Jean Piaget, and the interviewer was to pay close attention to the interviewee, to refrain from arguing or offering advice, to listen for and test the validity of patterns in the interviewee's responses, and to treat all responses as confidential. Interviews conducted along these lines would begin to answer the question that Mayo had defined as critical: how does the worker's psychological state relate to his or her productivity? The answer, when combined with findings from a further and more precise exploration of the relation between physiology and labor, might provide a new foundation for industrial relations.

In July, 1929, Western Electric accepted Mayo's approach, and by the end of the year Mayo was convinced that he was involved in a "major revolution in industrial method," comparable in its impact to the Industrial Revolution. "If all fear of bully-ragging can be taken out of supervision, and if a majority of supervisors are trained interviewers," he wrote to a Hawthorne associate in October, 1929, "industry will enter upon a new and undreamed era of active collaboration that will make possible an almost incredible human advance."

By 1930, the research team had grown to thirty, and almost half of the Hawthorne workers had been interviewed. Three young Harvard professors—Fritz J. Roethlisberger, W. Lloyd Warner, and Richard Meriam —visited the Hawthorne Works for the first time that summer, and Roethlisberger was soon deeply involved in the Hawthorne research. As part of an understanding between Harvard and Western Electric, it had been agreed that Roethlisberger would replace Mayo as Harvard's principal researcher at Hawthorne, thereby enabling Mayo to write the official account of the researches. Warner, who held a joint appointment in the Business School and the Department of Anthropology, was to assist Western Electric in the sociological aspects of the continuing studies, including a new "Bank Wiring Room" project, which explored the progress of affinities and antagonisms in working groups.

**A Mayo graph plotting the effect of rest periods on worker productivity. Mayo gradually came to emphasize the qualitative, rather than the quantitative, aspects of the workplace.**

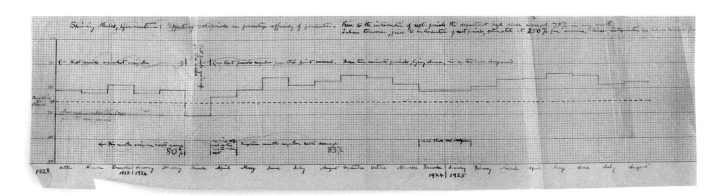

W. Lloyd Warner, formally employed by Mayo's Department of Industrial Research in the fall of 1931, wanted to use Harvard sociology students to study the Hawthorne Works' environs of Cicero, Illinois—a plan proposed by Western Electric, but ultimately deemed impractical. Research based on this idea, however, was eventually carried out in Newburyport, Massachusetts, and produced the famed "Yankee City" series of studies.

Both the Yankee City studies and Bank Wiring Room experiments illustrated a key difference between Mayo and Warner. Warner, as an anthropologist, was primarily interested in the status, structure, and standing of a social situation—its stable elements. Mayo, by contrast, emphasized the dynamics of social change.

At work in the Bank Wiring Room, where W. Lloyd Warner first studied the informal organization of small work groups.

The Business School's Dean was pleased with the progress of the research, which seemed to contradict prevailing stereotypes of the industrial workplace and its effect on the worker. "We cannot make an individual stupid," Donham wrote in his 1932 report to President Lowell. Summarizing the results of the Hawthorne research to that date, Donham challenged the commonly held view that an "atrophied individual" was the inevitable result of the monotony of industrial production. The worker's problem, it seemed, was of a different sort: "We may make him dissatisfied, psychoneurotic, or restless if working conditions and outside influences are such as to disturb his emotional status. It is urgently necessary that industry should give as much attention to human as it has to material inquiry."

But Donham was only too aware that his call would go unheeded. Industrial research was a precarious venture in the best of times; now its most promising model —the Hawthorne research—was being swamped by external circumstances. The Depression had hit Western Electric, and Hawthorne, hard. In January and February of 1932, the company made four successive cuts in its manufacturing schedule and announced plans to lay off 5,000 workers. Within six months, a third of the firm's 40,000 employees were laid off, including most of those being studied.

At the outset of the research, Mayo could argue persuasively that the very vagueness of his inquiries was a virtue, allowing the investigation to pursue the unexpected leads suggested by empirical evidence. Now, vagueness and indirection—and an expensive corporate research apparatus based on those premises —could no longer be justified. After severing his last formal ties with Western Electric, Mayo determined in 1932 to write a full account of the Hawthorne studies. Glaucoma prevented him from doing so, however, and the task of chronicling the Hawthorne studies eventually fell to Harvard's Roethlisberger and Western Electric's Harold Wright and William Dickson.

*Management and the Worker*, published in 1939, became an unexpected bestseller, and established the Hawthorne experiments as classics in their field. Almost immediately, academic critics charged the Hawthorne researchers with both ideological and methodological shortcomings—and thus began a debate which still continues. But *Management and the Worker*, and the work it described, indisputably defined a new field of social research. In the process, it shaped the research agenda and methodology of the Harvard Business School, and validated Wallace Donham's concept of field-based empirical research, aimed at addressing key social and industrial issues.

## A slow and hard process

Edmund P. Learned, the youngest member of the School's Marketing faculty, had suffered through three cases of whooping cough in his family while trying to complete his HBS doctoral dissertation on schedule. Proud of his work, he was therefore taken aback when Dean Donham encouraged him, in a conference in the fall of 1929, *not* to publish the dissertation—and was particularly surprised at the rationale Donham offered.

In the recent past, Donham explained, he had conducted a small experiment: he had asked ten lawyers each to cite six great law books. Combining the lists, he found ten books mentioned consistently. "When he reflected on this list," Learned later recalled, "he noted certain common elements. Each [author] had selected an area for study in breadth and depth; none had rushed into publication; each wrote articles for the law journals from time to time; [and] eventually each published the great book that reflected the wisdom of 20 to 25 years of research and reflective thought."

Seven years later, in a memorandum to himself, Donham confessed that he had urged a similar strategy on his faculty, and reflected on its results.

"We have written no first-rate books," he noted, "nor have we written much. Declaratory writing by members of a business faculty who are interested in the concrete study of case material is a slow and hard process involving common sense, judgement, and wide experience with many situations. We have for fifteen years deliberately slowed down such writing, at the cost of some loss of standing in the community and among university colleagues in other fields. We have preferred to do this rather than to write prematurely. My personal influence has been exerted in this direction."

The strategy did not always sit well with members of the faculty. In the previous year, Professor Malcolm McNair had presented a report on research to a faculty meeting. Case research was all-important to the course for which it was carried out, McNair conceded, "but outside that course the knowledge obtained by the collection of cases is not made generally useful. It tends to remain in a somewhat unorganized form in the instructor's mind. In other words, we have not followed *through* the case system as a means of research."

One problem identified by McNair was the inordinately time-consuming process of case book revision. It was a process with which Melvin Copeland, for example, was painfully familiar. By 1934, Copeland was faced with the task of producing the *fifth* edition of *Marketing Problems*— first published only twelve years earlier. Such circumstances led McNair to suggest the abandonment of printed and bound case books, in favor of looseleaf versions.

"Members of the faculty," McNair said flatly, "should definitely plan to do more writing of a declaratory nature." Faculty members should "plan more or less regularly and systematically to deal definitively with specialized topics or narrow segments in their particular fields, perhaps largely in the form of monographs and articles. Senior members of the faculty, however, may be expected from time to time to write books of broader scope."

It was not until the end of the decade that such books began to emerge. It was in the spring of 1939, for example, that the Harvard University Press published *Management and the Worker*, an account by HBS Professor Fritz J. Roethlisberger (with coauthor William Dickson) of the research at Western Electric's Hawthorne plant. With the help of a timely account in *Reader's Digest*, the book became an unexpected bestseller.

Three years later, Neil H. Borden finally synthesized years of research and a huge mass of data into *The Economic Effects of Advertising*, which was immediately recognized as a classic in its field. Borden's book—as the summary of an academic career, and the result of sustained, research-oriented case investigation—also represented a resolution of the contrasting research strategies advocated by McNair and Donham, and set a high standard for postwar project research at the School.

"*The most outstanding study of industrial rela... been published anywhere, any time.*" — PERSON...

## MANAGEME[N]T AND THE WORKER

### F. J. ROETHLISBERGER
### WILLIAM J. DICKSON

**Fifteenth Printing**

**Preparing for the pot of gold: few suspected in 1930 that the hardest economic times were still to come.**

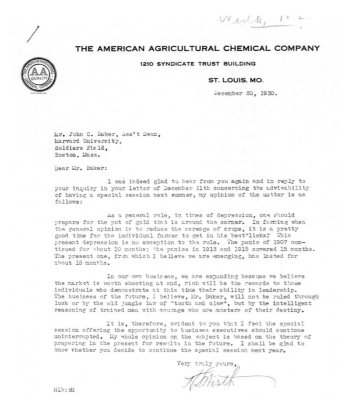

"IF I WERE STARTING LIFE OVER AGAIN, I am inclined to think that I would go into the advertising business in preference to almost any other," wrote the governor of New York in a 1931 *Printer's Ink* article. "It is essentially a form of education; and the progress of civilization depends on education."

Franklin D. Roosevelt chose an unlikely juncture to write optimistically about the advertising business. Within the previous two years, the industry's total volume had shrunk by a third; within the next two years, it would suffer an equally large decline. Roosevelt was not the only optimist, however, as Paul T. Cherington had demonstrated in the pages of the same magazine several months earlier. "The recovery is as inevitable as the rising of the sun," Cherington wrote, "and we should not be concerned with when it is coming but how to be ready for it when it does come."

By any ordinary calculation of the business cycle, in fact, optimism would have been well placed in mid-1931. It had been almost two years, after all, since the calamitous stock market crash — the panic of late

October and early November, 1929, that had resulted in a $30 billion aggregate investor loss. Historical experience suggested that the economy should soon be turning upwards, in response to accumulated demand and the depressed price of manufactured goods.

On the whole, President Hoover subscribed to the assumption that the marketplace would right itself. Bank failures were increasing, it was true — from 1,326 failures in 1930 to 2,294 in 1931. A visit from the Harvard Business School's Dean Donham and Professor John F. Ebersole, alarmed about the banking situation, failed to alter the thinking of the president's advisors. Even in the prosperous 1920s, they argued, an average of 700 banks failed each year. Hoover, furthermore, had minimized the consequences of the economic turmoil by engineering a remarkable compact on November 11, 1929. That day, he had met in the morning with Henry Ford, Alfred Sloan, Owen D. Young, Walter Gifford, and other leading industrialists, and had extracted from them pledges to support existing wage levels, and to divide available work equally. In the afternoon, he had used these pledges to persuade John L. Lewis and other labor leaders to forego strikes and wage increases for the duration of the compact.

After two relatively tranquil years, however, the compact collapsed, and wage cuts became widespread. The economy's downward spiral intensified, as the nation's 550 largest industrials suffered a 68 percent decline in net income between 1929 and 1931. Industrial production in 1932 stood at half its 1929 level. Unlike earlier economic crises, furthermore, this was a disaster of international proportions. Trade among the industrialized nations shrank by almost two-thirds.

Hoover, finally spurred to action in early 1932, doubled federal spending on public works projects, and established a "Reconstruction Finance Corporation," making $500 million available for loans to banks, railroads, and manufacturers. But an economic and psychological paralysis was now firmly entrenched. In only three years, business had fallen from grace in the eyes of the public; increasingly, business and businessmen were reviled. Hoover had been dubbed the "Great Engineer" for his notable relief efforts during the World War; now the nickname was used contemptuously.

George F. Baker died in May, 1931. He was eulogized in the HBS faculty minutes as "an exemplar of the tradition which the School hopes to carry on and spread throughout the business world."

Six years later, Dean Donham asked George F. Baker, Jr., to donate one of his father's personal possessions to the School. Such a keepsake, he said, would be passed down from dean to dean. Baker obliged with his father's pen stand. "It is in somewhat battered condition," he wrote, "but that probably makes it all the more attractive."

Within the year, the younger Baker himself was dead, victim of an acute appendicitis attack suffered while at sea on his yacht.

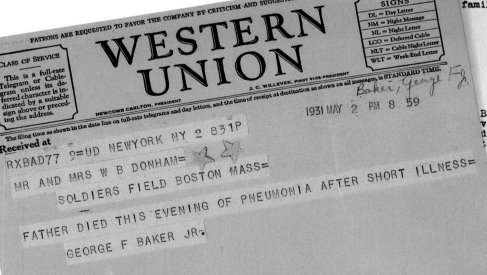

FEB 6 1937

2 Wall Street
New York

February 5, 1937

Dear Wallace:

I am sending you my father's inkstand which he had on his desk for over forty years, right up to the time of his death. It is in somewhat battered condition but that probably makes it all the more attractive.

I am also sending by separate parcel the inkstand which Senator Aldrich used up to the time of his death and which his family gave to the late Harry P. Davison, and after the death of Mr. Davison his family gave it to me.

Yours faithfully,

Geo. F. Baker

B. Donham, Esq.
vard Business School
diers Field
on, Mass.

WESTERN UNION

CLASS OF SERVICE
This is a full-rate Telegram or Cable-gram unless its deferred character is indicated by a suitable sign above or preceding the address.

NEWCOMB CARLTON, PRESIDENT          J. C. WILLEVER, FIRST VICE-PRESIDENT

PATRONS ARE REQUESTED TO FAVOR THE COMPANY BY CRITICISM AND SUGGESTION CONCERNING ITS SERVICE          12018

SIGNS
DL = Day Letter
NM = Night Message
NL = Night Letter
LCO = Deferred Cable
NLT = Cable Night Letter
WLT = Week-End Letter

The filing time as shown in the date line on full-rate telegrams and day letters, and the time of receipt at destination as shown on all messages, is STANDARD TIME.

Baker, George F. J.

1931 MAY 2 PM 8 59

Received at
RXBAD77 9=UD NEWYORK NY 2 831P

MR AND MRS W B DONHAM=

SOLDIERS FIELD BOSTON MASS=

FATHER DIED THIS EVENING OF PNEUMONIA AFTER SHORT ILLNESS=

GEORGE F BAKER JR=

WESTERN UNION GIFT ORDERS SOLVE THE PERPLEXING QUESTION OF WHAT TO GIVE.

The Tennessee Valley Authority—one of Roosevelt's most controversial experiments—supplied an interesting example to public and private utilities.

Offering radically low power rates, the TVA increased power consumption in its districts by an average of almost 200 percent between 1934 and 1942, thereby making a profit on its energy. During the same period, national average consumption increased only 63 percent.

Roosevelt wasted no time in implementing his various experiments. The Works Progress Administration (WPA), for example, was created in April of 1935.

Eight months later, it had 2.7 million workers on its payroll.

"The only thing we have to fear is fear itself," Roosevelt proclaimed on March 4, 1933, in his first inaugural address. In fact, the banking crisis had intensified over the previous several months, and only a small percentage of the nation's banks were functioning normally that day. The new president declared a national bank holiday, and in his first "fireside chat" a week later, attempted to persuade the nation that it was "safer to keep your money in a reopened bank than under the mattress."

The initial three months of Roosevelt's first term were later recalled as the "Hundred Days"—significant for the record number of important pieces of legislation passed by the special session of Congress. Roosevelt had defined two short-term goals: to stabilize the nation's failing agricultural system, and to foster "industrial self-government." He had powerful allies in his pursuit of the latter goal, since leaders in business and government alike had reached the conclusion that traditional competition was ineffective and inappropriate, given the prevailing economic conditions.

The established body of antitrust law, however, prevented the degree of industrial collaboration needed to stabilize prices, control production, and curb marketing excesses. As secretary of commerce, Herbert Hoover had lobbied hard on behalf of cooperative trade associations, but the Supreme Court had ruled in the mid-1920s against information-sharing that might be used to restrain production. When General Electric's President Gerard Swope approached President Hoover in 1931 with a similar scheme—although it was now a plan born out of crisis, rather than prosperity—Hoover had declined to support it.

The banking crisis: Internal Revenue Service officials announced in early March that despite bank failures, personal checks were still being accepted for income-tax payments.

Roosevelt, however, embraced the concept. After protracted negotiations with both business and labor, the president's draftsmen devised the "National Industrial Recovery Act" (NIRA), which Congress passed in June of 1933. The law provided for "codes of fair competition," to be written primarily by trade associations. These codes were to be reviewed by the National Recovery Administration (NRA) to ensure that they were not designed to foster industry monopolies. Once approved, a code would apply to all producers in a given industry, who could then be punished for non-compliance.

The business community was generally apprehensive about the NIRA, but recognizing the need for action, accepted the government's intrusion into the private sector. The Act contained one clause which many businessmen found particularly objectionable—the controversial Section 7-A, which for the first time guaranteed to workers the right of collective bargaining, free from employer interference. In return for this concession, however, businesses subscribing to an approved code were exempted from antitrust regulation. Within a month of the passage of the Act, over two hundred industries had submitted codes for approval by the NRA. The codes approved by the NRA all prohibited child labor and acknowledged labor's right to collective bargaining. Most established a work-week and minimum wage, and many specified unacceptable (and already illegal) trade practices: false advertising, bribery, and so on.

The NRA was only one of many highly visible—and often controversial—initiatives that came early in the new president's first term. The Civilian Conservation Corps created temporary work for 250,000 single men between 18 and 25 years old. The creation of the Tennessee Valley Authority in May, 1933, began a large-scale dam building project, and for the first time put the federal government in direct competition with private industry in the field of power generation. A quiet "divorce" of the dollar from gold led to a 40 percent devaluation of the dollar within a year, and a more competitive position in relation to other currencies already off the gold standard.

But the NRA had a special symbolic importance, establishing as it did a new cooperative relationship between business and government. Government for the first time tacitly acknowledged that the large business organization was not necessarily an economic evil; business acknowledged that government had authority—at least during periods of economic crisis—in realms previously reserved for business alone.

The symbolic impact of the NRA also reached into the daily lives of Americans. Adherence to an NRA-approved code enabled a business to display the NRA emblem: a blue eagle with the slogan "NRA—We do our part." Within four months of the passage of the NIRA, over 90 percent of the nation's commercial and industrial firms had done so. In the same period, almost three million workers were rehired, and the nation's purchasing power reversed its downward trend. By the end of the Hundred Days, with the active and visible intervention of the federal government into nearly every sector of the economy, few Americans felt, as they had a year earlier, that the nation lacked a leader.

# What assistant deans do

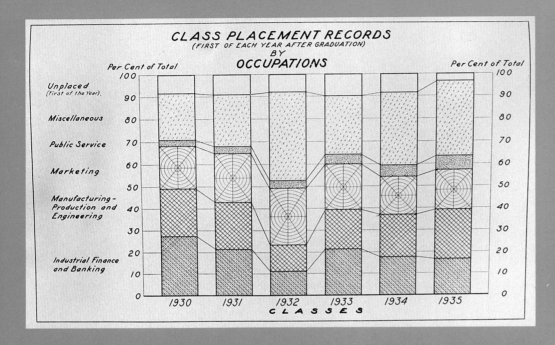

CLASS PLACEMENT RECORDS
(FIRST OF EACH YEAR AFTER GRADUATION)
BY
OCCUPATIONS

**Placement—a key function of the assistant deans in the 1930s —reflected the impact of the Depression. More graduates reported employment in "miscellaneous" categories, while fewer went into manufacturing, banking, and finance.**

In a letter of November, 1922, Harvard's President Emeritus Charles W. Eliot asked Dean Wallace Donham what function the Business School's three assistant deans performed. It was an administrative title, Eliot confessed, with which he was not familiar.

"Our three assistant deans," Donham replied, "Mr. David, Mr. Biddle, and Mr. Borden, are engaged like myself in a combination of functions, — partly teaching (Professor David teaches Retail Store Management, and Mr. Biddle Investment Banking); partly internal administration (the entire coordinating work of building up student relations is handled through this office); partly financial (Mr. David and Mr. Biddle as well as I myself have devoted a good deal of time to financing the case system); partly making industrial contacts (all of us devote much time to this and Mr. Borden is now at the General Electric Company for a year, working on the gathering of teaching material, namely, cases, under an agreement with them and at their expense); partly placement (the problem of placing men who graduate from the School is not serious today but during the [1920–22] depression it was very serious, and

will always require a good deal of attention if we are to continue to fit men into proper environments.)"

For the assistant deans, seated in a row of desks outside the Dean's office, informality was the rule. They were meant to be available to students in a way that Donham himself—at first because of time pressures, and later for health reasons—was not. As Donham's letter to Eliot implied, the assistant deans were responsible for student relations, fundraising, college recruiting, and special assignments. Placement of graduating students, particularly in summer jobs between the first and second years, required constant solicitation on the part of the assistant deans. The faculty, at first skeptical of Donham's innovation, was gradually persuaded of the usefulness of the assistant deans. By 1932, for example, the faculty Committee on Economy recommended against cuts in the ranks of assistant deans, having concluded that professors could not carry on the School's routine office tasks as efficiently as the assistant deans.

**Borden**

**Bates**

**Malott**

**Doriot**

**Case**

Clinton P. Biddle was Donham's closest confidant, as evidenced by a 1937 note from Donham to Biddle regarding a research grant and a library acquisition. Biddle's sudden death in 1939 created great difficulties for the Dean, who had delegated extensive authority to him.

After Biddle's death, his portrait was hung above the fireplace in the Dean's office.

Biddle

Baker

Donham had an additional practical reason for maintaining his corps of assistant deans. Young graduates of the School could be retained in this capacity as possible future faculty candidates, without formal commitment on either side. For their part, the assistant deans were generally pleased with the career opportunities afforded by the post, as well as with the chance to work for Donham. They frequently traveled with the Dean, thereby becoming acquainted with Donham's influential advisors in the business community; they also formed close personal relationships among themselves.

"Five years ago," wrote Assistant Dean Biddle in 1925, declining a tentative offer of the presidency of Ohio University, "a group of us headed by Mr. Donham set out to make the Business School the outstanding accomplishment in education for this half of the twentieth century. . . . We have not yet accomplished our goal, but as I look back over the five years of struggle in building up confidence of the business men, in creating a morale among our students and graduates, and in financing our experimental research work from hand to mouth and week by week, I believe that the hardest part of our task is over."

The subsequent careers of Donham's assistant deans suggest the caliber of men attracted to the post. Georges F. Doriot and George E. Bates, for example, made the successful—and, for most, difficult—transition from administrator to academic. John C. Baker, Everett N. Case, and Deane W. Malott all eventually served as university presidents, prompting one journalist to dub Harvard's business school the "School for Presidents." Biddle, having served as de facto dean following Donham's 1927 heart attack, was appointed the School's first associate dean in 1931. His influence with Donham was enormous, and he helped contain the occasional problem created by the Dean's impetuous nature. Had Biddle not died suddenly in 1939, he might well have succeeded Donham in the deanship.

The post did in fact go to another former assistant dean, Donald K. David, a close personal friend of Clinton Biddle. "It is a real pleasure to me to have Mr. David return," Donham wrote to a friend and former co-worker of George F. Baker, Jr., in 1941. "He combines the training in the School and intimate knowledge of it with successful business experience in a way that I think would have been very satisfactory to George, who was, I believe, very fond of him."

**"The most appalling feature** of this depression," Wallace Donham told the assembled first-year class three days after Roosevelt's inauguration, "has been the lack of leadership, both political and business." Former President Hoover, said Donham, had abdicated his authority early in his term by not addressing the issue of Prohibition; Congress had unfortunately followed suit. Now, with the ascent of Roosevelt, there was "a real basis for hope."

To Donham, as to many Americans, the summer of 1932 had presented little basis for hope. The paralysis of the Hoover administration had only intensified as the Depression had deepened. In response—acting on the impulse to do *something*—the Business School's Dean had initiated a "commodity study," strongly requesting all faculty members in residence to participate in a large-scale study of commodity prices. The scheme, generally regarded by the faculty as misguided, was abandoned after a week of intensive activity.

But the Dean retained the urge to act, and to use the School's resources to address the national crisis. It seemed to Donham, Mayo, and others that the social collapse they had anticipated was now upon them, well before the needed correctives were in hand. The future was obscure, Donham wrote in 1933, but neither the business community nor the School could afford to look backwards. "Business will assume new relationships to the civilization of which it is a part," he noted, "and business education must not only follow developing changes, but should contribute through its faculties and through its graduates to the sane development of these new relationships."

Europe and America, Donham concluded reluctantly, must now "turn toward great centralization of power in efforts to exercise control over the complexities of industrial civilization." Only experience would show how far that centralization should proceed. One thing, however, was certain: America could not depend upon its accustomed laissez-faire approach to the marketplace, because "the social cost of rapid progress in the scientific mechanization of industry is too high, and the resulting instability too great."

Donham cautioned against holding individuals responsible for the nation's loss of social and economic balance. "No one," he argued, "could deplore more deeply than the Faculty of this School the abuses of the period of wild expansion just preceding the depression.

No one could be more shocked by the evidence of personal disintegration in high places." But a focus on punishment would be futile, for "the search for personal devils too often diverts attention from the critical social problems which create these personal devils."

Given the sobering circumstances, the celebration of the 25th anniversary of the Harvard Business School—marked on April 10, 1933, in the University's Memorial Church—was muted. Following an invocation by Bishop William Lawrence, Donham spoke on "The Failure of Business Leadership and the Responsibility of the Universities."

"To say that the atmosphere was one of pessimism would be inaccurate," the Harvard Business School *Bulletin* reported, "but it was plainly evident that the speakers and the audience felt, and in large part understood, that the University, the Business School, and the country at large had definitely bade farewell to a state of things that probably would never be seen again."

As the *Harvard Crimson* reported on March 6, 1933, "Harvard Square lacks cold cash," due to the banking crisis.

Just before the Massachusetts banks closed, HBS Professor Arthur Stone Dewing withdrew $30,000 in gold from a Cambridge bank. Dewing, a popular finance professor, had long speculated in and managed small local utilities. This led to conflict with Wallace Donham, who thought that Dewing's outside commitments were adversely affecting his teaching. It was apparently this latter conflict —and not Dewing's highly visible gold withdrawal— that led to his resignation from the faculty.

At the next 25th anniversary-related event, held three days later in Baker Library, Professor Philip Cabot noted that in 25 years the School had graduated some 4,000 men, who had now taken their places "in the industrial structure of the nation." Nearly all were employed, he pointed out, suggesting that their training must have been valuable to them and their employers. Like Donham before him, though, Cabot emphasized that an education for the acquisition of wealth alone was neither a real education nor a safe education. "All the addresses," the *Bulletin* reported, "either expressly or by implication pointed out that there must be other things than the purely material."

While Donham was heartened by what he termed the "magnificent conviction" of President Roosevelt to depart from tradition, he remained distressed about the business community's seeming paralysis. On the day of his Memorial Church address on that subject, he received a letter from his friend Wetmore Hodges— a former Business School faculty member then in business in San Francisco—which paralleled his own thoughts on leadership and the impact of the Depression.

"Somebody told me the other day that I was becoming a radical," Hodges confided. The accusation had arisen, he explained, because he had questioned such basic tenets of capitalism as adherence to the gold standard. "My answer was that far from being a radical, I was a loyal officer of the capitalistic army who was reporting to headquarters from the front; that we had better start now to lay out some orderly line of retreat."

Hodges reported that he had found in most businessmen an "abhorrence" of even discussing basic economic questions. It seemed, he noted, that Americans had tacitly accepted the premise that their economy was designed to serve those who were "clever enough and agile enough" to acquire wealth. But another possible premise—that the economy should enable all the nation's citizens to be comfortably clothed, fed, and housed as a result of their labors—justified "letting our thoughts run in a lot of new directions."

"There are over 300,000 people in the State of California today living by barter," Hodges continued. Recounting his experiences serving a community shelter during the past winter, he wrote, "I have seen a good deal of roving groups of unemployed boys who have taken possession of buildings and defied the

"Farewell to a state of things that would probably never be seen again": a transition from the exuberant 1920s (above, the "Discussioneers of 1925–1927") to the somber 1930s (below, the Century Club, 1933).

*Applied economics: an unsuccessful transplant*

In his 1958 history of the Harvard Business School, economist and HBS faculty member Melvin Copeland reviewed the School's various pre-World War II efforts to teach economics, and to apply economic theory. He concluded that those efforts were largely unsuccessful, and offered an explanation for that failure.

"Over a period of 25 years," Copeland wrote, "a variety of attempts were made to adapt the 'principles' of conventional economic theory to instruction in the Business School. . . . As I now see it, the assignment to transplant the 'principles' of conventional economic theory, as it then stood, to instruction in business administration was

very difficult, if not impossible, to carry out effectively. Most of the economic theory concerning the business firm was restricted to hypothetical states of equilibrium under restrictive sets of static assumptions which completely ignored many of the most significant elements of business strategy and behavior, as well as many of the most important issues involved in the decisions facing an active business executive.

"Most of the theory was worked out under conditions of so-called 'perfect' competition, in which there were assumed to be so many producers and sellers of each completely homogeneous product that no business executive had any price decisions to make, and no

problems of marketing strategy, product mix, or sales promotion. Even the theories of 'imperfect' competition developed in the early 1930s ignored many of the most important aspects of such problems. Because of the static assumptions, the theories had little relevance to the issues posed for business executives by the continuous dynamic *change* in conditions, which is one of the most important characteristics of business in the real world."

police to move them out. I have seen something of the young communists' party. All this has given me an opportunity to see at first hand the existence of conditions, and the existence of a state of mind among the greatest sufferers from the present situation, which I find surprisingly unappreciated by men in my own walk of life."

Hodges suggested that another twelve to eighteen months of current economic circumstances would effectively transform the unemployed — then suffering patiently — into destructive radicals. His conclusion was blunt: "Too long a hesitancy in acquiring a new conception of economics will lead to revolution."

HERBERT HOOVER CONFERENCE
HARVARD BUSINESS SCHOOL CLUB
SAN FRANCISCO. SEPTEMBER 27. 1935

**Former President Herbert Hoover delivered an off-the-record analysis of the U. S. economy and the New Deal when he was made an honorary member of the**

**HBS Club of San Francisco in 1935. One of Hoover's sons, and later a grandson, attended the Business School.**

IT WAS THIS "NEW CONCEPTION" which the Business School faculty had struggled for nearly a decade to formulate. Its overall failure to do so, particularly in light of the deepening economic crisis, had helped to revive old arguments about the place of business schools in academia. Abraham Flexner, a writer, social critic, and member of the Rockefellers' General Education Board, published in 1930 a critical study entitled *Universities*. His arguments echoed those that Thorstein Veblen had put forward ten years earlier.

"Modern business does not satisfy the criteria of a profession," Flexner wrote. "It is shrewd, energetic, and clever, rather than intellectual in character; it aims — and under our present social organization must aim — at its own advantage, rather than at noble purpose within itself."

But where Veblen was inclined toward generality, Flexner took specific aim at an institution which the General Education Board had helped bring into being: "The Harvard Business School raises neither ethical nor social questions; it does not put business on the defensive; it does not even take a broad view of business as business."

Asked by a prominent Business School supporter to comment, Donham wrote that Flexner's views were "so far away from my own conception of our philosophical job that I was not even annoyed by it." The Dean acknowledged that he might be prejudiced, but he believed that "the Business School plans go at least as far in the direction of a philosophical conception of its position in civilization as does the thinking of many of the older departments in our universities."

The implicit question remained, however: where was the refutation to Flexner's charge that the School was "unimaginative and short-sighted"?

"There is a firmly held point of view in this School," Donham wrote, "which in part starts with me, and for which I would be willing to assume the whole responsibility, were it not for the fact that so far as I know there is no dissent among any of my associates. We have felt for the twelve years that I have been here at the School that to start criticizing policies before we know enough about business to give a foundation for such criticisms would result in two things. In the first place, it would result in half-baked unconstructive attitudes on our part. In the second place, it would wholly

## Toughmindedness and loyalty

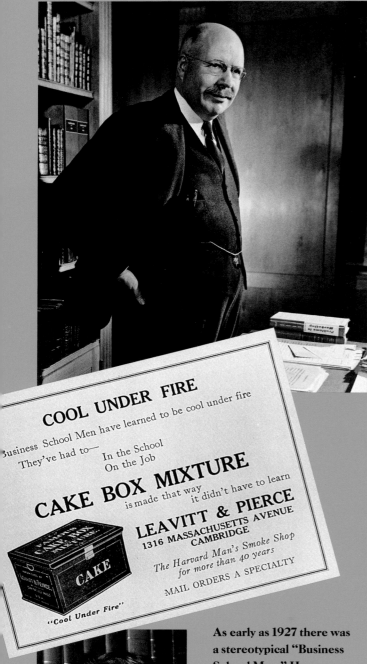

**McNair: on toughmindedness.**

COOL UNDER FIRE

Business School Men have learned to be cool under fire

They've had to — In the School
On the Job

CAKE BOX MIXTURE

is made that way
it didn't have to learn

LEAVITT & PIERCE
1316 MASSACHUSETTS AVENUE
CAMBRIDGE

The Harvard Man's Smoke Shop
for more than 40 years

MAIL ORDERS A SPECIALTY

"Cool Under Fire"

**As early as 1927 there was a stereotypical "Business School Man." He was, according to a Leavitt & Pierce copywriter, "cool under fire."**

**Lewis: on loyalty.**

At what point did the "Harvard Business School" become a distinctive entity? At what point did the phrase—and the institution—acquire a strong emotional component, both for its supporters and detractors?

The answer is complicated, and perhaps artificial in any summary form. At Harvard, the completion of George F. Baker's new campus focused significant attention on the School for the first time since its founding. The gift of the new campus, and the drama of the architectural competition, also received national media attention. Larger trends contributed, as well. At Harvard, as in broader educational circles, business became the focus of intense scrutiny during the euphoric 1920s and the turbulent 1930s; for better or worse, the Business School also gained visibility.

The rapid progress of the case method also garnered new attention for the School. By the late 1920s, the Soldiers Field campus was considered by visiting European educators to be a necessary stop on the tour of American business and business education. In the same period, of course, critics began to single out the School for individual attention, and that too suggested its growing symbolic significance.

More elusive still is the emergence of the particular brand of loyalty displayed by the alumni of the Business School. Individual testimonials, of course, were volunteered throughout the School's early history—or were secured as needed for particular ends. By the end of the 1930s, however, graduating students of the School, as well as members of that decade's earlier classes, were demonstrating a consciousness of themselves as a cohesive and distinctive group, and many displayed a very powerful sense of loyalty to the School.

This self-consciousness, perhaps retarded in its development by the Depression, seems to have been an outgrowth of the School's own sharpened sense of purpose and identity in the 1920s. While far from monolithic, the School's faculty in that period developed a rare degree of consensus regarding its methods and its values. These were well articulated by Professor Malcolm McNair in a preface to the 1941 school yearbook. The essay—entitled "On the Importance of Being Tough-Minded"—was reprinted in the alumni *Bulletin*, because, according to that magazine's editor, it "so clearly indicates the purpose of the Business School."

"For two years," wrote McNair, "the Business School has tried to make you tough-minded. We have forced you to acquire knowledge by the hard route of the case method instead of the easy route of the textbook and lecture." Rather than providing students with a specific body of knowledge, wrote McNair, the School offered a means of analyzing a situation, working out a program of action, and carrying out that program.

Don't look for the easy job, McNair counseled; don't look for easy answers; and don't play it safe: "Do not use your Business School training to seek a stodgy, conservative safety, because, paradoxically, when all business tries to play it safe there is no safety for any business."

The following year, Professor Howard T. Lewis contributed a yearbook preface entitled "The Cost of Loyalty." He noted the special alumni loyalty that the School enjoyed—a loyalty which was already perceived as unusual. That circumstance, he wrote, was significant for two reasons: first, because the School must be "in some measure at least, deserving of such esteem"; and second, because this loyalty was—or should be— "a force for good within the community to which the graduate goes."

In the late 1930s, Dean Donham attended a reunion of MBA classes from the 1920s. One alumnus startled the Dean with a blunt statement: "You didn't teach us anything in the Business School."

"I will accept that," Donham replied, "but in which sense do you mean it?"

"Well," came the response, "I studied a great number of cases with care, sought my own interpretations of them, discussed them with other members of the class, went into the classroom, where we argued them with the instructor, modified my conclusions, and reached what I thought were good working conclusions not only on the cases but on the subject matter we were discussing. And in ten years of experience I have never met a problem on all fours with any case I studied, or reached any conclusion that was controlled by the class discussion."

"I'll accept that," Donham said again, "but what did the School do for you?"

"That is simple," replied the alumnus. "It gave me a sense of assurance that I could tackle any problem, either because I had the experience to justify handling it myself, or because I knew in what direction to turn in situations where my experience was inadequate."

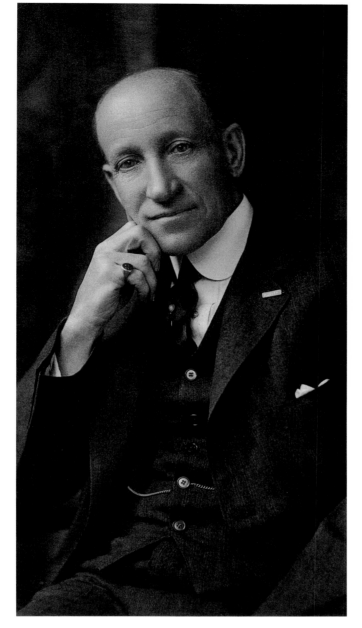

Philip Cabot, HBS Professor of Public Utilities. Cabot nearly died of diabetes, but was saved in 1923 by the introduction of insulin. His subsequent career at the Business School—iconoclastic and energetic—reflected his close brush with death.

"One never knows where Phil begins," commented his brother Richard with wry affection, "and where nervous prostration leaves off."

Sprague takes the oath of office. He later left the Treasury Department in a dispute over monetary policy.

destroy any chance we might have of making constructive comments on business, as we come to know enough about business to do so with some assurance. We stay here only because we feel we have this chance."

Three months later, in a letter to a friend, Donham reiterated the theme: "We have been going very slowly in this School on large social problems, and while we try to talk about the things as problems, I have been repeatedly asked by men, 'Well, we agree with you, but what do we do about it?' The reason for going slowly has been dual. First, we have felt that until we know more about business, anything we did would be half-baked and might well be so ill-considered that it would deserve the appellation 'red' or 'pink.'"

"We are just beginning to feel," he concluded, "that we know enough about business to make broader generalizations."

During President Roosevelt's first term, this incipient confidence—that the School could soon take a leadership role in the nation's affairs—began to manifest itself in the activities and writings of individual Business School professors. Surviving faculty members of the period recall the 1930s as a decade of unusual energy and intellectual excitement, despite straitened financial circumstances. Most active, of course, were those professors who strongly agreed or strongly disagreed with the initiatives of the New Deal. In April, 1933, banking authority O. M. W. Sprague was sworn in as executive assistant to the secretary of the treasury. In the fall of 1933, Professors Sumner Slichter, Philip Cabot, and Richard Meriam all contributed in different forums to the public debate on the National Industrial Recovery Act. Donham's *Business Adrift* represented his own first effort at broad generalization—although many readers found the result confusing. Elton Mayo's *The Human Problems of Industrial Civilization*, a compilation of his 1932 addresses in the prestigious Lowell Lecture series, reached a larger audience, bringing the preliminary findings of the Hawthorne research to public attention for the first time.

The Mayo research also provided intellectual foundations for an experiment in educational leadership undertaken by Professor Cabot in the first four months of 1935. Cabot had earlier been instrumental in organizing the School's first executive education programs, begun in the summer of 1928. These "Special Sessions" (in such fields as public utility management, accounting, and railroad transportation) had proven popular with businessmen and their sponsoring companies, but were suspended after the summer of 1930, a casualty of corporate economies in the face of the Depression. Cabot had enjoyed his contact with executives in the Special Sessions, however; and while convalescing from a severe heart attack in the winter of 1933–34, he had devised a new plan. He was interested, he informed Donham that spring, in sponsoring a discussion group for businessmen, who would meet monthly to examine the new relationships between business and government.

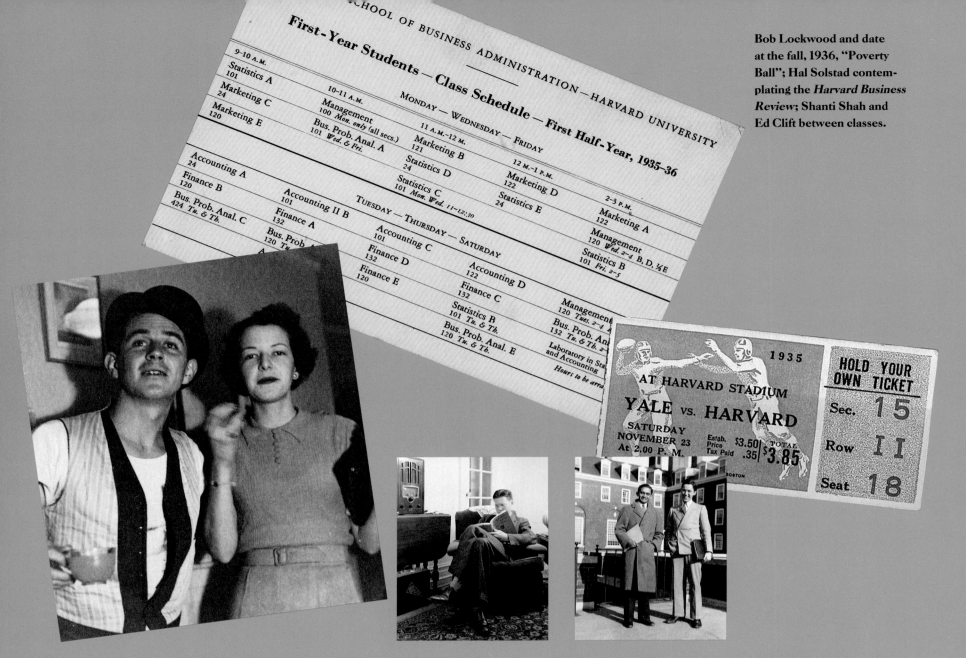

| | 9-10 A.M. | 10-11 A.M. | 11 A.M.-12 M. | 12 M.-1 P.M. | 2-3 P.M. |
|---|---|---|---|---|---|
| | Statistics A 101 | Management 100 *Mon. only (all secs.)* | Marketing B 121 | | |
| | Marketing C 24 | Bus. Prob. Anal. A 101 *Wed. & Fri.* | Statistics D 24 | Marketing D 122 | Marketing A 122 |
| | Marketing E 120 | | Statistics C 101 *Mon. Wed. 11-12:30* | Statistics E 24 | Management 120 *Wed. 2-4 B, D, ½ E* |
| | Accounting A 24 | | | | Statistics B 101 *Fri. 2-5* |
| | Finance B 120 | Accounting II B 101 | | | |
| | Bus. Prob. Anal. C 424 *Tu. & Th.* | Finance A 132 | Accounting C 101 | | |

MONDAY — WEDNESDAY — FRIDAY

TUESDAY — THURSDAY — SATURDAY

| | | |
|---|---|---|
| Bus. Prob. Anal. 120 *Tu.* | Finance D 132 | Accounting D 122 |
| | Finance E 120 | Finance C 132 |
| | Statistics B 101 *Tu. & Th.* | Management 120 *Tues. 2-4* |
| | Bus. Prob. Anal. E 120 *Tu. & Th.* | Bus. Prob. Anal. 132 *Tu. & Th.* |
| | | Laboratory in Statistics and Accounting |

*Hours to be arra...*

Bob Lockwood and date at the fall, 1936, "Poverty Ball"; Hal Solstad contemplating the *Harvard Business Review*; Shanti Shah and Ed Clift between classes.

1935
AT HARVARD STADIUM
YALE vs. HARVARD
SATURDAY NOVEMBER 23 At 2.00 P. M.
Estab. Price $3.50 Tax Paid .35 TOTAL $3.85
BOSTON

HOLD YOUR OWN TICKET
Sec. 15
Row II
Seat 18

## Hard times, hard facts

The Great Depression changed the lives of the Harvard Business School's students, particularly in the realm of personal budgets. In the 1920s, for example, there were not enough HBS students interested in waiting tables to fill available jobs in the dining halls. In 1933, by contrast, the School increased the number of waiters' jobs from roughly 100 to 135, and there were still many more applicants than jobs.

School administrators were concerned about a possible social stratification among the student body—a schism between the servers and the served—and in 1932 polled the waiters to find out, in part, if they perceived "any tendency on the part of students being served to regard waiters as their inferiors." The answer was overwhelmingly in the negative, although one waiter elaborated pointedly: "Harvard, Yale, and Princeton men in Mellon naturally are rather difficult. The rest hail from wide open spaces and are quite cordial."

It was estimated by School officials in that year that the average HBS student could exist on a budget of $1,200. This figure included $600 for tuition, $150 for room rent, $280 for board, $35 for books and supplies, and $135 for incidental expenses. First-year students could borrow $300 for tuition from the School's Loan Fund—but only after successfully completing their first semester. In their second year, they could borrow up to $600. By 1934, the Loan Fund had loaned out $375,000, all told; its repayments in that year

were expected to total $80,000; its loans exceeded $90,000. The difference was made up, for the most part, by alumni donations.

The School made efforts to reduce costs in many areas; for example, the board charge was reduced from $10.50 to $8.00 per week in 1933. Nevertheless, many students found it cheaper to eat off-campus. (The popular Cottage Farm Grille on Memorial Drive, for example, offered a full lobster salad dinner, from soup to pie, for a dollar.) But the HBS food was generally acknowledged to be of a high quality, and the food service was undeniably convenient. It was, evidently, also high in cholesterol: in a 1937 interview, the steward of the dining halls revealed that the Business School's 1,000 students consumed five tons of

meat, 11,000 eggs, and 500 gallons of milk each week. In the process, he reported disapprovingly, they broke up to 2,000 pieces of glassware and china each month.

In short, at least a third of the students lived on tight budgets and required financial assistance from the School, but the remainder did not. Almost 40 percent of the students registered in 1937, for example, had cars. And even those who had to scrimp noted that the economic hard times tended to cut both ways. In a wryly composed personal financial statement, one student wrote that he had no trouble finding dates "whose gold-digging instincts are practically atrophied."

Some aspects of HBS life evolved concurrent with, but independent of, the Depression. The parietal rules estab-

lished with the opening of the Soldiers Field living halls in 1926 stipulated that female guests in the dormitories had to be accompanied at all times by an "older lady." In 1932, that rule was modified to allow male chaperones; and in 1937, unchaperoned visiting hours were inaugurated: "Women guests may, with written permission from the Dean's office, be entertained in the students' rooms in the Living Halls between 1 p.m. and 7 p.m. on Saturdays, Sundays, and holidays."

The original plan for the campus had included an athletic building, which had been dropped as a cost-cutting measure. This left Business School students without access to wintertime exercise, except for skating. This was a circumstance which particularly concerned Dean Wallace Donham. Eventually, time at the University's Hemenway Gymnasium was reserved for HBS students on Tuesday and Thursday nights. Winter also presented other hazards: until 1939, none of the pedestrian ways were macadam. Instead, wooden boardwalks were erected between the buildings —walkways which were frequently slippery and congested.

The *Harbus*—the student newspaper which began publishing in October, 1937— periodically surveyed HBS students to determine their purchasing power and spending habits. A 1939 survey suggested that HBS students spent roughly $470,000 per year on non-School related expenses. Of that total, 33 percent was spent in Harvard Square, 20 percent in Boston, and 47 percent elsewhere. The average HBS student, it seemed, bought two new suits each year.

Upon graduation, of course, the typical Business School student found himself back in the real world—where the Depression reigned. The School's aggressive placement effort was consistently successful, but average starting salaries dropped from $1,750 in 1931 to $1,450 in 1932. One 1931 graduate counted himself lucky to secure a job pumping gas at a salary of $80 a month. A 1937 graduate sent a letter to *Harbus* readers the following fall, with some trenchant advice:

"The thing that [HBS] men trying to get a footing in the business world generally find to be of most value is this: a genuine spirit of humbleness, a willingness to learn new routines and tasks, a thorough realization of the fact that you are a complete novice, and that your business school training is worthless, per se."

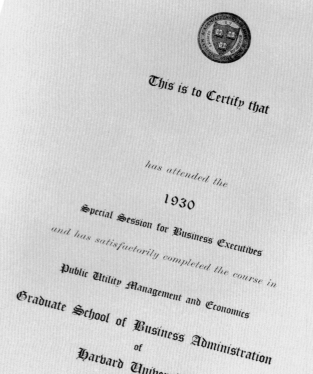

This is to Certify that

has attended the

1930

Special Session for Business Executives

and has satisfactorily completed the course in

Public Utility Management and Economics

Graduate School of Business Administration
of
Harvard University

Public Utilities
Summer Session
Harvard Business School
1928

Donham endorsed the plan enthusiastically, and the series began in January, 1935. Seventy business executives, mostly from eastern cities, spent one weekend a month for four months discussing such topics as "The Social and Governmental Problems which Industrialists and Business Men Must Face in Order to Help Stabilize our Industrial Situation." The sessions were held on the weekends, Donham noted in his 1935 report, "so that the men would lose as little business time as possible." Participants paid a total of $12 for the weekend: $7 for room and board, and $5 for tuition. Cabot purposefully recruited participants from high—but not the highest—executive ranks, hoping to influence those executives who would soon have greater responsibilities.

The series, which came to be known as "the Cabot Weekends," was well received by participants, and was repeated each year until interrupted by the Second World War. Businessmen and industrialists kept abreast of the faculty's research into economic and social issues, and at the same time helped shape that research. As one participating professor later recalled, he and his peers received a much-needed "currency of reality" from the Cabot Weekends.

Concurrently, the work of the Hawthorne researchers won its first real recognition and acceptance in the larger Business School faculty. Henderson, Mayo, and their junior colleagues had remained largely isolated at the School, despite Donham's steadfast support. The tacit endorsement of Mayo's work by the iconoclastic Cabot—who shaped many of his weekend meetings around talks by Mayo and Roethlisberger—was an important development in the School's intellectual history. Furthermore, the enthusiastic response by businessmen toward the Hawthorne findings suggested that the School might pursue new directions in executive education—a turn of events that was hastened by America's entry into the Second World War.

In the summer of 1928, 170 businessmen attended one of five six-week courses offered by the Harvard Business School. The courses were a mixture of functional and specialized offerings: Finance, Marketing, Retail Store Management, Public Utility Management, and Transportation. About one-quarter of the students were

sent by their companies, and their average age was 34. Half of the class were college graduates.

The courses were well received, and 224 men attended the 1929 summer sessions. By 1930, though, the effects of the Depression were beginning to be felt.

The courses were shortened to one month, but enrollment nevertheless dropped to 156. The special sessions were suspended after 1930.

Philip Cabot, a key force behind the Special Sessions, was interested in the challenge of educating executives—although he found six weeks too short a period for effective teaching.

Donham and Cabot in conference: a frame from a 1929 movie produced by Harvard for use by its alumni organizations.

THE SCHOOL'S URGE TO PROVIDE LEADERSHIP, spurred by the deepening economic depression, also led to a number of educational initiatives, several of which were aimed at producing graduates with new combinations of skills. The Depression soon provided additional incentive for these innovations, as School enrollment began to decline. For a brief period, the economic downturn had encouraged students to apply to the Business School: 1,098 applications were received in 1931, for example, compared with 695 in 1928. But the following year saw a 36 percent drop in applications (to 697) and a 13 percent decline in enrollment. Also sobering was the gradual decline in the percentage of eligible second-year students who decided to return: from almost 90 percent in 1929 to just over 80 percent in 1933. Under pressure from the Visiting Committee to help unemployed college graduates, and with an eye toward additional tuition income, the School in 1933 revived the "extra session," enrolling MBA students in January who would work through the summer and graduate the following June.

**The "extra sessions" inaugurated in 1933 revived a policy of mid-year admissions which had been in effect from 1922 to 1927. Like the extra sessions of the 1920s, those of the 1930s provided extra tuition income, and a means of testing proposed innovations in the MBA curriculum.**

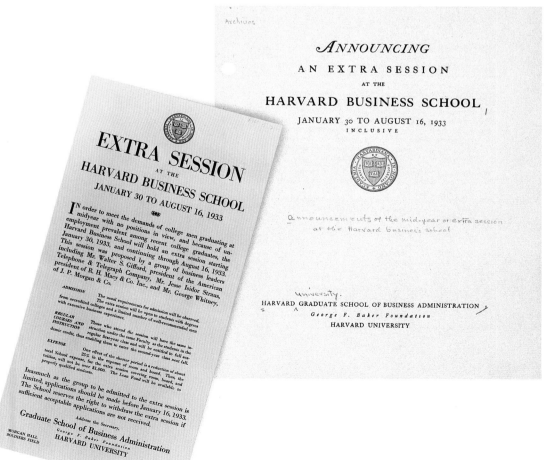

But the most ambitious of Donham's initiatives in the mid-1930s refocused attention on the earliest conceptions of the School: as a school of public *and* private business. "This is a school of business administration," began a confidential memorandum from Donham to the faculty, dated October, 1934. "It should remain that and nothing more." The Dean qualified this limitation, however, by arguing that the expansion of the scope of government necessarily broadened the agenda of the Harvard Business School.

The School had two new obligations, Donham argued: first, to train businessmen to deal effectively with such new or reinvigorated agencies as the Federal Trade Commission and the Interstate Commerce Commission; and second, to train people to staff those agencies. Donham recounted his recent conversations with the Department of Government's Professor Archibald Coolidge, who had argued more than a quarter-century earlier that Harvard's new professional school should address the public service. "The time has come," said Donham, paraphrasing Coolidge, "when the country cannot carry on its programs unless it gives competent men careers. Careers in public service must develop." Donham also noted that William Ziegler, donor in 1927 of a chair in international relations, had broadened the mandate of the chair—as yet not fully funded—to include all aspects of the relationship between business and government.

At a subsequent faculty meeting in December, 1934, the Dean won approval for seven courses, either new or reoriented, with a focus on public policy. These were to be taught by six relatively senior professors —J. Anton de Haas, Harry Tosdal, Clyde Ruggles, Nathan Isaacs, John Ebersole, and Deane Malott— whose efforts in the public policy field would soon be complemented by those of the anticipated appointee to the Ziegler chair. The faculty also authorized the hiring of a staff member to teach a new course entitled Industry in Government—although Donham had asked for a course called Government in Industry.

The Dean was successful in securing faculty approval for the plan in part because, as he noted, few additional staff members would be needed to implement it. The largest expense incurred, it seemed, would be for case research in public affairs. Donham

## Harvard and Yale: a brief marriage

In 1931, HBS faculty member George E. Bates, then an assistant professor, turned down a full professorship at the Yale Law School. His career, he told the Yale authorities, was at Harvard. Undeterred, Yale then proposed that Bates—an economist by training—conduct research and teach a law course jointly with Yale Law School Professor William O. Douglas.

The collaboration was successful, and Bates proposed to HBS Dean Wallace Donham that Harvard consider an expansion of the relationship. Donham readily agreed. Several graduates of both Harvard's Law School and Business School had already begun distinguished careers, and it

seemed sensible to encourage the trend by devising a shorter business-law curriculum. In fact, Donham had contemplated such a collaboration with the Harvard Law School —his own alma mater—but that school's dean had made it clear that he had little use for the Business School.

Nathan Isaacs, the senior law authority on the Business School faculty, took over negotiations with Yale in the summer of 1932. His counterparts at Yale were Charles E. Clark, Dean of the School, and Professor Douglas. "We are now at the stage," Douglas wrote to Isaacs in the fall of 1932, "where we want further information and exchange of ideas with you and your associates." Harvard had economic as well as intellectual incentives for participating in such an exchange. Yale had agreed to reimburse Harvard for Bates's time—at a juncture when Donham and his assistant deans were struggling to make ends meet.

Donham visited Yale shortly thereafter to promote the project and to work out administrative details. He and Clark adopted a plan whereby Harvard would admit into its first-year class a number of men then completing the first year at the Yale Law School. These students would then finish their law degrees at Yale, where they would also take a Business Policy course taught by HBS professors. Students completing the program would receive a Yale degree and a Harvard certificate; the question of a Harvard degree was deferred.

The Harvard and Yale corporations approved the plan in early 1933. A year later, on February 13, 1934, Deans Donham and Clark jointly taught the first session of the first seminar at Yale. That session was evidently a success;

however, subsequent enrollments in the program were discouragingly low. "Only three students of the seventeen that we had expected have definitely decided to take the combination course," Professor Isaacs complained in a letter to a Yale counterpart. "I am wondering whether the experiment can really be given a fair trial on such a basis."

In fact, enrollments in the program never rose to an acceptable level—in part because Yale ceased to promote it after key faculty members, including Douglas, departed, and in part because participating students received no Harvard degree. The Business School faculty officially ended its involvement in the program in November, 1938, and it was not until 1969 that the Business School entered into a new law-and-business collaboration: this time, a joint degree program with the Harvard Law School.

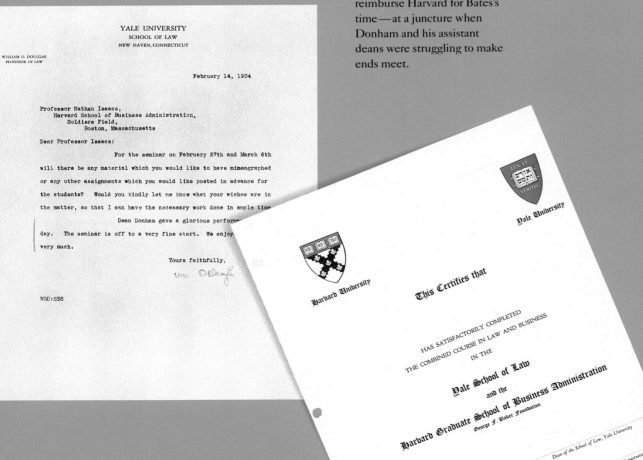

Students in the Harvard-Yale program received a Yale degree and a Harvard certificate.

A school of public and
private business: a step
ahead of the "academic
stampede."

The Shift  **193**

assured the faculty that he would willingly take responsibility for raising the needed funds. In fact, he argued, the "public business" initiative might make his job easier. "While it puts on me the burden of raising a larger sum for research than I would have had to raise without the program"—as he informed George F. Baker, Jr., in an October note explaining the initiative—"it will, I confidently believe, make the actual raising of the money easier, and fortunately the lines on which we wish to do research at the present time fall naturally in this general area."

While Donham set about raising the research money, the School's administrators made a special effort to publicize their new initiative in public policy. In response, scores of government officials and industrial leaders offered support and advice. In late January, 1935, Donham informed President Roosevelt in a letter that the School was being transformed into a school of public, as well as private business—a necessary step, he said, "if we are to avoid social revolution." Donham also informed Roosevelt that Harvard's newly installed president, James B. Conant, was deeply interested in the plan, "as a first step in his comprehensive plans for training men for Government service in a number of great departments of the University."

Donham and the Business School had correctly anticipated, by about six months, a widespread movement among the various schools and departments at Harvard into the field of training for public service. Those other schools were equally aware of the national problems—and the local opportunities —created by the expansion of government. In fact, Harvard's Faculty of Arts and Sciences was then offering some fifty courses in "government," and another several dozen courses with a public policy focus were being taught by the Departments of History, Government, and Economics, and the professional schools.

"The academic stampede to gain an acknowledged position on the Harvard road to a career in Washington," President Conant later recalled, "had been set off by Dean Wallace B. Donham's decision to expand the objectives of the School of Business Administration." Donham had admitted privately to Conant that the Depression and the New Deal discouraged many prospective students from pursuing business careers, and

GRADUATE SCHOOL
OF BUSINESS ADMINISTRATION
GEORGE F. BAKER FOUNDATION
HARVARD UNIVERSITY

*A School of Public and
Private Business*

SOLDIERS FIELD, BOSTON, MASSACHUSETTS
DECEMBER, 1934

had argued that the Business School's methods of instruction could easily be adapted to training for positions in government. Donham's contention, according to Conant, "was not well received on the Cambridge side of the Charles River. My first introduction to a deep-seated distrust between most of the members of the Business School and a majority of the members of the economics department was in connection with reaction to the Business School announcement about training for government work."

In a speech to the Economic Club of New York in the spring of 1935, Conant was more circumspect, describing the "comprehensive attack" then being launched by Harvard on the whole range of public policy problems. The Business School's initiative in public administration, he said, was one effort to provide training for "non-technical positions" in the expanding government. At the same time, he emphasized, the Business School would "continue its program of instruction in private business administration."

John Maynard Keynes's *General Theory of Employment, Interest, and Money* (1936) provided a rationale for many New Deal policies, and greatly influenced the faculty of Harvard's Littauer School.

In addition to training for the non-technical public administrator, Conant also envisioned Harvard training for technical specialists in government (such as engineers, foresters, and urban planners), as well as graduate internships in government offered jointly by various University departments and professional schools. Internal documents from the period suggest that there was general agreement among Harvard administrators that training for the non-technical public servant should be patterned on the Business School case method. This would, they realized, necessitate major expenditures on case research in the new field.

Again, Donham had anticipated this challenge, and was already cultivating a possible donor: Lucius N. Littauer, a member of Harvard's Class of 1878, and a glove manufacturer and former congressman from upstate New York. Working in concert with representatives of several other Harvard departments, Donham tried to persuade Littauer to endow a "School of Public Administration" — which, as Donham saw it, would serve as Harvard's *research* arm in the field of public administration. If Littauer would provide an endow-

Lucius N. Littauer, benefactor of Harvard's original School of Government.

ment for research, the Dean argued, existing schools could contribute faculty time and the necessary physical space.

But Littauer, to Donham's great disappointment, decided upon a different sort of gift to his alma mater. Announced in December of 1935, his $2 million pledge provided $500,000 for a building, and $1.5 million for the endowment of a School of Public Administration. An endowment of this size, as a discouraged Donham pointed out in a letter to a friend, would yield some $60,000 annually. This income would enable the School to support its building, a dean and small administrative staff, a faculty of three, and a library — but no research.

"Nevertheless," he noted, "if during the early years of the School while its resources are limited, it is realistic in its approach to the relation between government and business, it will be so because we can help it in its research and teaching."

In accordance with the plan outlined for the new school by a University planning committee, Donham lent to the School of Public Administration the part-time services of Professors Isaacs, Bevis, Ruggles, and Slichter, and also assigned additional Business School faculty members to conduct occasional seminars there. It seemed to Donham and others, however, that the new school had neither the resources nor the administrative inclination to address the pressing issues of the day. For the remainder of the decade, as the Littauer School became increasingly identified with the emerging Keynesian economics — and thereby became influential among New Dealers seeking a theoretical base for their various *ad hoc* policies — the Business School continued to conduct its own experiments in the field of training for public administration.

"In this particular case," Donham wrote to Conant in 1937, regarding Lucius Littauer, "I have every reason to believe the donor intended originally to make a large addition to his gift either during his life or at his death. Without such a gift from some source, it is my judgement that the new school cannot be a high-grade school of training for public administration."

Harvard's first doctoral diploma in business. Some HBS faculty members feared business's response to the concept of a "business doctor" — which led the School to settle on "Doctor of Commercial Science," rather than "Doctor of Business Administration."

The Doctors Donham at younger brother Paul's wedding. Both Philip Donham (far left) and Richard Donham (far right) specialized in corporate management; the latter subsequently served as dean of Northwestern University's business school.

## A *little bit out of line*

Early in 1922, Dean Wallace Donham explained to his predecessor, Edwin Gay, why he felt the School needed its own doctoral degree, distinct from the joint "Doctor of Business Economics" program then offered by HBS and the Department of Economics. First, he noted, the School wanted to require previous business experience of its doctoral candidates—"a little bit out of line with the regular Ph.D. requirement." Second, HBS didn't want to insist on French and German proficiency, since there were sometimes other, more relevant languages for its doctoral students to master. And finally, Donham reported, the School was

"overwhelmed with requests for teachers." In the previous year, 55 colleges and universities had asked HBS to supply them with instructors in business.

That year, Harvard's governing boards authorized HBS to grant the "Doctor of Commercial Science" (DCS) degree, in addition to the joint degree with the economics department. It was not until 1928, however, that Charles I. Gragg was awarded the first DCS degree. The delay was in part the result of the burdensome set of degree requirements prescribed in 1922, but was also due to the teaching and

administrative responsibilities assumed by HBS doctoral candidates. During a faculty discussion of the subject, Professors Copeland and Sprague in particular emphasized the "problem of young men on the staff who were required to devote all their time to work for the School when they should be devoting half their time to study for the doctor's degree."

The School's second doctoral degree was awarded in 1933 to Stanley F. Teele, whose dissertation examined functional specialization in retail stores. A year later, Dean Donham's oldest son, Richard, earned his DCS. In 1936, Philip Donham was also awarded the doctoral degree. Both Donham sons specialized in the field of corporate management.

But the School's relatively unproductive doctoral program remained a source of concern throughout Donham's tenure. In fact, only 49 people earned the DCS before 1950, and only two (including the popular accounting professor Thomas H. Sanders) completed the joint degree program with the economics department. Until well after World War II, the School found itself unable to "export" teachers—and thereby influence business education at other schools— and often had to recruit its own faculty members from other institutions.

# On presidents and revolution

A. Lawrence Lowell concluded a quarter-century of service to Harvard, and of support for its Business School, in 1933.

While the latter years of his tenure were troubled first by his role as an arbiter in the Sacco and Vanzetti affair, and later by the Depression, Lowell felt that he turned over to his successor a university in excellent fiscal and intellectual health.

At their April 10, 1933, meeting, the Harvard Business School faculty paid tribute to A. Lawrence Lowell, soon to retire as Harvard's president. On that occasion, Professor Melvin Copeland spoke for the faculty:

"President Lowell, your tenure in office has covered practically the full quarter of a century since this School was established. During these years every member of the faculty has felt that you were a real partner in this intellectual adventure of learning how to train young men for the profession of business administration.

"You have sat through our faculty meetings when the whole faculty gathered around a small table in the old Colonial Club, to discuss laboriously the deficiencies of ill-chosen students. As our faculty has increased in size, you also have been patient with our groping experiments in pedagogy and administration. You have helped us to develop in the traditions of the University."

Lowell, in response, also recalled early HBS faculty meetings, and noted that he had made a point of attending every such meeting when he was not absent from Cambridge. There were, he said, three kinds of faculties: those which always agreed unanimously to every proposition and thereby missed the benefits of discussion; those whose differences could not be brought into harmony; and those—like the Business School's—with the ability to air differences of opinion in open discussion and "arrive at an agreement on the subject under fire."

Lowell's resignation ended the intimate ties of 25 years' standing between the president's office and the Business School. Unlike Lowell and Eliot before him, Harvard's new president—James Bryant Conant—had played no part in the creation and development of the School. Conant was a distinguished organic chemist, a member of the first generation of research chemists to be attracted in large numbers to positions in industry. In 1917, Conant and two Harvard friends had set up a commercial laboratory to manufacture needed war chemicals, with tragic results: the plant exploded and burned, killing one of Conant's partners. This experience helped persuade Conant to stay in academia. "I had learned first hand," Conant later recalled, "something about the hazards of free enterprise."

Conant assumed the Harvard presidency in the midst of the nation's economic crisis, only six months after Franklin Roosevelt's inauguration and the national bank holiday. Lowell had left him a university in relatively good financial health. (The president emeritus, in fact, had to be discouraged from boasting about the University's financial position. He had announced in one semi-public setting, for example, that Harvard "needed no more money, and probably never would.") But Conant wanted new professorships to ensure the high quality of Harvard's faculty, as well as scholarships to broaden the range of students at the University. This led him to his first sustained contact with the Business School.

"For that purpose," recalled Conant, "a small, secret informal committee was formed. Not for the last time, a former professor of the Business School, Donald K. David"—who had left the School's employ in 1927 for a position in industry—"was recruited to lend a helping hand. He was one of my oldest friends and certainly my most loyal and helpful one."

Two years passed before the campaign was announced publicly as the "Three Hundredth Anniversary Fund of Harvard University." By late 1935, the worst of the Depression had passed, and Harvard's supporters seemed reasonably receptive to a fundraising drive. On the other hand, Harvard's more conservative alumni were irritated by the University's identification with Roosevelt's New Deal programs. "Though many more Columbia professors were active in Washington than Harvard professors," Conant wrote, "the wrath of many was focused on Harvard." In part as a result of this sentiment, the campaign progressed slowly. By 1940, only three "University Professorships"—a key component of Conant's plan—had been funded.

The fundraising effort forced a consideration of substantive questions about the work of the University, and the function of the Business School at Harvard. The president had identified four "quadrants" of the University—biological sciences, physical sciences, social sciences, and arts and letters—for specific fundraising initiatives; in addition, he wanted to secure "mobile funds for instruction and research not allocated to any department," which would endow University Professorships. Donham had argued unsuccessfully that individual research initiatives, like that of Professors Mayo and Henderson, or perhaps a broad study of tax policy, would be more attractive to prospective donors.

"I know that I don't have to tell you that I am keenly interested in the whole question of the social sciences in this University and in providing them with adequate funds," Conant's letter continued. "At the same time, I am rather confused in my own mind about this whole area"—which in Conant's scheme included the Business School. "I am particularly troubled about the social sciences becoming too 'applied,' too vocational, and our spending too much money in efforts which are not really within the scope of the university."

The president then praised a speech given at the recent commencement exercises by one Robert Hutchins, who had argued that the professional schools, lacking intellectual ties to the "fundamental problems of metaphysics," had no valid place in the university setting. Hutchins had proposed that university-based research should seek to illustrate metaphysical principles, rather than to gather empirical data—a proposal that clearly contradicted the model of the professional schools.

Donham, in response, registered his "strong dissent" from Hutchins's position. "I am very far from being convinced that one should start with metaphysics and gradually drift when forced in the direction of reality," he wrote—in effect summarizing the School's unhappy experience with applied economics in the 1920s. "I distrust intensely principles divorced from facts. Indeed, I question whether there are such things—at least outside mathematics—as 'principles' which are not based explicitly or implicitly on facts or assumed facts."

"The net effect of [Hutchins's] talk," Donham concluded, "is to include among the subjects which are taboo everything in the social sciences that has a realistic chance to be useful."

Donham had not previously found himself in the position of having to offer, to the president of the University, a rationale for the existence of the Business School. Equally unusual, and no doubt discomfiting to both Donham and Conant, was the Dean's role in a dispute that erupted three years later. President Conant had, through a series of well-intentioned missteps in the area of faculty promotions, fostered an open rebellion among the Arts and Sciences faculty. By the fall of 1939, that faculty was considering a challenge to the authority of the president and governing boards, proposing to restructure the faculty appointments process. Dean Donham met with Conant, and told him that the president had not only lost the confidence of a majority of the Arts and Sciences faculty, but was now jeopardizing a tradition at the heart of the Harvard system.

"The only thing for you to do," Donham told Conant, "is to admit frankly and openly at the faculty meeting that you have made mistakes—and you have made mistakes—and ask the faculty not to attempt a revolution in the Harvard constitution because of your own errors. In my experience, if one admits a mistake to a faculty group, they will usually rally in support."

Conant did not appreciate the advice. After considerable soul-searching, however, he decided to follow Donham's prescription. Before the largest Harvard faculty group ever assembled, Conant apologized, and urged the Arts and Sciences faculty not to make a hasty decision with long-term consequences for the University.

"When I finished," he noted, "there was silence. Someone moved that the [restructuring] motion be laid on the table; by voice vote, which sounded unanimous, the tabling motion was carried. Dean Donham was proved to have been right."

ANOTHER REFLECTION of the School's urge to provide social leadership—and also to protect overall enrollments—was the short-lived "third year" plan, which commanded much of Donham's attention in the early 1930s. The plan was an outgrowth of the School's ill-fated tutorial program, which had been started in the fall of 1929 to give more attention to outstanding second-year students. The tutorial program was abandoned after two years, in part because the business literature necessary for tutorial study didn't exist, and in part because it was difficult to justify allocating up to one-half of the second-year faculty's time to approximately a tenth of the second-year students.

Even before the official demise of the tutorial program, Donham attempted to persuade the faculty to approve a third year for selected students, during which these students would receive specialized training and conduct research. At the end of the third year they would receive a Doctor of Commercial Science degree. The faculty had misgivings: some of its members preferred to concentrate on problems in the existing curriculum, while others thought the existing tutorial system and doctoral program served the needs Donham was identifying.

"This third year," Donham argued before the faculty in December of 1931, "will be devoted to an effort to train men with capacity for leadership in problems of the relation of business to civilization. As the basis for such training is worked out, it will inevitably affect radically the instruction given in the first two years, and bring more consistent emphasis on the social objective of the School."

The faculty approved the plan at that meeting, and the Dean was given authority to set up an appropriate third-year structure when economically feasible. The announcement of the School's intent—made public in Donham's annual report the following month—earned an effusive editorial accolade from the *Boston Herald*, which supported the concept of "a picked body of men" for specialized business research. "The community expects more from Harvard than from any other college or university, and Harvard usually gives it. The Business School, young as it is, stands at the head of such institutions in the United States."

The School's Committee on Instruction, headed by Donham, made a preliminary report on the third-year proposal to the faculty in February, 1933. It suggested a wide-ranging research agenda, which might include such diverse topics as biology, sociology, and government. President Lowell, then two months away from retirement, made a pointed comment regarding this proposed agenda. "The President admonished us," the faculty secretary noted, "that this was a business school, and should always remain a School of Business Administration."

One interesting aspect of the report was its description of a course of study for the "specialist in general relationships." This course would serve "the administrator who is not and cannot be a specialist but who must make use of specialists at all times." The problem of specialization, and the use of specialists, had been identified by Alfred North Whitehead, among others, in the 1920s. The subject increasingly came under study by School researchers, and eventually served as the cornerstone of an institutional focus on the general manager.

**President Lowell's 1933 caution**—that HBS was first and foremost a school of business administration—was not forgotten, notwithstanding the wide-ranging HBS educational experiments of the 1930s. Manufacturing continued to be a mainstay of the MBA curriculum, and the nation's industrial corporations became an increasingly important base of support for the School.

In 1936, for example, in conjunction with Harvard's 300th anniversary, the Plymouth Motor Company donated to the School a diorama of their principal manufacturing facility. In the accompanying photograph, Dean Donham (left), Associate Dean Biddle (third from left), and Manufacturing Professor Georges F. Doriot (to Biddle's left) accept the gift on behalf of the School.

Visions and realities: despite the economic straits of the Depression, Dean Donham hoped to improve the Soldiers Field campus with a boat landing and bell towers on the river dormitories — as depicted in an air-brushed photograph from the period. The reality was very different: Donham had to ask the Harvard Corporation to adjust its formula for calculating HBS building maintenance reserves, thereby freeing up $19,000 for case research between 1932 and 1934.

Meanwhile, Harvard had its own agenda. In April of 1932, the University's comptroller suggested to Donham that "the dust from the parking space and road back of Baker Library and Morgan Hall is blowing into the building so as to be rather objectionable."

School Secretary F. E. Heard agreed, noting that dust was bad for both books and stenography equipment. "Of course some day," she added, "I think it would save expense to have the roadway surfaced."

But the third-year plan was soon deferred, and then deferred again, in the face of the deepening depression. As the need for business research intensified, the resources to support it decreased correspondingly. The last public statement regarding the third-year initiative appeared in Donham's 1937 report, a full six years after it was first announced. "Business has suffered loss of prestige during the past eight years," the Dean wrote, "and business leadership has failed at a critical juncture. It is essential that this failure shall not occur again. . . . It is regrettable that we are forced to plan rather than to perform in this critical area, because of lack of funds."

BETWEEN 1919 AND THE SECOND WORLD WAR, a lack of funds — or the prospect of such a shortfall — was generally the rule when new departures were considered by the administrators of the Harvard Business School. The opening of the new campus in 1927, and the resulting infusion of dormitory rental income, temporarily changed this circumstance: in the two years before the

1929 stock market crash, the School made an average profit of $90,000 per year, and these surpluses were used to retire the School's debt to the University for cost overruns on the original campus.

By the early 1930s, however, Donham faced new capital expenditures: completing the top floor of Morgan Hall, finishing the Dean's House, building wings on the rear of Baker Library, and refitting Glass and Sherman Halls for use by married faculty members. He needed an additional $50,000 per year for new faculty salaries (enabling the School to reduce the size of sections from 200 students to 100 students), and he further anticipated the need, over the course of the following decade, for an additional $100,000 annually to meet the costs of an older faculty, new scholarships, and so on.

To support research — which, with the library, had been one of the School's activities most vulnerable to periodic budgetary crises — Donham and members of the School's Visiting Committee devised "The Two Hundred Fifty Associates of the Harvard Business School," a program apparently based on an innovation

The Shanghai Club, 1934.

A 1926 HBS alumni meeting announcement: "Three Dollars Covers the Entire Cost."

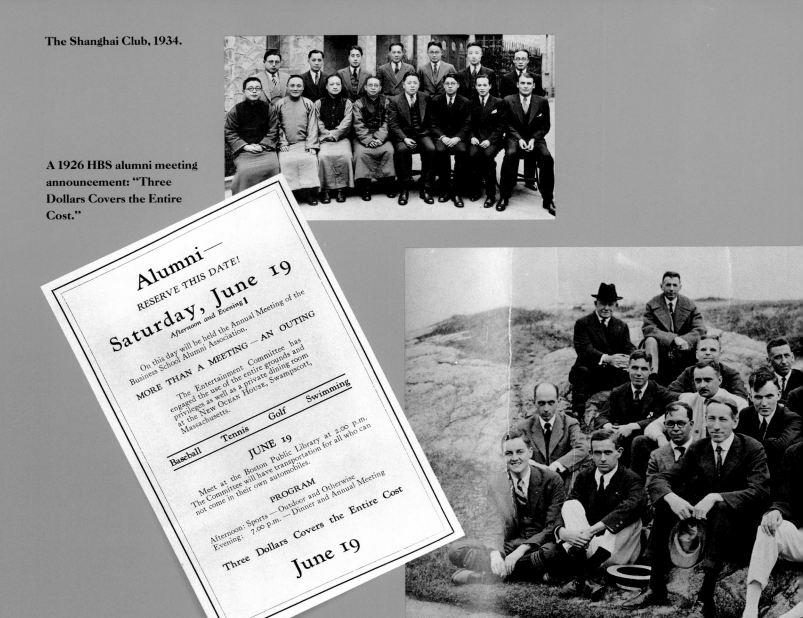

Alumni—
RESERVE THIS DATE!
Saturday, June 19
Afternoon and Evening!
On this day will be held the Annual Meeting of the
Business School Alumni Association.

MORE THAN A MEETING — AN OUTING

The Entertainment Committee has
engaged the use of the entire grounds and
privileges as well as a private dining room
at the NEW OCEAN HOUSE, Swampscott,
Massachusetts.

Baseball    Tennis    Golf    Swimming

JUNE 19

Meet at the Boston Public Library at 2.00 p.m.
The Committee will have transportation for all who can
not come in their own automobiles.

PROGRAM

Afternoon: Sports — Outdoor and Otherwise
Evening: 7.00 p.m. — Dinner and Annual Meeting

Three Dollars Covers the Entire Cost

June 19

## Common service for a common goal

The Harvard Business School Association was organized in 1914 by four HBS alumni and one current student; their goal was "to advance the interests and increase the usefulness of the Harvard Graduate School of Business Administration and to promote business education in general."

Four of these five charter members of the HBSA were graduates of Harvard College, and were therefore well aware of the College's sophisticated alumni outreach program. They were also aware of the advantages of the informal "network" of the College's alumni, and they concluded that Business School alumni would benefit from similar opportunities for affiliation. In 1916, the HBSA published its first *Directory of Former Students*—a 48-page document containing 392 names.

"There exists among the alumni a strong feeling of loyalty to the School," HBSA President Eliot Mears wrote in 1916, in the *Harvard Alumni Bulletin*. "They realize that the institution must and will be judged by their work in the world, and they are ambitious not only for themselves but for the School."

At first, the University's alumni magazine, which included a Business School section, remained the principal vehicle for communication between the School and its alumni. In January, 1925, however, the "Bulletin of the Harvard Business School Alumni Association" (later the HBS *Bulletin*) began publication. The rationale for the new magazine, as explained in its first issue, was not only to keep

alumni in touch with each other and with the School, but also to provide a form of continuing education to interested graduates. The magazine was to include "actual problems used for written reports in the School," as well as summaries of cases and statistical studies prepared by the Bureau of Business Research. "I believe that to do this is an essential part of our service to our graduates and to the community," Dean Donham wrote in that issue. "A sense of unity, of a common service for a common goal, can only be achieved with the help of a constantly aroused intellectual curiosity."

The early and mid-1920s also saw the growth of a network of local HBS clubs sponsored by the HBSA. The School's New York and Boston alumni had held informal

luncheon meetings since 1916, and had soon established the first organized Business School alumni clubs. They were joined by Chicago, Cleveland, and Philadelphia shortly after the World War, and within a few years by Detroit, San Francisco, and Los Angeles. The efforts of the local clubs, and no doubt the publicity surrounding the gift and construction of the new campus, led to a steady growth in HBSA membership. In 1925, 40 percent of HBS alumni were members of the HBSA—a higher proportion of active alumni than was enjoyed by any other Harvard graduate school. Within a year, that number had climbed substantially, to 56 percent.

The student Loan Fund, supported by the HBSA and annual fundraising efforts by the Dean, grew out of a decision early in Donham's administration to give loans, rather than scholarships, to HBS students. In March of 1922, President Lowell approved the plan, accepting Donham's argument that Business School students should be prepared to pay for their education.

A 1922 HBS alumni outing in Swampscott, Massachusetts.

While the HBSA had held an annual meeting in most of the years since its founding, these were purely social events until 1931, when the organization sponsored its first educationally oriented reunion. Over five hundred alumni and HBS students attended the weekend event, which, according to the HBS *Bulletin*, included "very frank and pertinent talks" by Dean Donham, former Dean Gay, and Professor Philip Cabot.

For both the School and the HBSA, the Depression era was one of retrenchment. The HBSA's efforts to raise money for the student Loan Fund were suspended in 1932, although Dean Donham was able to use the $13,700 that they collected in that year as "collateral," and thereby to persuade the University to contribute $100,000 to the Loan Fund. Individual clubs, however, did continue to sponsor scholarships and loans for deserving HBS students, and the number of active clubs also increased over the decade of the 1930s. The founding of the Paris and Shanghai clubs in 1934 marked the beginning of the internationalization of the HBSA, and reinforced the incipient internationalization of the School.

The strong bonds between the School and its alumni, in fact, at times prevailed in the face of other deeply held loyalties. As a 1942 issue of the *Bulletin* noted with grudging admiration, the naval officer with highest rank among the HBS alumni was Tomokazu Mogi—a vice admiral in the Japanese Navy. The vice admiral, the *Bulletin* also noted, had paid his membership dues to the HBS Club of Tokyo through October, 1942.

HBSA President Marvin Bower with Dean Donham, 1942.

**The first meeting of the Two Hundred Fifty Associates of the Harvard Business School was held in December of 1930. Contributions from the Associates funded case research in the difficult Depression years.**

*PROGRAM*

❖

*Members of the Two Hundred Fifty Associates will meet in the Faculty Club which will be open the entire day for their use.*

9 A.M. TO 1 P.M.    Members are invited to visit the various classes.

*Anyone who so desires may be accompanied to class by a man from the Harvard Business School staff.*

1.15 P.M.    Lunch in Faculty Club with members of the Faculty of the Harvard Business School.

3.15 P.M.    Business Meeting, Living Room of the Faculty Club. Mr. Jesse Isidor Straus will preside.

4.00 P.M.    Professor Melvin T. Copeland will discuss "Present-day Problems in Distribution." Living Room, Faculty Club.

7.30 P.M.    Dinner, Faculty Club. Speakers, President A. Lawrence Lowell, Dean Wallace B. Donham, and Professor Elton Mayo.

has been chosen a member of the Two Hundred Fifty Associates of the Harvard Business School on this _____ day of _____ nineteen hundred thirty

PRESIDENT

DEAN

at the California Institute of Technology. The plan created a nonprofit association under the laws of Massachusetts, for which certain members of the Visiting Committee would serve as trustees. Each of the 250 members of the group would contribute $1,000 annually, in the form of a personal gift; these funds would be held by the trustees and made available to the School for research activities.

The plan was promptly approved by the Visiting Committee, and, later in 1929, by Harvard's governing boards. Donham and Assistant Dean John C. Baker, with key assistance from Visiting Committee chairman Jesse I. Straus, set out to recruit members for the new association. Members of the Visiting Committee signed up 35 Associates, and Harvard's agents recruited an additional 164 members. Only the contributions of these Associates (which totaled $344,000 in the organization's first two years, and almost $550,000 over the course of a decade) kept the School's research and course development activities alive through the Depression years.

A second response to the financial exigencies of the Depression, resorted to only with reluctance, was the expansion of the student body between 1930 and 1932 from 1,000 to 1,100. While the additional income was welcome, the strain on existing resources was not. "We do not intend to set aside our general [enrollment] policy again, even if we can," Dean Donham wrote subsequently, "because we have found from experience that such a large enrollment affects our educational efficiency. We are not organized to teach 1,100 students."

But this increased enrollment, combined with gifts, enabled Donham to build up the School's

**Jesse I. Straus, a key supporter of the Harvard Business School in its first three decades, later served as U. S. Ambassador to France.**

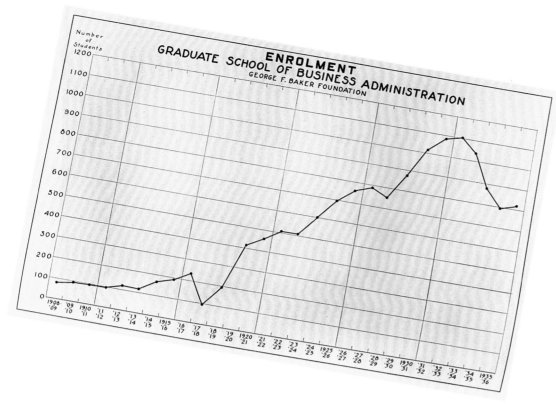

**Peaks and valleys: enrollment was a critical variable for HBS—in the 1930s and subsequent decades—because of the School's relatively small endowment.**

financial reserves significantly: from $40,890 in 1929 to $232,380 in the fourth year of the Depression. These reserves were expended gradually, over the course of the 1930s. In combination with the efforts of the faculty Economy Committee—which reduced the School's annual operating costs by $125,000, to approximately $840,000—the reserves enabled the Business School to avoid net deficits throughout the Depression.

Yet it was clearly discouraging for Donham, after building a campus and increasing the School's endowment from approximately $500,000 in 1919 to almost $3 million, to report cash reserves in 1938 of only $24,000. He felt, as he had informed President Conant, "a personal responsibility to finance the activities of this School as they exist when I retire. Otherwise, my successor might be seriously embarrassed." After almost two decades of nearly constant fundraising, Donham found himself, by his own estimate, spending 80 percent of his time soliciting new funds.

No immediate solution presented itself. With Conant's approval, he developed in 1938 a proposal intended for the trustees of George F. Baker's public trust, whereby the trust would establish a "stabilization fund" of $250,000. Such a fund would be used to flatten the unpredictable peaks and valleys of the Business School's income. The proposal, apparently not forwarded to the Bakers, reflects Donham's increasing weariness with his tasks. "I am 61 years old, and severely limited by considerations of health in the amount of time I can work each year," he wrote. "I ought to be giving a large part of my time to studying the relationship of the School to the social changes going on around us. For several years this has been impossible."

IN SPITE OF THE EVER-PRESENT FINANCIAL WORRIES of the 1930s, Donham and his fellow faculty members were in fact devoting considerable attention to the development of the School's conceptual base. The steady progress of the Rockefeller-funded Mayo and Henderson research had provided, as Donham wrote in a 1937 memorandum to Henderson, "a conceptual scheme by which we could attack problems of human behavior." By the mid-1930s, the Mayo research—which had extended its scope from the purely psychological into the physiological, and later into the socio-anthropological—was becoming integrated into the School's curriculum, although Mayo himself remained outside the mainstream of the Business School culture. Philip Cabot's innovative Industry and Government in the United States, first offered in 1934, was based in large part on Mayo's research.

"Five years ago," Donham noted in a 1937 letter to President Conant, who was then trying to secure another extension of the Rockefeller grant, "our required second-year course in Business Policy devoted its attention to logical problems of business policy. Now in practically every topic considered the human aspects of problems are given primary emphasis. There is also a distinct filtration of the work into other courses."

What Mayo, and to a certain extent Henderson's Fatigue Laboratory, had accomplished was to suggest a conceptual model to replace the discredited model of applied economics. The approach of the medical clinician, defined most broadly, seemed a much more workable basis for business research and teaching than did economics. The physician, in a sense, replaced the economist; the "clinical method" supplanted the illustration, through case research, of established economic theory.

But the Mayo approach was still an important step away from a workable theory of administration. Administrators had to *act*, and while Mayo's research helped them do so—by suggesting the means whereby policy could be successfully implemented through human organizations—administrators also had to be able to appreciate and employ the contributions of specialists, in order to devise sensible policies. Administrators, as Donham and the faculty gradually came to phrase it, needed to act in the present, with reference to the past, and in anticipation of the future.

## A *bad type of attitude*

By a show of hands, twelve HBS professors in attendance at a November, 1926, faculty meeting indicated that they thought the first-year students were being overworked. Five professors voted in the negative.

The issue had arisen because first-year students earlier in the fall had petitioned for a reduction in their workload. In a meeting with representatives of the Dean's office, the students claimed to be spending more than 70 hours per week on their studies. A faculty review of the students' grievances concluded that their analysis was correct. Students were required to devote approximately 72 hours per week to their school work: 24 hours for report writing, 15 hours in class, 9 hours for accounting preparation, 18 hours for other course preparation, and 6 hours for statistics laboratories.

Report writing emerged as the most objectionable obligation, and the reports for the Business Policy course were a particular focus of ire. These assignments were handed out on Fridays, and completed reports, averaging several pages in length, were due on Saturday of the following week.

"If report-writing is an end in itself," concluded a group of junior faculty members in December of 1926, "it is now receiving too little attention, but if it is a means to an end (i.e., a means of presenting part of the subject matter of the course), it is now overemphasized." In the following month, first-year instructors agreed to reduce the number of written reports, and to monitor the total workload in the first year.

The report-writing issue arose again a year later, this time in relation to the second-year curriculum. The Committee on Instruction concluded that it was "excessive in amount and not altogether satisfactory in character."

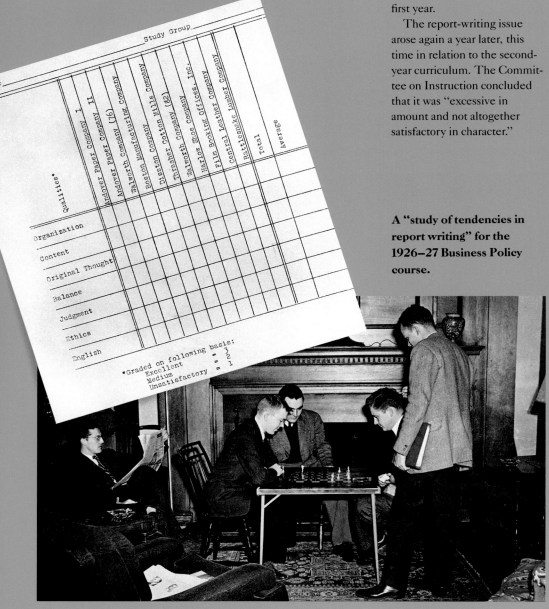

**A "study of tendencies in report writing" for the 1926–27 Business Policy course.**

The committee suggested that beyond a certain point report writing was simply "routine work," and therefore wasted effort. This prompted a debate over the definition of "routine" —a debate which Professor Sprague ended by stating that routine work was that beyond what was absolutely necessary to the development of writing skills. Sprague, typically, had identified an unwelcome truth. Remedial instruction in writing skills had gradually gained importance relative to the development of analytical skills.

In addition to consuming disproportionate amounts of time, the proliferation of reports also contributed to the development of a "bad type of attitude" on the part of the students, according to a 1931 report of the Committee on Instruction. More reports, more exams, and "too much grading and petty policing" had created a situation which needed remedy. Significantly, the committee attempted for the first time to set an absolute limit on reports: no more than one a week, they suggested. "Written reports," the committee concluded, "should be regarded primarily as a means of developing in students the power to assemble facts, analyze situations, and arrive at conclusions, in good written form, on relatively short notice."

The Depression helped reinforce this tendency. In 1932, for example, three of the School's 16 graders—previously assigned full-time to help professors review written work —were reassigned to other tasks. Not all HBS faculty members, however, were satisfied with the downgrading of the report-writing function, or with the reduction in the students' work load. Donham, for one, continued to feel that report writing made up for deficiencies in the case system.

"The only place where we give the type of training which requires ten hours or more," Donham noted in a 1935 letter to President Conant, "is in the written reports. These reports have much the same relation to our work as, for example, the laboratory work has to the first two years of a medical course. While he may grumble, our student is at heart willing to spend a large amount of time on these reports. The reason, I believe, is his discovery that the more time he puts on them, the more he gets out of his work in accomplishment per hour."

Report writing, and the attitudes it engendered, was an issue that would not subside, and the School soon found itself again committing substantial resources to the grading of written reports. By the early 1940s, for example, some $50,000 per year was needed to pay 28 full-time graders. The ever-proliferating written report remained the focus of much criticism. Decrying the "superficial habits" developed by the students in response to "so much written work," one faculty observer employed a logic in 1942 which would retain much of its force over ensuing decades:

"Does not business itself suffer from haste, pressures, throwing straws in the air, and snap judgements? Perhaps a hectic graduate course is a preparation for a hectic business career."

**The issue of report writing merged inevitably with larger questions at the "Busy School," as HBS had come to be known. In his 1930 report to President Lowell, Dean Donham expressed his concern about the health of students "subjected to steady pressure work such as we have here."**

**The Student Club— across the Baker Library lawn from the Faculty Club —was designed to give HBS students a relaxing environment for study breaks.**

With the death in December of 1941 of Philip Cabot, the death two months later of L. J. Henderson, and the retirement of Wallace Donham five months after that, Elton Mayo found himself increasingly isolated at HBS. The "heirs" of his intellectual tradition had left Harvard—some for the war effort, and others permanently.

Curiously, Mayo's reputation outside Harvard was then growing. He was the subject of a *Fortune* cover story ("The Philosopher of the Picket Line"), among other public notices. But his disdain for the Business School's social traditions had reinforced his intellectual isolation. Even his personal idiosyncrasies were subject to misinterpretation as a result. His long goose-quill cigarette holders, for example—often cited as an affectation—were actually a necessity: his glaucoma was aggravated by cigarette smoke.

Mayo postponed his own retirement until 1947, hoping to reestablish a core of younger faculty members in sympathy with his ideas. The effort was successful. In the spring of that year, a "Mayo Weekend" was held. It was attended by some sixty executives and academics with an interest in Mayo's work.

Speakers included Mayo, Donham, and George Lombard—one of the cadre of junior professors who, with Fritz Roethlisberger, later helped reinforce the Mayo tradition at Harvard.

In his memorandum to Henderson, Donham defined administration as "the determination and execution of policies involving action. Such policies must be conceived by men. Such action must be effected by human organizations, and is important because it affects human beings."

It was an organizing principle of deceptive simplicity, and remarkable durability. "It forces us to face facts realistically," Donham concluded. "By keeping our attention on the facts as a whole, it enables us to get far greater values out of the specialized social sciences than we could before. . . . We minimize metaphysical abstractions from assumed facts and from arbitrarily selected segments of facts."

It was also a conceptual scheme largely out of step with prevailing trends in business education, and in the broader society. The Wharton School, for example, installed a new dean (Joseph Willits, an original sponsor of Elton Mayo) in 1933, and subsequently embarked upon a deliberate effort to reconstruct itself as a school of applied economics. In the same period, the federal government turned increasingly to economists, such as Harvard's influential Alvin Hansen and Seymour Harris, for social prescriptions.

This trend in particular was deplored by the Dean of Harvard's business school. "The emphasis in the thinking in both public and private affairs," Donham told the December, 1937, graduating class of the U. S. Department of Agriculture's graduate school, "on the economic aspects of the situations that develop is, in my opinion, most unfortunate." That emphasis, Donham explained, failed to consider "the most important variables in practically every problem, and because it ignores them, it leads to action which would not have been taken if the problem had been conceived more broadly, and more premises had been taken into account."

## Rare and treasured items

**Herbert Somerton Foxwell, progenitor of two impressive collections of early economic and business literature.**

An anonymous Baker Library memorandum-writer of 1929 described the Library's collection—the product of a ten-year "dragnet"—as a "very large and bulky collection, without the rare and treasured items which we should have." The Business School's library, the staff member concluded, "was lamentably lacking in the sort of material that gives distinction to a library." The solution proposed in the memorandum was the purchase of Herbert Somerton Foxwell's 20,000-item collection of early economic and business literature.

The author of the memorandum was most likely Charles C. Eaton, who had come across Foxwell's collection in England in 1927. Foxwell, 81 years old in 1929, was a retired professor of moral science and political economy at St. John's College, Cambridge. In the late 19th century, Cambridge University had been a crucible for the emerging discipline of economics, and the long and sometimes bitter economic debates between Foxwell and Alfred Marshall—his senior colleague on the Cambridge faculty—fueled Foxwell's passion for book collecting. By the turn of the century, Foxwell

had acquired an impressive collection of early economic and business literature, despite his modest academic's salary. That collection was sold in 1901 to the Worshipful Company of Goldsmiths in London, on the occasion of Foxwell's marriage, and Foxwell immediately began building a second collection with the proceeds of the sale. By the late 1920s, this second collection had largely duplicated, and in some areas surpassed, the first.

**"Truths of the Day," or, "The Great Demon Money": one of several popular early 19th-century images issued by Charles Pellerin on the evils of money. Prints such as this were often hung in shops, cafes, and private homes.**

**"I feel I can leave the matter in your hands,"** Claude W. Kress wrote to Dean Donham in 1936, "to make this addition to the library what both you and I would like it to be."

In 1927, Foxwell indicated to Eaton his willingness to sell his collection; however, he was then at work on a bibliography of economic literature, and wanted to keep his collection until his death. Two years of difficult negotiations followed. They were concluded in April of 1929, when Donham made a personal commitment to purchase the collection upon Foxwell's death. This was only possible, Donham later recalled, because George F. Baker, Jr., agreed to guarantee the agreed-upon purchase price of between $100,000 and $125,000. Donham assured Baker, whose family had already been so generous to the School, that he would never be called upon to honor the pledge.

The School's new librarian, Arthur Cole, had mixed feelings about the acquisition of the Foxwell collection. Cole was inclined to rationalize the collecting policies of the various Harvard libraries that had an interest in business and economics; by his reasoning, Foxwell's treasures probably belonged in Widener. Nevertheless, it fell to Cole to maintain relations with Foxwell following the 1929 agreement. In 1934, for example, Cole visited England, and reported to Donham that Foxwell had "failed markedly in the last year or two. . . . [He is] still up and around but he can walk only with the greatest difficulty."

By this point, Donham himself may well have been experiencing qualms about the impending acquisition, although in his public comments he remained firmly committed to it. The agreement to purchase the collection had been reached at the high-water mark of the School's fortunes in the late 1920s, and even though the money for the purchase was not then in hand, it had seemed at that time not too great a challenge to raise it. Now, as Foxwell's health declined in the midst of the deepening Depression, the prospect of raising over $100,000 was daunting.

Foxwell's death in 1936 forced the issue. Donham called in John C. Baker, one of his assistant deans, for a conference on the subject. "I had known," Baker later recalled, "of the negotiations for the collection—almost all faculty members did—but I had not realized the demanding terms of the agreement: cash payment due [to Foxwell's daughter] immediately upon delivery of the books. As Dean Donham recounted to me the details of the contract, I recognized the awkward situation he faced. He needed to raise quickly a very substantial sum of money in a difficult period, possibly without enthusiastic faculty support."

Baker suggested Claude W. Kress, president of the S. H. Kress Co., as a possible underwriter for the Foxwell acquisition. With Baker's encouragement, Kress had earlier donated $15,000 to a Bureau of Business Research study of chain stores, and had supplied detailed statistics on operating costs for his own stores. Kress had subsequently joined the School's Visiting Committee at Donham's invitation, and was well aware of the School's deteriorating financial position in the mid-1930s.

The day after a dinner meeting with Donham and Baker regarding the Foxwell collection, Kress made an unexpectedly generous gift: not only would he contribute up to $100,000 for the acquisition of the collection, but he would also pay up to $50,000 for the construction of a specially appointed room to house the collection. "It has been my deepest wish to have our Library one of the great libraries of the world," Donham wrote to Kress in December of 1936, expressing his gratitude. "I believe our library with your gift now becomes one of the great libraries."

The "Kress Library of Business and Economics" officially opened in 1938, in an extension of Baker Library built for that purpose. Claude Kress continued to demonstrate his interest in the library, commissioning a special bookplate (based on Albrecht Durer's design for the original Kress family coat of arms) and broadening the collection with gifts in specific areas. Gifts arrived from other quarters, as well. The widow of Boston newspaperman Hugh Bancroft, for example, contributed over 300 items pertaining to the "South Sea Bubble," the infamous 18th-century speculative scandal. Homer B. Vanderblue, a member of the School's faculty in the 1920s, donated to the Kress Library his unique collection of "Smithiana"— materials by and about Adam Smith, including over 180 editions of the *Wealth of Nations* in 14 languages.

In 1972, an ambitious microfilming project was begun in London and Boston. It combined the two original Foxwell collections —the 30,000 titles in the Goldsmiths' Library, and the 20,000 titles in Kress —as well as some 17,000 additional titles added subsequently to the Kress collection, and now constitutes the most extensive early economics research library in existence.

**Homer Vanderblue, collector of Smithiana, taught Business Economics at HBS from 1923 to 1929.** Known for his sharp wit, Vanderblue was fond of directing HBS students' attention to a series of prints on his classroom walls—Hogarth's "Idle and Industrious Apprentices."

**WAR DEPARTMENT,**
WASHINGTON.

August 14, 1923.

Dr. Wallace B. Donham,
Dean, Harvard University,
Cambridge, Massachusetts.

My dear Dr. Donham:

With reference to your letter of July 31, 1923, setting forth the advantages of the School of Business Administration for officers of the Army, there are two branches in the War Department, namely, the Quartermaster Department and the Finance Department, which are largely concerned with the business of administration of the Army, and I am pleased to inform you that I have caused copies of your letter to be referred to these two departments for their information and such action in detailing officers from their respective branches to take the course at your institution as may be deemed most beneficial to the service.

I appreciate very much your bringing this matter to my attention and sincerely hope that the state of our finances and personnel will permit the War Department to send a larger representation to your school in the future.

Very truly yours,

Secretary of War.

**Secretary of War John
Weeks (above, left) helped
establish the Army Indus-
trial College in Washington,
and sent prospective College
instructors, among others in
the military, to HBS for
training. This longstanding**
**relationship—as well as
memories of procurement
mishaps in World War I—
led to new ties between
HBS and the War Depart-
ment in the late 1930s.**

GRADUALLY, IN THE LATTER HALF OF THE 1930s, the general perception of national economic crisis subsided. Although the Depression was far from over, industrial production in 1936 finally exceeded that of 1929, and President Roosevelt could boast in that same year that not a single bank had failed—the first such unblemished record in 55 years. Toward the end of the decade, however, the economic debate began to be overshadowed by a debate on a different subject: the appropriate American response to the aggressions of Germany, Italy, and Japan.

Bitter memories of the Great War were still fresh in many people's minds, and there was a widespread sense that America had somehow been "tricked" into participating in that war—perhaps by the British, or perhaps by arms manufacturers. The "war to end all wars" had led only to rearmament, and therefore disillusionment. "A number of us who were too old or too scared to fight prostituted our talents by making posters inciting a large mob of young men who had never done anything to us, to hop over and get shot at," wrote James Montgomery Flagg, designer of the "I want *you!*" posters

featuring an aggressive Uncle Sam. "We sold the war to youth."

In the May 21, 1940, issue of the Harvard *Crimson*, hundreds of Harvard undergraduates signed their names to a statement declaring their determination "never under any circumstances to follow the footsteps of the students of 1917." That earlier generation of students, the statement said, had indeed been "sold" the war, and were unfortunate dupes. The May 31 *Crimson* carried an angry response from the Class of 1917: they had *not* been tricked, they said; they had fought for principles.

Harvard's President Conant was astonished to hear undergraduates—even British nationals—arguing that Nazi rule in England would be an acceptable price to pay for the break-up of the British empire. It was in defense of that empire, these students feared, that America would be drawn into a new global war. Conant argued forcefully throughout 1940 for American preparedness, in response to which his office was picketed by students, and *Crimson* editorials portrayed him as a warmonger.

**Louis Johnson's sudden resignation from the War Department contributed to what Dean Donham termed a "very curious set of conditions."**

By March of 1939, Donham and other faculty members at the Harvard Business School had already concluded that American intervention in the widening war was inevitable, and the School began to prepare itself for that outcome. A series of meetings in the fall of 1939 between Business School administrators and officials of the U. S. Army's Planning Division led to a "memo of understanding," signed on behalf of the Army by Associate Secretary of War Louis Johnson. The memorandum outlined, in general terms, a plan for the relocation of the "Army Industrial College" to Soldiers Field.

There was by that juncture a long history of collaboration between the School and the armed forces. In the early 1920s, the War Department had established a school (which became the Army Industrial College) for the training of selected Army officers in business affairs. The Navy Supply Corps had simultaneously set up its own "School of Application" to provide similar training for naval officers. Donham had been particularly involved in the creation of the Army school, and had recommended that Army officers be sent to the Business School in preparation for teaching at the Army Industrial College—a practice already observed by the Navy. Over the subsequent nineteen years, the Army had sent 135 men to the Business School, and the Navy 55. By the end of the 1930s, half of the faculty of the Army Industrial College were Business School graduates.

The nation's defenses, nevertheless, were woefully inadequate to meet the growing international crisis. The armed forces were small and relatively untrained, while the Depression had weakened or destroyed much of the American industrial capacity. This hard reality

led to a query from Secretary Johnson's Planning Division, late in 1939: could the School develop new courses related to defense production and procurement? The response was positive. Working with the Army Industrial College, and drawing upon the case research of several Washington-based Business School faculty members, Donham was able to announce the inauguration of two such courses in the fall of 1940: Industrial Mobilization, and Economic Problems of National Defense.

In June, 1940, Secretary Johnson informed Donham that the "situation was developing so fast that he expected to order the arrangement [to relocate the Army Industrial College] into effect in about six weeks," as the Dean recorded in a note to himself. Donham was therefore stunned when Johnson resigned a scant three weeks later, and his successor announced that he could not commit resources to the project so early in his tenure.

During the difficult months that followed, in the fall of 1940 and the winter of 1940–41, the Business School contemplated three crucial questions. First, *should* the faculty be kept intact—an explicit goal of the Industrial College relocation plan—or should it be allowed to disperse, as in the previous world war? Second, *could* the School be kept intact, if dispersion were not determined to be in the national interest? In other words, could a sufficient enrollment and operating income be maintained, and enough faculty members retained at Soldiers Field? And, third, how should instruction be altered, taking into account not only immediate defense needs, but also postwar needs?

In practical terms, the proposed Army Industrial College relocation had guaranteed that all available

**The last-minute failure of the Army Industrial College to relocate to Soldiers Field prompted a debate over the Harvard Business School's methods and goals.**

seats at the Business School would be filled for the duration of the "emergency." Now there was no such guarantee, and given the incipient draft psychology, the School might soon face the circumstances it had faced in the fall of 1918: no civilian students, and no alternative to civilian students. In November of 1940, therefore, Donham invited the faculty Committee on Instruction to a meeting at his home. The gist of his comments that evening was circulated subsequently in a memorandum to the faculty.

Donham pointed out that while the School constantly urged business to examine its assumptions in the light of changing conditions, the School had never taken its own advice. "Have we not the same obligation," he asked, "to maintain an organization so elastic that we can move rapidly as conditions change?"

Building toward what he knew would be an explosive proposal, the Dean outlined a number of external conditions that had changed around the School. Large fortunes were rapidly disappearing; the middle class was far weaker than it had been a decade earlier; national demographic trends were less and less favor-

able to institutions of higher learning; the School's endowment might conceivably earn less income, or even become valueless.

"Our enrollment suffers," he continued. "I anticipate a serious further drop in enrollment next year, and a calamitous drop the following year, unless we do something designed to meet the needs of youth swept up in the necessity for militarization. We cannot rely on officer training to meet the emergency, nor would this be an answer to the long-term trends." These conclusions, he reported, paralleled those of President Conant, as stated at a recent meeting of graduate school deans. The president had warned that the University's various schools should develop plans to cope with unprecedented declines in enrollment.

In response, Donham outlined a radical departure. The School, he argued, should admit 750 first-year students, rather than the 600 students accepted under normal circumstances. At the end of the first year, qualified students—up to two-thirds of the class—would go on to the second year. The remaining third of the students, however, would receive three months of

**The Business School claimed just over 10,000 alumni at the outset of World War II. Of these, the vast majority were Americans, living principally on the coasts, in the Northeast and Midwest, and in Texas.**

**Outside the United States, Canada and China boasted the highest numbers of HBS alumni: 132 and 51 respectively. Russia —not being home to any HBS graduates—was not named on the accompanying map, but Lithuania, with one resident HBS alumnus, was.**

specialized training, and be awarded a "Bachelor of Commerce" degree in their field of specialization.

In a second memorandum, dated February 7, 1941, the Dean explained that his proposal was designed to address both educational and financial problems. It was clear, he reiterated, that fewer and fewer people would be able to invest two years (and $2,500, all told) in a business education. Furthermore, the first-year program was of demonstrable value to many students. "Fundamentally," he wrote, "the plan proceeds from pride in the fact that one year in this school means so much, and assured confidence that we can do a really important job in twelve months."

The Dean then discussed what would later come to be called "the screen." In about 15 percent of its decisions on admissions, he observed, the School made mistakes, "to such extent that we scare these men out during the first year, or refuse them the chance to go on into the second year." But perhaps not all of these unsuccessful students *deserved* to fail — perhaps, Donham suggested, they were the victims of unrealistic expectations.

Could not the School return to the original point of its "functional" curriculum orientation—which, Donham said, actually reflected the departments of industries as they had existed in the early 1920s? Marketing, for example, was designed to help students perform tasks within a firm's marketing department. Why not use the first year to train students to identify and solve such departmental problems, and the second year to address higher-level functions? Donham cited the example of bank managers: why should the School train 100 percent of its graduates to do what only 5 percent of bankers actually do—especially when it was "clearly indicated by our records that our low-stand men have no hope of getting into this 5 percent"?

Finally, Donham reminded the faculty of the School's financial prospects in that ambiguous winter of 1940–41: "Budgetwise we would be better off, as we make money on the first year and lose it on the second year. We would, of course, charge proportionate tuition for the summer months, and we would make our dormitories work in the summer. We might reasonably expect a steady net revenue from dormitories of $115,000. Our expected revenue this year is $81,000, and next year under $60,000."

As the Dean had anticipated, his plan for a bachelor's degree aroused bitter opposition within the faculty. "We did not wish to lower the quality of our instruction," the vice chairman of the Committee on Instruction later recalled. "We felt that the mission of the Harvard Business School could only be accomplished by a two-year program." Furthermore, the faculty was then at work designing a training program recently commissioned by the Army Quartermaster Corps, which would help fend off a fiscal crisis.

But many professors agreed with the Dean's analysis of the School's financial situation. In January of 1941, the faculty authorized Donham "to take steps immediately to make reductions in the staff." Clearly, a new program had to be developed—a task which the faculty undertook early in 1941, while Donham was on his annual Florida vacation. The result, after a protracted and sometimes acrimonious debate, was twofold: the continuation of the four-term MBA program, and the authorization of an "Industrial Administrator" (IA) program. The latter was conceived of as a three-term program, to be offered in twelve months of continuous

**A 1941 announcement of the Industrial Administrator program was careful to note that the School's MBA program would continue to be offered, and that applicants to the IA program had to "satisfy the School's customary admissions standards."**

## TRAINING FOR DEFENSE INDUSTRIES

A TWELVE MONTHS' COURSE

AT THE

## HARVARD BUSINESS SCHOOL

First Session Beginning September 22, 1941

The regular two-year program leading to the degree of Master in Business Administration is continued as heretofore. The twelve months' National Defense Plan of Study is offered as an alternative for the duration of the national emergency.

PURPOSE    Faced with the necessity to increase production of vital materiel in defense industries, this country is confronted with a shortage of men trained in industrial administration and management. To help fill this need and to accelerate its contribution to the national defense effort, the School is offering this twelve months' National Defense Plan for the duration of the emergency.

CONTENT    The Plan includes training in the basic administrative areas of accounting, business statistics, industrial management, finance, and marketing. Work is concentrated mainly on administrative problems in factory management, cost accounting, budgeting, and procurement. Special material secured with the active cooperation of the Army Industrial College in industrial mobilization, war-time procurement, priorities, and the economic problems of national defense is discussed.

DEGREE    Those who successfully complete the course are awarded the professional degree of Industrial Administrator.

ADMISSION    Students admitted to this twelve months' National Defense Plan of Study must satisfy the School's customary admission standards as administered for candidates for the regular two-year course.

For additional information concerning the National Defense Plan of Study, address

The Secretary

GRADUATE SCHOOL OF BUSINESS ADMINISTRATION

GEORGE F. BAKER FOUNDATION
HARVARD UNIVERSITY

114 Morgan Hall
Soldiers Field

Boston, Massachusetts

training. It was designed for men "going into government service or into industries connected with National Defense," according to the faculty secretary—in other words, for those who could not or would not commit themselves to more than a year of specialized training. Drawing most of its elements from the MBA program, the IA curriculum emphasized production at the expense of marketing and policy issues. Budgetary control was included only in limited applications, such as factory cost accounting.

The IA program successfully addressed the need to link the School's curriculum with war-preparedness training, while also taking into account Donham's concerns for the immediate needs of the School. The wisdom of the compromise was soon apparent. While MBA enrollment dropped from 850 in the fall of 1940 to 501 in the fall of 1941, the School's total enrollment declined only modestly—from 869 to 809. The enrollment deficit was made up by the 295 students in the recently admitted Industrial Administrator class, which

**"Now that America is at war,"** began a 1942 IA circular. The IA program was offered in three separate sessions in calendar year 1942.

IA literature emphasized that work in "essential war industries" was a critical component in the national war effort—a point also made in the federal government's "Give 'em both barrels" campaign.

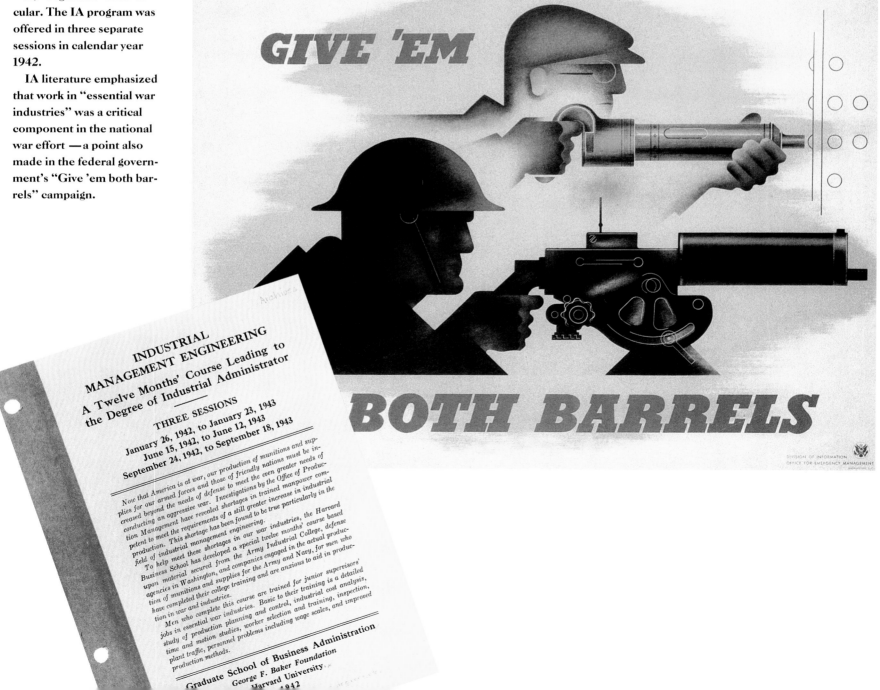

enrolled its first students only six months after receiving faculty and Corporation authorizations. In order to begin the program on such short notice, the faculty had voted unanimously to work on a twelve-month basis without additional compensation, and had worked all summer securing new case materials.

In summarizing these events in his next report to President Conant, Donham was studiously neutral—except for a compliment to his faculty for their hard work and dedication. "In the history of national crises," he added, "not the least significant chapters are those which recite the efforts of universities and professional schools to adjust their programs of instruction and research to certain immediate and compelling facts, without doing violence to their long run objectives and obligations. The problem is one of perspective and balance."

AT THE MAY 8, 1942, FACULTY MEETING, Wallace Donham announced that the Corporation had accepted his resignation as Dean, effective July 1. He discussed his plans to remain at the School afterwards as a faculty member, and reported that he had asked the Board of Overseers to change his title from "George F. Baker Professor of Business Economics" to "George F. Baker Professor of Administration." Such a change, he said, would be in keeping with what he considered the aim of the School: the teaching of administration.

Associate Dean Donald K. David—Donham's designated successor—thanked Donham, and stated his intention to call upon the retiring Dean for advice and guidance.

Professor Elton Mayo spoke next, on behalf of the faculty. He expressed the faculty's sense that in the preceding twelve years, the School had passed through two crises: a major economic depression, and an unprecedented conversion from the tasks of peace to those of war. "In both situations," said Mayo, "the foresight, courage, and intelligence shown by the Dean have been worthy of the word 'remarkable.'"

A series of articles in the subsequent issue of the Harvard Business School *Bulletin* recounted, from several perspectives, Donham's many accomplishments in his long tenure as Dean. Former Assistant Dean Everett Case—then recently named president of

Colgate University—applauded Donham's efforts to prepare the School for World War II. Business historian N. S. B. Gras cited the curricular innovations that had occurred during Donham's 23-year deanship, and Melvin Copeland traced the development of the case method. Librarian Arthur Cole noted Donham's sustaining interest in Baker Library, and the risks he had taken on its behalf. Elton Mayo again cited Donham's vision, manifested early in his tenure. ("At this time of which I write," recalled Mayo, "there were many who laughed at Dean Donham and his pretensions for the new school of administration.") J. E. Le Rossignol, then head of the Association of American Collegiate Schools of Business, labeled Donham a "new type of dean"—not a converted economics professor, but a businessman with firsthand knowledge and a sense of how to provide a "combination of theory and practice which makes for maximum production at minimum cost."

HARVARD UNIVERSITY
GRADUATE SCHOOL OF BUSINESS ADMINISTRATION
GEORGE F. BAKER FOUNDATION

OFFICE OF THE DEAN

SOLDIERS FIELD
BOSTON, MASSACHUSETTS

May 7, 1942

Professor Edwin F. Gay
Huntington Library
San Marino, California

Dear Gay:

The purpose of this letter was to give you advance notice of a bit of news but I learn from Arthur Cole that you are starting back to California the first of the week and meantime he does not know where to address you. Therefore before this can reach you the public announcement will be out that I have resigned as Dean of the Business School to take effect July first.

I am staying on as Baker Professor and hope through relief from the administrative work to find time to do a lot of things in which I am interested. The pressures involved in keeping the School adjusted to the developing national emergency have made the job burdensome, particularly this year, and now that David has returned and had a half year to get into the swing of things, I feel very comfortable about turning the Dean's job over to him.

Cordially yours,

W. Donham

Dean

The final *Bulletin* essay was contributed by Alfred North Whitehead. The aging British philosopher described Donham as one of those unrecognized heroes who initiate "a shift in the ways of looking at the existing activities. The result is a change which makes all the difference, although the nation hardly notices what has happened."

This shift, Whitehead elaborated, was a transition from "decisions once based on the personal interest of industrial leaders" to a more complex objective, within which the sociological effects of the organization on industrial activities must be taken into account.

"The shift has been a slight one," he concluded, "although essential for social stability. When effected, it seems obvious; and for this men, like Dean Donham, who initiated it are apt to lose the gratitude which they deserve. The thanks of posterity go to belated people, who struggle with revolution which should never have occurred."

**The outgoing and incoming Deans. Donham had considered remaining at his post until 1944—his 25th anniversary in the deanship—but was dissuaded for two reasons. First, his own stamina was limited, and second, Associate Dean David was evidently uncomfortable in his role as "apprentice dean."**

Business historian N. S. B. Gras first contemplated writing a history of the Harvard Business School in 1929, but it was not until 1940 that Gras began gathering material for the projected study. At one point, Gras found it useful to try and summarize the policies of Dean Wallace B. Donham, who had so influenced the School in the previous two decades. He came up with 28 principles—reproduced below—and asked Donham to comment. Donham gave his qualified approval to the list, which was, in his opinion, only a partial summary. Furthermore, according to Donham, they were management policies, as opposed to educational policies.

In retrospect, the list seems overly sensitive to the issues of the early 1940s, and it was, as Gras noted, "written in ten minutes." It is, nevertheless, a revealing portrait of a manager:

- Don't worry about things beyond your control.

- Let a good man work out his own salvation, and a poor man hang himself.

- Don't let a good man go sour, but shift him when necessary.

- Young instructors improve by being given a chance to teach more than one subject.

- Let the young instructors work to their limit, but guard the older men because of their health.

- Provide professors with assistance, so as to save their time and the School's money.

- Emphasize the School's income rather than its outgo.

- The School must always be kept close to business to survive.

- The School has had more success with business than with other educational institutions. This must be corrected.

- The time may come when the School may have to give more attention to governmental administration, civic and military.

- Make the students feel that the School is theirs. They have to pay for what they get, but they receive genuine service.

- The faculty improves by constant association, such as at the Faculty Club of the School.

- Faculty meetings are not only the occasions of discussions of policies, but educational exercises for all concerned.

- The faculty meetings should be carefully planned, because a large group can easily waste its time.

- In controlling a body as large as the School, the best method is to discuss matters with leaders among the students and faculty. If the leaders cannot be persuaded, there is little use of going farther with a new plan.

- Avoid departments within the School, because they tend to interfere with the School's elasticity.

- Discipline among the students is essential, but it should be based upon a discrimination between the important and the unimportant.

- The School should do more for the students' and the faculty's health than just provide tennis courts. Someday a gymnasium will be possible.

- When a member of the faculty or the staff proves unsuited to the School's work, get him a better job on the outside.

- Faculty members can be divided into groups: those who overwork and those who take life too leisurely. The former should be assisted; the latter tolerated where necessary.

- Close personal ties of appreciation among faculty, students, and staff are marks of efficient organization and should be encouraged in a school, as in a factory.

- Give a teacher a good office, service, and a position of respect, and he will repay the efforts and the investment.

- Among all, there must be a developed sense of fairness. Where that has failed, the School has suffered.

- The School, having grown up in an era of prosperity, must now prepare for a time of adversity. Scholarships will help meet costs and help bring a better selection of students.

- For the average student, a departmentally-minded man, the School can do less in the second year than in the first year. Accordingly, a lower degree such as B.B.A. should be instituted.

- Away beyond the main work of the School, as at present constituted, is a great opportunity to build up a school of research (above the level of cases) which will be at the level of doctoral work, and which may be provided for at some favorable moment.

- Boston has never been a source of either inspiration or funds for the School. The great issue now is as between New York and Washington. The West has been too long neglected.

- Working out nice policies for the School is a pleasant exercise, but the only useful one is to coordinate needs with opportunities.

**The manager in an informal pose.**

SOONER THAN HIS AMERICAN CLASSMATES, Robert Gueiroard learned how the Second World War would be fought. He was three months into his second year of the Harvard Business School's MBA program—in November, 1939—when he was ordered by the French government to return home for military duty.

The transatlantic crossing took seventeen days. Gueiroard's ship was overloaded with American warplanes, also bound for France. Like others in the convoy, it presented an obvious target for German U-boats. Two ships were lost to torpedoes before the convoy reached Le Havre.

Gueiroard, son of a prominent Paris publisher, went directly to a French military school for training in tank warfare. He was commissioned as a second lieutenant in the Tank Corps, but his training was cut short by the German invasion of Belgium in the spring of 1940. France itself was soon under attack, and Gueiroard found himself second in command of one of the "Groupe Franc"—mechanized units assigned to protect retreating French infantry divisions.

Gueiroard's group of 250 men commanded some of France's best motorized equipment:

**Overleaf:**
**Retreads Frank Coburn,**
**Albert Church, Jr., and**
**James Moran: members of**
**the School's first executive**
**education class.**

**The cathedral at Rouen—**
**near where Robert Guei-**
**roard's mechanized unit was**
**destroyed—rises undam-**
**aged above the ruins of the**
**French city.**

medium and light tanks, scout cars, motorcycles and a variety of trucks. Nonetheless, it was regarded as a suicide squad and consisted entirely of volunteers. Experience soon showed that the Groupe Franc's reputation was justified. In less than two months, after fierce fighting along the River Somme and near the industrial city of Rouen, a hundred of the men in the unit were dead, fifty wounded, and eighty taken prisoner. By the time France surrendered on June 22, only seventeen of the original members of the unit were still fighting.

One of those survivors was Robert Gueiroard, who was released from the defeated French army in August, 1940. He secured the papers he needed in order to leave the country, but found he couldn't risk crossing Spain to reach Portugal, and freedom. (Under pressure from Berlin, the Spanish government was then interning former French soldiers, even those holding valid Spanish visas.) In desperation, Gueiroard ran the English blockade of the Mediterranean aboard a small cargo boat, which landed in Algiers. He reached Tangiers by train and Lisbon by plane. In Lisbon, he joined his American wife and together they sailed for the United States.

Gueiroard reentered Harvard's MBA program, and early in 1941, contributed some reflections on his experiences to the Business School's alumni magazine. He called his article "'Blitzkrieg Tactics': A Warning to the United States."

Simply put, Gueiroard's warning was that warfare had changed dramatically, and that "Fortress America" was no longer the invulnerable bastion it had traditionally thought itself to be. The First World War had been a battle fought from trenches, in which advances were often measured in yards. But the Germans had now developed a new strategy, designed to defeat the French and British before they could mobilize their superior industrial resources. The blitzkrieg employed two weapons—the tank and the plane—in new ways. These mechanized forces probed the enemy's defenses, bypassing strong points and attacking weak points.

"The best way and the only way to stop tank divisions is to use a larger tank division," Gueiroard wrote, "[and] the only effective active defense against a plane is another plane. If the Germans had not had such a superiority in the air, our troops would not have been submitted to such continuous destruction."

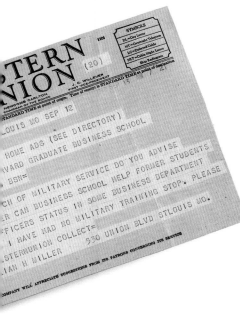

From the days of the prewar "national emergency," the Business School was deluged with requests for draft-related information from alumni. In fact, the School composed a standard response to incoming telegrams concerning the draft: "We are not recommending any specific branch of service. Cannot assist alumni secure reserve officer's status."

What was the lesson that the United States should draw? "The world is growing smaller," Gueiroard suggested, "[and] isolation is an illusion." The Germans had used only 120,000 well-equipped soldiers and a few thousand pilots to conquer all of France. America's defenses against a German assault would have to be spread across an entire continent—probably a hopeless position. Even so, America persisted in its inappropriate isolationist posture. Americans continued to produce luxurious automobiles, for example, when they should instead be manufacturing trucks and tanks for their army.

"I wonder," Gueiroard concluded with evident pessimism, "whether the people of this country are ready to accept the sacrifices which are required, if this country is to be saved?"

Franklin Roosevelt in May, 1940, following an address to Congress in which he called for an annual aircraft productive capacity of 50,000 planes.

IN FACT, THE LESSONS of the blitzkrieg were not lost on all Americans. In May of 1940, President Roosevelt astonished a joint session of Congress by calling for a national productive capacity of 50,000 planes per year. The aviation industry, then working under a congressional mandate to deliver 5,500 planes annually, was as surprised as the Congress. Only 46,000 planes had been produced, in total, in the 22 years since the end of World War I. As a result of this proposal, Roosevelt (like Harvard's President Conant, then also arguing publicly for preparedness) was condemned variously as an interventionist, a warmonger, and a dupe of the British.

But Louis A. Johnson, assistant secretary of war, elaborated on Roosevelt's theme in a June, 1940, address to some 300 members of the Harvard Business School Alumni Association. "England and France were not prepared to produce planes in quantity," Johnson said bluntly. "Germany was. And in that fact alone we find the principal reason for heart-breaking defeats to one side, and astounding victories for the other."

He recounted the history of American military aviation in World War I. Even though Congress had appropriated $640 million—a "staggering sum for those days"—industry had for the most part failed to deliver planes in time to affect the course of the war. It proved impossible to produce large quantities of "handmade" aircraft; it proved equally impossible to set up mass-production facilities on short notice. Nevertheless, Johnson noted, certain achievements of the American aviation industry (and the military) were not to be overlooked. America entered World War I with 55 planes, and ended it with 22,000. Its engine capacity went from almost nothing to 33,000 units annually. Its pilot corps went from 35 to 35,000.

Even as he spoke, Johnson told his audience, Germany was producing planes at the rate of 4,000 per month. Furthermore, the Third Reich planned to increase that rate of production to 6,000 planes per month by the end of the summer. In that context—a likely German output of some 72,000 planes annually—Roosevelt's proposed quota seemed modest and even conservative. "Will any intelligent, patriotic American tell me," Johnson asked, "that we in the United States cannot equal Germany's effort?"

A 1937 meeting of the
German-American Bund
in Madison Square Garden,
New York City. American
isolationism and pro-
German sentiment greatly
complicated efforts—

including those by HBS
administrators—on behalf
of preparedness.

The assistant secretary of war was convinced that America could, in fact, exceed Germany's maximum output. Further, America would *have* to do so: "Let me issue this warning. It is my firm conviction, after serious thought and study of what has taken place abroad in recent times, that if we cannot do it, the safety of this country is indeed in jeopardy. Airplanes have proven themselves engines of destruction far beyond expectation. Air forces have proven themselves in recent months to be controlling factors in the fortunes of war; and the fortunes of war, at the present stage in civilization, determine the freedom of nations."

Gradually, the nation's government prepared itself for this new kind of warfare. In September of 1940, Congress passed the first peacetime draft legislation in American history. Over 100,000 students had received vocational-school engineering training at government expense that summer, in an experimental program sponsored by the U.S. Office of Education; this effort was greatly expanded in October, with a congressional appropriation of $60 million, and renamed the "Engineering Defense Training" program. In his 1941 State of the Union address, Roosevelt asked Congress to approve a "lend-lease" plan, which would make war materials available to selected nations, including Britain and China. Passed in March, Lend-Lease provided $7 billion for the production of "defense"-related materials, and effectively put an end to the nation's formal stance of neutrality.

Isolationism still flourished, though, despite new threats from Germany—and, increasingly, Japan. Colonel Charles A. Lindbergh, a national hero since his solo transatlantic flight in 1927, proclaimed in September of 1941 that the nation was being pushed into war by a cabal consisting of Jews, the British, and the Roosevelt administration. In the ensuing public uproar, Lindbergh was forced to resign his commission in the Army Air Corps. But Lindbergh's public utterances reflected the private thoughts of many, across a wide spectrum of political convictions: pacifists, communists, fascist sympathizers, and members of the isolationist America First Committee.

ENGINEERING, SCIENCE, AND
MANAGEMENT WAR
TRAINING

John W. Studebaker was
U. S. Commissioner of
Education from 1934 to
1948. In December of 1943
—after Harvard's retraining
program had established
itself—Studebaker asked
HBS Dean Donald David
to join his national advisory
committee on war training
programs.

In internal government
memoranda, Harvard's pro-
gram was first described as
an experiment, and later
as a model.

The Japanese surprise attack on Pearl Harbor—
on December 7, 1941—had two significant short-term
effects. First, it gave the Japanese military a naval and
aerial advantage that would last well into the following
year. The Navy lost 150 of the 202 planes it had sta-
tioned at Pearl Harbor, as well as many ships; the Army
lost 97 of its 273 planes. More important, however, the
"sneak attack" instantly mobilized American public
opinion in support of war, which was declared by both
Japan and the United States on December 8. (Three
days later, Germany and Italy also declared war on the
United States.) America had been attacked, and could
no longer fight by proxy; now its full military and industrial resources had to be brought to bear on the conflict.

"Pearl Harbor," wrote U.S. Commissioner of Education John W. Studebaker in 1943, "may be said to stand
figuratively as a bench mark in the mobilization of the
nation's resources, both of material and manpower."
Studebaker had since 1934 overseen the U.S. Office of
Education, which had been transformed by the dramatic events taking place on the world stage. For years
a relatively somnolent branch of the Federal Security
Agency, Studebaker's agency in 1940 had begun contributing to the effort to put American industry on a war
footing. The "Engineering Defense Training" program
was an immediate success, underwriting the training
of some 137,000 workers in short, intensive courses
between October, 1940, and June of the following year.
In this period, employment in the domestic aircraft
industry doubled, and the number of machine-tool
workers increased by almost 50 percent.

Engineering Defense Training was designed to be
elastic, responding to the changing needs of defense-
related industries. It was in effect not a national program, but a large collection of local programs, focusing
initially on engineers: how could enough engineering
skills be marshaled to supervise a massive expansion of
armament production facilities? The answer seemed
to lie in breaking down engineering functions into their
component tasks, and training less skilled workers
to perform those tasks. Typically, a school discovered a
need for defense training which it was able to meet, and
asked the Office of Education to authorize a course
to meet that need. With preliminary authorization in
hand, the school then publicly announced the course,
which was offered only if an agreed-upon minimum
enrollment was attained.

The system worked well. "Whenever there was
an expressed need for engineering defense training,"
Studebaker reported in 1941, "some nearby college was
willing to set up the necessary courses to satisfy it." By
the summer of 1941, over 140 colleges, including institutions in almost every state, had participated in the
program. The evident success of the program—and the
new imperatives of war—led Congress to expand it
again in the summer of 1942. Now called the "Engineering, Science, and Management War Training"
program (ESMWT), the expanded effort now also
sought to train chemists, physicists, and "production
supervisors in fields essential to the national defense."

# *Black-outs and dim-outs*

The surprise attack on Pearl Harbor forced Americans to take civil defense seriously for the first time. If Hawaii could be successfully attacked, were not coastal cities in the continental United States—including Boston—also vulnerable?

In response, the city of Boston hastily created a metropolitan-area system of defense "precincts," which oversaw civil defense efforts. An indefinite "dim-out" was decreed, designed to minimize the nighttime glow of the city. In addition, regular black-outs were held on short notice.

Soldiers Field was no exception. Professor Ralph M. Hower was appointed "precinct warden," and several junior faculty members (including Robert S. McNamara, the future secretary of defense) were named alternate wardens. The School participated in the dim-out by requiring its students to keep their venetian blinds fully closed at night; students who failed to comply were threatened with loss of their campus living privileges. "It was realized, of course," as the notes of one wardens' meeting recorded, "that these restrictions would have to be altered during the warmer months."

The relaxed attitude implied in that comment had earlier gotten the School in some difficulty with local authorities. The city's first black-out was called for ten o'clock on the night of February 17, 1942. All was appropriately dark at Soldiers Field until fifteen minutes into the twenty-minute exercise. At that point, a Business School student threw a handful of firecrackers out of a McCulloch Hall window, briefly illuminating the campus. A local barber and Allston precinct warden reported the incident to police, apparently elaborating on the length and seriousness of the infraction; the next day, a local newspaper complained about the antics of "pampered college students."

University officials were annoyed; they had hoped for a model performance by the Business School. HBS administrators were apprehensive that the Law School's Dean Landis, who was head of the national civil defense effort and openly hostile to the School's wartime programs, might bring the incident to the attention of the Army and the Navy, both then in contractual relationships with the School. He did not do so; furthermore, the Navy ensigns then training on the campus had been pointedly indifferent to the black-out.

"A second tryout came on Thursday the 19th," Professor N. S. B. Gras noted in his diary, "and was a great success. About ninety wardens were present as well as University representation, Associate Dean David, and several police officers. The students had been duly instructed and impressed. The failure turned into a success.

"In the belfry of Baker Library was a warden with a telephone attached to the switchboard and to the entrance of Baker. Just before the end he reported that someone was leaving a car [behind the library] and was smoking a cigarette. Hower says this was Associate Dean David!

"The futility of a local black-out was apparent from the fact that the lights of Cambridge were reflected in the S. of B. windows."

By the following summer, black-outs had become part of the routine at Soldiers Field. At a July, 1943, faculty meeting, for example, Professor Richard Meriam was presenting a key report of the Subcommittee on Objectives regarding the future of the School. "The major interests of this faculty," Meriam was telling his colleagues, "are in the area of private enterprise. . . . As a part of this faculty's work in the area of private business, we should give some attention to the subject of public administration." At just that moment, the lights went out. Forever immortalizing the episode in the memories of those in the room, Meriam proceeded to recite the rest of the report from memory. The faculty then dutifully debated its contents. The meeting was later summarized as follows: "The Secretary regrets that these minutes do not contain a record of the Faculty's discussion of this question, which continued in the dark from 8:55 to 10:40 p.m. during an Air Raid black-out."

**Robert S. McNamara, alternate warden of the HBS civil defense precinct, served on the Business School faculty from 1940–45. He and faculty colleague Myles Mace taught in one of the School's experimental wartime programs, and later served as lieutenant colonels and chief statistical officers with the 8th Air Force in England.**

**McNamara's band: the insignia from the armband worn by HBS precinct and alternate wardens.**

Engineers remained supremely important: having built or rebuilt the staggering number of factories needed for the war effort (over $25 billion worth, including equipment, between 1939 and 1945), they would now design new weapons and the machines needed to produce them. (Henry Ford had confidently announced in June of 1940 that his plants could produce a thousand planes a day. To his subsequent dismay, he discovered that only 3 percent of his existing machinery could be converted to airplane production.) Similarly, an enlarged pool of chemists and physicists would be needed in the field of weapons development. But more and more pressing, in early 1942, was the need for skilled production supervisors.

"The rapid expansion of aircraft construction, shipbuilding, manufacturing of machine tools, munitions, and other essential war industries created a serious problem in plant management," Commissioner Studebaker wrote of the two-year period culminating in the spring and summer of 1942. "Some industries increased their personnel many times within a few months, thus creating an unprecedented need for leadmen, supervisors, assistant foremen, and foremen."

Women at work in the Chrysler Corporation's De Soto bomber plant. Automobile manufacturers were surprised to find how few of their manufacturing processes and machines could be converted to aircraft production.

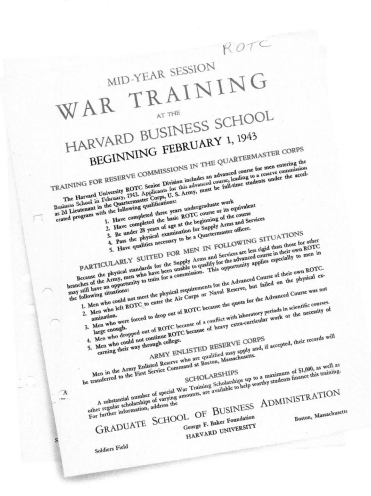

AT THE MAY 20, 1942, MEETING of the Harvard Business School faculty, Dean Wallace Donham reported on the School's ever-changing relationship with the federal government. He apologized for already having taken a series of unilateral actions without adequate faculty consultation, but said that the fluid circumstances in Washington necessitated this approach. He discussed the possibility that the Army might expand its existing Quartermaster Corps ROTC unit at Soldiers Field, and described additional military programs which might be established in conjunction with the MBA program.

Then Donham, six weeks from retirement, proposed the last major initiative of his deanship. The faculty should give immediate consideration, he said, to a government-sponsored retraining program. He suggested that the faculty be prepared to admit, in the coming September, "a group of older men to take selected courses as a means of accomplishing the conversion from peacetime to wartime employment."

Associate Dean Donald David, who would shortly succeed Donham, proposed in turn that the administrative heads of the first-year MBA courses study the proposal and report back to the faculty as soon as possible. The faculty approved, and, in the months following, an ad hoc committee led by Professor Malcolm McNair pursued the idea. They considered three basic questions. First, did the School have the resources to offer such a program? Second, would industry support this kind of course, at least to the extent of hiring its graduates? And third, would the federal government give official sanction to the course under its Engineering, Science, and Management War Training program?

It was hard for the professors investigating the problem to imagine how the first question could be answered affirmatively. The sheer number of students already enrolled in civilian and military programs at Soldiers Field was itself a considerable obstacle: over 1,300 students were then living in dormitories designed for 900; over 5,000 meals were being served daily in facilities intended to produce half that total. Furthermore, the School found its administrative resources taxed by calls and letters from alumni—up to a hundred a day—seeking advice about getting into defense industries. Finally, despite Donham's best efforts, faculty ranks had been depleted, since a half-dozen professors had already been called to war service in Washington. These logistical problems would certainly have to be overcome before the Business School could take on any new assignment on the scale Donham was proposing.

Some sectors of industry, on the other hand, seemed receptive to the idea of a retraining program. Austin Grimshaw, an assistant professor in the Industrial Management area, conducted a survey of the war-training needs of defense industries. The need for war production supervisors was obvious, he reported, and Harvard would do well to address that need. Even now, what was missing from many production lines was experienced supervisors at the foreman level and above. At the same time, increasing numbers of executives were becoming available as nonessential industries closed down. If the Business School could design a course to retrain executives for supervisory production positions, Grimshaw suggested, industry would certainly support it.

**The Business School _Bugle_, which published at unpredictable intervals, appeared in July of 1942 with a barbed commentary on the cramped quarters at Soldiers Field: "Army-Navy Orders _All_ Officers to Train at School."**

**The changing of the guard: at a military review on the steps of Baker Library, the Business School is represented by outgoing Dean Wallace Donham, incoming Dean Donald David, and Assistant Dean Cecil Fraser. Fraser was an invaluable aide to both Donham and David in the war period.**

The University goes to war. Following Pearl Harbor, President Conant pledged the full resources of the University to the war effort. In the following years, Harvard's alumni engaged in symbolic acts—like scrapping the iron fence outside the Boston Harvard Club— and Harvard's departments offered a variety of training programs in support of the war.

Largest of these was the Naval Communications group, which housed and trained over a thousand officers at a time in the Yard. (The Business School's Supply Corps school was the University's second largest military program.) Harvard's normal prewar dormitory population was 4,500; by December of 1942, it had increased to almost 6,500. Some anticipated military contracts did not materialize, but most did; and as a result, Harvard fared better than many American colleges and universities during the war years.

**Naval Science cadets in front of Memorial Hall.**

**The Department of Military Science and Tactics, 1943.**

**"This fence gone to war."**

**Army Communications exercises, July, 1943.**

## Scaling up

At the April 25, 1941, Business School faculty meeting, Dean Donham announced a decision reached the previous month by the Army's Quartermaster Corps. For the first time, the Corps would establish a Reserve Officer's Training Course (ROTC) at a graduate school—the Harvard Business School. Donham also relayed welcome news from the Navy, which had decided to send Supply Corps personnel to Soldiers Field for training. These developments followed by only a month the School's decision to inaugurate the Industrial Administrator program. In combination with the IA program, they effectively guaranteed that the School's faculty could remain intact during the war.

Two months later, the Dean called three members of his administrative staff into his office: Charles A. Anderson, Robert N. Anthony, and J. Sterling Livingston. All were members of the MBA Class of 1940 and had joined the School's research staff in the previous year. Each was young and unmarried. "We have just signed a contract with the Navy Supply Corps," Donham told them, "and as part of that contract, we are to furnish three faculty members to that school. You three are volunteering for the job. You'll go down to North Station this afternoon to be sworn in to the Navy."

The Navy Supply Corps School at Soldiers Field opened on June 26, 1941. At the opening ceremonies, two rear admirals and other dignitaries heard Donham call for unity of purpose in the face of the national emergency: "This emergency gives us a chance to pull together. Even when we have won this war we shall keep our freedom only if we learn to work together."

In fact, the Business School and the Supply Corps School worked more in proximity with each other than together. Anderson, Anthony, and Livingston were the exceptions; 12 of the school's 15 faculty members were career naval officers. The school's curriculum concentrated on disbursing, supply, accounting, and related subjects; 450 probationary ensigns attended each of the four-month sessions, which were offered year round. For the first session, Baker Library's reading room was divided into four classrooms— the only way the School could provide the Navy students with adequate table space for their various manuals, forms, and working reports.

Within the year, the Navy decided to double its Soldiers Field allotment of ensigns-in-training, and therefore needed substantially more space. In the summer of 1942, the Navy built Carpenter Hall, a two-story building with ten large classrooms, on Harvard's playing fields. Six of the twenty tennis courts behind Morgan Hall soon gave way to Cowie Mess Hall. Carey Cage, a small University gymnasium, received a new roof, floor, and speaker's platform, and became Potter Auditorium. This enabled all 800 Supply Corps students to attend lectures simultaneously.

"We do not teach these officers," Dean David noted in the summer of 1944, by which time the Supply Corps school had graduated some 3,500 ensigns, "but we do house and feed them, and we feel fortunate in having this group of outstanding officers living and associating with us here."

**Carey Cage is transformed into Potter Auditorium.**

The Quartermaster ROTC unit, by contrast, built no buildings and was essentially a modification of the prewar MBA program. Business School students added military training to their MBA curriculum and agreed to take the School's several courses in defense mobilization. They received specialized instruction in the duties of the quartermaster and took field trips to nearby military installations. At the end of a two-year course of study, they received MBAs and were commissioned as second lieutenants in the Quartermaster Corps. The ROTC unit was relatively short-lived, however, since the War Department announced in June of 1943 that it was activating all reserve officers and terminating its ROTC courses.

In his wartime journal, business historian N. S. B. Gras analyzed the School's strategy for contributing to (and surviving) the war:

"1. The School first got the Navy students and faculty to use equipment.

"2. And it arranged the Industrial Administrator [program] for civilian war work. This promises to dry up.

"3. Number 1 above does not employ the S. of B. faculty, and Number 2 threatens to disappear.

"The new development is to have S. of B. faculty do the teaching for the government. This was begun with the Air Corps under Learned [and will] be developed in the retraining course to begin 2/1/43."

As Gras suspected, the Army Air Forces Statistical School did indeed become the model for subsequent HBS war programs. Although the four-month Navy Supply Corps school continued to graduate more officers than all the other HBS military schools combined for the duration of the war, each of those other programs nevertheless demanded considerably more time from HBS faculty members.

The Army Supply Officers Training School, for example, began in April of 1943. This three-month program, headed by Professor Malcolm McNair, was designed to prepare officers for "higher duties of supply work in the Army." Members of the 200-officer contingents sent regularly by the Army to Harvard learned the language, fundamental problems, and points of view of business managers in order to make themselves more effective procurers of supplies and equipment.

"Officers with this training," reported the HBS *Bulletin* when the course was inaugurated, "are essential to avoid waste, to cut through to the heart of the problem in anticipating and reporting shortages of food, clothing, and equipment on a rapidly changing and far-flung front, and, at the same time, to avoid being overwhelmed and rendered ineffective by becoming involved in a mass of unnecessary reports and details."

Of more ambitious scope was the Navy Supply Corps Midshipmen-Officers' School, established in February, 1943. The "Mid-Off" program was an extension of the Navy's V-12 program; it was in effect a combination of the first-year MBA curriculum and the existing courses offered by the Navy

Supply Corps School. In order to staff the Mid-Off program (which first brought future HBS Professor Abraham Zaleznik to the School), the faculty voted in December of 1942 to discontinue twelve courses not related to the war effort. The Mid-Off program, as it developed in the four classes begun in rapid succession over the following year, presented the Business School with an unanticipated problem. The first and second classes consisted for the most part of college graduates with two or three years of business experience. Members of the third class typically had no business experience, while many members of the fourth class had not completed college. "It now seems probable that we shall soon be receiving trainees eighteen or nineteen years old," Dean David wrote in 1944. "Thus for the first time we have been asked by the Armed Services to give advanced professional training to men who we should normally feel were not sufficiently mature to handle this work effectively."

The answer, David suggested, might lie in smaller classes and the allocation of more faculty time to individual students. "The change in age and experience of the midshipmen-officers has added a third objective to this program," David continued. "That is, to mature the judgement of these officers. For instance, the faculty has found that it has to place greater stress on the matter of human relations in all aspects of its instruction, in order to supply what these men might otherwise have gained by some years of experience in Navy, industrial, or other organizations."

Dean David subscribed to and expanded upon Wallace Donham's strategy for keeping the HBS faculty intact during World War II. The plan involved bringing the Navy, Army Air Force, and Quartermaster Corps to Soldiers Field.

Supply School students entering Carpenter Hall, a temporary building constructed by the Navy to provide ten additional classrooms for its expanded program.

Administering the Navy courses—which trained huge numbers of students at Soldiers Field—required a full complement of office workers.

Vocalist Patsy Garrett was named "Sweetheart of the Corps" when she—and Fred Waring's Pennsylvanians—entertained the Quartermaster ROTC at a February, 1942, military ball.

The MBA/ROTC program included field trips to local military establishments.

Based on the success of the HBS Quartermaster ROTC program, the Army set up similar programs at eight other American universities.

FROM IRON ORE TO COILS AND SHEETS

Quartermaster Corps students received training in the metal-working process "from the raw materials to the finished products" — a Production process also taught to the civilian retrainees, among others.

In April, 1942, War Manpower Commission head Paul V. McNutt announced that he was creating a system of labor priorities designed to steer workers into the most important war industries. McNutt subsequently played a behind-the-scenes role in getting Harvard's civilian retraining program underway.

McNutt gained some notoriety at Soldiers Field for drafting faculty talent. Professors, according to a tongue-in-cheek HBS *Bulletin* account in the winter of 1943, were "looking apprehensively about every time they step out of Morgan Hall, fully expecting Mr. McNutt to spring on them from behind the nearest bush."

The prospects of working with the government, and of securing ESMWT approval for a graduate-level production course, seemed less hopeful. But there was one promising development early in 1942: President Roosevelt transferred authority over the ESMWT program from the Federal Security Agency to the War Manpower Commission. This meant that Paul V. McNutt, head of the War Manpower Commission and a personal friend of Donald David's, now had ultimate authority over ESMWT. Instead of confronting a skeptical or disinterested bureaucracy, the School might well find a sympathetic audience in Washington.

Early in August, David and Assistant Dean Cecil E. Fraser met with Fowler V. Harper, deputy chairman of the War Manpower Commission. Harper listened to a novel proposal: would the government agree to sponsor a retraining course for accomplished executives, of unprecedented length and comprehensiveness, taught by a graduate school of business administration? These characteristics all represented more or less radical departures from existing ESMWT programs; nevertheless, Harper was encouraging, and agreed to meet with Grimshaw to hear the results of his industry survey. After this second meeting, Harper was again receptive and offered suggestions about how to shape the course's curriculum. Based on this response, and after consultation with his faculty, David notified Harper in October of the School's decision:

"We are going ahead with the retraining program. I am having a faculty meeting to approve it this week. . . . As soon as the thing has official blessing here, we will prepare a memo for you in the hope that some official statement can come from the Governor or the Manpower Commission. . . . It is most gratifying to know that you will consider giving us such an official blessing. Indeed, it is a great satisfaction to have the Governor [McNutt] and yourself unofficially sanction it."

Washington's official sanction finally arrived in November, 1942. The War Manpower Commission emphasized that it considered Harvard's proposed course in "War Production Training" an experiment. The Business School planned to train up to 150 men between the ages of 35 and 60 "who have demonstrated through their business or professional experience the likelihood of being successfully trained." The course

would be long—fifteen weeks—intensive, and residential. Harvard would seek to make the retrainees immediately useful to the war effort by giving them not only a broad production background, but also an understanding of budgetary controls (accounting and statistics, for example) and formal and informal organizational structures.

"Prospective candidates for the retraining course," cautioned the official announcement, made in late November, "must appreciate that because of the type of work they may have been doing in the past, there will be a readjustment involved in adapting themselves to production work. One of the purposes of the course is to aid them in making this adjustment."

Corporate policymaking, however, was *not* to be included in the course: "The basic assumption . . . is that business policies are already established, and that the problem of management is to transmit these policies and make them effective throughout the human organization."

The principal architect of the retraining curriculum, as approved by the Washington authorities, was Professor Franklin E. Folts. Folts had been a member of the Business School faculty since 1928, in the Industrial Management area. He and University of Oregon colleague Edwin C. Robbins had been brought to Harvard by Dean Wallace Donham; their principal assignment was to introduce the case method to the Industrial Management field. (Recognizing the importance of the production function, the Business School faculty had in 1920 made Industrial Management a required course in the first-year curriculum.) Their first collaborative effort was a notable success: *Introduction to Industrial Management*, a combined case and text book published in 1933, was soon recognized as a classic, and remained in print through the mid-1960s.

Throughout the Depression years, Folts gradually shaped and refined Industrial Management. Two factors worked against the course during that period, however. The first problem was the Depression itself: overproduction and lack of demand had idled much of the nation's productive capacity. Then, too, many first-year students still assumed themselves to be destined for higher management positions; this was the second obstacle Folts faced. Like Business Statistics, another

**Frank Folts at the drafting table. Folts headed the faculty Production group from 1928 to 1960, and presided over several major revisions of the course.**

    Folts argued long, and most often successfully, that the Business School should provide a thorough grounding in operational issues. "It would be disastrous," he wrote to Dean David in 1943, "if we were to underrate the importance of training at the operating level as

an essential component of training for effective leadership in industrial management."
    But many students before and after the war considered such operational training overly specific.

**Judson Neff, co-designer of the Production Organization and Engineering (POE) course, checks a film title (right) and demonstrates appropriate uses for spot welds and arc welds on a model aircraft wing (below).**
    **POE attempted to bring the reality of the manufacturing process into the classroom. As a result, it was one of the first HBS courses to depend heavily on instructional films, which depicted various production techniques.**

required and generally derided first-year course, Industrial Management seemed overly functional, and therefore perhaps beneath the consideration of future captains of industry.
    In response to this latter objection, Folts and others in the Industrial Management area developed a broad-gauged production course in the years immediately preceding the Second World War. For example, during the first four weeks of the course as taught in September, 1940, introductory cases emphasized that factory

problems had to be considered as an integral part of larger corporate issues. The second half-year emphasized problems of organization and personnel. "It was felt," as one junior faculty member wrote of the course, "that a major part of the task of higher executives is guiding the course of human beings who differ in interests, skills, and responsibilities, and that the student should have an understanding of the relationships that exist when people work together."
    The impending global war placed new demands on the nation's industrial capacity, and by extension on the Business School's Industrial Management and other production courses. The Industrial Administrator (IA) program, inaugurated in the fall of 1941, was a first step toward meeting these demands. It presented a condensed version of the MBA curriculum in twelve months, with special emphasis on procurement. In connection with this effort, Judson Neff, an engineer and 1936 graduate of the MBA program, returned to the School in 1941 to help Folts design a new and more appropriate production course. The result was Production Organization and Engineering (POE), organized for the first run of the IA program.
    "The content of Production Organization and Engineering," according to a 1942 Harvard Business School *Bulletin* account, "was determined by going to industry and finding out from the sources of origin specifically what supervisory training was needed. As a result the course is completely down-to-earth. It takes up problems at the point where the *what-to-do* has been determined, and confines itself to training in the *how-to-do-it* area." Students in POE focused on the techniques and equipment of the workplace: shop sketching, blueprint-reading, job analyses, time studies, and so on.
    "No description of the POE course would be revealing," the *Bulletin* continued, "without mention of the new and varied equipment that the School has provided for the work. Machine tools, calipers and micrometers, a wide variety of fixed gauges, decimal stop watches, and thousands of feet of moving pictures of shop operations are new additions to the Business School resources. To students of POE, these are now commonplace materials of the Business School on a wartime footing."

"Boys who never expected to taste a sample of higher education are now eating and sleeping in luxurious Eliot House"—a July, 1943, *Boston Herald* report on Harvard's wartime activities. In fact, President Conant's position on wartime use of University facilities led to friction with the Business School.

## War Revolutionizes Harvard In Rush to Train U. S. Officers
### 4500 Alert Army, Navy Students Come from All Levels of Society
**By Arthur Sampson**

*The January, 1947, New Yorker pointed archly to the Business School's first postwar deficit.*

In the immediate aftermath of Pearl Harbor, Harvard's President Conant pledged the full resources of the University to the war effort. In a message to President Roosevelt, he also made it clear that Harvard intended to make no profit on its wartime activities.

This stance, while commendable in the abstract, created immediate practical problems for the Business School. The University treasurer interpreted Conant's decree to mean that all Harvard dormitory space would be rented to military programs at a rate which would only cover operating charges and an adequate reserve for maintenance. "I objected strenuously to this point of view as applied to the Business School buildings," Dean David noted in an October, 1942, memorandum, "and pointed out that under the terms of the gift of the Baker endowment, and certainly of the Straus Hall endowment, that there was expected to be a return on dormitories which would form an endowment fund for the purposes of the Business School. I felt that if the Corporation carried out what he suggested, they would be, in effect, violating the terms of these two important gifts. In addition, it would take a very substantial amount of Business School income away, to a point where we could not hope to operate without showing large deficits."

The University did not agree, and within two years, the School was indeed showing operating deficits as a result of the loss of dormitory revenues. School income and expenses roughly balanced during the war years, at approximately $1.5 million; the shortfall was made up by a dramatic increase in annual gifts to the School—from $100,000 in 1941–42 to $673,000 in 1944–45. (Income from endowment funds, by contrast, remained at roughly $145,000 throughout this period.) Part of the increase resulted from the revised Associates program, which for the first time encouraged corporate gifts to the School. But equally important was Dean David's own consummate skill at fundraising.

An unending series of annual deficits, however, was not a prospect that David contemplated happily. In his 1945 report to President Conant, he noted that without a dramatic change in circumstances, the School would have to operate at a $500,000 annual deficit. There were, as Deans Gay and Donham had pointed out many times previously, only three sources of additional income: higher tuition fees, more unrestricted gifts for immediate use, and more endowment income.

The Business School's tuition rates were already the University's highest. If they were raised substantially, David noted, then new scholarship money would also have to be raised. Otherwise, entire economic groups would be excluded from enrolling at the School. On the subject of annual gifts, David was firm:

"No organization or institution can safely preserve an independent, detached, and impartial position if it must depend every year, regardless of general economic and business conditions, on the generosity and support of others." Nor could the School look forward confidently to a period of vigorous growth and a position of intellectual leadership, David added, if it had to rely on an annual gift total of $500,000.

"Thus we come very directly to the conclusion," David wrote—in a year when the School's endowment was less than $3.8 million—"that the School must obtain additional endowment to provide at least $500,000 [annually] in free funds available for the general educational purposes of the School. In view of the return currently and prospectively available on invested funds, I place the new endowment requirements of the Business School at approximately $15 million."

More negotiations with the University were to follow. Initially, the Harvard Corporation was willing to allow David to seek only $8 million in new endowment funds, of which $3 million was to be allocated for building construction and maintenance. This smaller sum would not have enabled the Dean either to raise faculty salaries significantly, or to build needed classroom and dining facilities. Finally—in 1948—David was authorized by the University to begin a campaign for $20 million.

A retread triumvirate: Eugene Zuckert (left) served as the program's administrative head, and Frank Folts (right) designed the curriculum and led the faculty

group assigned to the program; with Dean David, they initiated and nurtured the retraining program—the forerunner of executive education.

Almost a Complete Break **233**

AT LEAST ONE NEWSPAPER, the *New York Times*, greeted Harvard's announcement of a "War Course for Businessmen" with approval. In a November 30, 1942, editorial, the *Times* pointed out that the war economy had "uprooted many civilian concerns," and had "left stranded any number of valuable businessmen. Unfortunately, too many of the executives are of middle age or beyond, and therefore find it doubly difficult to make the necessary adjustments. . . . Dean David and his associates are to be congratulated for the step they have taken."

Dean David's top aide on the administrative side of the proposed War Production Training course was Eugene M. Zuckert. Zuckert, a graduate of the short-lived Yale Law School/Harvard Business School joint training program, had been recruited to the Business School's administrative staff in 1940 from the Securities and Exchange Commission. During the summer of 1942, Assistant Dean Zuckert had helped persuade the Office of Education to authorize the retraining program; now, several months later, he had principal administrative responsibility for launching the course. It was an important assignment: as David told his faculty in the first week of December, the retraining course might well represent the School's only direct contact with business during the war years.

Even then, however, David knew that all was not well with the course. Because of the delay in securing Washington's official sanction, Harvard had less than three months to find and sign up the hoped-for 150 businessmen "left stranded" by the war. Throughout the fall of 1942, the School had assumed that Harvard's name, combined with the widespread desire to contribute to the war effort, would be sufficient to populate the course. In fact, only a few dozen inquiries had been received by early December. It seemed that few

executives were willing to spend nearly four months at Harvard at their own expense—even though tuition would be paid by the government—if there was no guarantee of employment afterward.

David and Zuckert faced a dilemma. The retraining course was scheduled to begin in six weeks, and the Office of Education was prepared to cancel the course if its enrollment was too low. In the second week of December, David called Zuckert in for an emergency meeting. "We have to *do* something, Gene," the Dean told his assistant in no uncertain terms. "I think you ought to get your ass out into industry."

Zuckert, therefore, found himself boarding the midnight train from Boston's South Station. His plan was to travel across New York State and on into the midwest, visiting selected companies in cities along the way. He intended to propose a slightly modified version of the original retraining plan: now, Harvard's friends in industry were supposed to identify "stranded" executives in their own cities, and pay their expenses while they attended Harvard's retraining course. The sponsoring companies might (or might not) hire the retooled executives when they returned home.

But officials at General Electric and Kodak—Zuckert's first two stops—were not persuaded. The program, they told him, was too broad-gauged. Furthermore, anyone who was valuable enough to warrant four months of intensive training was probably *not* stranded. Such an executive, they pointed out, would have already found war-related work, perhaps only recently, and wouldn't be an appropriate candidate for a four-month leave of absence.

Zuckert's next stop was Buffalo, headquarters of the Curtiss-Wright Corporation. Curtiss-Wright was then manufacturing all three major components of the aircraft—airplane, engine, and propellor—in fifteen huge plants in the east and midwest. Between 1940 and 1944, Curtiss-Wright was second only to General Motors as a recipient of prime war contracts. These two companies, along with Ford Motor and two other aircraft companies, won more than a fifth of all government munitions contracts in the Second World War, totaling over $184 billion. In addition, through the Defense Plant Corporation program, the government invested over $358 million in Curtiss-Wright's manufacturing facilities.

## General, admiral, greeter, host

"Mr. David has this summer completed all requirements for our degree of MBA," Acting Dean Lincoln Schaub informed Harvard's President Lowell in 1919, "and is a man whose record in this school has been exceptionally good."

Donald K. David, who managed to impress the overworked Business School faculty in the difficult months following the Armistice, was born in Moscow, Idaho, in February of 1896. A 1916 graduate of the University of Idaho, he spent a year in the family retail business, then enrolled in Harvard's MBA program.

Joining the Business School's research staff shortly after his graduation, David was appointed to the faculty several months before the arrival of Dean Wallace Donham, who quickly put him to work on various administrative tasks. But David also involved himself in the School's academic affairs, working as an instructor in Marketing and helping to set up the new Retail Store Management course. In 1926, he was promoted to Associate Professor of Marketing.

David evidently enjoyed the academic life. In the mid-1920s, for example, he turned down a job in business which promised both profit sharing and a $25,000 salary—a sum at least four times his Harvard salary at the time. Nevertheless, he was lured away from the Business School faculty in 1927 by an offer of the executive vice presidency of the Royal Baking Powder Company. The offer grew out of David's close personal relationship with William Ziegler, Jr., son of the founder of the Royal Chemical Company. David relocated to New York City, where he made many of the contacts which would later serve the Business School so well. Following the merger of Royal Baking Powder with Standard Brands, David in 1932 was elected president of American Maize Products Company, where he remained until 1941. Late in that year, he was appointed to the School's William Ziegler Professorship in Business Administration—a chair which he had persuaded Ziegler to fund in 1927.

"Executive" is how Dean David described his occupation on a 1930s-vintage passport. It was a self-description which he continued to employ during his term in the Harvard Business School deanship. His role at Harvard, as he saw it, was to plan for the institution's needs ten years in the future, and to support his faculty to the greatest extent possible.

**Donald and Beth David pose informally on the lawn in front of Baker Library. Beth David helped establish the Dean's House as the center of the Business School community—which was considered by many to be an extended family.**

**David's, Inc., of Moscow, Idaho. Donald K. David spent a year after college in the family business, and then attended the Harvard Business School.**

**Harvard's President Conant (above, left) described Dean David as "one of my oldest friends, and certainly my most loyal and helpful one."**

**In his autobiography, Conant praised David for destroying the "curtain of suspicion and disrespect" which had traditionally separated Harvard's business school and economics department, and for David's success with executive education. "As presiding officer**

**of the faculty," Conant recalled, "I had an opportunity to learn through informative debates about the ambitions of the School. Thus I was aware of the methods of instruction which had been initiated under Dean Donham and carried forward to still more effective use under Dean David."**

**Dean David observed to a faculty colleague that his professional life had been punctuated by three major reorganizations: at Royal Baking Powder, American Maize, and the Harvard Business School. Coming in at the top, he further observed, was harder than starting at the bottom.**

David was brought back to Harvard by Dean Donham, who intended David to be his successor. By David's own admission, he was unaccustomed to being second-in-command and was uncomfortable in his temporary role as understudy to Donham. The apprenticeship was terminated after six months, when Donham resigned, and Harvard President James Conant named David to the deanship. It was, for Conant, both an easy and a difficult choice: he and David had been close personal friends since the early 1920s. While he agreed with Donham that David was the best man for the job, he also feared the appearance of personal favoritism. He therefore sought and received assurances from the business community concerning David's qualifications for the job.

The new Dean got mixed reviews from his faculty during his first months in office. He was commended for decentralizing the School's administrative structure and for soliciting a wide range of opinion; at the same time, some professors wondered if these trends might not be going too far. ("One year I was a member of the

Committee on Instruction," as a faculty member noted in the fall of 1942. "The committee met once and listened to Donham. One member asked a question and was squelched. Now"—under David—"everybody talks, and perhaps no one will get anywhere.") But David was, according to most observers, forceful, dynamic, and immensely charming in one-on-one encounters. A successful businessman in his own right, he was entirely comfortable with, and accepted by, his peers in business.

In one sense, David's role in the Second World War period was custodial. His predecessor had succeeded in capitalizing on the School's existing ties with the military and the government and had thereby managed to keep the faculty intact in the first difficult years of the war. Much of David's energy, clearly, was devoted to carrying out Donham's initiatives in this area. On the other hand, in the frenetic and distracting atmosphere of wartime, David faced major new tasks. First, he had to work with his faculty to develop a postwar conception of the School. Second, he had to help build consensus for that conception, which would carry the School into the late 1940s and early 1950s.

Toward the end of 1944, a friend from David's New York days took the Dean to task for failing to keep in touch. The tone of his letter was bantering; David responded in kind. "There was a fellow," he wrote, "who left the hurly-burly of New York to come to the academic calm behind the ivied halls of Cambridge. Phooey! As it turned out, he has become a traveling man, a greeter, a pocket-picker, a third-rate speechmaker, and a stooge."

In a more contemplative letter to another friend, David addressed many of the same issues, which seemed to be defining his new life:

"As you know, we have been training only men for the services these last years. . . . With five instructional programs going, each with its own faculty and administration, the place is really a six-ring circus. I have had to be general, admiral, greeter, host, and money-raiser all at the same time, but the job is a fascinating one and I have enjoyed it, even though it is the most active and pressing one I have ever had."

The Curtiss-Wright complex in Buffalo produced Warhawk fighters, C-46 transports, and various other pursuit, observation, trainer, interceptor, and scouting planes for the Army Air Forces. It occupied a huge complex of hangars, many only recently completed, and in late 1942 employed many thousands of new workers. On the bitterly cold morning of December 16, therefore, the Harvard Business School's emissary to Curtiss found himself in a setting of intense activity and seeming chaos.

Peter Jansen, director of the airplane division, listened in silence to Zuckert's proposal. "Let me get this straight," he finally responded in a pronounced Dutch accent. "I should go downtown and get *dumbkopfs*, send them to your school, and hire them when they get back?"

"Mr. Jansen, that is exactly right," Zuckert replied.

"Tell me," Jansen continued wryly, "why I should go downtown to get *dumbkopfs*, when I have so many right here?"

The idea, although obvious in hindsight, simply hadn't before been considered: that companies could send their *own* employees to be retrained. Zuckert agreed to the tentative proposal and arranged to return the following week with Professor Frank Folts. Folts, in turn, greatly impressed a gathering of sixteen Curtiss-Wright engineers and personnel officers, and the company committed itself to sending up to a dozen men to the first retraining course.

Other companies—notably the Bell and Lockheed aircraft companies—soon followed Curtiss-Wright's lead, although not without further recruiting on Zuckert's part. "The scope of the course has been expanded," Zuckert explained to Bell's comptroller in early January, 1943, "at the request of numerous companies in war industry, so that they may send to us men of demonstrated executive ability whom the training would fit to shoulder more responsible positions with the companies sending them. We believe that this upgrading at such a high level represents a training of unprecedented character, highly significant to companies now in war industry or in the process of conversion."

**Negotiating by telegram: Curtiss-Wright seeks an extension of a deadline for a retread's application (left). Given the circumstances, the School was happy to oblige.**

**Four months later, Assistant Dean Zuckert was again recruiting at Curtiss-Wright (below), this time for the second retread program.**

In a subsequent letter, Zuckert also stressed the advantages of the School's unusual approach to instruction: "Under the case method, men acquire facility in effective analysis and the habit of making decisions. The use of actual problems of companies enables us to give vicariously the benefit of a lot of experience in a short amount of time."

Finally, the assistant dean explained the strengths which the course would derive from its residential nature. As evidence, Zuckert cited the students sent to the MBA program by the armed forces over the previous two decades, who had benefited greatly from "continuous informal contact between students. We know from our experience in the case of the older Army and Navy men we have trained since the last war that this is particularly true in the case of more mature individuals."

PAUL V. McNUTT, CHAIRMAN of the War Manpower Commission and overall head of the Engineering, Science, and Management War Training program, came to the Harvard Business School on February 1, 1943, to address the "retreads"—as they were almost immediately dubbed—on their first day of school. Three weeks earlier, the Business School faculty had voted to stop offering second-year MBA courses immediately, and to suspend the first-year program in June in favor of military programs and the new retraining course. McNutt, therefore, would be speaking to the first members of the only civilian program to continue at the Business School after May.

The 121 retreads were a disparate group. Two out of three were self-sponsored—many of them the result of a last-minute surge in applications. One had operated a successful automobile dealership in Boston; another had been a mural painter in the employ of the Works Progress Administration; still another had run a dance academy. The company-sponsored contingent of retreads—34 of the 121—represented 19 firms located mostly in the east and midwest. Collectively, the retreads averaged 42 years of age. Their median salary in the previous year had been nearly $7,000. Except for a few "commuters," they were housed in Wigglesworth Hall, the newest dormitory in Harvard Yard.

"This course to me is an important development," McNutt said at the beginning of his short address. "With its broad curriculum and objectives, its supervised study, and case method of presentation, it is nowhere duplicated in the country. One of the principal bottlenecks facing industry today is trained manpower at the executive and supervisory level. Never has the country needed administrative talent with a broadened outlook more than now."

McNutt also expressed his satisfaction with "the number of companies who have sent representatives to take this course, despite the heavy pressure on their executive forces. . . . I shall watch the development of this course with personal interest, and with confidence in its success."

The media served notice that they, too, would be watching the retreads with interest. "They are called 'retreads,'" as the *Boston Herald* reported the following Sunday, "in the conviction that they will go a good deal farther if a little refinishing work is done on them. But

these retreads are made of a material far rarer and more valuable than rubber. They are men, and they make up the most unusual and promising class that the Harvard School of Business Administration has ever seen."

The *Herald* concluded its generally laudatory feature with a challenge to a hypothetical business executive: "Think it over, Mr. Executive, if you want to help the war effort where you can be of most value. You must be between 35 and 60, although [Harvard] will allow a little leeway. You must have college training or the equivalent. You must have some executive ability, proven in the give-and-take of business life.

"You must be able to study in the classroom for forty intense hours a week—and do your homework, too. You must be eager to devote your abilities to the winning of this war."

And finally, academia expressed interest, and not a little skepticism. "Frankly," as a Cornell professor wrote to Zuckert, "if it wasn't Harvard which was advertising this War Production Retraining course, I would say it couldn't be done. Fifteen weeks to train an ex-college professor or life insurance salesman is certainly a healthy assignment."

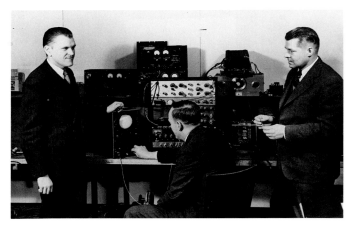

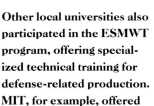

**Harvard was not the only local university working with the Office of Education.**

**Other local universities also participated in the ESMWT program, offering specialized technical training for defense-related production. MIT, for example, offered**

**drafting courses related to radar (above), and instructed students in the use of telemetry test equipment (right).**

The first retraining class, May, 1943. "Except for a handful of commuters," noted the HBS *Bulletin*, "the men are living together in Wigglesworth Hall, newest dormitory in the Harvard Yard. The value of such an arrangement has already made itself felt in the group spirit."

Almost a Complete Break    **239**

HARVARD GRADUATE SCHOOL OF BUSINESS ADMINISTRATION
RETRAINING CLASS ···· FEBRUARY - MAY 1943
Presented to Class by AMPCO METAL, INC., MILWAUKEE

*Boston Herald*

**'Harvard Plans Retraining of Executives**

20 Nov 1942

**Would Aid Them To Positions in War Production**

Harvard business school will offer a 15-week, full-time retraining course to business executives who wish to shift from occupations not now vital to the war effort to positions in war production fields.

In approving the program, Chairman McNutt of the War Manpower Commission said the need for training in business and industrial management to serve the expanding war effort was critical. The university's contribution would be a long stride toward meeting the need.

One hundred and fifty men between 35 and 60 will be accepted for the tuition-free training, which will start Feb. 1, 1943, and be conducted on a daytime, 40-hour-week basis by the regular faculty of the business school. Tuition will be subsidized by the federal government through the Engineering, Science and Management War Training Program of the United States Office of Education.

Applicants, who must have two years of college training, will be selected after interviews on the basis of qualifications demonstrated in their business experience. It is expected that many of those enrolled will be housed and take their meals in the business school buildings. Although the government will pay tuition, living costs and the charge for textbooks will be the responsibility of the students.

The course will seek to enable men not familiar by experience or training with work in production to adjust themselves to some job in that field useful to the war effort.

Dean Donald K. Davis of the business school said: "We believe that this new educational enterprise will be a material contribution in the rounding out of Harvard's part in the war effort. The business school is at present almost entirely a military institution. As a business school, we are conscious of the adjustments that must be made on the home front. In our desire to aid in the great task of transferring executives who have demonstrated their capabilities in the business enterprise in peacetimes to useful, responsible roles in the production of goods necessary to win the war, we are hopeful that there will be substantial results.

"It is not intended that this will qualify men for any specific kind of job. But the effort will be made to give trainees a knowledge of the tools and techniques in the production field. The complete new type of course will be run in consultation with those now in war industries whose advice is sought in connection with organization of the program.

"The War Service Advisory Bureau at the Harvard Club of Boston will assist the business school in receiving applications and inquiries concerning the course. Selection of

The *Boston Herald's* November, 1942, announcement of the proposed retraining program. "The course," reported the *Herald*, "will seek to enable men not familiar by experience or training with work in production to adjust themselves to some job in that field useful to the war effort."

**HARVARD BUSINESS 'RETREADS' REVEL AT MOCK GRADUATION**

Poking fun at professors and awarding honorary degrees, "retreads" of Harvard Business School last night staged a mock commencement at the Harvard Club. Officially known as students of the War Production Training Course, who entered the school from business life to smooth their entrance into war industry, the "retreads" have had 14 weeks of courses and enter their 15th and final lap tomorrow.

Dean Donald K. David of the Business School was awarded the degree of absentia, although he appeared on the platform to don a golden crown. Wallace B. Donham, dean emeritus, made a brief speech, declaring simply, "I'm just a sheer abstraction."

Skits were presented in weird costumes by Robert Ewens of Milwaukee, William Dunn of Toledo, O., Gordon Strong of Milwaukee, Henry De Forest of Arlington and Ferdinand Heinhard of Newark, N. J.,

whose name revived an ancient Harvard call.

Walter Leitch of Springfield was master of ceremonies. Irving O. Reynolds of Toledo was chairman of the class committee, with Raymond Zindle of Brookline as his aid, and Paul Johnson of Cleveland led the singing. More than 100 trainees, who, after long years of business life, have been studying the production methods and soon will enter war work, attended the dinner. Prof. Franklin E. Folts, head of the retraining course, was among the guests. Irving L. Wallen of Boston wrote special songs.

From the first session of the retraining course, participants demonstrated a strong sense of solidarity and cohesiveness. On May 8, 1943, for example, the outgoing "retreads" sponsored a dinner and mock graduation ceremony.

Former Dean Donham attended the dinner, and delivered his shortest address on record: "I'm just a sheer abstraction."

A SECOND EXPERIMENT, also conceived at Harvard in the spring and summer of 1942, was equally a "healthy assignment." Like the retread program, the Army Air Forces Statistical School attempted to put the resources and accumulated experience of the Harvard Business School to new tasks.

The expanded air forces that America took into the Second World War can be considered an outgrowth, in part, of a series of tragedies in 1934. In February of that year, President Roosevelt for political reasons canceled all existing government airmail contracts with private air transport firms. The Army Air Corps then assumed responsibility for offering a greatly curtailed airmail service between selected cities, although it was ill-equipped to do so. Its planes were few and outmoded, especially in comparison to the commercial airlines; severe winter weather across the nation in February and March made the assignment all the more hazardous. Within a month, ten Air Corps pilots had died in airmail-related crashes.

"The whole operation," according to one military historian, "focused attention on the Air Corps as nothing else could have, short of war." The public outcry and congressional hearings which followed led eventually to the creation of the General Headquarters Air Force (GHQ) in March, 1935. While still part of the Army, the new administrative structure was organized to promote the development of an effective and coordinated air corps. Congress also stipulated that the reinvigorated Army Air Corps should comprise 980 planes.

But the reality was quite different. In fact, the Army Air Corps then possessed only 412 planes, of which fewer than 200 were first-line combat aircraft. It lingered for several years in this state of precarious health, undercut by internal disputes and America's prevailing isolationist sentiment. In September of 1938, however, President Roosevelt—a former Secretary of the Navy who had only gradually been awakened to the realities of air power—gave General Henry H. ("Hap") Arnold authority to begin a massive build-up of the Air Corps. The German blitzkrieg in May, 1940, led directly to Roosevelt's public call for an annual productive capacity of 50,000 military and naval planes. The surrender of France in the following month effectively ended the debate. "All you have to do is ask for it,"

Massachusetts Senator Henry Cabot Lodge told General Arnold, when Arnold appeared before Congress to justify increased Army Air Corps funding.

Military aircraft production began to increase rapidly: from 402 per month in April of 1940 to 2,464 per month by December, 1941. But projections of the Air Corps' real needs also climbed astronomically. One 1940 program called for a grand total of 7,800 combat planes and 400,000 officers and men. Only shortly thereafter, a revised projection (and one which proved remarkably accurate) called for 63,000 planes and over 2 million personnel, to be in place by April of 1944.

In other words, in less than four years, the Army Air Corps would grow into one the world's largest enterprises. This called for major organizational changes. In June, 1941, for example, Army Chief of Staff General George C. Marshall created the "Army Air Forces" (AAF) to address growing chain-of-command difficulties within the expanding Air Corps, and named Arnold the Chief of the AAF. Arnold instituted a number of innovations, including a system for "subcontracting" to civilian aviation schools the immense task of pilot training. The 1st, 2nd, 3rd, and 4th Air Forces were established to train personnel and defend the continental United States; after Pearl Harbor, the 5th through 15th and the 20th Air Forces were set up to conduct overseas operations.

One of Arnold's largest challenges, as the ranks of the AAF swelled, was simply keeping track of who and where its personnel were. Furthermore, the AAF had to know which personnel had received which training, and then assign them appropriately. By the end of the war, 1.5 million people would have gone through AAF technical training courses, and a roughly equal number would have received some form of specialized aviation training: piloting, navigating, bombing, and so on. In addition, the AAF had to procure and deploy planes—over 230,000, by war's end—and the necessary spare parts. Finally, the AAF's logistical and combat operations had to be tracked and assessed in some way.

To meet these mounting challenges, Arnold decided—with the enthusiastic support of Assistant Secretary of War for Air Robert A. Lovett—to create a "Statistical Control Division" at AAF Headquarters in March, 1942. Arnold and Lovett envisioned a network of statistical officers, assigned to each AAF command,

Cecil E. Fraser, a 1921 graduate of the School, served two terms as an HBS administrator: from 1921 to 1931, and again from 1941 to 1947. He greatly assisted Deans Donham and David in their interactions with the federal government and the military during the early 1940s.

By all accounts, Fraser was not cut from the standard Business School cloth. He had, as one faculty colleague put it, "the common touch." Fraser derived satisfaction, for example, from dealing with local draft boards and politicians; he enjoyed spending spare hours chatting with officers at the police station in Cambridge's Central Square.

who could collect, organize, and interpret data concerning the status of personnel and equipment. In effect, they would serve as a rough equivalent of corporate controllers. The success of the German blitzkrieg was in part due to the existence of such a statistical system, although in a simplified form; and the problems stemming from the AAF's lack of such a system were already becoming painfully evident.

Arnold delegated this complex task to his staff assistant, Colonel Byron E. Gates, and promised Gates full backing if traditionalists within the Army raised objections to the proposal. Gates, in turn, sought out Major Charles B. ("Tex") Thornton, a former Department of Agriculture employee with an interest in statistics. Thornton was appointed to head the new Statistical Control Division, and he immediately began seeking a means whereby he could set up a control system such as Arnold and Lovett had envisioned.

Thornton was inclined to "subcontract" the training of AAF statistical officers, much as Arnold had contracted out for the bulk of pilot training, and he soon settled upon two possible homes for the proposed "Army Air Forces Statistical School" (AAFSS): the University of Maryland and the Harvard Business School. Initial contacts between the AAF and Harvard—arranged by Professor Georges Doriot in January, 1942—proved unproductive, and the ensuing negotiations were conducted with great secrecy. Harvard's representatives to the negotiations—Assistant Dean Cecil A. Fraser and Professor Edmund P. Learned—had only limited security clearances, and were convinced more than once that the AAFSS contract had gone to the University of Maryland.

But in early May, the AAF informed Dean Donham that Harvard had indeed been selected to organize the new school. AAF officials stressed that the Statistical School (or "Stat School," as it was soon known) had the highest military priority, and requested that Donham immediately dispatch a dozen faculty members to Washington for indoctrination. It was a matter of some urgency, they pointed out: the AAF planned to send its first class to Soldiers Field in June—only three weeks from that date.

THE HARVARD BUSINESS SCHOOL had some expertise in statistical techniques, of course, but none of it was directly relevant to the Stat School experiment. Two questions had to be answered immediately: what would the new school teach, and who would teach it?

The only faculty member then assigned to the Stat School project was Edmund Learned. Learned, a member of the MBA Class of 1927, was one of the first recipients of the Doctor of Commercial Science degree to earn a distinguished place on the Business School faculty. Although he had been trained in (and throughout the 1930s had taught in) the School's Marketing area, Learned had a quick and versatile mind, and an unusual ability to size up and recast an intellectual problem. As a result, he had been asked by Dean Donham to take on a difficult assignment in the spring of 1939: a revamping of the first-year Business Statistics course.

Edmund P. Learned served a catalyzing and integrating role on the Business School faculty. In the Second World War, he not only helped establish the Army Air Forces Statistical School at Soldiers Field, but also served as a Special Consultant for Program Control to the AAF's commanding general.

This latter position earned him, in 1945, an AAF Distinguished Service Medal. "He was responsible," noted General H. H. Arnold, "for reviewing on an annual basis all parts of the Army Air Forces program, and maintaining a proper adjustment among them, to insure a coordinated flow of aircraft, equipment, and trained personnel to meet commitments."

Business Statistics had been controversial almost since its inception in 1912. In marked contrast to the cohesive Accounting faculty, the Statistics faculty had disagreed on how to teach the fundamentals of their discipline: should they present statistics as understood and used by economists, or only as the science pertained to businessmen? Students, for the most part, loathed the course, which in the late 1930s concentrated on the calculation of averages, regressions, time series, and so on. Particularly distasteful to them was the "40-hour problem"—a long (and to many, pointless) laboratory exercise in which students assembled data on many years' worth of cigarette sales, ran them manually through tabulators, and developed time series showing seasonal, cyclical, and trend patterns.

Through Learned, Donham sought to resolve the longstanding problem of statistics once and for all. As Learned later recalled, "The Dean essentially said, 'Make the Business Statistics course one on the management use of figures in decision-making. Somehow find more time for this objective. Condense method if you can; reduce method if you must.'" Working with Professors Joseph L. Snider and Charles A. Bliss, Learned began a conceptual redesign of the course. Per Donham's directive, the emphasis was on *action*. "We sought to train our men for positions of responsibility that required statistical facts and analyses for diagnosis or action purposes," Learned wrote of the course. "We wanted men to develop judgement in the use of figures, and we aimed to train men to plan for and seek data, inside or outside the business, that would contribute to an intelligent solution of the problem under discussion."

Not coincidentally, the School's Accounting courses were then evolving toward the same goals. In 1936, Professor Ross Walker had first offered a second-year

research course called Aspects of Budgetary Control, which represented a departure from Harvard's previous courses in the field. Walker—who had left the faculty briefly in the early 1930s to serve as treasurer of a woolen mill—was an intensely practical thinker. He concerned himself with the aims, as well as the techniques, of managerial planning and control. In his teaching and his few published works, Walker emphasized the ways in which accounting might be used for internal, in additional to external, purposes. By so doing, he helped develop the rudiments of management accounting, which after the war would be combined with statistics to create a new course and a new field: Control.

The Industrial Administrator program—the School's transitional mobilization course, organized in the summer of 1941—presented an unusual opportunity for a synthesis of these emerging concepts. The faculty group charged with developing the twelve-month curriculum perceived the need for a course in Management Controls. Again, Donham called upon Learned. "I want this course," Donham told Learned, "to be a combination of the control concepts represented by [Professor Richard] Meriam in Industrial Management, by Walker in the advanced accounting field, and by you and Bliss in Marketing and Statistics." Furthermore, Donham said, he wanted the Human Relations concepts then being taught by Professors Elton Mayo, Fritz Roethlisberger, and Benjamin Selekman to have a prominent place in the new course.

Donham promised Learned that he could expect help from Meriam, Walker, and Roethlisberger; but Learned soon found that his senior faculty colleagues were unable to help, owing to prior commitments and illness. Instead, Learned began his course development work with two young assistants: George F. F. Lombard, from the Human Relations group; and John D. Glover, an instructor in Harvard's economics department who had volunteered for defense-related work. Learned, Lombard, and Glover, drawing upon the School's contacts in industry and government, revised existing cases and developed new ones in an effort to achieve the synthesis that the Dean had articulated. The Management Controls course development effort continued through the winter of 1941–42, and the course was first offered to Industrial Administrator students in May of 1942.

**Ross Walker, who helped invent the field of Control, taught at the Harvard Business School from 1926 to 1959. Although he wrote only four books, his influence was felt internationally.**

**According to a colleague, Walker helped bring accounting "out of the green-eyeshade era to become a tool of general management."**

At a meeting of the
President and Fellows of Harvard College
in Cambridge,    February 15, 1943

Voted to grant leave of absence to the following persons:

Assistant Professor Myles L. Mace, without salary, from ✓
March 1 to July 1, 1943, for Government service.

Assistant Professor Robert S. McNamara, without salary, ✓
from March 1 to July 1, 1943, for Government service.

Jerome D. Greene,
Secretary

Dean Donald K.

**In March of 1943, HBS Professors Myles L. Mace and Robert S. McNamara— members of the Stat School teaching group—began their first European tour of duty on behalf of the Army Air Forces.**

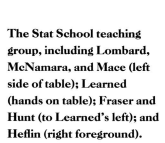

**The Stat School teaching group, including Lombard, McNamara, and Mace (left side of table); Learned (hands on table); Fraser and Hunt (to Learned's left); and Heflin (right foreground).**

"Because the School was faced with the necessity of organizing the course rapidly to meet the emergency situation, the actual construction of [Management Controls] was started before the area which it was to cover was clearly defined," Lombard wrote the following year. "The fact that its parts go together as well as they do can only be explained by the consistency with which the students are drilled in the point of view behind the course. For no matter what particular aspects of management responsibilities are being discussed, the emphasis of the instruction is always to get the student to make a diagnosis of the situation, and to take action in the light of that diagnosis."

IT WAS THIS EXPERIENCE, both practical and theoretical, that recommended Learned and the Business School to the Army Air Forces. Clearly, the "actual construction of the course" to be offered by the Stat School would be started before the subject was fully defined. Furthermore, the active use of statistical techniques and the emphasis on both diagnosis and action were precisely to the point. And while the AAF had not previously contemplated training in human relations, Major Thornton had no objections to including the subject in the Stat School curriculum.

When Donham learned in May of 1942 that the AAF had selected Harvard, Learned was relieved of his teaching responsibilities. At once, he and ten junior colleagues went to work—in Washington, and at a half-dozen bases around the country. The task they faced was imposing. Not only would they work with the AAF to create a new type of school, without the benefit of field manuals or other formal precedents; but they would also help the AAF set up a new reporting system, whereby information developed by a contemplated network of thousands of statistical officers, in commands around the world, would be sent directly to the headquarters of individual Air Forces. The information would there be consolidated, analyzed, and subsequently forwarded to the office of Thornton, Chief of the Statistical Control Division.

"Among the required adjustments"—as Dan T. Smith, a junior member of the faculty team, later wrote of the experience—"was a temporary repression of traditional academic perfectionism." In fact, when over 100 statistical officers-in-training gathered at Soldiers Field in June for the school's first five-week session,

In their five (later eight) weeks of training, the Stat School's students received not only classroom instruction, but also a practical introduction to sidearms.

A Stat School class. The Stat School was housed in Mellon Hall and instructed in Baker Library classrooms.

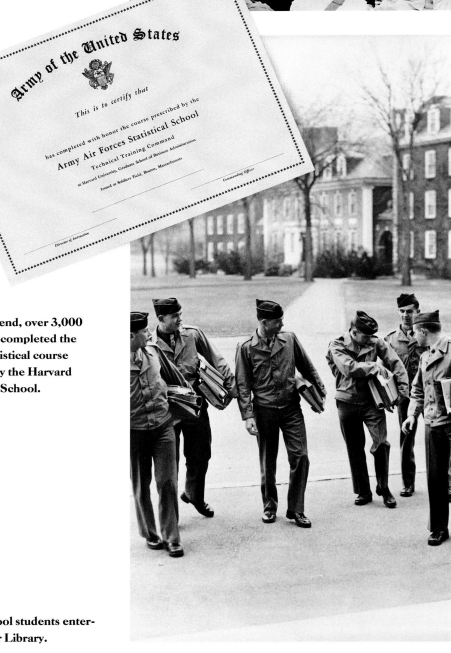

By war's end, over 3,000 men had completed the AAF statistical course offered by the Harvard Business School.

Stat School students entering Baker Library.

teaching material was in hand for only three weeks' worth of classes. While that material was being presented, other researchers were still scrambling in the field, developing cases and related materials for the final two weeks of the program. But this ad hoc approach had an obvious benefit: case research could serve course development purposes and, simultaneously, provide practical assessments of the needs and potential of the statistical control system itself. Eventually, this dual role received formal recognition, and Business School faculty members associated over the long term with the Statistical School were designated as "Special Consultants" to the AAF.

Lieutenant Colonel John F. Heflin, a former military school headmaster, was appointed commandant of the Statistical School. He worked closely with academic head Learned. ("You were the military head of the school, and I was the academic head," as Learned noted in a letter to Heflin after the war, "and never once did we have any basic difficulty agreeing on our respective spheres of influence.") Together, Learned and Heflin shaped and reshaped the school and its curriculum, in response to field data and in recognition of the changing needs of the Air Forces. At first, the military was most interested in securing useful and uniform information on personnel; gradually, emphasis shifted to *using* the personnel most effectively. Similarly, as the advantages of centralized and standardized personnel information became obvious, the techniques were extended to aircraft status, spare parts inventories, and training and operations analyses.

The curriculum (which was lengthened to eight weeks in 1944) came to be divided into two roughly equal parts. In the first half, officers learned elementary statistics and their uses: ratios and percentages, cross-classification, averages and measures of dispersion, times series, and correlation. Instructors emphasized the dangers of superficial or unjustified inferences—cautions to be heeded in the second half of the course, during which students were assigned a series of "analysis problems." Actual data (disguised for security reasons) and a proposed plan of action were presented; students had to assess the feasibility of the plan based on the data. In no case was there an implied "school solution." Instead, as Dan T. Smith later noted, the

In 1949, George Lombard reflected (in the third person) on his approach to researching the Umpteenth Fighter Squadron case: "He thought it especially important that he disrupt the working activities of the squadron as little as possible, so that he would be free to come back over and over again. In this respect his behavior had to differ from that of most research agents collecting cases for most courses."

analysis problems were designed "to encourage initiative and imagination, and to develop (or at the very least show the need for) initiative and judgement."

Realism and pragmatism were emphasized throughout—in part because they were stated objectives, but also because the ongoing field research into AAF operations constantly pointed up their importance. Bad statistics, or the improper use of good statistics, could be dangerous. Early in the war, for example, two Business School researchers visited a small AAF base outside Boston. The fighter squadron at this particular base was one of three which shared responsibility for keeping planes aloft at all times over the Roosevelt estate in Hyde Park, New York. The squadron commander at the base assured the Harvard researchers, as he had assured Washington, that he had thirty planes which could "fly, fight, and bomb" on a moment's notice. His analysis, it soon emerged, was based on the reports of crew chiefs, who in turn made their separate estimates assuming that they had unlimited access to a common inventory of crews and equipment. But this was a fallacy, since no two planes could share a pilot, a propellor, or a weapon. In fact, as the researchers discovered, the squadron commander at one point in time had only a *single* plane which he could depend upon to fly, fight, and bomb.

This same base—actually only a pair of fighter strips set at right angles in a cornfield—was soon revisited by George Lombard, then researching the human and organizational challenges of the rapidly expanding AAF on behalf of the Statistical School. Lombard made almost daily visits to the base over the span of six weeks, early in 1943. He tried to observe as much as possible about the human interactions at the base without disrupting normal routines. He recorded not only what various individuals said, but also what they did; and how what they did affected the work of others around them.

This was a different kind of research, which drew upon the lessons of the Western Electric experiments of the 1930s to assess and depict the inherent complexities of a human organization. Lombard quickly perceived a collision of values and a pronounced incompatibility between old and new types of warfare. The "old guard" in the Army, for example, placed great emphasis on the morning report, a daily personnel summary which dated back to Revolutionary War days.

More recently commissioned officers, however, tended to dismiss the morning report as time-consuming and irrelevant. For one thing, it failed to link the availability of people and the availability of machines. Furthermore, the sheer scope of the AAF, and the nature of its new assignments, made "counting noses" a nearly hopeless task. In 1943 alone, for example, the AAF produced 65,000 pilots, 14,000 navigators, 14,000 bombardiers, 82,000 aerial gunners, and 530,000 technicians, many of whom reported for duty without official assignments. The result, in many cases, was chaos.

Small as it was, the air base being studied by Harvard's researchers offered homely examples of these same growing pains. One morning, for example, Lombard accompanied the adjutant—the staff officer responsible for personnel and administration, and a career officer—on a tour of the base. Crossing the cornfield, they came upon a private who was tending a small fire. The young man was evidently boiling some water.

"What are you doing, soldier?" asked the adjutant.

"Just making some hot water to wash my socks, sir," replied the private sheepishly.

"Why aren't you on duty?" the adjutant demanded. "What's your assignment? What are you supposed to be doing?" The questions were critical ones, given the severe manpower shortages faced by this and similar units across the country.

"I don't *have* an assignment, sir," came the response. "I don't know."

The Stat School marching in formation. "Originally," wrote HBS Professor Norman Gras in 1943, "they were told that they were the rag-tag and bob tail of the whole [Soldiers Field] outfit; they decided to change and they did."

THIS WAS NOT WARFARE as it was then being taught at the Army Air Forces' Officer Candidate School in Miami. There, young officers-in-training spent three months studying military strategy—war as it *should* be fought—and going through a rigorous physical training. Simultaneously, they were evaluated in terms of their backgrounds and any special talents. At the end of the first six weeks, some were selected for specialized training at certain schools under contract to the AAF. One of these was the Statistical School at Harvard.

In charge of such classification at Miami was AAF Second Lieutenant Kenneth R. Andrews. Andrews had been drafted in June, 1942, as he neared the end of his graduate work in English at the University of Illinois. He had soon become an AAF bureaucrat by default: typing, shorthand, and other incidental skills resulting from his graduate education were in short supply. Every six weeks, therefore, Andrews faced the unenviable task of classifying some 3,000 AAF officer candidates for their next postings. Some were easy to assign, such as meteorologists, radar technicians, physicists, and other specialists. The vast majority, though, had been accountants, clerks, and other types of office workers in the civilian economy. Somehow, this group had to be divided up with reasonable fairness among the available postings.

In the fall of 1942, however, Andrews noticed a pattern emerging which he considered unfair. Representatives of Harvard's Statistical School, which obviously had the blessing of headquarters in Washington, would come down to Miami every six weeks and select the cream of the new officer crop for instruction at Harvard. Worse, they would pointedly turn down the less distinguished candidates whom Andrews attempted to press

upon them. Harvard's Professor Learned was particularly firm on this point. The situation was further complicated by the fact that Harvard was known to be a desirable posting—for one thing, there were no dawn drills—and some of Andrews' officers-in-training went to great lengths to apply for and get assigned to the Stat School.

So Andrews took unilateral action: he began withholding certain applications from the Harvard interviewers. The tactic was soon discovered, however, and Andrews fully expected the well-connected Learned to go over his head and seek redress. Instead, Learned chose to approach Andrews and explain his position: Harvard was training second lieutenants, he said, who would have to go out and tell majors and colonels how to run their business; therefore, they *had* to be good. He proposed a compromise—Andrews could join the interviewing board, and in that context he could make his case for alternative candidates or postings. Andrews accepted the proposal, and the system soon began to prove itself effective, particularly as the young second lieutenant gained a better understanding of what the Statistical School was trying to accomplish.

That understanding was greatly enhanced in the fall of 1943, when Andrews himself accompanied the most recently selected class of Stat School trainees from Miami to Harvard. The first case that the incoming students were asked to consider, on their first day at Soldiers Field, was "The Umpteenth Fighter Squadron" —a rich, complicated, and jarringly realistic summary of George Lombard's study of the fighter squadron in the cornfield. The case raised numerous human and

**The stacked rifles of the Stat School, on the Baker Library lawn.**

organizational issues, including impetuousness, failure to delegate authority, lack of persuasiveness, violation of the chain of command, and a general lack of coordination—in short, the reality that most of the statistical officers would soon encounter firsthand.

First taught in the summer of 1943, the Umpteenth Fighter Squadron case was already celebrated for the heated classroom sessions it provoked. In fact, the Business School community had begun to look forward to these bimonthly events. Typically, the consensus of the first hour of discussion was simple: "Court-martial everybody!" (In fact, an AAF general in Washington once asked Learned to reveal the identity of the disguised base and its commanders, so that they *could* be court-martialed; Learned moved quickly to quash that initiative.) But eventually, other voices would begin to be heard in the classroom: "But that doesn't make sense. It's obviously not that simple."

Andrews was impressed. He attended six classes in a row and found each to be superbly taught. Reflecting on his undergraduate and graduate days, he realized that he had never before encountered even two excellent teachers in a row. He realized further that the subject matter at hand was not, in fact, statistics; but rather *administration* in the broadest sense. The statistical officers were being trained to assist their superiors in making informed decisions; therefore, they had to understand the problems and responsibilities faced by those superiors.

Eighteen months later, Andrews—a future Business School professor—was himself enrolled in the Stat School. He later applied his training in the Pacific theater, where members of the school's first class had already demonstrated their utility. In Australia, for example, they helped create a statistical control system

for the 5th Air Force. Lieutenant General George Kenney, chief of Allied Air Forces in the Southwest Pacific, described the system as "the answer to my prayers," and other AAF commands in the Pacific requested statistical assistance as a result.

Similar reports came in from other fronts. The 8th Air Force, which conducted controversial daytime raids on Germany and ultimately contributed to the defeat of the Luftwaffe, depended heavily on its network of statisticians. Its commanding officer, Lieutenant General Ira C. Eaker, wrote to Learned in December, 1943, to congratulate Harvard on the "great contribution" it was making to the war effort: "The statistical officers you have trained and sent to us are a fine lot, and reflect the excellent training they have received at Harvard."

The AAF statistical control system had a major impact for two reasons. First, through a system of new and modified reports, new types of information were generated. A much improved daily report on aircraft status, for example—the so-called 110 report—enabled strategists to know with great precision which planes could indeed "fly, fight, and bomb." Second, the information developed was used much more objectively, since it flowed up to Air Force headquarters through a parallel and largely independent command structure. This model of statistical control, furthermore, was adopted after the war by numerous companies. Perhaps the best known example is the Ford Motor Company, which employed former Stat School researcher and faculty member Robert S. McNamara in precisely this capacity.

To Professor Learned
and Harvard Business
School with all
good wishes —
Ira Eaker
Lt Gen USA

**Robert A. Lovett, Assistant Secretary of War for Air, worked with the Business School's Edmund P. Learned to create the Army Air Forces' Statistical Control Division. In 1967, the former officers of that division announced the creation of an endowed professorship at Harvard: the Lovett-Learned Professorship of Business Administration.**

By the end of the European war, the Statistical School had trained more than 3,000 officers. Assistant Secretary of War for Air Robert A. Lovett thanked Dean David in January, 1945, for that accomplishment, and also for the School's assistance in setting up a worldwide control system: "The present statistical control system of the Army Air Forces was set up within a space of time far shorter than I had believed possible. We have not only been enabled to apply modern business statistical methods to our intricate problems, but in conjunction with the School, we have devised various new techniques which will be of interest to government and industry after the war."

This lesson—the apparent transferability of certain management techniques and attitudes—had not been lost on the Harvard Business School. "We have found the development of this [Statistical School] curriculum very interesting," Dean David informed the dean of the Littauer School in February, 1944, "because it has shown the usefulness and applicability of various principles of administration in an entirely new sphere of activity."

**The Stat School's brain trust: Edmund Learned, AAF General Trubee Davison (a prominent backer of the School in Washington), Cecil Fraser, and Major John F. Heflin.**

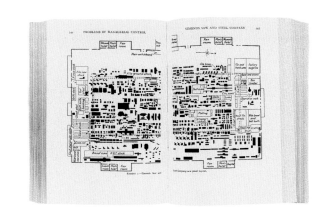

THE SUMMER OF 1942 also saw the birth of a third initiative at the Harvard Business School, in addition to the retraining program and the AAF Statistical School. But while those two educational experiments were conceived by Wallace Donham, the retiring Dean, the Business School's aviation research program was evidently inspired by Donald David, Donham's successor in the deanship.

When David left the School in 1927 to become executive vice president of the Royal Baking Powder Company, relatively little research was being conducted by the School's faculty. Even case research had been curtailed, due to budget constraints arising during the construction of the Soldiers Field campus. Elton Mayo's research and the work of the Fatigue Laboratory had just gotten underway; the Two Hundred Fifty Associates of the Harvard Business School, a group of wealthy individuals organized to provide a stable source of research funding, had not yet been conceived. Most faculty publications at that time tended to take the form of casebooks, or combined case and textbooks such as Folts' and Robbins' *Introduction to Industrial Management*. The only industry studies were those being carried out by the Bureau of Business Research; these were statistical in nature and were largely for the edification of the subject industries themselves.

Not much had changed by the winter of 1941–42, when David returned to the School as dean-in-training. The Depression had had a severe impact on the nascent Two Hundred Fifty Associates program—and, by extension, on the School's research capabilities. Dean Donham's effort to create a separate research institute (in the guise of a Littauer School of Government) had failed. In fact, only the sustained support of Elton Mayo and Lawrence J. Henderson by the Rockefeller Foundation had kept organized research alive at the School during the Depression. Even the defense mobilization effort begun at the end of the 1930s had of necessity concentrated faculty attention on case research and course development.

David was well aware of this history, both as an intermittent member of the School's Visiting Committee and through personal contacts with Donham and others on the faculty. He shared Donham's sense that the School had a responsibility to serve both business and society. Like Donham, he felt that the School was uniquely positioned to do so. "I have been amazed since my return here," he wrote to a friend in February, 1943, "to see the influence the School has with such diversified groups, including not only management, but labor, government officials, and the public as well. This is probably because there are comparatively few entirely independent agencies in the country that can be relied upon. We are a school of private business and are known as such. We operate under the banner of a great institution. I believe that we have both the obligation and the opportunity to carry on a research program that will be of real value and importance [during] the late war and post war period."

But while Donham and David shared certain convictions about research, their motivations were different. Whereas Donham felt that the School had to protect industrial capitalism from its own excesses in the context of the turbulent (and potentially radical) Depression era, David saw new problems. First, government was now a major player in the national economy, to an extent that would have been inconceivable only a few years earlier. By 1943, for example, the government had invested over $20 billion in industrial plants, and had acquired land for defense purposes exceeding the total acreage of New England. Early in his deanship, David shaped a question which he found particularly troubling: in the transition period at the end of the war, and in the postwar era, would America look to private enterprise or public enterprise for answers to pressing economic problems?

Furthermore, the spectre of renewed depression still loomed. Unemployment had declined dramatically, but only because of the intensified war production effort. What would happen when the war ended, war production ceased, and several million veterans began seeking employment? As David saw it, only unprecedented investments of capital in relatively exposed and risky ventures—new businesses, small businesses—could begin to meet the challenge.

"Where are the answers to these questions of the transition period," David asked the New England War Conference in the fall of 1943, "which will so vitally affect the future of all of us? . . . The logical answer lies in a word common to all of you: research. Free, honest, objective, and unfettered economic and administrative study. The only democratic way to answer these

Cartoonist Francis Dahl of the *Boston Herald* was a local institution. His 1943 HBS *Bulletin* cover lightly depicts what Dean David saw as the central postwar challenge to American industry and the Business School: creating an economy that would provide sufficient employment opportunities.

Two deans and a director: in two very different eras, Deans David and Donham called upon Professor Melvin T. Copeland to direct the School's research efforts. David and Donham shared a vision of business research, and collaborated in 1942 on a plea for corporate support of such activities.

problems is specific research"—with widely publicized results—"to give the American public facts with which to judge accurately where they want to stand on fundamental issues."

But the nagging practical problem, as David well understood, was to finance such a research program. The School had insufficient endowment income to support a large-scale research effort, and its administrators had decided twenty years earlier that they should not seek to finance research through tuition charges. Annual donations from wealthy individuals—the original model of the Two Hundred Fifty Associates—had proved inadequate during the Depression years. On the other hand, public perceptions of the role of the corporation were changing, and it seemed increasingly feasible in certain circumstances for corporations to make gifts in support of research without risking stockholder suits. "It is necessary, therefore," David wrote in early 1943, "to depend upon corporate support, and this corporate support can be justified only if we can show a return to stockholders for money spent."

Therefore, much as Edwin Gay and Arch Shaw had done three decades earlier, David and his advisers contemplated the industries which might serve as the focus of their proposed research. They quickly agreed on the aircraft industry. "At the School," David later recalled, "we felt that this was an industry we should study and examine; in a few months it had experienced a growth which ordinarily would be spread over several decades."

That growth could fairly be described as staggering. In 1939, the output of the aircraft industry totaled some $200 million, mostly for foreign purchasers. By 1943, output exceeded $20 billion, of which some $12 billion was produced by the manufacturers active in 1939. Even allowing for the high inflation of 1942–43, therefore, the prewar manufacturers experienced a dizzying expansion of output. By contrast, the highest prewar production in the automobile industry had totaled just over $4 billion.

In the first weeks of his deanship, David drew heavily on the advice of his predecessor. Together, David and Donham prepared a School "position paper," which David would use to persuade the aircraft industry, among others, to support Business School research. In the previous twelve years, as they noted in their paper, individuals, corporations, and foundations had

## Draft dodgers and disaster

The November, 1942, fire at Boston's Cocoanut Grove night club killed hundreds, including several Business School students. The Cocoanut Grove was a club favored by many at Soldiers Field.

"Is This the Army?", the HBS Quartermaster Corps musical, was staged only once: on the night of November 28, 1942. Some 1,200 people attended that evening—and therefore did not visit the Cocoanut Grove.

"There is a thought," N. S. B. Gras wrote in his journal, late in 1941, "that the School may be leaving itself open to the charges of attracting students who want chiefly to escape being drafted. Many of them may be willing to serve, but prefer something other than peeling potatoes in a camp. They would gladly offer their special abilities—as rounded out at the School."

Harvard's President Conant was sensitive to criticisms of American universities as havens for draft dodgers. In June of 1940, he made a speech in favor of universal compulsory military training; in Senate testimony the same month, however, he urged exemption of "men whose work in engineering, chemistry, physics, medicine, or dentistry is found to be necessary to the maintenance of the national health, safety, or interest." Conant argued fur-

ther that not only current practitioners, but also students in graduate schools devoted to those disciplines, should be exempted.

Conspicuously absent from Conant's proposed list of draft-exempt professionals were administrators. For the most part, the government's draft policies paralleled Conant's ideas. Business school students, including Harvard's, were not exempt; if called to service, they were expected to report for duty after finishing the school year during which they were summoned. Even the students in the Business School's Industrial Administrator program, being trained specifically for work in defense industries, were not necessarily draft-exempt. Nevertheless, the School was sensitive, in the weeks and months following Pearl Harbor, to charges by Harvard undergraduates and others that its MBA program was helping young men avoid the draft.

As a result, the faculty voted in 1942 to require each applicant for admission to the School to sign an agreement: if the student was admitted and then offered the chance by one of the armed services to apply for a commission, he would apply. He would then accept the commission, if it was offered. Furthermore, if the student was found to be physically unfit for military service, he would accept a position in a war-related industry.

Despite this step, suspicions lingered in the University. President Conant, for example, instructed his treasurer to spend a week at the School and report on the relevance and efficacy of the School's war-related programs. Even the early military programs, including the Navy Supply Corps School, were suspect. "Recently," Gras wrote in mid-1942, "some Harvard College students spoke loudly at a Harvard Square restaurant about the Navy men of the School of Business using the United States uniform to screen draft-dodging. This became so offensive that one of the officers threw his beer into the face of one of the offenders, who thereupon retired. Trouble may lie ahead."

In fact, disaster lay ahead, in which the Business School only narrowly avoided a deep involvement. On a cold Saturday night in November, 1942, near Boston's Park Square, the Cocoanut Grove nightclub caught fire. Over 700 people—many of them Holy Cross alumni, celebrating a football victory over rival Boston College—were in the club, which had a legal capacity of 400. Over 450 people died in the fire, for the most part because fire exits were locked, obstructed, or otherwise inadequate.

The Cocoanut Grove was a club favored by many at Soldiers Field, but especially by the MBA students and the Navy Supply Corps officers. The fatalities that night included three recent HBS graduates, two MBA students, and an ensign in the Navy school. The list of Business School casualties might well have been enormous except for four factors. First, the Quartermaster Corps that night gave the sole performance of its musical comedy, which was attended by 1,200 people. Second, because of an infraction earlier in the day, the Supply Corps ensigns were confined to quarters until 10:00 p.m. (Many arrived at the Cocoanut Grove in time to help with rescue operations.) Third, officer candidates in the Army Air Forces Statistical School were facing final exams in the following week; many decided to remain at Soldiers Field and study. And fourth, the Harvard Business School Association had on the previous evening sponsored a large dance for Business School students. Many students evidently decided not to go out on the town two nights running.

"But the point here," Gras noted (in a journal entry entitled, "Did the Deity Save the School?"), "is that normally at least fifty School soldiers, sailors, or civilians would have attended the club with their wives or girl friends. . . . Had fifty men and wives lost their lives, the School would not have received future favors from Washington."

contributed $1.5 million to Harvard "for the realistic study of business problems. But of this amount, corporations, who are, it is believed, the most deeply concerned, have only contributed $321,000, of which $157,000, or roughly 10 percent, was available for general research. The balance was spent for research projects"—such as the cost studies conducted by the Bureau of Business Research—"of direct benefit to the contributing corporations."

The two Deans pointed out that in 1939 alone, industry spent in excess of $300 million on scientific research. By contrast, business and universities, working jointly, had spent only $1 million on "first hand study of the rapid material, human, and social changes resulting from the advance of science and technology."

David and Donham reiterated the obvious: that mobilization required the entire Business School teaching and course development effort to focus on the needs of the military and war industry. "But it should not occupy the same proportion of intellectual effort," they argued. "For the objectives of aiding industry, a longer range view is essential, and the School is eager to extend such studies if corporations wish its experience and its independent point of view. . . .

"We estimate that the School would require about $250,000 per year if it is to bring its experience and abilities effectively to bear on broad studies of war trends and postwar conditions.

"It is the opinion of eminent legal counsel," the Deans concluded, "that corporations, through their directors, have the right to make contributions to the School for such purposes chargeable to operations."

David's next step was to call upon the School's tenuous ties to the aircraft industry and to forge new ones where possible. At that point, the School's relationships with both the aircraft industry and the air transport industry were relatively distant. To the extent that they did exist, it was mostly due to one Business School faculty member: George P. Baker.

Baker was a protege of James J. Hill Professor of Transportation William J. Cunningham, who had for years been grooming Baker to succeed him in the Hill professorship. Decades earlier, Cunningham had encouraged Baker's boyhood interest in trains—for example, he had taken him on several tours of the Boston and Albany roundhouses near Soldiers Field—and in the 1920s, it was Cunningham who advised

**Baker spent two years on the Civil Aeronautics Board, at the end of which he was commended for his "outstanding public service."**

**After a year in his new position with the Office of the Quartermaster General, Baker was promoted to Chief of Staff.**

**George P. Baker and family, circa 1944.**

In the Second World War, the HBS Fatigue Laboratory investigated, among other things, the performance of protective clothing under extreme climatic conditions (below).

Many of these experiments were conducted in collaboration with the Climatic Research Laboratory, in Lawrence, Massachusetts. Toward the end of the war, members of the Harvard faculty posed with their Lawrence counterparts (below, center).

Baker to secure a graduate degree in Harvard's economics department. When Professor George B. Roorbach died suddenly in 1934, Baker (then an instructor in Harvard's economics department) was asked to teach Roorbach's course in Water Transportation on a part-time basis.

Baker expanded the School's transportation curriculum in 1938 with a new course in Air Transportation, using research funds contributed by the Guggenheim family. In 1940, he successfully argued that the School should collaborate with Harvard's engineering department to offer a short-lived "Master in Engineering Administration" degree program, graduates of which would be trained "for work in the air transport industry."

Another important connection was made when Baker became friendly with Professor Ross McFarland, who joined the staff of the Fatigue Laboratory in 1937 to participate in their studies of the physiological effects of work at high altitudes. McFarland was soon working closely with physicians of United Air Transport Company (later United Airlines) on the problem of oxygen deprivation. This was before the era of cabin pressurization, and above 10,000 feet, United's pilots tended either to fall asleep or become exhilarated. As a result, United was conducting a series of experiments, to which McFarland contributed. Was it safer, the researchers asked, to send pilots out on constantly varying routes, on the theory that those pilots wouldn't grow too cocky over unknown territory? Or was it safer to have pilots fly the same route, year after year? A group of Fatigue Laboratory publications, resulting in large part from this work, attracted a modest amount of industry attention in the late 1930s.

Baker also had personal ties to several key figures in the aircraft industry. One was Robert E. Gross, president of the Lockheed Aircraft Company, who had been at Harvard College with Baker. Another was Courtland Gross—several years behind his brother and Baker at Harvard—who by the late 1930s was in charge of the Vega Airplane Company, later absorbed by Lockheed. A third was William A. M. Burden, assistant secretary of commerce for air, whom Baker had met when Burden was a business executive. At the government's request, Burden had helped rid several South American national airlines of German influence; he also had one of the world's most extensive private collections of aviation literature.

**Lockheed's Robert E. Gross.**

Aviation researcher Lynn Bollinger, who remained on the School's faculty until 1954. Bollinger greatly impressed Lockheed's president, Robert E. Gross, who in February of 1945 asked if he could "borrow" Bollinger from Harvard for six months.

Dean David was loathe to refuse a favor to Gross, who had been instrumental in supporting the School's aviation research. Nevertheless, he said no: "Bollinger has many commitments, and the government has just approached us for more studies."

DEAN DAVID DREW UPON all of these contacts when, in July of 1942, he created the "Air Research Advisory Committee," which the Commerce Department's William Burden agreed to head. "Because of our own inexperience at the School in matters pertaining to the air," David wrote in a letter that month to Robert Gross, "we will need a good deal of advice, but we have selected the committee with some care."

The committee held its first meeting in August, in Burden's Washington office, and blocked out a plan of action. Members of the group would seek industry support for a Business School study of material control in the aircraft industry. The study would begin as soon as possible, probably before the hoped-for resources were in hand. The School's researchers would focus on developing data and conclusions which would facilitate the production of war planes. Published reports were to be completed and published as rapidly as possible and circulated in mimeographed form.

In October, 1942, the aviation research began in earnest. It was conducted principally by Professors Lynn L. Bollinger and Tom Lilley, who set off on the first of numerous visits to aircraft plants across the country. Bollinger was a 1936 graduate of the School, who had returned to Soldiers Field in 1939 as a research assistant; his lifelong interest in flying made him an obvious candidate to lead the research effort. Lilley, a classmate in the MBA program, had returned to Harvard earlier in the year specifically to participate in the project.

During the winter of 1942–43, Bollinger and Lilley (assisted by up to a dozen part-time researchers) conducted extensive field studies, and Dean David and the Air Research Advisory Committee continued to seek industry backing. Financial support was crucial, but access for Harvard's researchers was equally important. In February, David visited the major aircraft manufacturers in the west, seeking $10,000 per company to match the anticipated contribution from the east coast manufacturers. "In each case," David reported to a friend, "they seemed genuinely interested in our research program, and opened their plants to our staff."

Guy W. Vaughan, president of Curtiss-Wright, thanked Dean David in a mid-1943 letter for the School's retraining effort: "I am sure that their term with you will be of great benefit to us, and we all appreciate what you are doing to train men to a higher rank of intelligence and ability."

Vaughan also made reference to the School's aviation research: "The reason we supported your effort is our firm belief that you will make a very intelligent and unbiased survey which should, in the long run, pay dividends, and [we] are therefore very glad to be able to do so."

**At the start of World War II, Ralph Damon was president of Republic Aviation Corporation, and in July of 1943 was named vice president and general manager of American Airlines. Damon was a key backer of Dean David's aviation research, and helped to recruit additional industry sponsors for the studies.**

**Donald W. Douglas, president of Douglas Aircraft, served on Dean David's Air Research Advisory Committee, and argued in favor of a study of "the problem of re-employment of the industry's wartime labor force."**

There were disappointments, of course. "We are probably a little self-satisfied at the moment," an official of the Beech Aircraft Corporation wrote, declining Harvard's request for cooperation, "because of the fact that for more than 100 days our airplanes have moved according to their predetermined plant schedule without a single deviation of as much as ten minutes in any case." But few major aircraft companies could make such a claim in that period of overwhelming expansion, and most welcomed and supported the research effort.

Publications soon began to emerge under the auspices of the Business School program. A preliminary study on the "Financial Position of the Aircraft Industry," for example, was produced in the summer of 1943. It proved immediately useful to a vice president of American Airlines, who wrote to Dean David in September to "compliment your research staff on the preliminary figures of the financial report which I have seen, and around which I am weaving my testimony [on contract renegotiation] before the House Ways and Means Committee this Thursday." Shortly thereafter, the results of Bollinger's and Lilley's initial investigations were published as "Material Control in Aircraft Plants." Professors Howard T. Lewis and Charles A. Livesey subsequently contributed "Materials Management: A Problem of the Airframe Industry."

Proposals for research projects came from a variety of sources, including industry, government, and the researchers themselves. Each proposed investigation was discussed in advance with the Air Research Advisory Committee, which insisted that all proposed studies had to have a realistic chance of being useful *at the time of publication*. "No matter how thorough a research study may be," as one internal memorandum noted, "it will be of little use if there is no interest in the subject on the part of the public or industry." This imperative kept researchers focused on the short term, and on the month-by-month needs of a rapidly changing industry. As the memorandum went on to elaborate, it seemed "unwise and undesirable to set forth a firm program of future subjects for the next two or more years."

THIS SHORT-TERM FOCUS was a practical necessity, given the changing needs of the sponsoring companies in the midst of unprecedented expansion. It also seemed a realistic approach to aviation research as the industry began to approach its inevitable contraction. In fact, one of the original justifications offered by Dean David for a large-scale study of aircraft manufacturing was that such a study might help avoid the sorts of economic disruptions which had followed military contract terminations at the end of the First World War.

Rumors of industry collapse, in the later years of World War II, far preceded the reality. "Ironically enough," the supervisor of Curtiss-Wright's Engineering Personnel Bureau complained in a November, 1944, letter to a Business School administrator, "the rumor seems to circulate at the time when our demand for engineers is greatest." Curtiss-Wright then had need of 123 additional engineers, metallurgists, and mathematicians. Over 80 of these positions, the supervisor asserted, had "post-war possibilities."

Three months later, Lockheed's Robert Gross informed David that although the war was obviously winding down, the armed forces were still increasing their demands on his company. The contracts were lucrative, and certainly welcome; but company officials were increasingly anxious about their inability to allocate people to the task of long-range planning. Short-term windfalls, in other words, might entail long-term perils. "We are afraid," Gross continued, "that the very people who load us with work and problems now, leaving us no strength with which to plan, will be the first to criticize us if upon cessation we do not have a plan."

In fact, the Army Air Forces began considering the related problems of contract cancellation and surplus aircraft disposal as early as the summer of 1943. In September of that year—several months before production actually peaked—the AAF asked Harvard's small cadre of aviation researchers to undertake a study of the disposal of surplus aircraft and components. "Expert research was needed," as Assistant Secretary of War for Air Robert Lovett later noted, "to ensure that the disposal methods to be adopted by this government would not impair the ability of the Army Air Forces to maintain in the future the high standard of equipment essential for the defense of the nation." The resulting report was submitted on March 23, 1944—the day it was due—and its findings were accepted in full by the House of Representatives' subcommittee on war contracts.

A year later, in March of 1945, the AAF asked Harvard to undertake an even larger study, this time specifically concerning the imminent demobilization of the aircraft industry. The Business School agreed, although members of Dean David's Air Research Advisory Committee had already begun to express displeasure at the AAF's regular disruption of the specific studies which were tailored to industry needs. Of particular interest to sponsoring companies was a study of postwar airport financing—an investigation about to be suspended once again in favor of an AAF study. At an April meeting of the committee, David explained that while the war continued, the School's first obligation had to be to the military. Young researchers working on strictly civilian research projects, furthermore, were extremely vulnerable to the draft. "The critical draft situation," David explained, "is the most immediate reason that the study was so quickly undertaken." The School, he further explained, did not plan to undertake any additional studies for the AAF.

In fact, Harvard was to undertake one more study for the AAF: "Preserving American Air Power." This study followed the AAF's cancellation on V-J Day—August 14, 1945—of some $9 billion in aircraft production contracts. The Business School's researchers considered difficult questions. What size should the peacetime air force be? How could the government stimulate technical progress in aviation and also maintain a large enough productive capacity to meet emergencies? What further plans should be made to minimize economic disruption in the transition from war to peace?

The answers, according to participants in the study, were in the end elusive and unsatisfactory. Much of the research program was made moot by the sheer scope of industry retrenchment in the latter half of 1945. In that short period, an additional $11 billion in AAF contracts were canceled. By the end of the year, only 16 of 66 plants were still producing aircraft. Industry sales in 1944 exceeded $16 billion; three years later, they would total only $1.2 billion. In the same three-year span, the AAF shrank from 2.3 million people and 72,000 planes to 300,000 people and 10,000 planes. The growth of the civil aviation field, while unexpectedly strong, offset only a small fraction of the lost military market.

Harvard's aviation studies continued until the end of the 1940s, concentrating for the most part on issues of commercial aviation. Lynn Bollinger's research team produced several books on subjects such as airport terminal financing and personal aircraft usage patterns. A related series of books, concerning the effects of taxation on business, was initially supported by the Air Research Advisory Committee, and later by the Merrill Foundation. The first book in this series, *Effects of Federal Taxes on Growing Enterprises*, was researched and written by two graduates of Harvard's economics department, J. Keith Butters and John V. Lintner.

It was through Butters and Linter, in fact, that the aviation studies had an enduring impact on the Business School. Economists, and especially Harvard economists, were regarded with great suspicion by many on the Soldiers Field faculty. For example, Dean David and Melvin Copeland (the Business School's director of research since the fall of 1942) took pains to distinguish the work of the Business School from that of the Harvard economics department. Nevertheless, David evidently saw a place for economists in his scheme for an expanded research effort, and persuaded Copeland in 1943 to hire Butters, who had specialized in public finance issues. Butters in turn persuaded Copeland that the School would do well to employ Lintner, who, as a junior fellow in Harvard's Society of Fellows, was available to the School at no cost. Both Butters and Lintner (who formally joined the faculty in 1945) soon distinguished themselves not only as researchers, but also as teachers—a crucial step toward their full integration into the Business School community.

Effect
of
Federal Taxes
on
Growing
Enterprises

J. KEITH BUTTERS and JOHN LINTNER

**Taxation was first proposed as a subject for HBS research in the mid-1930s, when Dean Donham became interested in identifying topics suitable for large-scale investigations.**

**Initiated as part of the aircraft and aviation studies, Butters' and Lintner's taxation research eventually received independent backing from the Merrill Foundation.**

Frank Folts in conference with retreads, and with Dean David at the first retread graduation ceremony.

"Mature men of business and the professions can be taught, want to be taught, and enjoy it," a college professor and member of the first class wrote to Dean David afterwards. "There is much foolish thinking along the lines of 'an old dog,' etc. ... Yet if I closed my eyes to the thin hair and forgot the business titles, I saw men behaving much as my students of 19 and 21 years of age."

THE BUSINESS OF THAT COMMUNITY, as it defined itself toward the end of World War II, was specialized education: primarily of members of the armed forces, but also of business executives participating in the retread program. It came as a shock, therefore, when Curtiss-Wright informed the Business School in January, 1944, that it was dropping out of the retread program. The decision in no way reflected a decreased workload in the company's production facilities; indeed, the case was just the opposite. The company had in fact sent a representative to the previous run of the executive retraining program, in the fall of 1943, only to recall him to Buffalo after six weeks.

"You are no doubt aware," wrote Curtiss-Wright's coordinator of training, explaining his company's decision, "that the manpower shortages which have come about through the Selective Service demands, and through the increase of our obligation to our schedule, make the loss of even one man who is qualified to take your work at a profit to himself almost impossible. . . . We appreciate very much the opportunity of having

some of our men take the Harvard training. It is indeed unfortunate that the demands of war make it impossible for others to attend."

This was an unusual setback for a program which by most measures was proving remarkably successful. At a lunch with faculty colleague N. S. B. Gras in the previous October, Professor Frank Folts had offered a candid assessment of the retraining effort which he headed. The third class of retreads was entering that day. Its 83 members were evenly split between "independents"—those who sponsored themselves in the course—and company representatives. The second class had just gone out into industry and, contrary to the expectations of some, its independents had had little trouble finding war-related employment. The School's novel concept of executive retraining seemed to be proving itself. Perhaps most important, it was clear that men twenty and thirty years out of school could still learn—a dubious assertion, to many, before the retread experience.

# *Scaling down*

President Conant with officials of the Navy Supply Corps School. "The great success of the Business School during the war years in training supply officers for the armed services," Conant wrote in his last report as Harvard's President, "might be said to justify those who see this faculty of the University as the one academic group which knows how to teach 'administration.' I realize, of course, the strenuous objections that many graduates of our Law School now serving the Government in administrative posts would make to any such contention."

At the end of World War I, American manufacturers held 24,000 uncompleted contracts for war supplies and the government owned over $6 billion worth of surplus war materials. Six contentious years passed before the last of these contracts were settled, and the bulk of the surplus equipment disposed of.

In 1943, HBS researchers anticipated that the Second World War was in the process of generating ten times as much postwar surplus, and related economic troubles. "The whole pattern of American industry in the next critical decade," according to an internal HBS memorandum from the period, "will be vitally affected by the way in which these industrial demobilization problems are handled."

Government officials agreed. "It is sufficient to say," the secretary of war told a House subcommittee in October of 1943, "that we must realistically face the fact that unless industry, upon the termination of its war production contracts, is enabled to reconvert rapidly to normal peacetime production, a disastrous hiatus in the industrial economy of this nation will result." In other words, without a rapid and fair termination of war contracts, a sensible disposal of government-owned plants and equipment, and a rapid reconversion, the national economy might well slip back into its depressed prewar state.

The national defense also had to be considered. Following the First World War, an oversupply of obsolete aircraft engines had for a decade discouraged research and development in the field. Aware of this history, Assistant Secretary of War for Air Robert Lovett

asked HBS aviation researchers, in late 1943, to suggest how the government might dispose of surplus aircraft in ways which "would not impair the ability of the Army Air Forces to maintain in the future the high standard of equipment essential for the defense of the nation."

In June of 1944, as an outgrowth of both this study and the success of the AAF Statistical School, Lovett asked the Business School to set up an "Army Air Forces War Adjustment Course," designed to address the increasing backlog of unsettled contract termination cases. For the first time, the School said no to the AAF: there simply weren't enough instructors available, School officials said, unless the AAF permitted a reduction in the size of the Statistical School. AAF officials, in turn, vetoed that proposal but suggested a compromise: HBS professors could retain several distinguished officers from the next graduating class of the Stat School to serve as instructors, enabling an equal number of HBS professors to take on the new course. The School agreed. Two months later, 200 AAF officers arrived at Soldiers Field for eight weeks of training in "war adjustment." Professor Pearson Hunt headed the teaching group.

"Class discussion on actual cases of war adjustment," reported the HBS *Bulletin* that summer, "are supplemented by field trips to important contracting plants. Officers are given work in procurement to develop the background necessary for understanding of relationships between the contractor and the Army Air Forces

which are relevant to the termination and property disposal problems."

The *Bulletin* used almost identical language to describe a Navy contract termination course, also inaugurated at Soldiers Field in the summer of 1944. The Navy asked for and got a four-month course for 200 students, to be offered at eight-week intervals. "Although this development did not come as a surprise," Dean David noted in his annual report, "the School had not anticipated 400 officers at one time."

Nor had the School anticipated the difficulty of teaching this new breed of student. Unlike the officer candidates in the Supply and Stat Schools, many of the men in the Army and Navy surplus disposal schools were experienced officers, returning from active duty in theaters of operations around the world. They averaged 35 years in age and their median prewar salary had been almost $7,000—roughly equal to the civilian retrainees, or retreads, then at the Business School. Most had anticipated an early release from military service; they did not relish the prospect of four months of intensive training, followed by an indefinite period of responsibility for surplus disposal. For the first time, HBS faculty members found themselves teaching large numbers of students who weren't particularly happy to be at Soldiers Field.

This fact, among others, led to the faculty's decision late in 1944 not to honor yet another AAF request: this time, to set up a training program in surplus disposal for selected civilians in the federal bureaucracy. As Dean David noted at a November faculty meeting,

Congress was reconsidering the recently passed Surplus Disposal Bill and might well amend it. Furthermore, the Navy's surplus disposal course might soon be opened to civilians. And finally, the faculty saw no reason to create competition for its contemplated "Advanced Executive Training Program," which was then being broadened to include work in surplus disposal.

The executive training program, in fact, did not ultimately concern itself with surplus disposal—in part because the sponsoring Office of Education was uncertain whether its authorization covered the subject. Furthermore, the rapid progress of the war in late 1944 was leading even the armed forces to reconsider their surplus disposal plans. The AAF War Adjustment Course was, in fact, only offered twice; it held its second and final graduation ceremonies on November 25, 1944. While the Navy course continued until the following year, the abrupt termination of the AAF course—in the same month that the School was asked by the AAF to create its civilian-oriented surplus disposal program—convinced HBS professors that they should avoid involvement in future surplus disposal courses.

HARVARD UNIVERSITY
CAMBRIDGE · MASSACHUSETTS

THIS IS TO CERTIFY THAT

has completed the course of instruction in
ARMY AIR FORCES WAR ADJUSTMENT
as prescribed by
HEADQUARTERS, ARMY AIR FORCES
given at the
Graduate School of Business Administration
Harvard University, 23 September 1944

_Commandant, HQ AAF._          _Administrative Director_

## How papa's mind works

At a December, 1942, meeting of a HBS library committee, the subject of labor-related documents arose. Should the School collect such documents? If so, toward what end?

Dean David then volunteered his own opinion. He intended, he said, to develop labor studies at the School—even including studies in cooperation with the relatively radical Congress of Industrial Organizations. David wanted it understood that the School did not exist only to study corporations.

In fact, David had already acted on this intention in other quarters. He had hoped to include trade unionists in the war industry retraining (or retread) program: "I would much prefer not to have the whole group made up of management," he stressed in a 1942 letter to Anna M. Rosenberg, New York regional director of the War Manpower Commission. But late in the year, Rosenberg informed the Dean that organized labor was cool to retraining: "A great many of them are skeptical, however, and it will take time for us to convert all of them."

David, however, had a persistent vision of the School and the University as both a meeting-ground for adversaries and a crucible for new types of communication, both formal and informal. Others at the University shared this view. In the summer of 1942, therefore, three separate Harvard units—the Business School, the School of Public Administration, and the Department of Economics—collaborated in a unique experiment. They proposed to establish a "Trade Union Fellowship Program," which would provide selected labor leaders with an opportunity to spend a year at Harvard. The plan combined elements of a similar labor program at Yale and Harvard's Nieman fellowships in journalism.

As proved to be the case with the retraining program, labor leaders had reservations about the proposal. HBS Professor Sumner H. Slichter, who served as informal head of Harvard's joint initiative, was apprised of some of them by the Education Committee of the International Ladies' Garment Workers' Union. First, he was told, the proposed stipend would not provide adequate support for a Fellow's family. (The unions, unlike the companies which would soon sponsor many of the retreads, felt they could not afford to subsidize Harvard's experiment.) Furthermore, potential Fellows might jeopardize their draft deferments if they gave up jobs in defense industries for a year of study at Harvard. Two of the labor leaders selected for Yale's program, in fact, had decided at the last minute not to attend, for precisely this reason.

**Sumner Slichter (lower left) with a postwar Trade Union Fellowship Program faculty group. Three Harvard departments collaborated in the experiment, although the Business School soon assumed overall responsibility.**

HARVARD UNIVERSITY
TRADE UNION
FELLOWSHIP PROGRA

Sponsored by

THE COOPERATING LABOR ORGANIZAT
THE LITTAUER SCHOOL OF PUBLIC ADMIN
THE GRADUATE SCHOOL OF BUSINESS ADM
THE DEPARTMENT OF ECONOMI

In cooperation with the participating La
Organizations, Harvard University announces
an intensive thirteen week program for trade
representatives.

Eventually, these problems were resolved. Harvard offered to pay all costs for course development; the unions agreed to split the cost of tuition. Only candidates with secure draft exemptions or numerous dependents were considered; the unions decided to help support those dependents, where necessary. The public announcement of the program, made in August of 1942, stressed that it had been designed in cooperation with labor leaders and had close parallels in other fields. "I have put in a paragraph about the army training at the Business School, the Sloan fellowships at MIT, and the Nieman fellowships," Slichter told Dean David concerning the announcement, "so that the unions would realize that they are not being picked out as especially needing this kind of help. They are sensitive on that point."

Labor's responses to the announcement ranged from enthusiastic to noncommittal. One Birmingham, Alabama warehouse workers' union asked Slichter for help in securing a fellowship: "The cost of organizational work in the deep South has drained our treasury so that we are only able to pay for our current needs. The labor movement in the South needs leadership so badly, more so than I can convey in a short letter to you. The people are here who want to take the lead, and we are trying desperately within our limited means to provide them with the opportunities."

The Brotherhood of Locomotive Firemen and Enginemen, based in Cleveland, thought the program would "contribute much toward the trade union movement. However, in our branch of the railroad service, we are being strained to the utmost to provide a sufficient number of men to meet the transportation demands resulting from increased volume of war materials and supplies and the handling of troops." As a result, they said, they could not participate.

But thirteen labor leaders, selected by their own unions, did arrive at Harvard in September of 1942. Five of the thirteen lived in Business School dormitories—a crucial component of the experiment, in the estimation of HBS administrators. Only through close and prolonged contact, they felt, could a real exchange occur between the labor leaders and their business counterparts. The trade unionists took three courses together: Economic Analysis, Trade Union Problems and Policy, and Human Problems of Administration. They also took electives, and—beginning in February, 1943—were offered the opportunity to audit courses offered to the retreads. Seven of the thirteen Fellows elected to take Production Organization and Engineering, and most audited Management Controls.

"It is no secret," *Coronet* magazine reported in December of 1943, "that most of the members of the pioneer group came to Harvard a little in awe, more than slightly skeptical, and prepared for a certain amount of rebuff and snobbery. But the students found a faculty far from stuffy, men they could sit down with and trim at poker and gin rummy. In the classroom an informal atmosphere prevailed, and the fellows soon discovered they could air their problems and make their points in perfect freedom. In fact . . . they found a fertile field for missionary work on behalf of labor.

"What is best of all, perhaps, about the Trade Union Fellowship Program, they eat, live and study on equal terms with the boss's son at the world's richest university—and as one of the fellows put it, 'get an insight into how papa's mind works.'"

"Let me stick my neck out," Mark Starr—education director for the International Ladies' Garment Workers' Union—volunteered to *Coronet* magazine, "by saying that the Trade Union Fellowship Program is a unique milestone, and marks a new era."

Dean David, writing in his 1944 annual report, lauded the "exciting possibilities [which] are suggested by this very modest beginning." But the "exciting possibilities" were not realized, for the most part. In 1948, the program was shortened to thirteen weeks and offered on the same schedule as the Advanced Management Program, in an effort to encourage cooperation between the two programs. Although 166 trade unionists took advantage of Harvard scholarships between 1942 and 1954, the quality of applicants representing American unions was increasingly disappointing. The steady improvement in the number and caliber of the Advanced Management Program's participants, meanwhile, led to a troublesome imbalance between the two programs. Harvard also learned informally that several unions were alarmed at the effect of the program on some of their members: the returning Fellows seemed overly sympathetic to the needs and problems of management.

The Trade Union Fellowship Program brought both women and blacks to Soldiers Field. No women had previously attended classes taught at the Business School—although many had been taught by HBS professors in an affiliated Radcliffe program—and relatively few blacks had received MBAs.

The purposeful mixing of business and labor, in the retread and trade union program, was alternately exhilarating and exasperating for the labor representatives.

"Most [of the retreads] are intelligent people," one trade unionist wrote to a Harvard administrator, "and can be persuaded to accept a liberal view of the rights and privileges of the wage earners who make up the vast majority of the people who make this country great.

"Others, however, are so stupid that they have no opinion of their own, and rather than try to think for themselves, they choose to ape and parrot their bosses, believing in their stupidity that promotion will come to them through this medium."

SEVERAL MONTHS of sustained discussions came to a head on February 22, 1945, when the faculty met for a momentous session. Faculty members had two crucial votes before them. First, they would be asked to rescind all previous course authorizations, creating a "clean slate," as many professors had suggested. Second, the final report of the Committee on Educational Policy (CEP)—the "MBA Report of February, 1945" —would be presented for approval or disapproval. This report synthesized the work of the CEP's subcommittees on objectives and the transition period. If accepted, it would define the postwar conception of the Harvard Business School.

Dean David opened the meeting by making a number of procedural points and personal commitments. He argued once again for a school that would cultivate a sense of public responsibilities in its students, and produce risk-takers for the postwar economy. He applauded the concept of an integrated first-year program. He promised that if the CEP's report was approved, faculty assignments would be made through a consensual process. He further promised to make more time and funds available for sustained research by faculty members.

According to the notes of the faculty secretary, he then suggested that "the theory of interchangeability of personnel between courses is sound when applied to men at the level of assistant professors, and during the early portion of their term as associate professors, but that in the later instances men should be permitted to develop within their respective fields of specialization so that they may demonstrate in advance of being placed on tenure their capacity for further development." The practice of "interchangeability"—the rotation of even senior professors through the required first-year courses—had been a great convenience to the Dean's office since the early 1920s. But it had become increasingly burdensome to many on the faculty, including those who wanted to devote more time to original research in their chosen areas of specialization. This was especially important to junior professors, whose prospects for promotion were linked to the caliber of their research and writing.

David, like Donham before him, was convinced that interchangeability had in fact served the School well, by fostering a shared (if at times forced) understanding of the first-year curriculum. How, then, was

this positive outcome to be achieved, if interchangeability was to be deemphasized?

The answer lay in the CEP report, which Richard Meriam then presented to the faculty. Speaking for the committee, Meriam proposed a "real shift of emphasis" for the MBA program, which should in the future focus much more on "getting action through human beings, tasks and duties of operating executives, [and on] public responsibilities of enterprise." There should be, Meriam said, a single first-year course, entitled "Elements of Administration." Within that course would be six "subjects." Three of the proposed subjects (Production, Marketing, and Finance) had direct prewar antecedents. One, Control, represented a merger of the prewar Accounting and Statistics courses. Two other courses were considered new, and had only tentative titles: "Communication," an outgrowth of the wartime Management Control course; and "S.E.P.," which, as Meriam explained, was a "temporary label used to represent Social, Economic, and Political."

The point of the Elements of Administration proposal, Meriam emphasized, was to provide unity and flexibility. The effective operation of one overall first-year course would be a twofold challenge for all concerned: first and foremost an intellectual challenge, but also a faculty exercise in "getting along with one another."

Following a break for dinner, the faculty then considered each of the proposed "subjects" in turn. Production was described in the CEP report as integrating the managerial and technical aspects of that functional area. Marketing would place a new emphasis on action and on public and governmental responsibilities. The primary emphasis of Finance would be on "the financial implications of production, sales, and other policies and decisions." Some concern was expressed about the proposed Control course. William Cunningham, for example, argued that the stewardship role of financial accounting should not be lost in the new emphasis on its internal uses. Reflecting on the lessons of the Stat School and the retread program, Melvin Copeland responded that those responsible for the development of this new subject would not be able to think in terms either of accounting or statistics principles. Instead, they would have to keep in mind the demands of an entirely new function: Control. Henceforth, numbers would be used *actively* in management, in addition to serving the end of stewardship.

Richard Meriam teaching in a Baker Library classroom in 1946, a member of a faculty newly unified under the "Elements of Administration" curriculum. Meriam considered the revised curriculum to be, in part, a faculty "exercise in getting along with one another."

The crush of returning students immediately after the war not only tested the new curriculum, but also underscored the inadequacy of the School's existing classroom facilities.

The Communication course, which was to combine a new topic—Administrative Practices—with Communication (report writing), was intended to "give emphasis to the problems of securing understanding and effective response in a variety of administrative situations." The purposefully vague "administrative practices" label had been coined by Professor Edmund Learned, who, as de facto head of the new course, wanted to make a sharp distinction between the new course and its prewar antecedents.

The proposed Social, Economic, and Political course, like Communication, would serve to integrate the first-year program, emphasizing the social, economic, and political responsibilities of the administrator. This was the course which was to embody David's call for risk-taking, and to imbue in its students "a spirit of vigorous and courageous enterprise."

The second-year program was treated more summarily—in part because the faculty felt it had an additional year to plan a second-year curriculum, and in part because the Elements of Administration proposal relegated it to a secondary status. "The concept of an integrated and coordinated first-year program," David told the faculty that night, "which generates pressures on the second-year courses, is more desirable than one which permits the requirements of second-year work to influence materially the work of the first year." This was a purposeful reversal, designed to foster an overall "administrative point of view," and to minimize any undue influence exercised by strong functional area faculty groups. A new course, Administrative Policy, would (like its antecedent Business Policy) serve to integrate the Business School experience; now, however, it would have the advantage of building upon an integrated first-year curriculum.

After minor amendments were proposed and voted upon, the faculty was asked to take the unprecedented step of rescinding all previous course authorizations. It did so unanimously. Then Dean David moved that "the faculty adopt the MBA Report of February, 1945 and the recommendations contained therein." Again, the vote was recorded as unanimously in favor.

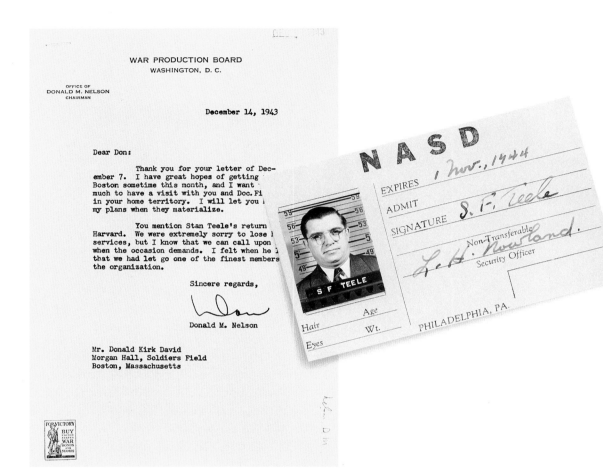

Stanley F. Teele's effective service in Washington was commended by War Production Board chairman Donald M. Nelson (facing page). When Dean David felt the need to expand the School's administration in 1945, he turned to Teele.

Teele had mixed feelings about the Elements of Administration plan. While applauding its stated goal of eliminating artificial separations between business functions, he was concerned about a looming pedagogical problem:

"From the beginning, if the student is to have the vicarious experience which is the essence of the case method, he must practice putting himself in the shoes of the people in the case. He must say 'I' and 'we' rather than 'they.' Students hate to do this; and it is doubly difficult for them to imagine themselves in the shoes of the chairman of the board of a great corporation."

"THIS IS A REPORT to the alumni on the present state of admissions to the Business School," began the special notice in the School's alumni *Bulletin* issued in late 1945. "It is also a plea for understanding of a serious problem."

The problem was simple: as a result of the atomic bombing of Japan and that nation's prompt surrender, the war had ended unexpectedly early. Veterans, supported by the year-old GI Bill of Rights, were returning in droves to the nation's educational institutions. Enough students to fill four or five graduating classes were converging on the nation's campuses in a single year, overwhelming many undergraduate institutions. Harvard's business school was also receiving a flood of inquiries, not only from potential first-year students, but also from returning and transfer students interested in a second-year program.

"The specific facts with respect to the Business School," reported the *Bulletin*, "are that as of November 10, just under 6,000 men have indicated, either by letter of inquiry or by a personal visit, an interest in coming to the Business School during 1946. Of this number, 2,700 have been specifically interested in the February entering date."

The Business School faculty had voted in April of 1945 to resume civilian instruction in February, 1946. Only a first-year program was then contemplated; the second year was to resume perhaps a year later. In its 37 years of existence, the School had awarded 7,757 degrees. Now it had almost an equal number of potential students expressing an interest in admission within the coming calendar year. Already, 500 completed first-year applications for February admission were in hand, with hundreds more evidently on the way. An additional 500 students, furthermore, had indicated their definite intention to return to Soldiers Field in the near future to complete their degrees.

In response, said the *Bulletin*, the School had decided to "stretch to the utmost." Temporarily, the maximum size of the entering class would be increased from 550 to 900. Enrollment would be spread as evenly as possible over three entering dates: February 13, June 11, and October 8. Students enrolling at those times would be able to complete the requirements for the MBA in sixteen continuous calendar months. Second-year students would be admitted in June and October,

Before adjourning the four-hour meeting, Dean David made one further announcement. Faculty approval of the report, he said, placed a new and heavy burden on the School's administrative apparatus. Therefore, he intended to ask Professor Stanley Teele to become a member of the Dean's office, specifically to help in the administration of the revised MBA program.

News of the curriculum revisions circulated only gradually, in part because the School was still not anticipating an imminent return to civilian instruction. It was not until the fall of 1945, for example, that David informed J. Hugh Jackson, Dean of the Stanford Business School, of the new Elements of Administration program. "That sounds like a most interesting development," Jackson replied, unwittingly summarizing the sentiments of many at Soldiers Field. "We cannot help but wonder, however, how any [faculty] group can handle 33 hours of classwork, and make reasonable preparation therefore. We shall watch this program with much interest."

and a limited number needing only one term to graduate would be admitted in February.

"It should be clearly stated," the *Bulletin* continued, "that the competition for places is resulting in the rejection by the Admissions Board of many men who, under normal conditions, would readily gain admission to the School." The School's admissions officers, in other words, found themselves caught in a dilemma. They anticipated a time when alumni would again be needed — as they had been before the war — to recruit suitable candidates for admission to the School. For the moment, however, many alumni recommendations were of necessity being ignored.

"We sincerely hope," the *Bulletin* account concluded, "that our alumni will understand the current predicament, and they will continue to search for

promising young men for the School. In the long run, there is no better source of high-grade applicants for the School than the active interest of our own graduates."

In some ways, the School's circumstances in the fall of 1945 resembled those of mid-1919. Veterans were once again returning in triumph, and in large numbers, from a bitterly fought foreign war. Again, they were impatient; their overriding concern was to make up for lost time — with their families, their educations, and their careers. The School's physical and intellectual resources would again be taxed to their full capacity.

But there were crucial differences, as well. The *Bulletin's* "plea for understanding" suggests one such distinction between 1919 and 1945. Now, important constituencies existed which supported — and expected responsiveness from — the Harvard Business School. Active alumni now numbered in the thousands, rather than the hundreds. Immediately after the First World War, the School was still in an arm's-length relationship with much of the nation's business community; when judged at all, the School was often judged by business to be too theoretical and too parochial. By

**A certificate of service, awarded by the Army Air Forces to Harvard in October, 1945, and symbolizing the new collaborative relationship between HBS and the government.**

**Edwin Gay: an internal focus.**

1945, however, the business community viewed the School as having significant responsibilities. When the faculty contemplated discontinuing executive education at the end of the war, for example, a number of companies simply insisted that the program be continued.

The School's relationship with the federal government, especially the military, had similarly been transformed from distant to intimate. Dean Donham had been convinced that Business School concepts of administration had both public and military applications. While the former assertion remained largely untested, the Statistical School experience seemed to prove conclusively the latter assertion. Furthermore, successes on the administrative side of the military had created a new network of supportive contacts in government. Instead of arguing with the conceptual base of Roosevelt's New Deal, the School was now positioned to interact creatively with the ever-growing federal bureaucracy.

The School also had new internal strengths. Twenty years of investment in the case method, and the field research it entailed, had produced a faculty and a curriculum that was fundamentally flexible and pragmatic. Whereas the First World War had distracted the School and dispersed its faculty, World War II clarified the School's objectives and indirectly opened its curriculum to new, more compelling organizing principles.

The School's leadership changed twice between 1918 and 1945, and each time its perspective broadened. Edwin Gay was necessarily preoccupied with building a place for the Business School within the University. Wallace Donham supplied a single-minded energy and vision, and strengthened and built upon the institution's tenuous ties with the New York financial community. Donald David used the Second World War to create national and—tentatively—global ties. In contrast to Donham, David was temperamentally inclined toward delegation and decentralization. He created a climate within which his faculty could think entrepreneurially about its teaching, research, and publishing activities. The School's innovative program in executive education, for example, was the direct result and beneficiary of this new climate.

**Wallace Donham: bricks, mortar, and vision.**

**Donald David: national and international perspectives.**

**Postwar, the School wanted to provide "the finest training for the maximum number of men," David wrote in the summer of 1945. "Surely the School's wartime record would soon seem incidental and would be quickly forgotten if our efforts on behalf of the men who have won this war were any less determined than our efforts in the officer-training programs."**

Only one professorship was established at HBS between 1927 and 1950: the Louis E. Kirstein Professorship of Labor Relations. Kirstein, a long-time friend of the School, was a vice president of Wm. Filene's Sons Company, a Boston retail firm, and chairman of the board of Federated Department Stores. He had long believed that business had a special responsibility to shape both social and economic progress, and that the School should offer its students training in ethical business conduct.

Kirstein's death in 1942 led his friends in both business and labor to inaugurate a campaign for a chair in his memory. The Filenes—company and family—made the biggest contributions, but many others, including labor unions, also subscribed.

The School's administrators made an explicit tie between the Hawthorne research of the 1930s and the proposed professorship: research into human and labor relations, they said, should be ongoing and systematic.

The drive was successfully completed early in 1944, and Harvard's President Conant announced the chair publicly in June of that year, describing it as a means whereby labor and business could meet on neutral ground.

Clear obstacles, and perhaps perils, loomed ahead. In the broadest terms, private enterprise had yet to prove that it could meet the postwar challenge of avoiding a disastrous relapse into depression. Closer to home, the School had operated continuously for five years. Its faculty was tired and overextended; few professors had managed a vacation since the summer before Pearl Harbor. Moreover, much intellectual groundwork for the new Elements of Administration program remained to be done. The surge in postwar enrollments would only exacerbate the problems of an overtaxed faculty.

The School's financial state was equally troubling. With the many distractions of the war years, Dean David could do little to augment the School's very limited endowment principal. Endowment income remained below $150,000 annually, and the School had the benefit of only four chaired professorships. Wartime deficits had been made up through annual gifts secured by Dean David; now David realized that budgetary imbalances would not end with the war. The School's first peacetime deficit since the mid-1920s seemed unavoidable in the 1945–46 academic year.

Future educational programs would be expensive, as David reported to President Conant toward the end of the war. Only additional endowment income could close the widening gap between the School's income and expenditures; therefore, David committed himself to raising an additional $15 million in endowment funds. It was an ambitious goal—a 300 percent increase in endowment principal. Furthermore, David assumed the difficult task of securing funding for a classroom building and dining hall, construction of which could no longer be deferred.

These were sobering challenges and responsibilities. And yet, as David had noted in 1944, there was at Soldiers Field "a certain impatience to get on with the job." The war had provided a clean slate, and in the process had created opportunities, as well as responsibilities.

Dean David realized that the latter part of his deanship would be largely devoted to augmenting the School's campus and endowment, which led him to appoint Stanley F. Teele as Associate Dean. They were an effective team: David as "Mr. Outside," and Teele as "Mr. Inside."

In 1951, they reviewed models of the expanded campus, which included a new classroom building and central dining facility.

"I have suggested to my faculty," said David, "that we should take the point of view that we are building a new school. We should address ourselves to the question: what kind of school do we want to have ten years from now?"

David's question provoked numerous and sometimes contradictory responses in the years that followed. As in the previous four decades, external circumstances produced both subtle and wrenching environmental changes. New constituencies placed demands on the Harvard Business School, and altered its plotted course in unanticipated ways. But significantly, David's question—what kind of school do we want to have ten years from now?—endured as an administrative and intellectual touchstone. Invention, and reinvention, were the natural result.

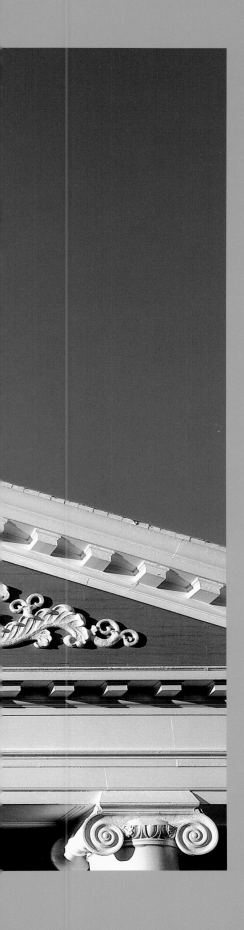

THIS HISTORY DOCUMENTS the first four decades of the Harvard Graduate School of Business Administration. Without question, it is the story of a pragmatic and protean institution, capable of assuming the roles that various constituencies have demanded of it over the years. At critical junctures, the institution has even invented new constituencies, ranging from New England's shoe retailers to the federal government. Necessity, clearly, has fostered this tradition of invention.

At several of these critical junctures, invention has in turn fostered institutional change on a large scale. Such change has not entailed simply adding a new element to an otherwise stable mix; most often, one means or end has replaced another. In fact, throughout the School's written records, as well as in the recollections of its faculty members, one encounters constant references to *change*: to radical departures, clean slates, and complete breaks. Change, rather than continuity, seems to dominate the institutional memory.

So let us weigh the impact of change, beginning with the concept of the "clean slate." There is ample evidence to suggest that the Harvard Business School, to an extent unique in the American academy, has been willing and able to reinvent itself. Edwin Gay's entire tenure, from 1908 to 1919, constituted an initial period of invention—a "simple scientific experiment," as he termed it. Gay and his faculty had to do nothing less than *define* the activities of a graduate school of business administration: what they would teach, how they would teach it, and how they would conduct research.

While the first years of experimentation were fruitful, the answers they presented eventually proved too limiting. For example, it became clear that a graduate school of business could not hope to offer specialized training across a range of industries. A broader conception was needed. In the early 1920s, therefore, Wallace Donham and his colleagues devised a functionally oriented curriculum. This new curriculum reflected the major functions of industrial concerns: production, finance, marketing, and accounting. The new curricular orientation proved to be much more durable, surviving largely unchanged until after the Second World War. In fact, elements of that curriculum's structure still persist today.

Donham and his faculty also reduced the School's eclectic mix of teaching styles, choosing to devote significant resources to the development of a home-grown "case method." And while the Bureau of Business Research's innovative statistical studies continued in the 1920s, most of the School's intellectual activity focused on the task of case research. In addition to Gay's three challenges—what to teach, how to teach it, and how to conduct research—Donham was forced by circumstance to ask an additional practical question: *where* to conduct the School's activities. The Soldiers Field campus, an artful blending of form and function, was the eventual result.

Donham's faculty took important strides in the 1920s, but they also made missteps, which in turn necessitated later adjustments. Simply stated, the School could not function as a school of applied economics (as the faculty defined its role in 1922). Case research repeatedly demonstrated the limitations of applying *only* classical economic principles to real business situations. Investigations in the field suggested that the human factor had been underemphasized in the study

of commercial and industrial life. To adjust this obvious imbalance, the School's research into human relations began. While at first only tentative, this initiative soon gained momentum, and eventually produced powerful results.

The next two occasions for institutional review and redefinition were presented by external circumstances. First, the Great Depression forced the School's administrators to develop new educational ventures. These initiatives gave the School an opportunity, however limited, to participate in the reshaping of the national economy; they also filled seats at Soldiers Field. Second, the impending American entry in the Second World War led Dean Donham to ask his faculty to approve a bachelor's degree program—in effect, to abandon the School's exclusive orientation toward graduate education. The faculty rejected the plan, but in so doing accepted responsibility for devising an alternative. Donham, it turned out, had asked a crucial question: "Have we not the same obligation [as industry] to maintain an organization so elastic that we can move rapidly as conditions change?"

The war itself prompted new sorts of experiments at the School: in the education of executives, in teaching methods, and in the organization of the faculty. It also called forth two events of both substantive and symbolic significance—the suspension of the MBA program in the spring of 1943, and an across-the-board rescission of all standing MBA course authorizations in February, 1945. Donald David, only recently installed in the deanship, began his notably successful tenure by presiding over the School's most thoroughgoing self-critique in its history. The core curriculum that resulted was a substantial departure from its prewar predecessor. As a result of lessons learned during the war years, the faculty gave formal recognition to new concepts in control and human relations. Henceforth, numbers would assume an active role in management, and the processes of management would not be considered apart from their human context.

This, in summary form, is a history of repeated institutional reinvention. Over the course of four decades, we see new intellectual constructs introduced and new opportunities seized upon. We see an institution winning a gradual (sometimes grudging) acceptance, first within Harvard University and the Boston

and New York business communities, and later in broader academic and business circles.

But is it entirely a history of clean slates and radical departures? On balance, it is not. Instead, the story is one of pragmatism, and of veiled continuities. Certainly Harvard's President Lowell intended a sharp break with the past when, in 1919, he appointed Wallace Donham to succeed Edwin Gay in the deanship. ("The school to succeed must be in close touch with the business world," Lowell had written in 1907; evidently Gay had not met Lowell's expectations in this regard.) But it is equally clear that Donham built in every possible way on the innovations of his predecessor — for example, in case-method teaching, in the integrative Business Policy course, and in the statistical studies of the Bureau of Business Research.

Jumping ahead twenty years: in 1941, as noted, the faculty turned down Dean Donham's request for a bachelor's program, despite compelling financial arguments in its favor. This constituted the first time the School's dean failed to win a major policy debate within the faculty. It suggests that by the early 1940s, many at the School had a strong conception of what the institution should and should not do. The School had an established intellectual "currency," and that currency was not to be devalued by a one-year bachelor's degree program.

Professor Malcolm McNair's 1941 essay, "On the Importance of Being Tough-Minded," helps to define that currency. "For two years," McNair wrote in the student yearbook, "the Business School has tried to make you tough-minded. We have forced you to acquire knowledge by the hard route of the case method instead of the easy route of the textbook and lecture." Four years later, Professor Sumner Slichter added to the definition, in a memorandum to fellow faculty members who were then reconsidering the core curriculum: "Something should happen to men who come to the Business School which could not happen to them anywhere else in the world, and which will leave its mark on them for the rest of their lives."

These two faculty comments hint at the most important development of the Donham era: the purposeful combining of a social and an intellectual agenda. The overriding goal was to foster in the School's students an attitude of professionalism, through both informal and formal learning processes. In effect, Donham and his colleagues grafted devices for socialization onto Edwin Gay's intellectual legacy. This explains, for example, the priority Donham assigned to a residential campus. "Without this," he wrote in 1922, "particularly with our lack of centralized administrative and teaching space, the faculty feel the great difficulty of developing the professional spirit without which we are hardly justified in having such a school."

The twofold agenda, intellectual and social, had many manifestations. Some of them endure today, albeit in disguised forms. For example: as part of the hoped-for socialization process, Donham insisted upon including dining rooms in each residence hall. When postwar economic conditions finally forced the School to employ a centralized dining facility, Donham's successors devoted considerable energy to refining a new device for socialization: the section. Through section organization, large groups of students could still create and experience an unusual social chemistry.

The metaphor of "grafting" suggests the persistence of an original botanical stock. In the case of Edwin Gay's intellectual agenda, the metaphor very much pertains. Gay's own writings were few, but he personally influenced generations of scholars, including many key figures who made their careers at the Harvard Business School. Melvin Copeland, for example, who helped invent the modern field of marketing and for many years directed the School's research activities, was a Gay protégé. Bertrand Fox, who succeeded Copeland as research director, also studied under Gay. In 1928, Gay recruited N. S. B. Gras for the School's faculty, and thereby helped initiate studies in business history, a field which thrives today at Soldiers Field and elsewhere. Simultaneously, Gay supported the research activities of economic historian Arthur H. Cole, who had a profound impact on the School as the head of Baker Library between 1929 and 1956. With Harvard economist Joseph Schumpeter, Cole also kept alive Gay's research interest in the "undertaker"—or, in contemporary parlance, the entrepreneur.

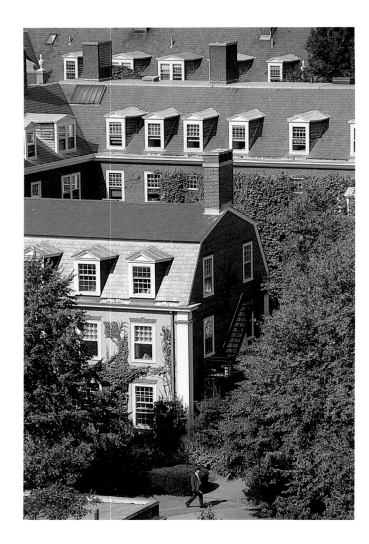

SOME READERS WILL no doubt feel frustrated that this volume fails to bring such broad generalizations up to date. How, for example, does Donald David fit into the historical traditions suggested above? Or, for that matter, Deans Teele, Baker, Fouraker, and McArthur after him? But documentation of these later decades is both difficult and far from complete; these questions will have to be left for a subsequent volume.

Suffice it to say that the conception of the School settled upon at the end of World War II has proved remarkably durable. This durability reflects the fact that the School's slate was *not* wiped clean, either up to that point or subsequently. At crucial junctures, the institution had a store of relevant wisdom and experience to draw upon. The lessons of the past remained very much alive, for example, in the discussions of 1944–45. (In fact, two members of Edwin Gay's original faculty, Melvin Copeland and William Cunningham, participated actively in those discussions. Between them, they represented 73 years of faculty experience.) By 1945, a strong and self-conscious institution operated at Soldiers Field. That institution was entirely amenable to evolution, and stubbornly resistant to revolution.

The same holds true today, despite myriad changes in the world beyond Soldiers Field in the latter half of the twentieth century. One such change lies in the sheer growth of the field of business education. In 1950, for example, American universities awarded approximately 4,300 MBA degrees. The Harvard Business School granted some 600 of these. Thirty-five years later, over 70,000 Americans received MBAs annually. While Harvard's class increased to over 700 in that interval, its percentage of the total dropped from roughly 15 percent to 1 percent. The nation supported 50 MBA programs in 1950; 35 years later, it supported 650. Corporations, moreover, have greatly expanded their internal training programs, and now spend more on education, broadly defined, than the combined budgets of all traditional academic institutions in this country.

One possible inference from these numbers—that the Harvard Business School's influence on graduate business education declined precipitously during that interval of explosive growth—is obviously incorrect. In fact, the 1950s and 1960s saw the School's influence

expand dramatically in the international arena. On the other hand, a number of other American universities took steps, particularly in the 1960s, to redefine and strengthen their MBA programs. Many of these efforts proved fruitful, and their products bore little resemblance to the ongoing experiment at Soldiers Field.

While only a handful of the schools involved were capable of sustained and productive research, those that were defined new fields and further distinguished themselves from Harvard's business school. By the 1960s, a prospective student of business could select from a range of pedagogical approaches; a scholar of business could choose to affiliate with a school based on its particular research orientation.

In other words, the wellspring of the Harvard Business School's uniqueness changed. Before the Second World War, the School was in part distinctive simply because it was the only fish in its pond. After the war, both the pond and its population grew tremendously, but relatively few of the new entrants patterned themselves on the Harvard model. Few, for example, adopted the case method as a basis for research and teaching, in part because of the expense it entailed. Similarly, only a handful made the study and practice of general management their goal. As business education evolved and expanded, the unique elements of the Harvard Business School's approach were thrown into increasingly sharp relief.

Even so, internal change proceeded apace on many fronts at Harvard. Perhaps the most significant development at Soldiers Field in the late 1950s and 1960s was the growth of the faculty, both in numbers and in range of interests. In 1946, for example, 98 individuals held faculty appointments at the School. Three decades later, this number peaked at 240. Beginning in the early 1950s, in part because of the encouragement and financial support of the Ford Foundation, the School made a series of faculty appointments designed to augment its competences in quantitative fields and the social sciences. New disciplines joined the School's research effort, and some of these gained a foothold in the curriculum. Concurrently, the faculty "barons" who had for years dominated certain teaching groups were beginning to relinquish the reins. This process only reinforced the impact of the purposeful recruitment of "outsiders."

Although decades have passed since that infusion of new interests, the merits of the experiment are still assessed and debated. What is undisputed is the change in social relationships—and to a certain extent, patterns of intellectual exchange—that has resulted from growth in numbers. In the mid-1950s, for example, the entire faculty still met and ate together on the second floor of the old Faculty Club. (Administrators, it should be noted, did not eat with the faculty, reflecting that era's more hierarchical social structure.) Within a few months of arriving at Soldiers Field, junior professors knew most of their colleagues on a first-name basis. "Everybody could pretty much understand everybody else," one emeritus professor recalled in an interview. "Interests and methodologies were sufficiently similar that if you sat down with people from another field, you would know them, and you could probably hang on to what was being talked about."

Increases in the faculty's ranks and in the range of its intellectual pursuits inevitably created a different environment. The transformation was hastened and reinforced by the swelling ranks of administrators and support staff at the School. (They numbered 235 in 1950, and 542 only fifteen years later). Like many other American communities in the postwar period, Soldiers Field became much more cosmopolitan. The values, virtues, and shortcomings of the small town were gradually replaced by those of the city. "As a social organization," one professor commented, "it was probably a more satisfying place [before the change]—unless one was at odds with the place. It was a homogeneous, live entity."

The student body in the 1950s was equally homogeneous. The typical MBA class (of approximately 600) was exclusively male and almost entirely white. About a quarter of the students arriving at the School each year had engineering backgrounds, and half were between 23 and 26 years of age. By 1980, the average class had grown to 780. Some characteristics of the student population had changed only slightly since the 1950s: for example, the proportion of engineers was identical, and the class had roughly the same median age (more than half between the ages of 23 and 26). But two significant changes, both resulting from policy decisions of the 1960s, had also occurred. Now, a quarter of Harvard's MBA students were female, and approximately 10 percent represented minority groups. To alumni, to senior faculty members, and to others in longstanding relationships with the School, this purposeful adjustment of the student mix constituted the most striking postwar change at Soldiers Field.

The School's financial circumstances have also changed since 1950. In his history of the Harvard Business School, Melvin Copeland cites Harvard President Eliot's assurance to Edwin Gay in 1908 that the School would soon be financially secure. Within five years, Eliot told Gay, the business community would fully support the work of the School. The prediction was made at regular intervals in ensuing decades. "As developments since 1949 show," Copeland wrote in 1957, "President Eliot was right in his expectation that the School would eventually receive strong financial support. He merely underestimated the time by about 35 years."

Copeland's summary was inaccurate in several respects. First, even if one accepts Eliot's premise—that the business community would eventually underwrite the School's operating expenses—that state of affairs certainly did not obtain in 1957. (The mistake can perhaps be explained by the fact that in the mid-1950s, the School was still reaping the harvest of Donald David's exceptional fund-raising efforts.) In ensuing years, furthermore, financial troubles intermittently threatened to restrict the School's activities. Budgetary problems in the early 1960s, for example, presented incoming Dean George P. Baker with an unwelcome priority. In response, he effected a remarkable 79 percent increase in the School's endowment, and increased its complement of chaired professorships from 13 to 35. Nevertheless, a business recession at the beginning of the 1970s again illustrated an underlying structural weakness at Soldiers Field. The School, as Lawrence Fouraker wrote in his first Dean's report, had "very soft sources of revenues against very firm commitments of expenses."

This recent history hints at the Harvard Business School's true financial circumstance and strategy, both before and since 1957. The School's income is derived principally from its educational programs. Other sources, including direct contributions from individual companies or industry groups, are distinctly secondary. The MBA program (and more recently, executive education programs) operates on a scale large enough that it generates substantial revenues when fully subscribed. Like most educational institutions, in other words, the School competes in a marketplace, and prospers when its "products" fill a large enough need.

But Harvard's business school has an advantage enjoyed by very few others. Harvard University has a longstanding policy which places "every tub on its own bottom," meaning that under normal circumstances, its graduate schools must pay their own way. This policy presents risks, as evidenced by President Eliot's ill-fated School of Veterinary Medicine. On the other hand, the "tub" policy allows individual schools to keep whatever surpluses they generate. Profits from good years can be used to offset deficits from bad ones; reserves can be used to retire outstanding debts, or to finance educational experiments. The School's willingness and capacity to innovate derive in part from this significant financial flexibility.

In 1917, Edwin Gay wrote that tuition fees covered "somewhat more than one half of the annual running expenses of this School, the remainder being supplied by endowments and gifts." With only minor qualifications, the same statement could be made today. Tuition fees now offset roughly half of the School's operating expenses.

It is tempting—perhaps it is human nature—to perceive false parallels with the past. Edwin Gay's Harvard Business School was a vastly different enterprise from the one which operates today. In Gay's time, for example, "tuition" meant income solely derived from the MBA program. Today, by contrast, income derived from executive education programs at Soldiers Field exceeds MBA tuition. Concealed within two broadly similar School "balance sheets," therefore, are entirely different ways of organizing a faculty and allocating institutional resources.

But it would be a missed opportunity to ignore the continuities which do exist. The School has not engaged in radical departures; nor has the accumulation of postwar changes at the School made it unrecognizable to friends from former decades. Readers with an impulse to understand the contemporary Harvard Business School should find ample reward in studying its past, since so much of that past endures today.

The last word belongs to Harvard's President Lowell. He, more succinctly than anyone else, defined the blend of high standards, adventurousness, and pragmatism that would come to characterize Harvard's business school. "I think," he wrote in 1907, "we had better do things that nobody else does; but we had better do them under the conditions that will be most likely to ensure success."

# Bibliographic notes

The material in this volume was derived mainly from primary sources, including interviews with principals, official records, and private correspondence. To encourage candor, interview subjects were promised either anonymity or the right to review direct quotations. In all cases, themes developed in individual interviews have been confirmed either by subsequent interviews or written materials. Each chapter has been reviewed by those most familiar with the period or themes contained therein; unless demonstrably wrong, their revisions have been incorporated in the text as published.

The basic reference for this period in the history of the Harvard Business School is Melvin T. Copeland's *And Mark an Era* (Boston: Little, Brown, 1958). An index of Copeland's book is available in Baker Library Manuscripts and Archives, along with some of Copeland's notes for the book. F. J. Roethlisberger's *The Elusive Phenomena* (Boston: Division of Research, Harvard Business School, 1977) provides a stimulating counterpoint to Copeland. Also valuable are N. S. B. Gras's various writings on the history of the School, and Edmund P. Learned's written recollections. These latter materials, drawn upon extensively in my work, can be reviewed with the permission of the curator of Baker Manuscripts and Archives.

Several types of official University and School papers were consulted extensively. These include the annual President's and Dean's Reports, faculty minutes, and subject and central administration files. Many key faculty members left their correspondence and other files to the care of the School, and these collections were drawn upon extensively. The Harvard Business School *Bulletin* provides a running record and official commentary on School activities beginning in the mid 1920s; the student-run *Harbus News* began publishing in 1937 and adds an additional perspective.

The Harvard Corporation restricts access to all University records which are less than fifty years old. In the case of individual school libraries, however, this restriction can be waived by the dean of the school in question. With Dean John McArthur's permission, therefore, I was able to draw upon materials from the 1930s, 1940s, and 1950s which would otherwise have been unavailable to me. Notes on this particular material—which have been deposited, along with other notes for this volume, in Baker Library's Manuscripts and Archives division—are subject to the fifty-year rule. Researchers should apply to the curator of Baker Manuscripts and Archives for permission to examine any other source materials.

Selected additional sources and reference materials are listed below by chapter.

## Chapter One

The University archives in Pusey Library were a key resource for this chapter. Of particular value were the papers of Harvard Presidents Eliot and Lowell, as well as Lowell's pre-presidential correspondence. (All excerpts from these papers appear with the permission of the University archivist.) For information on Harvard's alumni, the class records proved rewarding. Two alumni-oriented publications, the *Harvard Alumni Bulletin* and the *Graduates* magazine, also provided useful material.

Also consulted:

Peter Drucker, ed. *Preparing Tomorrow's Business Leaders Today*. Englewood Cliffs: Prentice-Hall, 1969.

Cleveland Amory. *The Proper Bostonians*. New York: Dutton, 1947.

Boston Chamber of Commerce. *Boston*. Boston: 1912.

Martin Green. *The Problem of Boston*. New York: W. W. Norton, 1966.

Paul A. Moreland. *A History of Business Education*. Toronto: Pitman, 1977.

## Chapter Two

Edwin Gay's personal papers are on deposit at the Huntington Library in California, and augment the official Gay papers at Baker Library. George Woodbridge's "Bible" — a 1923 document prepared for use in the 1924 fundraising campaign — provides useful insights on Gay's tenure as Dean of the Harvard Business School.

Also consulted:

Cecil E. Fraser, ed. *The Case Method of Instruction*. New York: McGraw-Hill, 1931.

Alfred D. Chandler, Jr. *The Visible Hand*. Cambridge: Harvard University Press, 1977.

Frederick Lewis Allen. *The Big Change*. New York: Harper & Brothers, 1952.

Herbert W. Heaton. *A Scholar in Action*. Cambridge: Harvard University Press, 1952.

Judy D. Dobbs. *A History of the Watertown Arsenal 1816-1967*. Army Materials and Research Center, 1977.

Arthur E. Sutherland. *The Law at Harvard*. Cambridge: Harvard University Press, 1967.

Joel Seligman. *The High Citadel*. Boston: Houghton Mifflin Company, 1978.

Frank Barkley Copley. *Frederick W. Taylor*. New York: Harper and Brothers, 1923.

Oscar Barck, Jr., and Nelson Manfred Blake. *Since 1900*. New York: Macmillan, 1974.

## Chapter Three

The Baker family, through George F. Baker III, kindly gave me access to material in the family archives. Sheridan A. Logan, a long-time employee of the First National Bank and the George F. Baker Trust, also provided information and guidance, as did interviews and correspondence with John C. Baker. The University's papers concerning the 1924 campaign are particularly thorough and useful. Woodbridge's "Bible," mentioned above, clarifies the School's perspective in 1923.

Also consulted:

William Lawrence. *Memories of a Happy Life*. Boston: Houghton Mifflin, 1926.

Sheridan A. Logan. *George F. Baker and His Bank*. New York: George F. Baker Trust, 1981.

Alfred Bigelow Paine. *George Fisher Baker*. New York: G. P. Putnam Sons, 1920.

## Chapter Four

Wallace Donham's two surviving sons, Philip and Paul, gave considerable assistance with this chapter. George P. Baker, Edmund P. Learned, Malcolm P. McNair, George E. Bates, and Georges F. Doriot also contributed supplementary materials and much-appreciated guidance.

Also consulted:

James Truslow Adams. *Our Business Civilization*. New York: Albert and Charles Boni, 1929.

Abraham Flexner. *Universities*, New York: Oxford University Press, 1930.

Alfred North Whitehead. *Science and the Modern World*. New York: Macmillan, 1925.

*Since 1900*, op. cit.

*The Big Change*, op. cit.

George P. Homans. *Coming to My Senses*. New Brunswick: Transaction, 1984.

*The Case Method at the Harvard Business School*, op. cit.

Richard C. S. Trahair. *The Humanist Temper*. New Brunswick: Transaction, 1984.

Stephen Fox. *The Mirror Makers*. New York: William Morrow, 1984.

**Chapter Five**

The National Archives provided access to Curtiss-Wright company records. Philip David gave permission to inspect Donald K. David's personal papers, held at Baker Library. Edmund P. Learned, George F. F. Lombard, Eugene M. Zuckert, George E. Bates, Kenneth R. Andrews, Robert N. Anthony, Lynn L. Bollinger, Clarence B. Nickerson, George P. Baker, Pearson Hunt, and members of the first "retread" class gave insight in the war years, as did several key faculty reports on the School's wartime experiences and postwar curriculum development. Several cases and related notes, particularly Lombard's "Notes on Field Work for the Umpteenth Fighter Squadron" and "Quaker Electric Company," proved useful. Robert Cuff gave helpful guidance on the national rearmament effort.

The Harvard Graduate School of Education library contains much relevant information on the ESMWT program, including the annual reports of the U. S. Commissioner of Education. These reports have been augmented by relevant congressional testimony, gleaned from records in Widener Library's Government Documents department.

Also consulted:

Carroll V. Glines, Jr. *A Compact History of the U. S. Air Force.* New York: Hawthorn, 1963.

G. R. Simonson, ed. *History of the American Aircraft Industry.* Cambridge: MIT Press, 1968.

John F. Heflin. *History of the Army Air Forces Statistical School.* Unpublished Army document, circa 1944.

*Since 1900,* op. cit.

# Photograph and illustration credits

**Chapter Four**

pp. 132-133: Baker Manuscripts and Archives
p. 134: Catherine Harris
pp. 135-136: Baker Manuscripts and Archives
p. 136: *(left)* Harvard University Archives
p. 137: *(top)* Baker Manuscripts and Archives
p. 137: *(center)* Elsie Copeland Brown
p. 138: Baker Manuscripts and Archives
p. 139: *(top)* University of Chicago Archives
pp. 139-140: Baker Manuscripts and Archives
p. 141: *(left)* Stephen Heard
pp. 141-145: Baker Manuscripts and Archives
p. 146: *(left)* Westinghouse Broadcasting and Cable, Inc.
p. 146: *(right)* Brown Brothers Photo
p. 147: University of Idaho Alumni Association, Inc.
pp. 148-150: Baker Manuscripts and Archives
p. 151: *(top)* Harvard University Archives
pp. 151-152: Stanford University News and Publications Service
p. 152: *(bottom)* Baker Manuscripts and Archives
pp. 153-155: Baker Manuscripts and Archives
p. 155: *(bottom)* Harvard University Archives
p. 156: *(top)* Baker Manuscripts and Archives
p. 156: *(bottom)* Harvard Law School Art Collection
p. 157: *(left) Boston Globe* Photo
pp. 157-160: Baker Manuscripts and Archives
p. 161: Bettmann Archive
p. 162: *(left)* Alfred Gras
p. 162: *(right)* Skolos Wedell & Raynor
p. 163: *(left and bottom right)* Baker Manuscripts and Archives
p. 163: *(top right)* General Electric
p. 164: *(left)* Francis A. Countway Library of Medicine
p. 164: *(right)* D. Bruce Dill
p. 165: Baker Manuscripts and Archives
p. 166: U.S. Department of the Interior, Bureau of Reclamation
p. 167: *(left)* Mahoning Valley Historical Society
pp. 167-169: Baker Manuscripts and Archives
p. 170: John F. Kennedy Library
p. 171: *(bottom right)* Georges F. Doriot
p. 171: Baker Manuscripts and Archives
p. 171: *(right)* Mary Morian/Albert Gordon

pp. 172-174: Baker Manuscripts and Archives
p. 174: *(right)* University of Chicago Library
pp. 175-177: Baker Manuscripts and Archives
p. 178: *(left)* AP/Wide World Photo
p. 178: *(right)* Copyright © 1933 by the New York Times Company. Reprinted by permission.
p. 179: *(left)* Tennessee Valley Authority
p. 179: *(right)* UPI(Acme)/ Bettmann Archive
p. 180: *(top)* Harvard Business School *Bulletin*
pp. 180-181: Baker Manuscripts and Archives
p. 182: *(left)* Harvard *Crimson*
p. 182: *(right)* Copyright © 1933 by the New York Times Company. Reprinted by permission.
p. 183: Baker Manuscripts and Archives
p. 184: Elsie Copeland Brown
p. 185: *(top)* Rockefeller Archive Center
pp. 185-186: Baker Manuscripts and Archives
p. 187: *(left)* Elizabeth Osborne
p. 187: *(right)* Boston Public Library Print Collection
pp. 188-189: Benjamin Hertzberg; Halsey V. Barrett
pp. 190-191: Baker Manuscripts and Archives
p. 192: *(top left and right)* Yale University Archives
pp. 192-193: Baker Manuscripts and Archives
p. 194: *(top)* Bassano/Camera Press. Courtesy Photo Trends
p. 194: *(bottom)* Lucius N. Littauer Foundation
p. 195: *(left)* Baker Manuscripts and Archives
p. 195: *(right)* Philip Donham
pp. 196-197: Harvard University Archives
p. 197: *(right)* Baker Manuscripts and Archives
pp. 198-204: Baker Manuscripts and Archives
p. 205: Copyright © 1986, Estate of Josef Breitenbach
p. 206: *(left)* Kress Library
p. 206: *(right)* Baker Manuscripts and Archives
p. 207: *(left)* Kress Library
p. 207: *(right)* Baker Manuscripts and Archives
p. 208: *(left)* National Archives
p. 208: *(right)* Baker Manuscripts and Archives
p. 209: National Archives
pp. 210-211: Baker Manuscripts and Archives
p. 212: *(top)* Library of Congress
p. 212: *(bottom)* Baker Manuscripts and Archives
p. 213: Colgate University Archives
p. 214: Baker Manuscripts and Archives
p. 215: Harvard University Archives

**Chapter Five**

pp. 216-217: Baker Manuscripts and Archives
p. 218: Heinrich Hoffmann. Courtesy Life Picture Service
p. 219: *(bottom)* UPI (Acme). Courtesy Franklin D. Roosevelt Library
p. 220: Photoworld/FPG
p. 221: *(top right)* National Archives
pp. 221-223: Baker Manuscripts and Archives
p. 223: *(right)* AP/Wide World
p. 224: Baker Manuscripts and Archives
p. 225: Harvard University Archives
pp. 226-229: Baker Manuscripts and Archives
p. 230: National Archives
p. 231: Baker Manuscripts and Archives
p. 232: *(top)* Reprinted with permission of the Boston *Herald*
p. 232: *(bottom)* Reprinted by permission; © 1947, 1975 The New Yorker Magazine, Inc.
pp. 233-234: Baker Manuscripts and Archives
p. 234: *(bottom)* Latah County Historical Society
p. 235: *(top)* Baker Manuscripts and Archives
p. 235: *(bottom)* Harvard University Archives
p. 236: *(left)* Smithsonian Institution Negative No. 86-56
p. 236: *(right)* Smithsonian Institution Negative No. 86-58
p. 237: *(top)* Baker Manuscripts and Archives
p. 237: *(bottom left)* Smithsonian Institution Negative No. 86-57
p. 237: *(bottom center)* Baker Manuscripts and Archives
p. 237: *(bottom right)* Smithsonian Institution Negative No. 86-59
p. 238: Massachusetts Institute of Technology Museum
p. 239: *(top)* Baker Manuscripts and Archives
p. 239: *(left)* Boston *Herald*
p. 239: *(right)* Baker Manuscripts and Archives
p. 240: Smithsonian Institution Negative No. 78-1648
pp. 241-248: Baker Manuscripts and Archives
p. 248: *(top right)* Smithsonian Institution Negative No. 86-53
pp. 248-250: Baker Manuscripts and Archives
p. 251: *(top)* AP/Wide World
p. 251: *(bottom)* Baker Manuscripts and Archives
p. 252: *(top)* George P. Baker
pp. 252-253: Baker Manuscripts and Archives

p. 253: *(bottom)* Lockheed Corporation
p. 254: Baker Manuscripts and Archives
p. 254: *(right)* Smithsonian Institution Negative No. 86-55
p. 255: *(top)* Smithsonian Institution Negative No. 86-50
pp. 255-267: Baker Manuscripts and Archives
p. 267: *(middle)* Mrs. Stanley F. Teele
pp. 268-271: Baker Manuscripts and Archives
p. 272: *(left)* Mrs. Stanley F. Teele
p. 272: *(right)* Baker Manuscripts and Archives
p. 273: National Archives
p. 274: *(right)* Mrs. Margaret Gay Davies
pp. 274-275: Baker Manuscripts and Archives
p. 276: Filene's
pp. 276-277: Baker Manuscripts and Archives

**Epilogue**

p. 278: Skolos Wedell & Raynor
pp. 280-285: Copyright © 1984, Nubar Alexanian

**Bibliographic notes**

p. 289: Copyright © 1984, Nubar Alexanian

# Index

A Delicate Experiment
*The Harvard Business School  1908-1945*

Designed by Logowitz + Moore Associates, Boston,
composed by Monotype Composition Company in Caslon 540,
printed by Daniels Printing Company on
Warren's Lustro Offset Enamel Dull, 100 lb. text,
bound by A. Horowitz & Sons in
Brillianta book cloth from Van Heek Textiles.